THE JEWS OF EDIRNE

STANFORD STUDIES IN JEWISH HISTORY AND CULTURE
Edited by Jessica Marglin and Daniel Schwartz

THE JEWS OF EDIRNE

*The End of Ottoman
Europe and the Arrival
of Borders*

JACOB DANIELS

STANFORD UNIVERSITY PRESS
Stanford, California

Stanford University Press
Stanford, California

© 2025 by Jacob Daniels. All rights reserved.

No part of this book may be reproduced or transmitted in any form or by any means, electronic or mechanical, including photocopying and recording, or in any information storage or retrieval system, without the prior written permission of Stanford University Press.

Library of Congress Cataloging-in-Publication Data
Names: Daniels, Jacob (Jacob Max), author.
Title: The Jews of Edirne : the end of Ottoman Europe and the arrival of borders / Jacob Daniels.
Other titles: Stanford studies in Jewish history and culture.
Description: Stanford, California : Stanford University Press, 2025. | Series: Stanford studies in Jewish history and culture | Includes bibliographical references and index.
Identifiers: LCCN 2024048951 (print) | LCCN 2024048952 (ebook) | ISBN 9781503641983 (cloth) | ISBN 9781503642911 (paperback) | ISBN 9781503642928 (ebook)
Subjects: LCSH: Jews—Turkey—Edirne—History—20th century. | Sephardim—Turkey—Edirne—History—20th century. | Borderlands—Turkey—History—20th century. | Edirne (Turkey)—Ethnic relations—History—20th century. | Turkey—History—Mehmed V, 1909–1918. | Turkey—History—1918–1960.
Classification: LCC DS135.T82 D36 2025 (print) | LCC DS135.T82 (ebook) | DDC 949.61/402004924—dc23/eng/20241213
LC record available at https://lccn.loc.gov/2024048951
LC ebook record available at https://lccn.loc.gov/2024048952

Cover design: Lindy Kasler
Cover art: Photograph of staff at Sultaniye Hospital, Edirne, 1912, Library of the Alliance Israélite Universelle (Paris), 7483; 1923 map of Turkey in Ottoman-Turkish script, Wikimedia
Typeset by Newgen in Garamond Premier Pro 11/15

The authorized representative in the EU for product safety and compliance is:
Mare Nostrum Group B.V. | Mauritskade 21D | 1091 GC Amsterdam | The Netherlands |
Email address: gpsr@mare-nostrum.co.uk | KVK chamber of commerce number: 96249943

For Mom—my original reader

Contents

Acknowledgments		ix
Maps: The Edirne Region		xv
	Introduction	1
1	Foundations of a Borderland Community: Mobility, Networks, and Economic Life	21
2	Liberty and Limits: Public Spheres on the Imperial Border, 1908–1912	53
3	The Eye of the Storm: Borderland Violence and the Jews, 1912–1918	90
4	Days of Blue and White: Hellenism and Zionism in Northeastern Greece, 1919–1922	122
5	Peacetime Violence: Completing Borderland Intolerance, 1923–1934	149
	Conclusion	177
	Epilogue: Bordering the Holocaust	182
Notes		187
Bibliography		265
Index		289

Acknowledgments

IT IS IMPOSSIBLE TO PINPOINT where and when the process of creating this book began. But if I had to try, I might say New York, 2014. It was there that three friends—Peter Constantine, Ali Humayun Akhtar, and Selim Karlıtekin—helped me find my intellectual path, and two scholars—Karen Barkey and Lisa Keller—guided my first project on Ottoman-Jewish history.

When I arrived at Stanford, I began working with Aron Rodrigue. Learning from him has been the privilege of a lifetime. He gave me everything I needed and—almost as important—nothing I did not. This book would not exist without Olga Borovaya, my witty guide to the world of Ladino sources. Like the best coaches, she pushed me to accomplish things I did not think were possible. Much of my growth as a historian occurred in the lamp-lit office of Steven Zipperstein. Among other things, his repeated advice to "give the reader a sense of place" has shaped my writing about Edirne. Ali Yaycıoğlu showed me how to approach Ottoman history in a way that is unconventional yet serious, creative yet rigorous. From Joel Beinin I learned that objective truth may be complicated, but integrity is not.

In addition to providing a generous publishing subvention, the Taube Center for Jewish Studies funded much of the research informing this book. The benevolence of the center is embodied in its associate director,

Shaina Hammerman, who has been a constant source of friendship and guidance. Eitan Kensky's expertise and geniality made Green Library a fun place to visit. My Hebrew teachers—Vered Karti Shemtov, Gallia Porat, and Shoshana Olidort—amazed me with their patience. And I was constantly guided by discussions with my wonderful Jewish history colleagues, including Daniella Farah, Beata Szymków, Joshua Tapper, Özgür Dikmen, Alin Constantin, Makena Mezistrano, and Nesi Altaras. May these discussions continue.

Studying a topic at the intersection of so many fields allowed me to work with brilliant scholars across programs, centers, and departments. J. P. Daughton helped me build the theoretical foundation that undergirds my work as a historian. Jovana Lazić Knežević taught me key themes of modern Balkan history. Burcu Karahan guided me through tricky Ottoman-Turkish texts. Workshops made possible by the Abbasi Program in Islamic Studies allowed me to learn from Kristen Alff, Vladimir Hamed-Troyansky, Uğur Peçe, Nora Barakat, Orit Bashkin, and other leading scholars of the late Ottoman Empire and modern Middle East. Emre Can Dağlıoğlu shared his historical insights and his skills in reading Riqʿah script. Basma Fahoum made sure I never missed the forest for the trees. Merve Tekgürler pushed me to think harder about Ottoman borderlands and my role as a historian. Padraic Rohan always seemed free for a long walk and deep discussion of Ottoman historiography. I am also indebted to the fantastic people who run the History Department at Stanford, including Art Palmon, Kai Dowding, Colin Hamill, Maria Annette Moreno-Lane, and especially Burçak Keskin Kozat.

Beyond Stanford, the wider Sephardi studies community (broadly defined) has been a fount of inspiration and support. The introduction to this book benefited tremendously from a session of the California Working Group on Jews in the Maghrib and Middle East (Cal JeMM). I am especially grateful to Matthias B. Lehmann and the current steering committee: Aomar Boum Emily Gottreich, Alma Heckman, Ethan Katz, Jessica Marglin, Susan Miller, Liron Mor, Aron Rodrigue, and Sarah Abrevaya Stein. Fellow Cal JeMMers Rachel Baron-Block and Rebecca Glasberg showed me what true colleagues look like: always generous and intellectually curious, never competitive or petty. I also received precious feedback at a symposium called "Jews amidst the Embers of the Ottoman Empire," held at the University of Washington in Seattle. I send my warmest thanks to the faculty organizers—Liora Halperin, Devin Naar, and Canan Bolel—and the graduate students who led a related initiative—Joana Bürger and Sasha Marie Ward. Before, during, and after the symposium, Julia Phillips Cohen and Devi Mays were extraordinary mentors and interlocutors. At the Center for Jewish History in New York, I attended a workshop called "New Sources in the Study of Women and Gender in Jewish History." Discussing my research with Dina Danon and others led to several breakthroughs. Additional thanks go to Devin Naar for helping me access the Sephardic Studies Digital Collection at the Stroum Center for Jewish Studies. And thank you, Louis Fishman, for always being so generous about sharing work in progress.

This book has been significantly shaped by the colleagues who joined me on panels at the Association for Jewish Studies (AJS) annual conference. This dynamic group of scholars includes Anabella Esperanza, Marina Mayorski, Tamir Karkason, and Ilan Benattar. On that note, I am grateful to be a recipient of the AJS's Jordan Schnitzer First Book Publication Award, which allowed me to include the five maps that follow (among other things).

This project was also motivated by a magnificent community of Ottomanists and scholars of modern Turkey. I have had rich conversations about Edirne with Pınar Odabaşı and Amy Singer, most recently at the Ottoman and Turkish Studies Association Annual Conference. Sertaç Şen and Kaleb Herman Adney taught me so much about interwar Thrace. And at the Intensive Ottoman and Turkish Summer School in Cunda, Turkey, Selim Kuru and Yorgos Dedes performed the miracle of teaching me to read Ottoman Turkish.

One of the most heartening parts of the research process was the enthusiastic support I received from scholars and archivists overseas. In Paris, Jean-Claude Kuperminc and Guila Cooper took good care of me at the archive of the Alliance Israélite Universelle. I am deeply grateful to all my friends in the sixteenth arrondissement.

In Turkey, my research journey began in the Istanbul office of Rıfat Bali, whose guidance saved me months of wrong turns. Also in Istanbul, Meliha Nur Çerçinli went above and beyond to help me locate documents in the Ottoman Archives. Upon reaching Edirne, I immediately visited Musa Öncel in a fifteenth-century stone *han*. Over tea, he gave me the rundown on local Ottoman-Turkish sources. At Edirne's Chamber of Commerce and Industry—a newer building—İsmail Eser unlocked his filing cabinet and handed me his dustiest *sicil* records. In the Edirne Public Library, Suat Pencik showed me the historical newspapers stored in the basement, and İsmail Demiray photographed the occasional article for me, after I had returned to California. In Edirne City Hall, Aydemir Ay helped me track down helpful sources and people. Later, Graham Lee gave me a first-rate walking tour of the city. I also managed to see the old *sicil* records in Tekirdağ's Chamber of Commerce and Industry, thanks to Ahmet Gürgürler. In Kırklareli, professors Ali Çakır and V. Türkan Doğruöz deepened my understanding of the region, and Barış Toptaş drove me to promising libraries and offices—teaching me much about his town along the way. In Lüleburgaz, I had the great fortune to meet Mustafa Gültekin, whose knowledge of local history is endless, as far as I can tell. Sharing a *rakı sofrası* with him and Gürsel Sezer was a highlight of my time in Turkish Thrace. While I have yet to meet him in person, İlkay Öz never hesitated to answer my questions about Edirne via WhatsApp (from Istanbul).

In Jerusalem, Tami Siesel and Yochai Ben-Ghedalia let me stay late at the Central Archives for the History of the Jewish People. Eyal Ginio introduced me to exciting sources at Yad Ben Zvi and the National Library of Israel, and Yaron Ben-Naeh welcomed me into his home to discuss my research. In a cafeteria at the Hebrew University, David Bunis helped me read Ladino documents written in the *soletreo* script. Two years later, he taught a fantastic Mediterranean Skills Seminar at the University of Colorado Boulder, under the leadership of Brian Catlos.

On my first trip to Greece, Yannis Glavinas bought me coffee in Athens and guided me through some Greek sources that appear in Chapter 4 of this book. Also in Athens, Zanet Battinou welcomed me to the library and archive of the Jewish Museum of Greece. A subsequent visit to that country brought me to the border town of Didymoteicho for an event called the "International Symposium on the Jews in Demotica before and after the Shoah." Thanks to the heroic organizing of Vasilis Ritzaleos, I was able to spend three days with a fabulous group of scholars from Greece, Israel, and beyond. Rena Molho and Thrasyvoulos Papastratis, especially, helped me rethink parts of my book project. Diamantis Myrtsidis taught me about the history of Balkan railways and, months later, took the photograph of the Edirne skyline that appears below. I am also grateful to Romilos Xatzigiannoglou, the mayor of Didymoteicho, for finding me a taxi to Bulgaria. That cab ride led to the opening paragraph of this book.

In the US, my archival research started at the American Jewish Joint Distribution Committee (JDC) office in midtown Manhattan. There, Misha Mitsel accommodated my requests with patience and skill. Down on 16th Street, I worked with superb archivists at YIVO/The Center for Jewish History. Even further down—in College Park, Maryland—David Langbart helped me prepare for a remarkably productive visit to the National Archives and Records Administration.

Special thanks are due to the editors I have worked with over the past seven years. Catherine Chatterley published my first scholarly article, which appeared in the journal *Antisemitism Studies* and contains the seeds of Chapter 5. A few years later, I was honored when Kerem Öktem and İpek Yosmaoğlu included my work in their superb volume *Turkish Jews and Their Diasporas: Entanglements and Separations*. That essay inspired Chapter 3 of this book. Sarah Abrevaya Stein, former editor of the series Stanford Studies in Jewish History and Culture, helped me find my historian's voice. I cannot thank her enough. At Stanford University Press, I was in the very good hands of Margo Irvin, Natalie Gabriela Rovero, and Kate Wahl. Their patience, knowledge, and professionalism made the publishing process as smooth as possible. This book reached its full potential thanks to the thoughtful, spot-on feedback of my two anonymous readers, to whom I remain grateful. While not acting in any official capacity, Mark Greif prompted me to rethink my book title during a chance encounter in San Francisco. And, in a Boston café, Kenneth Moss provided feedback on an early draft of my introduction (after treating me to a pastry).

Two other friends must be thanked. Cevdet Mehmet Kösemen helped ignite my interest in Ottoman-Jewish history by showing me around Istanbul—*way* off the beaten path. And Cem Dinlenmiş made the beautiful maps that appear below. Thank you both for years of inspiration.

Finally, I must thank my family. My wife, Duygu, never doubted that I would or should bring this project to completion—even though she bore the brunt of its all-consuming nature. My brother, Gabriel, showed me how to pursue a career that combines teaching with artistic work. My parents, Scott and Amy, instilled in me a love of knowledge without imposing their own worldviews, and they proved that people really can love their jobs. Extra thanks go to my mom, for proofreading my very first compositions. Let's see what she thinks of this one.

Maps: The Edirne Region

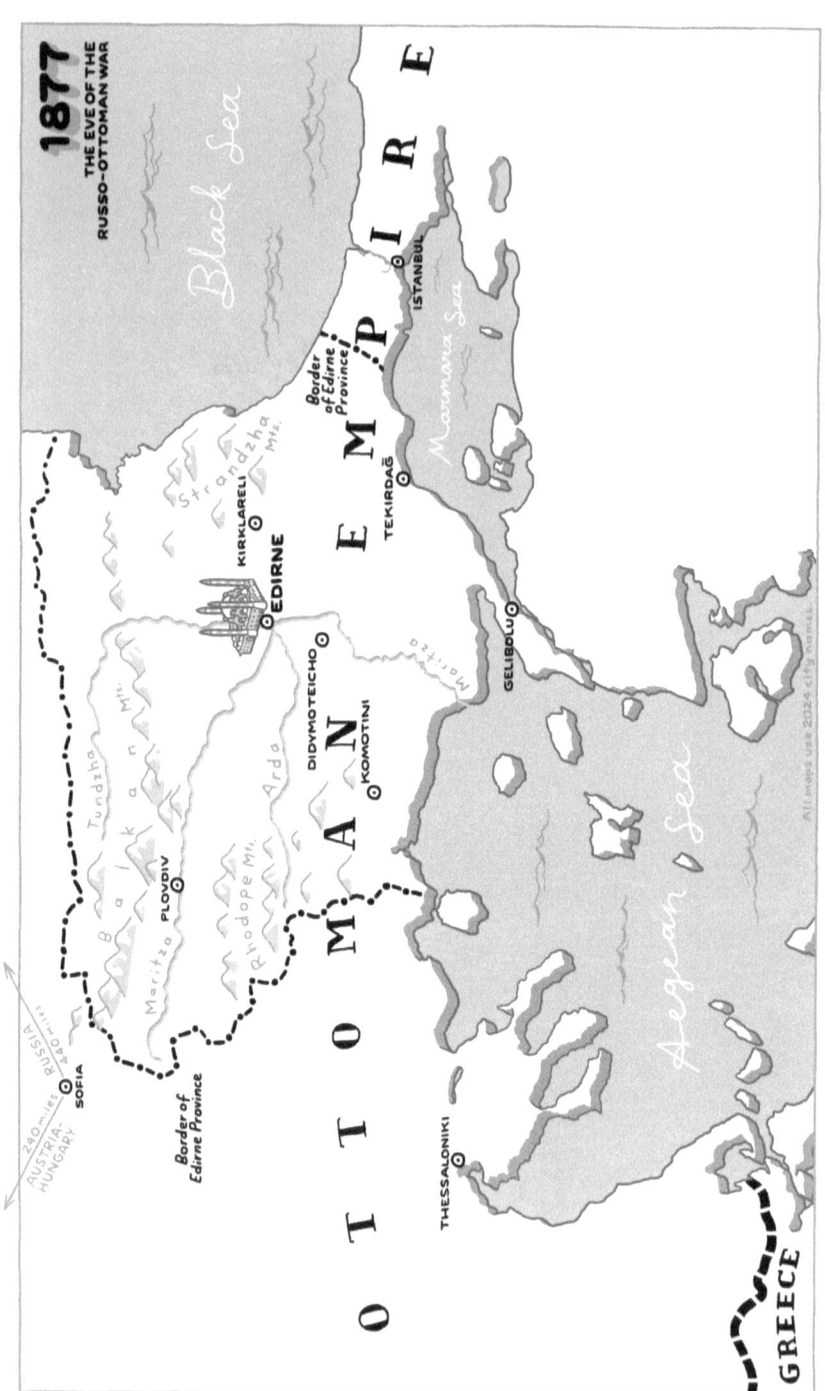

Map 1. The Edirne region in 1877

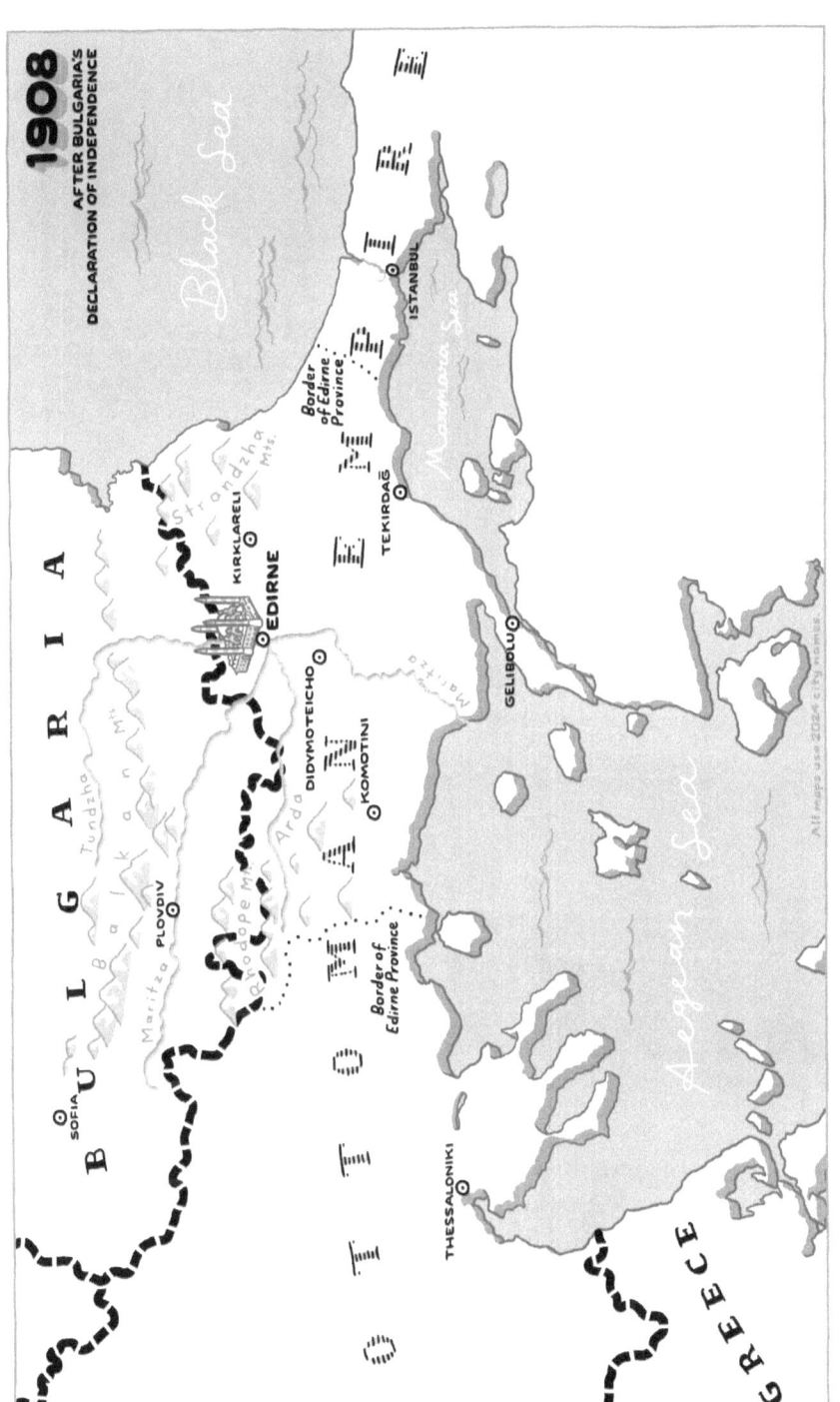

Map 2. The Edirne region in 1908

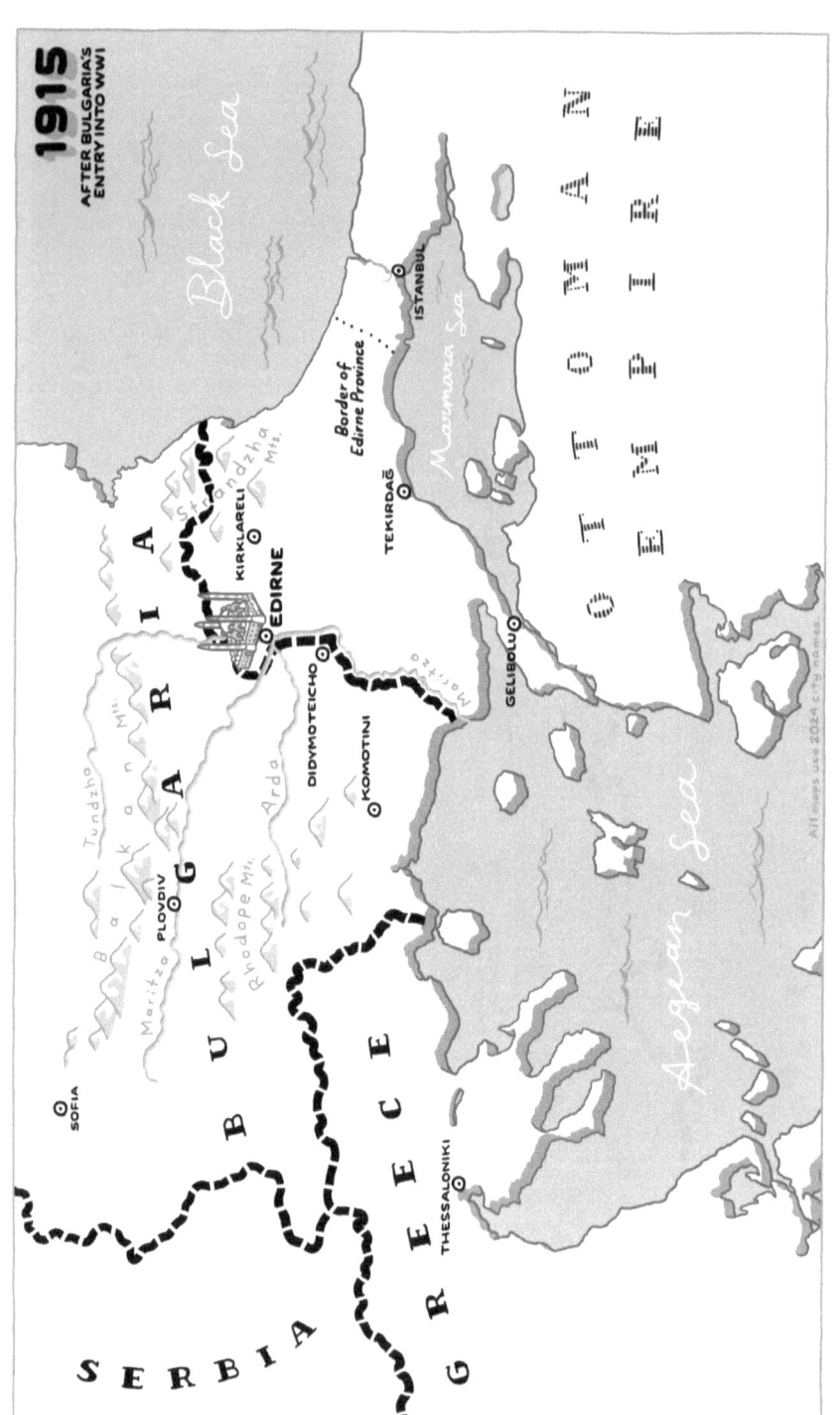

Map 3. The Edirne region in 1915

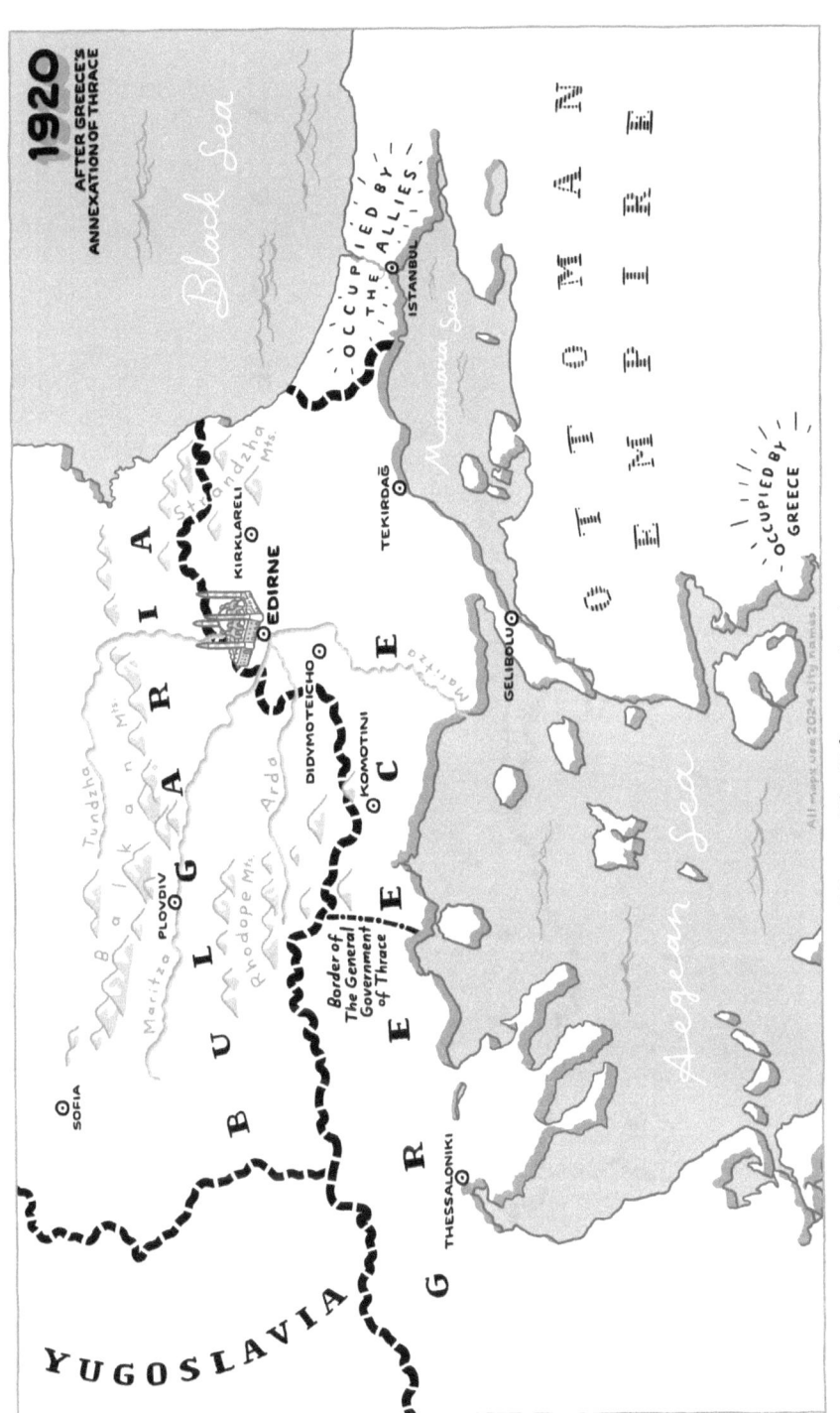

Map 4. The Edirne region in 1920

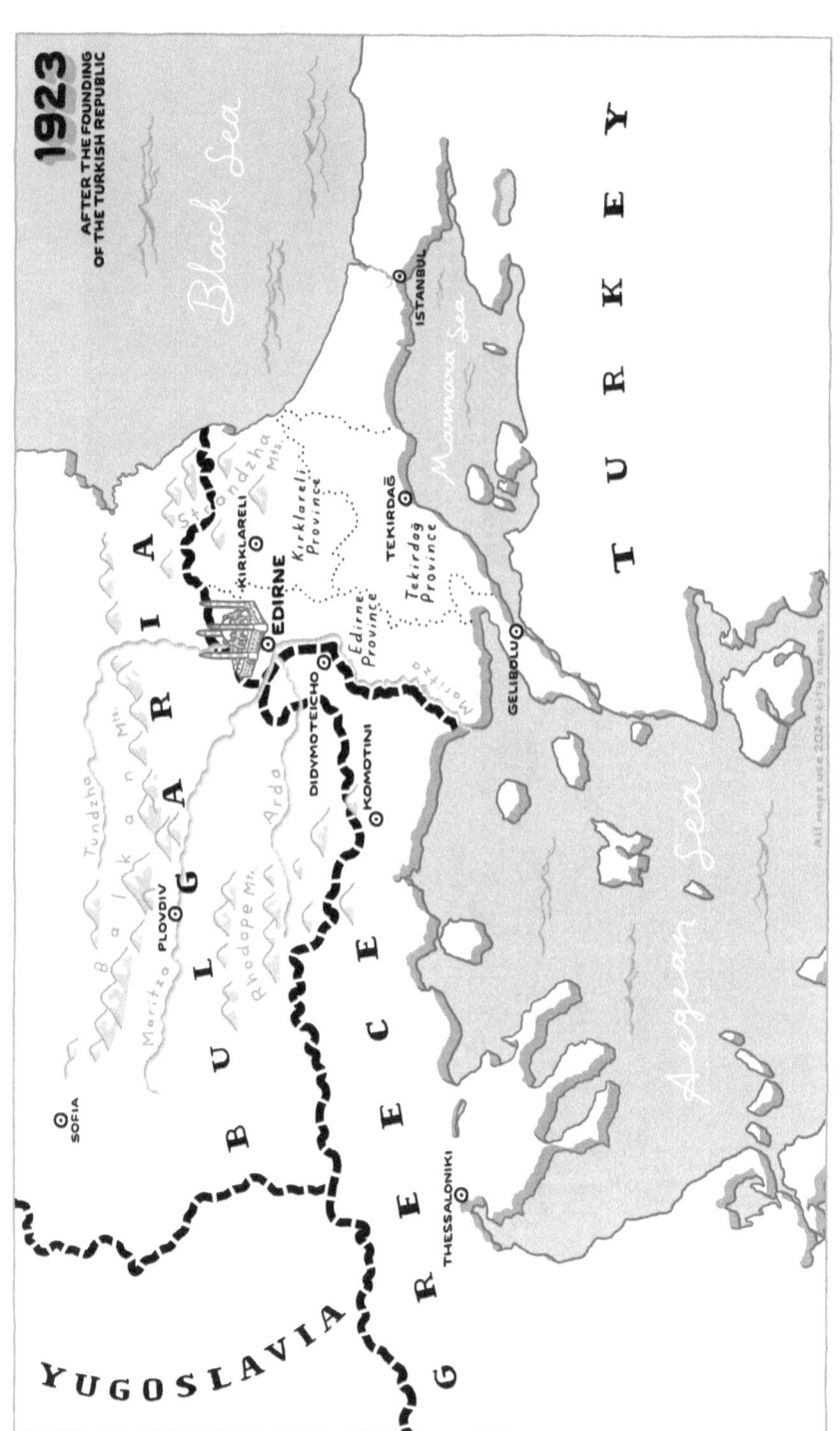

Map 5. The Edirne region in 1923

THE JEWS OF EDIRNE

Introduction

THE BEST VIEW OF EDIRNE, Turkey is from Greece. Should you find yourself approaching the border town of Kastanies on European route E85, scan the checkerboard of brown and green fields to the East. Beyond Greek Kastanies (Chestnut) and Turkish Karaağaç (Elm), between the Thracian plain in the foreground and the Strandzha Mountains in the background, a massive, four-minaret mosque looms on a hill over the sleepy borderland, pompously overdressed for the occasion.[1] This is Selimiye, the dominant feature of Edirne's otherwise modest skyline.

Upon its completion in 1575, Selimiye was the largest mosque in the Ottoman Empire. By choosing to build his namesake monument in Edirne (the former capital) instead of Istanbul (the contemporary one), Sultan Selim II may have been recognizing Edirne as the empire's second most important city. After all, it was the frequent home of the sultan's court and the staging ground for military campaigns that had pushed the imperial frontier to the meadows between Budapest and Vienna, seven hundred miles away. Historians list several factors that could have motivated Selim II to build his mosque in Edirne, but improving the view for people in a foreign country is not one of them.[2]

With a population of 180,000, Edirne is now a "secondary city" known mostly for its monumental Ottoman architecture and its border checkpoints with two European Union member states (Bulgaria and Greece).[3] Its difficult passage from central city to border town started in the nineteenth century, when the Ottomans began their piecemeal retreat from Europe. By 1908, an official state border existed just north of the city. Over the next fourteen years, that border would move back and forth across Edirne, wreaking havoc in the process. When the Ottoman Empire officially dissolved in 1923, the city found itself in a new country called the Republic of Turkey. At that point, the border stopped moving, but the borderland continued to be a place where "the future is always uncertain" (as a local Jew had said in 1910).[4] For Edirne residents, the first decades of the twentieth century were largely defined by the shifting position—and meaning—of the state border.

Compared to their Muslim and Christian neighbors, the Jews of Edirne—both the city and the larger province—experienced the border in ways that tended to be less bloody but more complex. On the eve of the 1908 Young Turk Revolution, Edirne Province was home to one of the world's oldest and largest communities of Ladino-speaking Sephardim (Jews who

Figure 1. Selimiye Mosque and the Edirne skyline, as seen from Greece. Photograph: Diamantis Myrtsidis.

traced their lineage to medieval Spain and Portugal). These people dodged a series of ethnic cleansing campaigns that targeted Muslims and then Christians in the period 1912–1922.[5] But in 1934, Jews across the region—which had come to be called Eastern Thrace—were attacked by neighbors in a week of violence that prompted a Jewish exodus from the borderland (but killed no Jews). The so-called Thrace Events (*Trakya Olayları*) remain the only case of mob violence against Jews in the history of the Turkish Republic.

How did Edirne's Jewish community survive the horrors of the last Ottoman decade only to unravel during the relatively peaceful years of the early Turkish Republic? That is a central question of this book. The answers have much to do with the border, the identities it could (and could not) generate, the violence it could (and could not) legitimate, and the survival strategies pursued by local Jews within this tricky matrix.

One of these Jews was the educator Rosa Mitrani (née Avigdor). In the photograph on the cover of this book, three rows of people sporting Red Crescent armbands sit before the military hospital in Edirne during the first phase of the Balkan Wars (1912–1913). In the center, surrounded by thirty-five mustachioed men wearing fezzes or turbans, two young women stare at the camera with an air of self-possession, hair up and hands folded. They are Rosa Mitrani and Angèle Guéron—local Jewish women volunteering in the service of their country, the Ottoman Empire. (Mitrani is sixth from the right.)[6]

An Edirne native, Mitrani had been running a Jewish girls' school in the town of Kırklareli, forty miles away.[7] More so than their coreligionists in other Ottoman provinces, the Jews of Edirne lived beyond the big city, in a constellation of small towns. Ottoman rule and the green expanse of the Thracian plain had made it relatively easy for merchants, educators, workers, and rabbis to travel and communicate across the *vilayet* (province). For decades or even centuries, this geopolitical situation tended to strengthen a network of Ladino-speaking communities that spanned Southeast Europe.

But as the camera shutter closed on Mitrani (and the other volunteers), her world was beginning to fall apart. The Balkan Wars would lead to a temporary occupation of Edirne Province and the permanent loss of the *vilayet*'s western half—home to thousands of Mitrani's coreligionists. In 1920, another foreign occupation would again force local Jews (and others) into new social, economic, and political orientations. Two and a half years later, the birth of the Turkish Republic would solidify Edirne's links to Anatolia but also its status as a border town. In the months and years after that photograph was taken, a series of border revisions threatened Mitrani's social and professional networks, while a succession of states each demanded her loyalty. She managed to navigate this landscape until 1935, when she left Edirne with her husband in the wake of the Thrace Events.[8]

The following chapters tell the story of Sephardi Jews trying to survive—and understand—the border. Some, like Mitrani, would ride out the wars and occupations of the very late Ottoman period and live as minorities in the northwest corner of Turkey. Others, like Guéron—the second woman in the photograph—would leave Edirne before the birth of the Turkish Republic. All of them, whether they realized it or not, had to confront the logic of modern nationalism that was reaching extreme conclusions in their province. The Ottoman borderland in Europe was a place where "debates on identity and the future of the empire started earlier and were more acute... than they were in the capital itself."[9] More broadly, late-imperial borderlands were ground zero for the forging of nation-states in much of Europe and Asia Minor, "the prime sites where contesting national myths, narratives, and identities [were] created."[10] The story of Edirne's Jewish community, then, occupies a central place not only in Sephardi history but also in the modern histories of Southeast Europe, Southwest Asia, and the larger Jewish world.

By following the Jewish community of Edirne—the city and the province, though the latter is a shrinking target—through the tumultuous period 1908–1934, this book offers fresh perspectives on the nature of modern borders, the place of violence in Jewish history, and the paths that ethno-religious minorities took from empire to nation-state(s) in much of the world at this time. Today, as borders, communal identities, and nationalism (including Zionism) continue to be highly charged topics in North America and beyond, Jews who inhabited the corner of a bygone empire serve as a remarkably relevant topic.

Middle East historians Jordi Tejel and Ramazan Hakkı Öztan write that "contrary to popular and traditional depictions of borders as areas where national sovereignty comes to an end," their work illustrates how "border areas and borderlanders become the very centres of influence, movements and tensions that transformed sovereignties into new forms."[11] Similarly, I hope to show that the northwestern borderland of the late Ottoman Empire was the cutting edge of a process in which the Turkish nation and Turkey's borders were simultaneously created. This is a very tainted distinction, as these developments were marred by the tragedies of displacement, dispossession, and mass killing. Innovativeness is not always a virtue.

But if the Edirne region played a violently radical role in the development of modern nationalism, its Jewish population was actively conservative.[12] Both phenomena were functions of the geopolitical situation, at every step of the way. When the 1908 Young Turk Revolution created new political options for Edirne Jews, the changing nature of the Ottoman-Bulgarian border prompted them to be circumspect in exploring both Zionism and a new Ottoman nationalism. During the wars and occupations of 1912–1922, new borders and ethnic cleansing campaigns were repeatedly used to justify each other. Meanwhile, local Jews survived by clinging to identities that were not implicated by (or in) these borders. Often, this involved solidarity with a community of Ladino speakers that had long inhabited a *continuous* Ottoman space but now existed across several *contiguous* states.

Caught in a ten-year territorial dispute between Greece, Bulgaria, and the Ottoman Empire/Turkey, Edirne was a place where Jews learned to keep a safe distance from the nationalisms of these states and to associate borders with displacement and disruption, not identity formation or national regeneration. Why should they have adopted worldviews that sanctified the border and the state at a time when both kept changing? Put negatively, the Jews of Edirne demonstrated "forms of Jewish thinking and choice defined not by ideological certainties but by recognition of weakness, danger, and the need to predict"—as Kenneth Moss sees in interwar Poland.[13] Stated more positively, in an age when demographic engineering and ethnonationalism were in vogue, the Jews of Edirne resisted these trends by supporting less fashionable political strategies (but with language that was very much in style).[14] To give just one example, the above-mentioned Angèle Guéron decried the "cruel law" of ethnic homogeneity that forced so many people from their homes whenever borders moved.[15] (Instead, she called for states to assimilate minorities through language policy.[16])

In the first quarter of the twentieth century, Southeast Europe was a place where demographic engineering was often practiced by parties claiming liberal and/or progressive agendas. Eleftherios Venizelos, leader of Greece's Liberal Party, was an architect of the 1923 Greek-Turkish population exchange.[17] In the Ottoman Empire after the 1908 revolution, the Committee of Union and Progress (CUP, İttihad ve Terakki Cemiyeti) positioned itself as a liberal party even as it discreetly pushed local Christians out of Edirne Province and replaced them with Muslims from Bulgaria.[18] This was a reversal of the ancien régime policy, by which the old *vali* (governor-general) and his director of political affairs—a Jew named Robert Mizrahi—had tried to stop mass migration into and out of the empire.[19] In Edirne's Jewish community, Mizrahi was unusual for reaching such a high station in government but typical in his reluctance to see the border as a sorter of ethnicities.

This conservative stance was not unique to local Jews. However, it seemed to become less popular among Muslims and Christians with every wave of ethnic cleansing that swept Edirne Province after 1912. Historians of the Balkans have shown how violence was often the cause—not the effect—of certain identities and worldviews.[20] Similarly, I suggest that people who were forced into or out of Edirne because of their religion/ethnicity began attaching new meanings to the border, as a result of this experience.[21] Those who were spared such a fate, however, did not change the "mental maps" that inform political and cultural identities.[22] At least, this is the sense one gets from the Jewish community's documents, which show a striking refusal to interpret the border as anything more than a physical hindrance in an arbitrary place.

In the late Ottoman period, the Jews of Edirne Province were, by and large, neither victims nor perpetrators of mass violence. But the latter was a heavy presence in their lives. For example, Jews in the port city of Tekirdağ were largely untouched by the Bulgarian occupiers in 1913, even as these soldiers committed "systematic massacres" in an attempt to "exterminate the Turks" (according to a Jewish observer).[23] A year later, Jews across the province watched with dread as their Greek Orthodox neighbors became victims of an ethnic cleansing campaign led by the above-mentioned CUP. When the persecutions ensnared a local Jew holding Greek citizenship— one Albert Alfassa—Jewish leaders in Edirne and Istanbul successfully petitioned the Ottoman government to let Alfassa stay in Edirne Province.[24] These examples—and others—support the widespread notion that violence was central to the Jewish experience in the eastern part of Europe during the first half of the twentieth century. But they challenge the assumption that such violence naturally targeted Jews.

It is tempting to say that Edirne Jews were "bystanders" to this local violence, but that would obscure the agency practiced by so many members of the community.[25] In their efforts to survive the borderland, the Jews of Edirne may have been politically moderate and—in the broadest sense—conservative. But they were hardly passive. Local Jewish politics were dynamic, in touch with global trends, and internally contested. From the two women who volunteered at Edirne's military hospital (1912) to the local chief rabbi who lobbied on Alfassa's behalf (1914); from the young men who fought in the Ottoman army (1912–1918) to the educators who turned their schools into bomb shelters (1912, 1920); from the Hebrew teacher who served in the parliament of Greece during that country's occupation of Edirne (1920–1922) to the community members who came to see Zionism as a neutral strategy in a sensitive borderland (1922)—local Jews reacted to violence and upheaval in ways that involved much more than "standing by."

This active yet cautious style had much to do with the region's tortuous journey "from empire to nation-state."[26] That popular phrase belies a more complicated, less linear story, in which Edirne went from (Ottoman) empire to (Bulgarian) nation-state; back to (Ottoman) empire; and then to (Greek) nation-state—before finally (it seems) finding itself in the nation-state of Turkey. Especially for Jews, this zigzag path would affect life at the destination. During the ten-year period that began in 1912, Edirne Jews learned that conspicuous patriotism could become a liability if/when their town changed hands and that, ironically, revamped versions of traditional Ottoman-Jewish identity tended to be the safest bet. This was a successful strategy until 1923, but it eventually clashed with the Turkish state's call for assimilation and assertive Turkish nationalism.[27]

For example, consider the case of Rosa Mitrani's husband, Moise. He directed Edirne's largest Jewish school from 1903 to 1935, constantly hiring (and firing) language teachers according to the political winds. He hired Turkish (and Hebrew) teachers after the 1908 revolution, Bulgarian teachers in 1913, Greek teachers in 1920, and Turkish teachers (again) after 1922.²⁸ Another example was Yuda Razon, who owned one of the few presses in Edirne (at the time). Beginning in 1910, he printed Edirne's Ladino newspaper, *La Boz de la Verdad* (The Voice of Truth), using the Rashi-Hebrew typeface. During the Greek occupation, a French-language Jewish newspaper rolled off his press. After 1922, Razon printed the Turkish newspaper *Paşaeli* (Pasha Province) using Arabic characters (the way Turkish was written until 1929).²⁹ For these two masters of adaptation, Turkish nationalism must have looked like the next chapter in the story, not necessarily the conclusion.

With time, Yuda Razon, the Mitranis, and other Edirne Jews may very well have changed their worldviews. But patience, it turned out, was among the borderland's scarcer resources. During the first decade of the Turkish Republic, certain people grew hostile toward their Jewish neighbors for reasons that entailed local economic factors, government agendas in Ankara, and developments across the Balkans. Local, national, and international issues intersected to spur an outbreak of anti-Jewish violence in the summer of 1934, prompting thousands of Jews to leave the region and dealing the community a blow from which it would never recover. Notably, most people who fled the violence went no further than Istanbul—at least for the time being. What they left was not the country but the borderland.

This book is about people who struggled to survive near a state border, though few of them were interested in immediately leaving the country. It is about a community that eventually died, though the blood of individual Jews was rarely shed. This book opposes the "lachrymose" conception of Jewish history—which emphasizes perennial persecution and remains central to Zionism, for example—but also challenges whitewashed narratives of Turkish-Jewish friendship—which continue to characterize the official position of Turkish Jewry.³⁰ If these statements appear paradoxical, we might need to view our topic through a different lens. While nation building, minoritization, ethno-religious violence, and the "othering" of Jews are all part of this story, the modern history of Edirne's Jewish community cannot be fully understood without an additional framework: the borderland.

So far, I have mostly used that term to denote territory near an international border, with the added connotation of local violence stemming from contest between states. These rather negative traits—remoteness from the center and absence of peace—are two essential elements of what I mean by "borderland" (or "borderlands").[31] Additionally, however, I use that word to evoke *some* of the more positive traits developed by the field of borderlands studies, which burgeoned in the 1980s and 1990s.[32] Inasmuch as it supplies meaningful categories of analysis and powerful ways to decenter the bounded state, borderlands studies is an inspiration for this book. With that said, the field has traditionally focused on the Americas, and this limits its applicability to my study. I would now like to discuss the similarities and differences between the borderlands category used in this book and the tenets of borderlands studies.

As a preface to this discussion, I should note that historians have recently tried to modify the borderlands framework and apply it to the worlds of the Habsburg, Russian, and Ottoman Empires—as well as their successor states.[33] But as an Ottoman borderland in Europe, Edirne represents a unique case that is rarely captured by these studies. The borderlands of Central and Eastern Europe were characterized by some traits that were rare in the Ottoman Empire, such as large Jewish minorities living among Christian majorities.[34] Meanwhile, borders in the post-Ottoman Middle East were, by and large, *not* born out of ethnic cleansing projects—a fact that differentiates these borderlands from those of Southeast Europe (including the Edirne region).[35] Oscar J. Martinez's crucial claim that borderlands everywhere "share many functional commonalities" must be balanced against the need to recognize geographic and historical specificity.[36]

Core to borderlands studies is the notion that a borderland is an "intermediary space" spanning at least two states.[37] Therefore, "the unit of analysis is the region on both sides of the border."[38] Scholars go on to posit that "borderlanders" on opposite sides of the boundary often have more in common with each other than with fellow citizens in their respective state centers. According to Martinez, "borderlanders stand apart, especially in relation to people who live in heartland regions, because of the singular world in which they live." This borderland-heartland distinction can be as important as class difference or the urban-rural divide.[39] In this vein, Tejel and Öztan describe the Turkish-Syrian borderland as a distinct "social institution," while Gloria Anzaldúa claims that the US-Mexico borderland forms something of "a third country."[40]

To be sure, many Edirne Jews operated in a continuous zone that extended across Ottoman and Bulgarian territory (or Ottoman and Greek territory, in some moments). Local Ladino journalists wrote about their trips to Bulgaria, while their counterparts in Bulgaria visited and wrote about the Ottoman side of the border. Edirne synagogue members who owed taxes to the Ottoman authorities could often be found doing business in Bulgarian cities. Jewish girls from relatively poor families in Edirne worked as domestics across the border (and sometimes found themselves in highly vulnerable positions). When Bulgaria and the Ottoman Empire joined the Central Powers in World War I, some Sephardi Jews played important roles in the alliance, earning "the freedom to cross the border" (in the words of an Ottoman official).[41] Greece's subsequent annexation of Edirne prompted Zionist agitators to tour the region; most, however, came not from the Jewish center of Greece (Thessaloniki) but from a city across the Ottoman-Greek border (Istanbul).

However, certain factors prevented Edirne Jews from inhabiting a full-fledged "border society."[42] One was the intensity with which nationalist projects were implemented by the Ottoman and Turkish states. Borderlands literature often implies a center-periphery dichotomy in which the capital neglects, marginalizes, or colonizes the borderland, while locals fight to defend their "border interests" (often by working with people across the boundary line).[43] But Edirne had been a so-called core province until the late nineteenth century, when Bulgaria effectively seceded from the Ottoman Empire.[44] As the buffer between Istanbul and a foreign state[45]—and as a region that had played a central role in Ottoman history—Edirne was hardly peripheral for the Young Turks who took power in 1908. From their official calls for patriotic self-sacrifice and intercommunal brotherhood to their unofficial campaigns of ethnic cleansing and demographic engineering, the CUP's nation-building program was implemented in Edirne with great force and significant local support. It is telling that many Young Turk leaders came from the Balkans and that Talat Paşa—arguably the empire's de facto leader after 1913—was from Edirne.[46]

Life for Jews in late-Ottoman Edirne was characterized by a central tension. On the one hand, they had a long history of operating in networks that had only recently been intersected by a border (a line they often ignored). On the other hand, they faced new demands from the Ottoman/Turkish state and survived repeated efforts to violently "unmix" the local population.[47] For them, one trait of the borderland was its central place in both an interstate society *and* a (Turkish) nation-building project, simultaneously. In fact, Edirne's centrality in narratives of Turkish nationalism had no equivalent on the Bulgarian or Greek sides of the border—a reminder that borderlands are rarely, if ever, symmetrical.[48] Reflecting that tension, this book focuses on those Jews who would go on to live in the Republic of Turkey but emphasizes their continued links with people who wound up in Greece and Bulgaria.

In addition to Edirne's place in nation-building agendas, another factor gave local Jews a borderland experience that complicates the literature: it was precisely *as Sephardi Jews* that they became "transnational borderlanders."[49] For the subjects of this book, living near the border did not lead to fluid identities, ethnic ambiguity, or a "consciousness of the Borderlands."[50] On the contrary, as Edirne became a borderland, the vagaries and violence of everyday life pushed local Jews even further toward regional Sephardi networks and identity.

To be sure, the typical Edirne Jew interacted daily with local Muslims and Christians. He or she was also a member of several nested communities—the Jewish community of Edirne, Edirne at large, the Ottoman-Jewish *millet* (semiautonomous ethno-religious community), Ottoman citizenry, the Ladino cultural community, world Jewry—and different levels of identity were emphasized depending on the context. But these conditions applied to Jews in many Ottoman cities and, therefore, can hardly be counted as borderland traits.[51] Furthermore, the sources produced by Edirne Jews contain very few self-conscious expressions of a borderlander identity.[52] In fact, I could not even find a Ladino word for "borderland." (The word *"frontyera"* was always used to indicate the border*line*.[53]) Equally scarce in the sources are signs of ethnic ambiguity. While this was an important theme within the Christian population of Southeast Europe, the boundaries between Sephardim and their non-Jewish neighbors were relatively clear, polyglotism notwithstanding.[54]

Together, these nuances bring us to another trait of the Edirne borderland: this was a place where a community could have clear boundaries even as it crossed state borders, where people experienced distinct borderland conditions without participating in an especially mixed "border culture."⁵⁵ While this applied to locals of all religions, the ethnic cleansing projects of 1912–1922 put an end to the interstate Christian communities and diminished the interstate nature of the Muslim community.⁵⁶ Meanwhile, about half of the local Jewish community managed to stay in Edirne through this transition from empire to nation-state(s). These people were unique in that their group identity first facilitated but later complicated their continued existence in the borderland.

If Edirne Jews did not identify as borderlanders or partake in a hybrid border culture, they did have other tendencies, in the cultural realm, that distinguished them from coreligionists in Istanbul and Izmir (for example). Notably, writers in Edirne were especially apt to make interstate comparisons. From the above-mentioned Angèle Guéron to the editor of Edirne's Ladino newspaper, Jewish commentators offered insightful, firsthand reports on the similarities and differences between Bulgaria and the Ottoman Empire (especially regarding Jews). Meanwhile, local Ottoman-Turkish newspapers offered analogous observations regarding Muslim life on both sides of the border.⁵⁷ It should hardly be surprising that in Plovdiv, Bulgaria—just over one hundred miles away—the Ladino and Turkish presses both wrote about Edirne. This tendency to compare—and be compared—constitutes another borderland trait that will appear in subsequent chapters.

Jeremey Adelman and Stephen Aron distinguish imperial/colonial borderlands from the "bordered lands" of the modern nation-states that eventually triumphed in the Americas and beyond.⁵⁸ Their scheme is helpful here, to an extent. Certain factors that came to characterize life in Edirne—the problematization of longstanding ethno-religious diversity, new cultural orientations forced on locals, a process of economic marginalization—reflect the rigid borders of the closed nation-state and, therefore, a type of borderland that differs from the interstate entity described above.⁵⁹ However, the defining traits of the Jewish borderland experience—centrality in two systems at once; congruence between international networks and intercommunal boundaries; a culture of making interstate comparisons—lingered after 1923. To quote Ebru Boyar and Kate Fleet, "perceptions of geography remained pinned to an imperial understanding."⁶⁰ This book, then, will often refer to Edirne as a borderland in the Republican period. If becoming a borderland was a gradual process, so was becoming a closed and homogenous national periphery.

In addition to putting Jewish history in conversation with borderland studies, this book encourages scholars to compare and connect the experiences of Jews across borderlands. In particular, I am thinking of what Omer Bartov and Eric D. Weitz call the "shatterzone of empires": the meeting points of the late German, Habsburg, Russian, and Ottoman empires, as well as the borderlands of their successor states (until World War II).[61] As a preliminary effort, I will draw a few comparisons of this nature.

From Central Europe to Anatolia, Jews across borderlands endured constantly changing sovereignty. On this score, the experience of Edirne Jews resembled that of their coreligionists in the Russian "Pale of Settlement." For example, the cities of Vilna (Vilnius), Grodno, and Pinsk were occupied by the Germans during World War I and by the Soviets shortly after—only to fall within the boundaries of newly created Poland. (Today, Vilnius is in Lithuania while Grodno and Pinsk are in Belarus.) Of the factors that inhibited Jews from integrating into these empires and nation-states, the instability of borders has received relatively little attention from scholars.

Another trait common to the Ashkenazi and Sephardi worlds was the tendency for writers to draw interstate comparisons. As mentioned above, Ladino journalists in Bulgaria and the Ottoman Empire regularly wrote about Jewish communities across the border. Meanwhile, Hebrew writers in the Habsburg, Russian, and Prussian (later German) states wrote similar articles, often for newspapers published in border towns.[62] I speculate that Yiddish writers did this, too. Historians interested in working with Jewish newspapers might consider comparing the comparers—that is, doing a comparative study of how Yiddish, Hebrew, and Ladino journalists evaluated life on both sides of the border.

Finally, Jews across borderlands were compelled to abandon old networks and accept new, bounded orientations in their cultural and economic lives.[63] The fall of the Russian Empire in 1917 broke up the cultural zone of *Lite* (Yiddish for "Lithuania") as the Jewish communities of Kovno (Kaunas), Minsk, and Vilna became Lithuanian, Soviet, and Polish (respectively).[64] When the Habsburg Empire crumbled, German-speaking Jews from Czernowitz (Chernivtsi) to Trieste to Prague were severed from their beloved Austrian *kulturbereich* and its beating heart, Vienna.[65] And when Poland annexed much of Upper Silesia in 1921, the local community was cut off from the Prussian cities of Breslau (Wrocław) and Berlin, home to Germany's leading centers of Jewish learning.[66] (Today, Wrocław is in Poland.) These painful separations should be counted among other, more famous factors that transformed Jewish life in the borderlands around this time— namely, antisemitism, the politics of assimilation, and state preoccupations with security.

Of course, Jewish life across borderlands was also marked by significant variation. For example, some places had been borderlands for decades or even centuries, while others *become* borderlands during and after World War I. The first category includes Habsburg Galicia, where Jews had lived near the boundary with Russia since the Partitions of Poland (1772–1795). After 1918, they found themselves in a new country (the Second Polish Republic) and near a new border (with the Soviet Union)—but still near *a* border.[67] This category also includes the Jews of Van-Urmia, a Neo-Aramaic-speaking people who had lived, for centuries, on both sides of the Ottoman-Iranian border but saw that lifestyle expire during World War I.[68] The second category includes the Jews of certain Russian cities—Vilna, Grodno, Pinsk, and Minsk—that were not so close to the empire's edge in the nineteenth and early twentieth centuries. After World War I, however, these people suddenly found themselves in border towns.

Another trait that varied across space was the intensity of anti-Jewish violence. It was especially high in what is now western Ukraine and southeastern Poland. During World War I, the Jews of Habsburg Galicia were repeatedly attacked by occupying Russian troops, while Jews on the Russian side of the border were deported en masse to the interior.[69] After the war, "genocidal violence" claimed the lives of over one hundred thousand Jews in today's Ukraine.[70] This stands in stark contrast to the story of Edirne Jews, the attacks of 1934 notwithstanding. Minsk was somewhere in the middle of this spectrum. Located in a part of the Russian Empire that had seen very few pogroms, the local community suffered anti-Jewish violence during the Polish occupation of 1919–1920 but then over a decade of physical security, thanks largely to a Soviet clampdown on antisemitism.[71]

Finally, it is revealing to compare the different paths that brought borderland communities to Zionism, which I define here as advocacy for a Jewish "national home" in Palestine and/or affiliation with the World Zionist Organization (established 1897).[72] In Eastern Europe, Zionism gained popularity in the late nineteenth and early twentieth centuries, often as an exit strategy for fleeing poverty and violence and/or as a movement entailing deep ideological commitments.[73] In its ideological form, Zionism was generally a response to antisemitism and the Jewish question.[74]

In Edirne, however, Zionism emerged later and for different reasons. It was slow to catch on after the Young Turk Revolution, even compared to the situations in Salonica (today Thessaloniki, Greece), Istanbul, and Bulgaria. Only after the Balfour Declaration (1917) did Zionist rhetoric became a language for Edirne Jews to work out a range of issues, many of which had more to do with class, gender, and interpersonal rivalry than with putting Jews in Palestine or establishing a Jewish state. In a disputed borderland where the only political certainty seemed to be the presence of *a* nation-state—as opposed to any *particular* nation-state—Jews discovered that sometimes the most prudent path was a diluted form of Zionism that combined talk of a Jewish home in Palestine with functional elements that resembled diaspora nationalism.[75] For the subjects of this book, modern nationalism was not an exciting chance to break with the past so much as a dangerous, obligatory game in which the safest strategy could be a version of Zionism that recalled the old *millet* system. This situation emerged from a confluence of Ottoman and borderland factors.[76]

The following chapters are informed by a variety of sources, including Ottoman/Turkish government documents and newspapers, reports of European diplomats and commissions, the Ladino press in Istanbul and Salonica, commercial yearbooks printed in Istanbul, publications of international Jewish organizations, and various memoirs and travelogues. But at the core of this book are sources produced by Jews who lived in Edirne Province between 1908 and 1934. These include local Jewish newspapers (printed in Ladino and French), French-language reports penned by directors of local Jewish schools, records from the chief rabbinate of Edirne, merchants' letters, correspondence between leaders of local Jewish communities in various small towns, and other notes written in the Ladino cursive known as *soletreo*.[77]

While my source base is diverse in terms of language and genre, most of the people who produced these documents came from an admittedly narrow range of social groups. By and large, those who left written records were rabbis, merchants, members of communal councils, school directors, and upstarts who founded Jewish newspapers. The voices of Jewish Edirne's porters, paupers, female silk-spinners, and orphans are hard to capture, though I always seek traces of their presence.

As a result, the sources tend to have a political skew.[78] Merchants, rabbis, educators, and editors were more likely than their working-class (or unemployed) coreligionists to write about subjects such as the Ottoman government's domestic policies, nationalist currents within the empire's non-Muslim communities, scandals in the Jewish communal council, the economic consequences of border revisions, and the pros and cons of foreign occupation. Surely, workers and housewives discussed these topics too. But for the communal elite, these were occupational matters that made their way into banal documents.

Fortunately, the nature of the sources harmonizes with another important characteristic of Edirne and its Jewish community: the way that international politics permeated everyday life in the borderland. The defining feature of Edirne in the late Ottoman Empire and early Turkish Republic was its proximity to the state border (and the implications of that situation). Any study of this community, no matter what the focus, must reckon with this fact. Edirne denizens could hardly distinguish the local from the international or the social from the political.

Throughout the Ladino-speaking world, Jewish Edirne was known for its rich cultural and intellectual legacy. Yosef Karo lived here in the sixteenth century, shortly before writing the last great codification of Jewish law. Beginning in the seventeenth century, a local musical tradition known as *maftirim*—the term denotes both the singers and the songs—combined Hebrew paraliturgical poetry with vocal melodies from Ottoman court music. The style later spread to Jewish communities in Istanbul, Izmir, and beyond.[79] In the late nineteenth century, Edirne became a regional center of the intellectual movement known as Haskalah (Jewish Enlightenment).[80] Local *maskilim* (proponents of Haskalah) printed Jewish newspapers, founded cultural associations, taught modern Hebrew, and founded a rabbinical seminary.

While these topics are certainly worthy of scholarly attention, they are not the focus of this book. Over the past few decades, cultural and intellectual approaches to Jewish history have illuminated the Ashkenazi and, to a lesser extent, Sephardi experiences of modernity. But for reasons outlined in this introduction—the absence of a hybrid borderland culture, the political skew of the sources, the links between Jewish identity and socioeconomic networks, state violence that curbed cultural production and violently altered local demographics—the story of this borderland community calls for other approaches.

The five chapters of this book are arranged chronologically, though certain thematic patterns do emerge. For example, the first and last chapters deal heavily with economic structures and mobility, while the middle three focus on politics, broadly defined. This reflects the nature of the sources—valuable economic data happens to be available for the earliest and latest periods—but also the different issues that characterized Jewish life at different times. For example, while geopolitics were inescapable in Edirne from 1912 to 1922 (Chapters 2–4), socioeconomic forces gave the Jewish community much of its shape before 1908 (Chapter 1) and exacerbated many of its problems after 1923 (Chapter 5).

Chapter 1 sets the stage for my narrative by establishing the structures of Jewish life in Edirne Province on the eve of the 1908 revolution. While readers might associate Ladino-speaking communities with densely populated port cities, the subjects of this book lived in the inland city of Edirne and a constellation of towns (which were hardly "provincial," if that word connotes ethno-religious homogeneity). In the late nineteenth and early twentieth centuries, railroads and other new technologies integrated this far-flung community in unprecedented ways. Meanwhile, the Ottoman-Bulgarian border remained a rather ambiguous entity that was not so different from the boundaries of Ottoman provinces or even city neighborhoods. In a world where, by our standards, geographic boundaries were negotiable but ethno-religious ones were firm, Jewish identity was largely structured around socioeconomic networks that extended into Bulgaria (but remained distinct from the larger Sephardi centers of Salonica and Istanbul).

Moving from structures to events, Chapter 2 deals with the consequences of two developments that shook the Balkans in 1908: the Young Turk Revolution and Bulgaria's declaration of independence (from the Ottoman Empire). The former led to new public spheres and talk of brotherhood between the empire's ethno-religious communities; the latter gave new strength and meaning to the border. The period 1908–1912 marked a peak in terms of population size and political energy for the Jews of Edirne, but with this energy came debates about gender roles and the distribution of resources and power in the community (among other issues). Meanwhile, an awkward contradiction developed between the state's call for social integration and the border's tacit demand for separation. In this context, Jewish leaders tried to avoid politicizing internal debates and to escape the polarization that was occurring in other Sephardi communities, seeking, instead, a middle path between revolutionary integration and the assertive Jewish nationalism of self-described "Zionists."

Things take a darker turn in Chapter 3, which introduces the themes of violence and departure. During the Balkan Wars, Turkish-speaking Muslims and, later, Bulgarian-speaking Christians became victims of ethnic cleansing. In 1914, Ottoman leaders used various means to expel Orthodox Greeks from the region. During World War I, thousands of Armenians from Edirne Province were sent to die in the Syrian desert, as part of a larger genocide orchestrated by members of the CUP. This was hardly a good period for local Jews, and many moved to Istanbul and the Americas. Still, they were spared the experience of forced displacement. As a result, they did not join their Muslim and Christian neighbors (or former neighbors) in attaching new meanings to the border but rather *strengthened* connections with Ladino speakers in Bulgaria. In a province that was suddenly emptied of its Christian population, the meaning of the borderland was changing for local Jews (even if the meaning of the border was not).

Chapter 4 covers Greece's annexation of the Edirne region—now called Eastern Thrace—which lasted from 1920 to 1922. After an eight-year separation, the Jews of Eastern and Western Thrace were reunited, this time under Greek rule (instead of Ottoman). Coming on the heels of the Balfour Declaration, this was the first—and only—time when Zionist discourse was prominent in Edirne's Jewish community. But even then, Zionism was less of an ideological commitment than a survival strategy (in the context of Greek occupation) and a common ground (in the context of intracommunal dust-ups). From 1920 to 1922, Zionism was acceptable to anti-Ottoman Greek authorities. And in 1923, it allowed Jews to plausibly tell the new Turkish regime that they had not been pro-Greek so much as pro-*Jewish*. (Meanwhile, most of Eastern Thrace's Greek Orthodox population fled across the border to Greece.)

With that said, Zionist expressions quickly became unacceptable in the new Turkish Republic, and Edirne Jews were soon accused of disloyalty, predatory lending, and refusing to speak Turkish. Chapter 5 surveys the state of the (diminished) community at a time when few Christians were left in the region and Turkish nationalism permeated all spheres of life, including the economic realm. The commercial void left by departing Christians was largely filled by Jews, a development that frustrated some Turkish-Muslim notables. Meanwhile, a series of international developments seemed to threaten the security of Turkey's northwestern border and to spur an influx of Muslims from the Balkans. In the summer of 1934, this perfect storm of local, domestic, and international factors led to an outbreak of anti-Jewish violence from which the community would never recover. The borderland was now a securitized space where communal life was virtually impossible for *all* religious minorities.[81] By some definitions, then, the region ceased to be a borderland.

Perhaps more than anything else, adaptation and moderation helped the Jewish community of Edirne survive the period 1908–1923. But those two traits were of limited use in the early Republican period. When the Jews of Eastern Thrace adjusted to the new demographic and economic landscape by filling commercial roles previously held by Christians, local Turkish newspapers responded with antisemitic tropes. When the revolutionary program of President Mustafa Kemal (Atatürk) sought to rapidly "Turkify" society, the moderate pace at which Jews replaced Ladino with Turkish—and left international networks for national ones—was too slow for some commentators.[82]

This brings up a final question: Had the Jews of Eastern Thrace acted differently, could they have somehow prevented the 1934 Thrace Events? To answer "no" is to rob our subjects of agency. But to answer "yes" is to blame violence on the victims (at least partially).

I am more inclined to commit the first sin than the second. If the strategies of adaptation and moderation failed the Jewish community after 1923, I doubt that a more committed and extreme approach to Turkification would have helped (or was possible). After the Young Turk Revolution and even amid the violence of 1912 to 1922—from the "eye of the storm," so to speak[83]—Edirne Jews exercised remarkable amounts of agency. This is an important theme of the book, especially Chapters 2–4. But after 1922, space for Jewish agency was narrowing in Thrace. We might count this as a final indicator that the age of imperial borderlands was giving way to a paradigm of closed national peripheries.

ONE

Foundations of a Borderland Community

Mobility, Networks, and Economic Life

IN 1876, EDIRNE PROVINCE WAS at the heart of Ottoman Europe, hundreds of miles from the neighboring states of Russia, Austria-Hungary, and Greece.[1] By 1915, it found itself at the edge of a rapidly shrinking empire, all but surrounded by a country that had not existed four decades prior. That year, soldiers manning the hilltop fortress in the city of Edirne (the provincial capital) could see Bulgarian villages dotting the Thracian plain.

For Edirnelis—the Ladino word, borrowed from Turkish, for residents of the city of Edirne—the encroaching border brought modern politics into their lives with an abruptness that was harsh even by the standards of early twentieth-century Europe.[2] State borders are political entities, by definition, and subsequent chapters of this book will explore how the moving, morphing border affected political choices and national identities for Edirne's Muslims, Christians, and especially Jews. At some point, local life and international politics became hopelessly entangled in Edirne.

But this chapter starts before that point. The 1908 Young Turk Revolution was a milestone in the transition from Ottoman Empire to Turkish nation-state.[3] On the eve of that event—and sometimes on its morrow—Edirnelis understood the Ottoman-Bulgarian border through lenses other than that of modern, territorial nationalism. After all, the legally ambiguous frontier was still in the process of becoming a state border, and other types of boundaries—between neighborhoods, communities, classes, or Ottoman provinces—remained formidable.[4] Compared to the world inhabited by most readers of this book, the *vilayet* of Edirne circa 1908 was a place where affiliation with (putatively) religious communities was strong, but identification with the state was weak; where regional trips were taxing, but international travel was not especially difficult; where upward social mobility was rare, but mobility across borders was common.[5] For denizens of the city and province of Edirne, the border was not the extraordinary entity it would soon become. Rather, it was one of several types of boundaries shaping everyday life.[6]

This, at least, was the case for the Sephardi Jews who are the subject of this book. I suspect that their Muslim and Christian neighbors also hesitated, at this time, to see the border as an essential divide between ethno-religious groups, though that hypothesis calls for further research.[7] Subsequent chapters argue that local Jewish attitudes toward the border eventually became unique. But I doubt this was the case before 1908 (or even 1912). While this chapter focuses on the Jewish experience, it invites comparisons with other local communities.

What, if not the border, provided meaning, structure, and limitation to the lives of Edirne Jews? If territorial nationalism was not the framework people used to situate themselves in the world, what was? On the collective level, what forces shaped the Jewish community of Edirne Province, and how did these interact with the border? The answers involve regional factors that were economic, geographic, demographic, and institutional (regarding religious institutions, especially). Only by studying these underlying structures can we glimpse the lived reality of Edirnelis and see how Jews in a constellation of towns maintained a supercommunity that spanned—and sometimes surpassed—Edirne Vilayet. Structures such as economic forces, mobility regimes, transportation infrastructure, educational networks, and religious institutions will help us understand this late-Ottoman community and the border that was slowly dividing it.[8]

As explored in later chapters, themes such as modern nationalism and social integration would soon become important (and controversial) for the local Jewish community. But such issues developed over other systems. In fact, the larger breakdown in intercommunal relations that came to characterize Edirne Province after 1912 was about politics and culture, to be sure, but also underlying socioeconomic factors that nationalism did not *replace* so much as *accumulate over*.[9] That is another large claim that exceeds the scope of this book, but I will support it with examples from the Jewish experience.

This chapter begins with a brief history of Edirne that focuses on commerce and mobility—two factors that were especially important in structuring local Jewish life. It shows how, in the period 1878–1908, the Ottoman-Bulgarian border developed from a combination of forces involving nationalism and states but also religious institutions and railroads. The next two sections describe Jewish settlement patterns in the city and province of Edirne, focusing especially on networks that bound the communities of about a dozen towns. The fourth section looks at socioeconomic strata *within* a typical Jewish community of the province, noting regional idiosyncrasies that distinguished the Jewish experience in Edirne from that in other *vilayets*. Switching from *actual* economic life to an occupational profile that was *desired* for the community (by some Jews), the fifth section discusses an ambitious agenda we might call "Jewish productivization." Finally, to give an early example of nationalist conflicts accruing over commercial ones, the last section turns to instances of "economic warfare" waged by various ethno-religious communities in the province shortly after the Young Turk Revolution.[10]

BECOMING A "BORDER PROVINCE": A BRIEF HISTORY OF OTTOMAN EDIRNE

On the eve of the Young Turk Revolution, Edirne Province was a place of contradictions. It was a "core" province in the sense that it neighbored Istanbul, had been in the empire for over five centuries, and hosted major state institutions such as the Ottoman Second Army.[11] At the same time, the empire's retreat from Europe was turning Edirne into a border province. According to Kemal Karpat's dichotomy, "core" provinces were "more Ottoman, Islamic and Turkish-speaking," while borderlands were "culturally, religiously and linguistically more heterogenous."[12] But Edirne had a (slim) Muslim majority *and* one of the empire's largest populations of Ottoman Christians (most of whom were Orthodox Greeks).[13] Geographically, the *vilayet* had hundreds of miles of coastline along the Marmara and Aegean Seas, yet commerce centered on inland networks. Even the border itself was something of a puzzle: de facto a boundary between Bulgaria and the Ottoman Empire, de jure it was a line between two Ottoman provinces. Demystifying these paradoxes calls for a brief history of the region.

In the second century, Roman Emperor Hadrian built a city over an old Greek and Thracian settlement near the junction of three rivers—the Arda, Tunca (Tundzha) and Meriç (Maritza). Hadrianopolis, as it was called, was strategically built on the Via Militaris that connected Constantinople (Istanbul) with Singidunum (Belgrade). For much of the Middle Ages, Adrianopolis—Greek speakers dropped the "H"—was a Byzantine city near the border with the Bulgarian Empire, though the latter occupied it at least once. In the 1360s, the city was conquered by the Ottomans, who called it Edirne and soon made it the capital of their rapidly expanding empire.[14]

In 1453, the Ottomans conquered Istanbul and moved their capital there. But the sophisticated provisioning systems that had developed around Edirne lasted well into the seventeenth century, when the city continued to host the imperial court.[15] Edirne also served as a staging ground for an army that, until 1683, was advancing into Europe. European diplomats and members of the Ottoman *askeri* class—military officers and civil administrators—demanded a range of goods that local merchants and artisans happily supplied. For example, many Jews produced or provisioned broadcloth, silk, and other fabrics for an *askeri* clientele in the early-modern period.[16]

Edirne's prestige largely stemmed from the presence of the sultan's court. When this institution returned to Istanbul in 1703, Edirne became—officially, at least—a typical city in the province of Rumeli (whose capital was Sofia). Even on the level of the district (*sancak*), the administrative center was not Edirne but rather nearby Çirmen (today Ormenio, Greece).[17] In terms of political status in the empire, the period 1703–1826 marked a low point.

Economically, however, things were moving in the opposite direction. The eighteenth century was a growth period for Edirne, as the city continued to benefit from the institutions and infrastructure that had developed in previous centuries. A locally dyed yarn known as "Edirne red" (*rouge d'Andrinople*) remained popular in Western Europe, and by the 1820s Edirne was exporting silk to England. Until 1817, French and English merchant vessels sailed to and from Edirne via the Meriç River, which linked the city to the Aegean port of Enez, downstream, and to Filibe, upstream.[18] (Called Philippopolis by the Greeks, Ottoman Filibe is today Plovdiv, Bulgaria.) From the mid-eighteenth to the mid-nineteenth centuries, the annual fair at Uzuncaova (today Uzundzhovo, Bulgaria) was among the largest in the empire, attracting merchants from Russia, Hungary, Poland, Germany, and Ottoman Anatolia. Local Jews were heavily represented, especially in the textiles trade.[19]

If the eighteenth century saw economic growth but an administrative downgrade for Edirne, the nineteenth century saw the opposite combination. On the one hand, the city became capital of a new province called the *eyalet* of Edirne in 1826—which became the *vilayet* of Edirne in 1867. On the other hand, the regional economy was faltering. The port of Enez silted up to the point that only small rafts could get from the city of Edirne to the sea.[20] The rise of the steamship and the opening of the Suez Canal (in 1869) helped create a global economy that favored ports and sprawling commercial empires at the expense of inland cities and trade fairs.[21] Meanwhile, during the Russo-Ottoman War of 1828–1829, Russia occupied Edirne and spurred many Muslims to leave.[22] On the heels of this, a silkworm epidemic struck the region, decimating the production of highly valuable silk cocoons.[23] By the late nineteenth century, observers were noting that Edirne was commercially inferior even to the smaller city of Plovdiv.[24] A Ladino newspaper in Salonica summarized the situation as follows: "Every year, *Andrinopole* has been moving a bit further back. Regrettably, its position in the interior of the country has caused it to gradually lose its former commercial importance."[25]

To these forces that hurt Edirne specifically, we can add one that affected the Ottoman Empire in general: cheap manufactures imported from Western Europe. As early as 1835, the British consul in Edirne was writing that "the import trade is perfectly free in every respect." He was exaggerating only slightly. The region was importing large quantities of cotton manufactures from England and woolen manufactures from the German states (while exporting animal hides, raw wool, rose oil, and other agricultural products to Western Europe). The consul added that local trade had recently "diminished" due to competition from the Danubian principalities (today's Romania), another consequence of British influence.[26] In 1838, trade agreements made between the Ottoman Empire and Britain—followed by other European countries—indefinitely extended the empire's low import duties, to the detriment of Edirne's spinners and weavers.[27]

A second, largely overlooked, consequence of these trade agreements was a two-tiered system of domestic tariffs (*iç gümrükler*). By 1840, the domestic tariffs that traders had always paid when transporting goods from one Ottoman region to another were effectively waived for foreign merchants but *raised* for Ottoman subjects (except those employed by European consulates). To facilitate revenue collection, customshouses proliferated throughout the empire.[28] The situation was disastrous for the inland merchants of Edirne and decried by a range of commentators, from the Young Ottoman (*Yeni Osmanlı*) ideologue Namık Kemal to the Bulgarian-speaking Edirne native Petko Slaveykov. In 1873, the latter wrote the following: "Once upon a time, Edirne had enjoyed a golden age in terms of inland trade. But in the face of a growing customs regime, the local economy began to lag."[29]

Domestic tariffs were lowered in 1874, but by then another crisis was brewing. At the time, Edirne Province was home to about five hundred thousand Muslims and eight hundred thousand non-Muslims.[30] Of the latter, most were categorized by the Ottoman state as *Rum*—Orthodox Greeks under the religious authority of the Ecumenical Patriarch in Istanbul. As such, the *Rum* constituted one of the empire's officially recognized ethno-religious communities, a structure known in Turkish as a *millet*.[31] Many *Rum* residents of Edirne Province were Bulgarian speakers, and some of them started to demand a separate Bulgarian church in the mid-nineteenth century.

Their goal was soon achieved. In 1870, Sultan Abdülaziz issued a *firman* establishing the Bulgarian Exarchate—an ecclesiastic district within the Eastern Orthodox Church, overseen by a special metropolitan in Istanbul called the exarch.[32] His jurisdiction began just north of the city of Edirne and extended to the Danube River, covering dioceses mainly in the provinces of Tuna (Danube) and Edirne. Additional dioceses could join the exarchate if two-thirds of the local Orthodox population voted to do so. In 1872, the exarch took the additional step of declaring his church to be autocephalous (self-headed). The Ecumenical Patriarchate ruled that the exarch had brought ethnonational criteria into ecclesiastical matters, and that this constituted a new heresy called phyletism.[33] In contrast, the Ottomans regarded the *Bulgar milleti* as a strictly religious category, hoping that it would not morph into a nationalist movement with separatist designs.[34]

But it did. The borders of the exarchate laid the rough parameters for the nation-state of Bulgaria that emerged from the Russo-Ottoman War of 1877–1878 (for all intents and purposes). During that conflict, Russian troops again occupied the city of Edirne, and hundreds of thousands of Muslims—plus a few thousand Jews—fled Bulgarian lands (for Edirne, Istanbul, and Anatolia).[35] The postwar settlement turned most of Tuna Vilayet into the Principality of Bulgaria—de jure an Ottoman vassal state but de facto an independent country. The settlement also made the northern half of Edirne Vilayet an autonomous province called Eastern Rumelia (Rumeli-i Şarkı).

In 1885, Bulgaria effectively annexed Eastern Rumelia.[36] Though statesmen continued to maintain the legal fiction that Bulgaria and Eastern Rumelia were under Ottoman suzerainty, European maps began to say otherwise.[37] Meanwhile, checkpoints and customshouses were established on both sides of Edirne Province's northern border. Train passengers soon had to endure inspection by customs officers when traveling between Edirne (the capital of Edirne Province) and Plovdiv (the capital of Eastern Rumelia).[38] By 1886, Bulgaria was busy doing the things that sovereign states were wont to do, even in an era known for rising free trade: establishing borders and tariffs that inhibited the flow of people, money, and goods.[39] As for the *vilayet* of Edirne, it had begun the painful process of becoming a border province.

But that is not the end of the story. After a tumultuous nineteenth century—which lasted through 1905, when a fire ravaged the city of Edirne—the region began to enjoy some positive trends. By 1908, the population was again growing, especially in the Jewish community.[40] The silk industry had been revived, thanks largely to investment and technology from the European-controlled Ottoman Public Debt Administration.[41] In the city of Edirne, the burned-out Jewish and Christian quarters were rebuilt along a grid plan, with wide, tree-lined streets replacing ancient warrens. Almost all of Edirne's thirteen wooden synagogues were beyond repair, so Jewish leaders decided to build one large house of worship that symbolized and facilitated a greater degree of centralization in the community.[42] Finally, as discussed in the next chapter, the 1908 Young Turk Revolution would bring new freedoms to Edirnelis of all religions, at least initially.

Between the Russo-Ottoman War (1877–1878) and the Balkan Wars (1912–1913), people on both sides of the new border generally adapted to its presence. By 1886, Bulgaria and the Ottoman Empire were already close trading partners.[43] As late as 1910, customs duties between the neighboring states were very low,[44] and even these were often dodged through smuggling.[45] The Ottoman archives show that, into the early 1900s, members of certain Edirne synagogues sojourned in "Bulgaria and Eastern Rumelia" to pursue the sugar trade and other business. Ottoman authorities only bothered them for the military exemption tax that most non-Muslims paid the state (until 1909, when universal conscription began in earnest).[46]

Crucially, Edirnelis were free to take the train to and from Bulgaria—so long as they had valid passports and the patience to endure customs checkpoints and disinfection procedures.[47] These hassles were not so different from those encountered on domestic itineraries. For example, the train ride from Edirne to Salonica entailed a long stop in Drama (today in Greece), where Ottoman authorities disinfected cars, inspected documents, and

Figure 2. The Great Synagogue of Edirne, after its 2015 restoration.
Source: CeeGee. Wikipedia Commons. CC BY-SA 4.0.

recorded the names of all passengers.⁴⁸ The authorities also tended to limit travel between Edirne and Istanbul, especially during the increasingly anxious reign of Abdülhamid II (1876–1909).⁴⁹ In 1906, the British consul in Edirne noted that Armenian and Bulgarian Orthodox residents especially were being denied the necessary documents for traveling to the capital.⁵⁰

Before 1908, Ottoman and Bulgarian authorities policed their shared border to collect revenue but also to prevent mass migration. Aside from a temporary expulsion of some Bulgarian speakers after a 1903 uprising, the authorities in Edirne generally did not try to expel Christians (or bring in Muslims).⁵¹ As the local British consul wrote in 1907, the *vali* and his director of political affairs—a Jew named Robert Mizrahi—prevented mass migration by pursuing "a strict application of the passport system at the frontier."⁵² In most cases, Istanbul did not revoke Ottoman citizenship from Christians who moved to Bulgaria, and the emigrants' tax burdens fell to relatives who remained in the empire. This policy caused headaches for officials in Bulgaria.⁵³ Little wonder that Ottoman and Bulgarian authorities both tried to control the flow of Ottoman citizens across the border by requiring passports.⁵⁴

Until 1908, the latitudinal line separating Edirne Vilayet from Eastern Rumelia was officially a border between two Ottoman provinces. While this was largely a legal fiction, Sofia's control of the border was truly limited, as the two regions were linked by the Oriental Railway—a Vienna-based company that was disinclined to take orders from Bulgaria.⁵⁵ (In the Balkans at this time, all railways in Ottoman successor states had been nationalized, while all railways in Ottoman provinces—including Eastern Rumelia—were still owned by European companies.⁵⁶) When the Young Turk Revolution triggered labor unrest throughout the empire, a strike among Oriental Railway workers spread from Istanbul to Eastern Rumelia, and management saw no choice but to beg Sofia for help—even at the cost of major concessions.⁵⁷ Seizing the opportunity, Bulgaria's state railway took over the line in Eastern Rumelia (and runs it to this day). This railroad nationalization encouraged Sofia to officially annex Eastern Rumelia and to declare Bulgaria's independence (on October 5).⁵⁸

In a way, the incident calls to mind Charles S. Maier's claim that railroads helped modern states establish *territoriality*—"the properties, including power, provided by the control of bordered political space, which ... created the framework for national and often ethnic identity."⁵⁹ Along with running schools, post offices, a telegraph agency, and other institutions that fully "pervaded" national space, running the railway—from the Serbian to the Ottoman borders—allowed Sofia to ensure that "no point inside the frontiers could be left devoid of the state's control."⁶⁰ Borders, railroads, and territory were intertwined issues. After a seven-month standoff in which troops gathered on both sides of the border, Ottoman leaders finally acknowledged the new reality: the northern edge of Edirne Province was also the limit of their empire.⁶¹

SETTLEMENT PATTERNS IN THE CITY

Though the Jews of Edirne Province were relatively spread out (compared to Jews in other *vilayets*), the city of Edirne was clearly their center. It had served this function for centuries. Greek-speaking (Romaniot) Jews inhabited the city in the Byzantine era, and Ottoman conquest led to an influx of Ashkenazi Jews expelled from France, Hungary, and elsewhere. This trend reversed when most of Edirne's Jewish community was moved to Istanbul in 1453 as part of Mehmed II's effort to repopulate his new capital through *sürgün* (forced relocation). But Edirne's Jewish population grew again after 1492, when Sephardim arrived from Spain and Portugal (often via other places).⁶² Through the early-modern period, Edirne saw the growth of a Jewish community whose origins were betrayed by the names of its thirteen synagogues: Buda, Germany, Sicily, Italy, Apulia, Portugal, Little Portugal, Catalonia, Toledo, Aragon, Majorca, Istanbul, and Exile (whose members also had roots in Italy).⁶³

For centuries, the city's Jewish center had been the Kaleiçi neighborhood—site of the old Byzantine city and, in Ottoman times, the non-Muslim quarter. The 1905 fire did not change this fact, but it prompted Jewish settlement in other neighborhoods to an extent that broke centuries of custom. The riverfront area of Tabakhane—named after the tanneries that operated there—became populated mostly by poor Jews, while nearby Sabuni and Tahtakale attracted a middling set. Hundreds of Jews moved to the leafy suburb of Karaağaç while the city was being rebuilt, and those who could afford the neighborhood tended to stay.⁶⁴ Populated mostly by Ottoman

Christians and citizens of European countries, Karaağaç was the site of the train station, the hotels for Oriental Express passengers, and the German, French, and Italian schools for the children of railway employees.[65]

On the eve of the Balkan Wars, the city of Edirne was home to about 55,000 Muslims, 20,000 Jews, 20,000 Orthodox Greeks, 10,000 Bulgarian Christians, and 6,000 Armenians.[66] Each community was linked to certain neighborhoods (*mahalles*). In a pattern that was typical for Ottoman cities, Muslims tended to live on the hill, while Jews and Christians lived closer to the water (the Tunca and Meriç Rivers, in this case).[67] The Kaleiçi quarter was divided into Jewish and Christian neighborhoods, the latter being subdivided into Greek, Bulgarian, and Armenian zones. Orthodox Greeks also clustered in the Yıldırım neighborhood, just across the Tunca, and Bulgarian Christians also lived Kıyık, a hilltop neighborhood overlooking Selimiye Mosque and containing Edirne's military fortress. Edirne's downtown was in the Sabuni neighborhood, where locals of all religions came to do business in the European-style city hall (completed 1900), the sprawling covered markets (Ali Paşa Çarşısı and Bedesten Çarşısı), and the redoubtable stone *hans* (caravansaries-turned-offices).[68]

The historical record says little about what must have been the norm: people were careful not to challenge the socioreligious order or cross sensitive communal boundaries. What the sources *do* reveal are the scandals that erupted in Edirne when the norm was occasionally broken. When a Bulgarian-Christian church opened in the predominantly Greek Orthodox Yıldırım neighborhood, the building soon burned down under suspicious circumstances.[69] And, as discussed in the next chapter, residents of the Jewish Quarter were so territorial that they had a gunfight with police after a building in their neighborhood was demolished by the municipality.

In most cases, the ethno-religious character of a given neighborhood was acknowledged tacitly. But in at least one instance, it was explicitly evoked. The story took place not in Edirne but in Dimetoka (today Didymoteicho, Greece), twenty-five miles south. In 1910, leaders of the local Jewish community announced their plan to build a new Jewish school. But Muslim notables protested, claiming that the proposed site was in a Muslim neighborhood. To their consternation, these objections were overruled by Ottoman authorities in Edirne and Istanbul. According to Eyal Ginio, the affair caused lasting damage to Muslim-Jewish relations in Dimetoka. "The *mahalle*," he writes, "served as the essential component of the [Ottoman] city's residential areas and the primary setting of communal life."⁷⁰ For some conservative voices, transgressing neighborhood boundaries was tantamount to transgressing the ethno-religious boundaries that continued to structure Ottoman society, even after the Young Turk Revolution.

SETTLEMENT PATTERNS IN THE PROVINCE

This excursion to Dimetoka brings us to a crucial topic: the towns that spanned Edirne Province. From 1878 to 1912, the *vilayet* was bounded by the Black Sea in the East, the Nestos (Mesta Karasu) River in the West, the Marmara and Aegean seas in the South, and the border with Bulgaria/Eastern Rumelia in the North. As the towns that dotted this region grew increasingly integrated, so did their small Jewish communities. By the early twentieth century, a veritable supercommunity had emerged, with borders that mostly mapped onto—but sometimes surpassed—the borders of the province.⁷¹ Both the shape of this community and the forces that bound it would have important consequences for Edirne Jews in the period covered by this book.

In some of these towns, Jews had arrived before the modern period.⁷² For example, Kırklareli, Dimetoka, and Çorlu were home to very old Jewish communities that only grew larger in the nineteenth century, when Jews from the city of Edirne increasingly chose to settle in places where they could be closer to suppliers of agricultural goods.⁷³ The fact that certain surnames came to proliferate in certain towns—Mitrani in Kırklareli, Djivre in Dimetoka, Barokas in Çorlu—suggests that people struck out from the city with their extended families.⁷⁴ While the Russo-Ottoman War of 1877–1878 sent thousands of non-Christians from the countryside to the city of Edirne, some of the Jewish refugees continued on to small towns in the eastern part of the province (such as Çorlu).⁷⁵

The nineteenth century saw the growth of existing Jewish communities but also the establishment of new ones. In Babaeski, Uzunköprü, and İskeçe, Jewish communities appeared after 1878.⁷⁶ (The first two towns are now in Turkey; the last is now Xanthi, Greece.) By 1907, over 35 percent of

Edirne Province's Jews lived outside the central district. For comparison, only 24 percent of the Jews in Aydın Province (home to Izmir) and 7 percent of the Jews in Selanik Province (home to Salonica) lived beyond the central district.[77] The dispersed nature and inland orientation of Edirne's Jewish community brought deep interaction with (non-Jewish) villagers and peasants—a dynamic that would persist into the 1930s.

Before 1912, the *vilayet* of Edirne consisted of six *sancaks*. The central *sancak* contained the city of Edirne and, just across the river, the suburb of Karaağaç. It also included Dimetoka, Mustafapaşa (today Svilengrad, Bulgaria), and Uzunköprü—home to the world's longest stone bridge (completed in 1444). Mustafapaşa and especially Dimetoka were home to vibrant Jewish communities closely linked to the one in urban Edirne. In a Ladino newspaper piece from 1904, a Dimetoka Jew described the relationship between the Edirne community and his own as that between "a mother and her daughter" (*una madre kon su idja*).[78] By 1910, about 950 Jews lived in Dimetoka and 600 in Mustafapaşa.[79]

Just east of the central *sancak* was Kırklareli, a majority-Christian district where Jews and Greeks were known for their homemade wine and raki (*rakı*).[80] Of the *sancak*'s 1,700 Jews, about 1,200 inhabited the namesake city, while the remainder lived mostly in the town of Lüleburgaz.[81] Edirne's Ladino newspaper referred to the Jews of Edirne and Kırklareli as "sister communities" (*komunidades ermanas*).[82] This extension of the family metaphor—along with evidence of socioeconomic ties—suggests that Kırklareli, Dimetoka, and Mustafapaşa were the three towns of the province whose Jewish communities were closest, in every sense, to the "mother" community in urban Edirne.[83]

Moving away from the border and toward Istanbul, one reached the *sancak* of Tekirdağ. The eponymous port city was the regional center of Armenian commerce and culture. Meanwhile, the local community of 1,500 Jews was notoriously poor.[84] The *sancak* of Tekirdağ also included the inland town of Çorlu, home to one thousand Jews who found themselves midway between the cities of Edirne and Istanbul.[85] Tekirdağ and Çorlu were important nodes in Edirne Province's Jewish network, as evidenced by their commercial orientations and their frequent appearances in Edirne's Ladino newspaper.[86]

Southwest of the central district is a region now called Western Thrace but then split into two *sancaks*: Dedeağaç and Gümülcine. The Dedeağaç district included the inland town of Sofulu (today Soufli, Greece), which enjoyed a thriving silk industry, and the port city of Dedeağaç (today Alexandroupoli, Greece). Known for decades as a "mere cluster of fisherman's huts," Dedeağaç was linked by rail to Istanbul and Edirne in 1873 and to Salonica in 1896. It was also connected to Istanbul by boat service.[87] In such a young town, however, the Jewish population never grew much larger than 300.[88]

Gümülcine, the only district in which over half the population was Muslim, was home to 1,290 Jews, most of whom lived in the eponymous center (today Komotini, Greece).[89] Traveling from the city of Edirne to the city of Gümülcine required—and still requires—circumventing the Rhodope Mountains along a route that hugs the Aegean. This is how a Jewish schoolteacher from Edirne arrived in 1901. He claimed that "half" of Gümülcine's Jews were "Salonikiyotes" (people who hailed from Salonica), an indication that he was approaching the western edge of Jewish Edirne.[90] The Gümülcine district also included the leafy town of İskeçe (Xanthi), a colorful collection of mansions, mosques, churches, and tobacco warehouses nestled in the foothills of the Rhodopes. Only in the late nineteenth century did Jews flock to this burgeoning tobacco entrepôt, especially from Edirne, Dimetoka, Salonica, and Serres.[91]

In the Jewish world I am mapping, the *sancak* of Gelibolu (Gallipoli) had the weakest connection to the provincial capital. Located on a peninsula between the Aegean Sea and the Dardanelles, Gelibolu had little in common with the other five *sancaks* of Edirne Province. For example, the economy centered on maritime trade, and the district was almost 70 percent Greek Orthodox. Though Gelibolu was home to a thriving community of almost 2,500 Jews, its relative independence and orientation toward Istanbul prompt me to keep it on the periphery of this study.[92] With that said, Gelibolu and Çanakkale (just across the Dardanelles) were among the towns that saw anti-Jewish violence during the 1934 Thrace Events—a fact that suggests lasting connections between this region and the core of Jewish Edirne.

Having mapped the province's subcommunities, we can now turn to the forces that linked these disparate clusters of Jews. What were the ties that bound the supercommunity of Edirne Vilayet? Leaving aside the Ladino press—discussed in the next chapter—I will explore four factors that held together this regional Jewish entity: the local chief rabbinate, commercial firms and institutions, a network of Jewish schools, and a new rail system.

For centuries, the Ottomans had allowed a local chief rabbinate to lead the Jewish community of Edirne. Initially limited to the city and its immediate hinterland, the rabbinate's jurisdiction—and tax base—eventually grew to include the entire province.[93] When the office holder died in 1722, the thirteen synagogues of Edirne could not agree on a replacement, and two chief rabbis were elected. The schism was mended by 1839 (at the latest), when a *firman* from Sultan Abdülmecid officially recognized Joseph Raphael ben Mordechai as *haham başı* (chief rabbi) of all Edirne congregations. The office suffered when, after 1878, much of its flock fell into the jurisdiction of the new chief rabbinate of Bulgaria (based in Sofia).[94] Nevertheless, the Edirne chief rabbinate continued to lead a community that numbered twenty-four thousand souls by 1907.[95]

In return for the right to collect revenues, the chief rabbi performed various duties. For example, he effectuated Jewish divorces by providing a document known as a *get*—a service that was especially important for smaller communities lacking a local religious authority.[96] The office was also a clearinghouse for information on people's marital status. If a young Jewish man arrived in a town claiming to be a bachelor, the president of the local community might ask the chief rabbinate in Edirne to confirm the claim. Also, each year the chief rabbi provided the various subcommunities with the *lulav*—a bundle of branches and fronds used ritually during the Sukkot harvest festival. Customarily if not officially, the chief rabbi of Edirne was expected to intercede with the *vali* on behalf of the Jewish community, should there be trouble from local authorities, Greek Orthodox merchants, Turkish newspapers, and so on. In short, the chief rabbinate united the Jews of Edirne Province by providing divorces (ironically), information, ritual objects, and a very old form of political representation. Of all the institutions and networks that gave form to the community, this one was most congruent with the shape of the province.

In contrast, examples from the previous section show that Jewish commercial networks often crossed the boundary of Edirne Province (and the

Ottoman Empire). Commerce also put Jewish merchants in close contact with Muslim and Christian peasants who sold cereals, sheep's milk, raw wool, and other agricultural products.[97] All these factors encouraged the formation of a regional Jewish community that was at once diffuse and tightknit, international and integrated with Ottoman Christians and Muslims.

The local silk industry was especially important. In the 1880s, European experts from the Ottoman Public Debt Administration began teaching Louis Pasteur's method for breeding silkworms, and the production of silk cocoons soared. Unlike the situation in Ottoman Macedonia, where most cocoons went to Italy (via the port of Salonica), cocoons produced in Edirne Province were often reeled into thread by local filatures.[98] Sericulture—raising silkworms and coaxing them to spin cocoons—was largely a Greek Orthodox profession.[99] Jews were more involved in the second stage of silk production: reeling cocoons into thread. In Karaağaç, the Azaria, Toledo, and Pappo families operated industrial filatures that reeled many tons of silk thread each year and employed six hundred people, mostly women and girls. The Azarias also owned a filature in Sofulu that employed eighty young women.[100] There, a Milan company opened an even larger filature in 1909, where it spun thread for export to Italy. The silk-reeling industry in Karaağaç and Sofulu was so large that cocoons were sometimes imported from Bulgaria, tax free.[101]

In addition to private enterprise, the regional economy was also structured around state-supported fairs. Weekly *pazars* and annual *panayırs* marked the calendars of merchants and peasants, Jews and non-Jews, Ottoman citizens and foreigners—all of whom convened on a regular basis to conduct business and socialize.[102] In the province's central district, Dimetoka hosted a livestock *pazar* on Thursdays, Ortaköy (today Ivaylovgrad, Bulgaria) hosted a *pazar* on Saturdays, and Uzunköprü hosted a livestock *panayır* just before Easter. In the district of Kırklareli, Vize hosted a livestock *pazar* on Fridays, a general *panayır* just before Easter, and a livestock *panayır* in late summer. In the Gümülcine district, the namesake city hosted a livestock *panayır* before Easter, and İskeçe hosted a Saturday *pazar*.[103] In the district of Gelibolu, Keşan hosted a Friday *pazar* dedicated to agricultural products, and Şarköy hosted a livestock *panayır* in August. In the Dedeağaç district, the town of Sofulu hosted a *pazar* on Saturday.[104]

The preponderance of livestock fairs reflects the extent to which the regional economy revolved around sheep and goats (and their products). Equally revealing is the scheduling of these events. *Panayırs* were often held before Easter, presumably because this was good timing for Bulgarian Christians—who usually raised the livestock—and Orthodox Greeks—who were prominent among the merchant class.[105] *Pazars* were often held on Friday, the empire's official weekend holiday and the Islamic day of congregational prayer (which is not a sabbath). *Pazars* were never held on Sunday, the Christian sabbath, but sometimes held on Saturday, the Jewish sabbath (as discussed below).

The Jewish community of Edirne Province was also united by a network of schools run by the Alliance Israélite Universelle, an international Jewish organization based in Paris. In 1867, as part of its larger mission to "regenerate" the Jews of Muslim-majority lands—and as its first foray into what is now Turkey—the organization established a boys' school in the city of Edirne. It had been asked to do so by a group of Jewish merchants who were inspired by the renowned Hebraist Joseph Halévy and his gospel of Haskalah (Jewish Enlightenment).[106] Three years later, a girls' school was founded nearby. By 1912, the Alliance was also running Jewish schools in the towns of Gümülcine, Dimetoka, Kırklareli, Tekirdağ, Gelibolu, and Çorlu. In all towns but the last, girls could enroll.[107]

Moise Mitrani, director of the boys' school in Edirne, became the de facto superintendent of this province-wide system. He could often convince his superiors in Paris to hire, fire, and transfer teachers, many of whom were from Edirne Province themselves. Less successfully, he tried to control discourse in the halls of the Alliance-affiliated clubs that appeared in many towns after 1908. In any case, Alliance schools and clubs continued to link the Jewish communities of Edirne Province to each other and to Paris.[108]

The chief rabbinate, commercial networks, and the Alliance school system all benefited from a fourth factor that structured social and economic life in this province: the railroad. Between 1873 and 1896, European companies built a rail network connecting Istanbul's Sirkeci Station to

Salonica in the West and Plovdiv in the Northwest.[109] From both points, passengers could continue as far as Paris. Meanwhile, Istanbul's Haydarpaşa Station was linked to the Anatolian interior. In Edirne Vilayet, railroad development only reinforced the inland nature of regional networks: the railway bypassed the province's two largest port cities (Tekirdağ and Gelibolu) but stopped in almost all major inland towns. (The exception was Kırklareli, at the foot of the Strandzha Mountains.) Largely the project of European interests seeking markets for manufactured goods, the railways were hardly designed to unite the small Jewish communities of Southeast Europe. That, however, was among their unintended consequences.[110]

At a time when the Balkan region was becoming synonymous with political fragmentation, the far-flung Jewish communities of Edirne Province grew increasingly integrated with each other.[111] Of course, this hardly meant that disparities within each Jewish community were disappearing. Economic inequality continued to be a salient trait of local Jewish life, into the final years of the Ottoman Empire.

CLASS: A BOUNDARY WITHIN THE COMMUNITY?

While the previous section took a macro-level view of the supercommunity that spanned Edirne Province, this one is a micro-level study of socioeconomic strata within the subcommunities. How did wealth translate to power in a typical Jewish community? In an empire where welfare and social services continued to be managed along religious lines, how did a Jewish community care for its members? What sorts of class conflicts and political agendas emerged from this system in the early twentieth century? The answers entail motifs common to Jewish communities throughout the empire as well as circumstances unique to Edirne.

As was the case in Istanbul, Izmir, and Salonica, the elite of Edirne's Jewish community consisted mainly of merchants. At the top of the ladder were the few whose activities extended into industry, an underdeveloped sector in the province.[112] This rarefied stratum included the above-mentioned families who ran silk filatures in Karaağaç and Sofulu. For context, the province's only other "industrial" operations—an admittedly vague category—were four gasoline-powered factories in the city of Edirne that made wool underwear (using Manchester machinery) and the flour mills that operated in several towns (using coal-burning steam engines).[113]

While a few of Edirne's Jewish merchants became industrial capitalists, most stuck to trading agricultural products on a wholesale basis. Sometimes they bought and sold semifinished goods, such as wool cloth woven in urban workshops. Other times they purchased raw agricultural products that they processed themselves, such as sheep's milk and silk cocoons.[114] In their dealings with Muslim and Christian peasants, merchants often secured lower prices by paying for goods well in advance, and many Jews were listed as both "merchants" and "bankers" in the commercial directories of the time.[115] Some of these merchant-bankers had offices in the city of Edirne, specifically in Rüstempaşa Kervansarayı, İki Kapılı Han, and other sixteenth-century Ottoman buildings in the Sabuni neighborhood.[116]

Notably, however, most of Edirne Province's merchants were Orthodox Greeks.[117] In commercial directories from 1905, 1909, and 1912, Greek names are more numerous than Jewish ones under most categories. (This was the case in all towns except for Dimetoka, which is the focus of this chapter's last section.[118]) Compared to the Greeks, the Jewish community did have a higher *percentage* of members working in trade. Still, of the 4,600 Jewish men who lived in Edirne's central district circa 1907, only about 140 were noteworthy wholesale merchants.[119]

In the city as well as the towns, merchants used their profits to help fund communal budgets. They also dominated the Jewish communal councils (*meclis-i cismani*)—the bodies of seven men that governed the local communities.[120] Circa 1912, the communal council in the city of Edirne was presided over by Joseph Jacob Pappo, one of the silk magnates mentioned above. The community's ad hoc general assembly (*meclis-i umumi*)—a larger body that convened a few times year—was led by a cereal merchant named Jacob Halfon.[121] Merchants also tended to lead the most important Jewish clubs in the city of Edirne, such as the Alliance-affiliated Cercle Israélite and the local chapter of the international Jewish organization B'nai B'rith.[122] To give just one example from the towns, the communal council in Çorlu was led by a cereal merchant named Bohor Behar.[123]

While merchants in port cities may have competed for the business of European companies, in Edirne the largest customer was the Ottoman army.[124] *La Boz de la Verdad*, the Ladino newspaper of Edirne, frequently announced the provisions needed by the army and the names of the merchants who had won the latest military contracts. In November 1911, for example, one Avraham Mordechai Efendi made the winning bid to provide the local army corps with raisins, salt, olive oil, onions, chickpeas, rice, sugar, and soap.[125] Around this time, a Jew named Nissim B. Samuel—honorary dragoman in the city's British consulate—worked as the Edirne agent for a British company that supplied grey cloth and blankets to the Ottoman military.[126] The association between local Jews and military provisioning was so strong that at one point the commandant of the Second Army hired "a Jewish banker of good reputation" to fix the contracting system, which had become rife with sweetheart deals.[127]

If Jewish merchants in the city of Edirne relied on the military and competed with Ottoman Christians, their counterparts in the towns did these two things even more intensely. In 1911, *La Boz de la Verdad* reported that in Kırklareli, where an army corps was headquartered, "all the Jews find themselves on good terms with the officers and do business with the army... but this means that when the army leaves Kirklisse [Kırklareli], the situation of our brothers worsens." In what was surely a reference to local Greeks—who composed about 40 percent of the district's population—the article added: "The economic situation of our brothers in Kirklisse is not as good as it was a few years ago, as wholesale commerce has passed into other hands."[128]

The situation was even more precarious in the border town of Mustafapaşa. In 1910, a Jewish visitor noted that "soldiers and officers in the garrison as well as villagers prefer to buy from Jews," even though the local population was mostly Muslim and Bulgarian Orthodox. He added that Jewish merchants often made loans to their customers, "even when some of these are insolvent."[129] But after an army reorganization occurred later that year, the director of Mustafapaşa's Talmud Torah (traditional Jewish school) reported that "everyone lives at the mercy of the army, which has diminished from six thousand to three hundred men. Supposedly, the few soldiers who remain will soon be sent to new barracks in Gümülcine." Indeed, six months later he wrote that many Jewish families were leaving for Gümülcine (and Çorlu). This "exodus" had "struck a decisive blow to communal tax revenues and the *gabela*," the latter being a sales tax on kosher meat that funded communal institutions.¹³⁰

In this case, one town's loss was another's gain. Between 1910 and 1912, the Jewish merchants of Çorlu and Gümülcine enjoyed the benefits of an increased military presence (the irony being that war would soon devastate their towns). Shortly after new barracks were constructed in 1910, a Jewish visitor to Çorlu noted that the community was in good order. During the summer and fall harvest season, he wrote, "several Jews, especially the president of the community, do a brisk business in cereals exportation" and end up supporting their poorer coreligionists.¹³¹ After an earthquake struck the region in 1912, a B'nai B'rith functionary visited Çorlu and lauded the local merchants for mitigating indigence in the Jewish community.¹³²

This orientation toward peasants and Ottoman soldiers, instead of the Europeans found in port cities, carried cultural implications. While debates about Western European culture certainly occurred in the Jewish community of Edirne, they were muted compared to those in Salonica, Istanbul, and Izmir.¹³³ In those places, Francos—Sephardim from the Tuscan port of Livorno—had dwelled for centuries as a Europeanized element within the Jewish community, and many Jews were citizens or protégés of European countries.¹³⁴ Relatedly, Jews in Ottoman port cities often adopted the fashions, consumption patterns, mores, and language (in every sense) of the French bourgeoisie.¹³⁵ But inland Edirne had never been a major destination for Francos and was home to a relatively small number of Jews holding foreign citizenship. Local Jewish merchants often hesitated to embrace bourgeois European culture, even as they supported the Alliance schools.¹³⁶ For example, Jacob Halfon, the above-mentioned president of the Jewish general assembly, did not know French. (Though this did not stop him from signing important petitions written in that language!)¹³⁷

After the merchants, a second upper class emerged among the Jews of urban Edirne, especially after 1908. This consisted of the bureaucrats and professionals—namely, lawyers, doctors, state functionaries, employees of the railway company, and agents of European financial institutions.¹³⁸ Many of these people had received a Francophone education in the Alliance schools. Of the twenty-five young men who graduated from the Edirne school in 1911, four would soon be hired by international banks (the Bank of Salonica, Deutsche Bank East, and a bank in Alexandria, Egypt), three by the Oriental Railway Company, one by Union Insurance, and one by Singer (as a sewing-machine salesman).[139] With that said, what was true for the merchants of Edirne was also true for the professionals: most were Christian, and those who were Jews represented a small fraction of their community.[140]

Most Edirne Jews were "small shopkeepers, brokers, peddlers, and workers striving to get by," according to the director of Edirne's Alliance boys' school. He estimated that this class represented three-fourths of urban Edirne's Jewish population.[141] A small number of Jews sold hardware, men's clothing, and other "manufactures" in the main bazaar. But most stalls in the sixteenth-century Ali Paşa Çarşısı were run by Armenians.[142] The school director's estimate is roughly consistent with a tally made eight years later by an international Jewish commission assessing the effects of the First Balkan War. Among the 3,307 Edirne Jews included in the survey, the most common "employments" were: peddlers (500), employees in commercial establishments (200), porters (200), dependents (200), butchers (150), master masons and helpers (150), tailors (120), dealers in hardware (120), petty tradesmen (120), army subcontractors (100), and manual laborers in various trades (100).[143]

This clustering toward the lower-middle class was not limited to the city of Edirne. A recent history of the Kırklareli community estimates that, in the late-Ottoman period, 65 percent of the Jewish population lived below the level of the merchants but above the level of the unemployed, often working as "peddlers, small shop owners with practically no capital, water carriers, and street vendors."[144] A 1901 report on Gümülcine described the occupational structure of that Jewish community as follows: "Except for a few commercial establishments that are in direct correspondence with Europe, one sees only small traders who earn a living with great difficulty. As is the case almost everywhere in Turkey, most [Jews] pursue minor commerce and peddling."[145]

As mentioned above, the port cities of Edirne Province were home to some of its poorest Jewish communities. In Gelibolu and Tekirdağ, many Jews worked as *hamals* at the docks, loading and unloading ships for a pittance.[146] The situation was especially bad in Tekirdağ, which suffered greatly when the railway linked the inland towns to the ports of Istanbul and Salonica.[147] Of the 115 Jewish fathers who sent their boys to the local Alliance school, the most common occupation was *hamal* (with twenty practitioners). According to the educator who made this tally, in Tekirdağ "it is the Jews who form the minority and whose situation is the least brilliant," compared to that of local Muslims and Christians (especially Armenians). He also described the Jewish quarter as "foul and unhealthy."[148]

In the Jewish communities of Edirne Province, the bottom rung of the economic ladder was occupied by those who could not find regular work and relied on the Alliance and communal welfare institutions to survive. Of the 1,077 boys enrolled in the city of Edirne's Alliance school circa 1911, more than 300 were classified as "poor" and therefore eligible for free lunch.[149] Similarly, the above-mentioned study of Kırklareli estimates that one in five local Jews required assistance from communal institutions.[150] According to *La Boz de la Verdad*, between 1908 and 1912 "hundreds" of young Jewish men left the province to seek work in the Americas, from where they could remit their earnings to their families in Edirne.[151] In 1911, the Alliance school director in Tekirdağ estimated that 120 young Jewish men had recently left town for the United States, fleeing poverty as well as military conscription.[152]

As discussed in the next chapter, the Young Turk Revolution inspired some upstarts in Edirne's Jewish community to briefly revolt against communal leadership. However, rhetoric of class struggle and calls for poverty reduction were largely absent. This was probably related to local factors that affected people of all religions. While Istanbul, Salonica, and Izmir were hit hard by the "Strike Wave" that came on the heels of the Young Turk Revolution, the only major labor action in Edirne was part of the larger Oriental Railway strike. (Relatedly, one of the few unions in town was a branch of the railway-workers' union).[153] By 1908, major socialist organizations existed in Istanbul, Bulgaria, and Salonica—the latter being home to Albert Benaroya's Socialist Worker's Federation.[154] But in Edirne, socialism was less prominent.[155] Neither endowed with heavy industry nor stricken by extreme poverty, neither galvanized by European radicalism nor enamored with bourgeois culture, the Jewish community of Edirne would debate its own set of issues in the years following the Young Turk Revolution.

In addition to economic strata, the category of women's work deserves special attention. For the Jews of Edirne, the largest employers of women and girls were the silk-reeling factories owned by the Azarias, Pappos, and Toledos. These industrialists had an arrangement with Edirne's Alliance girls' school, whereby students who completed a sewing class were put on a fast track to employment at the filatures.[156] Additionally, girls often worked in the homes of well-off Jewish merchants, sometimes across the Bulgarian border.[157] Silk reeling in the Ottoman Empire was a grueling, unhealthy job.[158] The dangers of domestic work, meanwhile, are reflected in the story of a fourteen-year-old girl from Edirne who was raped by two young men in Bulgaria. (The victim *and* the perpetrators were Jewish.[159]) While the entrance of Jewish girls into the workforce was a significant development of the late Ottoman era, it was not always a shining achievement for the community.

Of course, domestic workers freed up the woman of the house to pursue philanthropic projects. For example, the Jewish orphanage in the city of Edirne was run by women from notable families.[160] In addition to philanthropist, the other influential position available to Jewish women was director of an Alliance girls' school. Two of these existed in Edirne Province: one in Kırklareli and one in the city of Edirne.[161] In short, Jewish women and girls were largely excluded from middling careers such as shopkeeper, merchant, and professional. But they were present at both ends of the Jewish social spectrum.

JEWISH PRODUCTIVIZATION EFFORTS

Let us now shift the discussion from economic life as it existed to some idealistic efforts to change the status quo among the Jews of Edirne Province. Mostly, these were attempts to promote Jewish "productivization," a project that had roots in early nineteenth-century Western Europe, where "Jewish notables internalized the Enlightenment critique of the Jewish poor as sui generis and in need of drastic corrective measures." According to Derek Penslar, these notables sought to train Jewish youth in handicrafts and farming, "occupations thought to be archetypically productive despite their decline in the era of industrialization."[162] Productivization became a tenet of the Haskalah and was soon applied to Ottoman Jews in a way that reflected

European tendencies to read poverty "as proof of the moral deficiency of the 'Orient.'"[163]

While the Alliance and its French curriculum helped many students in Edirne attain desk jobs, the organization also tried to prepare young men to become artisans—a line of work that had been relatively uncommon among Ottoman Jews. Toward that end, Alliance school directors in the city of Edirne founded an apprenticeship program in 1878 and a mutual aid society for artisans around 1900. Similar initiatives appeared in Dimetoka.[164] Edirne's apprenticeship program was founded with help from Abraham Danon, a prominent local *maskil* whose Dorshei Haskalah society continued to support the program into the twentieth century.[165]

The apprenticeship program peaked in the years 1903–1911. In that period, 86 relatively poor students from Edirne's Alliance boys' school were assigned to patrons throughout the region, many of whom had worked as apprentices themselves. Sixty-five of these boys completed their four-year apprenticeships and went on to work as artisans.[166] However, according to the school director, the quality of their work was inferior to that of their Greek Orthodox, Armenian, and Muslim competitors. In fact, the large-scale building projects undertaken in the city around this time—the school of the Sisters of Agram (Zagreb), three government schools, a Greek Orthodox church, a Greek club (*syllogue*), the Great Synagogue, and the Alliance boys' school itself—recruited most of their workforce from Istanbul, and "not a single Jewish worker" could be found on the construction sites.[167] This was a missed opportunity indeed, as local wages for skilled labor tripled between 1905 and 1912, largely due to the building of new military barracks, road improvements undertaken by a French concern, and the military conscription of Christians (who had supplied much of the region's skilled labor, historically).[168]

Consistent with Haskalah notions of "productivization," some Jewish leaders believed that, in addition to learning skilled trades, Ottoman Jews should become farmers. In Edirne, the leading champion of Jewish agriculture was Samuel Loupo, director of Edirne's Alliance boys' school from 1883 to 1903. Loupo's initial goal was to provide agricultural work to Edirne Jews who graduated from the Alliance's two farm schools—Mikveh Israel in Ottoman Jaffa and the Djedeida school in French Tunisia. At first, he tried placing these graduates on farms owned by Edirne's Muslim beys, using the latter's Jewish bankers as intermediaries.[169] When that strategy failed, Loupo and a local Jewish banker founded a society dedicated to purchasing a farm in Edirne Province that would provide work for graduates of the farm schools, local Jews, *and* Ashkenazim leaving Eastern Europe. In a 1901 letter to Alliance leadership in Paris, Loupo listed the justifications for such a venture:

> the emigration of Jews from Romania and Bulgaria to Turkey and the West; the necessity of propagating a taste for working the land among our coreligionists in the East; the fact that agriculture is the principle source of wealth in this region; the frightening increase in begging [among Edirne Jews]; the profitability of small-scale farming; the aspirations of the Jews of Mustafapaşa to work in agriculture; the need to create a farming settlement for the two dozen students from Edirne who completed their studies at Mikveh Israel and Djedeida; the benevolence of the local authorities currently in power; the extremely good price of properties up for sale.[170]

Loupo realized that his dream farm could only be purchased with assistance from the Alliance and/or its sister organization, the Jewish Colonization Association (JCA). In his letters to Paris, he claimed that local Jews had a proclivity for working the land and emphasized that both Alliance farm schools were run by men from Edirne: Samuel Avigdor in Djedeida and Joseph Niego at Mikveh Israel. But in the end, Loupo's superiors had no appetite to invest in yet another farming venture. (The Alliance already ran Mikveh Israel and the Djedeida school, while the JCA ran Or Yehuda, near Izmir).[171] In 1903, when Loupo left Edirne to run Mikveh Israel, Edirne was still without a Jewish farming project.

Eight years later, the idea of establishing Jewish agricultural settlements in Eastern Thrace was briefly revived. This time, however, the drivers of the project came from abroad. In 1911, the governor of Edirne notified the interior minister of a "potentially dangerous and illegal" attempt by two "foreigners" to purchase land from Muslims near Tekirdağ, for the purpose of settling Russian Jews.[172] A year later, the interior minister received a similar communication from the *mutasarrıf* (regional administrator) of Çatalca, an independent *sancak* between the provinces of Edirne and Istanbul. Reportedly, the vice-president of the JCA was trying to buy a large farm in the town of Silivri for "Russian Jews expelled from their country." Both plans briefly came to fruition in 1913. In Silivri, an Italian citizen started a farm called Fethiköy Çiftliği that was worked by immigrants from Russia (Jewish *and* Christian), and a Jewish farm of some kind seems to have appeared in the Tekirdağ district.[173] However, this Jewish farming movement would be short lived, as the authorities soon decided that agricultural colonies in geopolitically sensitive regions should be reserved for *Muslim* immigrants.[174]

For the Jews of Edirne Province, the Alliance apprenticeship programs and the Jewish farming initiatives produced limited results, at best.[175] Far from changing the status quo, productivization efforts revealed the obstinacy of entrenched occupational structures. Instead of facilitating assimilation and a "normalization" of Jewish occupational profiles, these efforts probably *strengthened* the links between economic activity and ethno-religious identity.

ECONOMIC WAR BETWEEN COMMUNITIES

Strange as this might sound, one of the great dramas for Edirne Jews in the wake of the Young Turk Revolution was a livestock fair. By the early twentieth century, the above-mentioned livestock *pazar* in Dimetoka had become one of the province's main commercial events. In a *vilayet* that had more sheep and goats than almost any other, the value of animals that changed hands at this weekly event must have been enormous, by Ottoman standards.[176] In 1909, 1911, and 1914, certain interest groups tried to move the *pazar* from a weekday to Saturday, in what were clearly attempts to exclude Jewish buyers from the marketplace. By placing this story in the context of boycotts and other forms of economic warfare waged between Edirne's ethno-religious communities, we will see how nationalist conflicts that erupted after the Balkan Wars often grew out of more mundane rivalries.

In a sense, the above-mentioned efforts to turn Edirne Jews into artisans and farmers led to an early version of economic warfare. While they did not necessarily aim to hurt other groups, these programs often encountered resistance from non-Jews. From the start, the apprenticeship program struggled under "the tyrannical yoke of Christian patrons who, enjoying control of certain professions, hinder the success of the program by constantly threatening to dismiss [Jewish apprentices]."[177] And in 1896, the saddler's guild of Edirne rejected two Jewish apprentices on the grounds that saddling was a "Muslim trade."[178] Ethno-religious clustering in certain occupations was a very old phenomenon, but organized efforts to change these arrangements reflected a new and increasingly materialist way of thinking about the links between economic activity and ethno-religious identity.[179] In that sense, Jewish productivization efforts and economic warfare were two sides of the same coin.

Boycotts, properly speaking, first came to Edirne Province in the context of a rivalry between two Christian communities. After the schism between the Bulgarian Exarchate and the Ecumenical Patriarchate, Greek Orthodox boycotts of local Bulgarian businesses were "of not infrequent occurrence" (according to the British consul in Edirne).[180] In 1907, the director of Edirne's Greek Orthodox high school visited a village near Gümülcine and convinced local students and notables to stop patronizing a pair of Bulgarian Orthodox grocers.[181] Meanwhile, at least one outspoken Exarchist in Dedeağaç was boycotted by local Greeks until his business was ruined and he had to move.[182]

Immediately after the Young Turk Revolution, the Greek-Bulgarian rivalry spilled over to affect Jews.[183] In August 1908, the mayor of Edirne ordered all residents to welcome a delegation from Sofia by hanging Bulgarian and Ottoman flags from their windows. Members of the Greek Orthodox community refused to do so and "endeavored to bring pressure to bear on Jewish tradespeople to join in their refusal by threatening to boycott them."[184] Meanwhile, a Greek newspaper in Salonica "asked the Greeks to declare economic war against the Jews and stop buying from all Jewish merchants." There, too, Jews became collateral damage in a conflict between Orthodox Greeks and Bulgarian Christians.[185]

Only in October 1908 did the Muslims of Edirne first resort to boycotts. This was a response to Bulgaria's declaration of independence and Austria-Hungary's official annexation of Bosnia and Herzegovina. (Like Bulgaria, Bosnia-Herzegovina had been nominally Ottoman until 1908.) Unlike the previous examples, these boycotts did not target Ottoman communities but rather foreign states. In fact, Muslim, Jewish, and Christian port workers throughout the empire united in their refusal to unload

Austrian and Bulgarian goods.[186] In Edirne Vilayet, for example, dockworkers in Dedeağaç refused to unload Austrian steamers. Meanwhile, people in the city of Edirne joined an empire-wide trend by replacing the fez—typically manufactured in Austria—with locally made headgear.[187]

But as the patriotic boycotts wound down, economic warfare again became intercommunal (as opposed to international). In August 1909, a Jewish newspaper in Istanbul claimed that "various merchants" from Dimetoka had asked the administrative council of Edirne Province (*vilayet idare meclisi*) to move the weekly livestock fair from Thursday to Saturday. Reportedly, the chief rabbi of Edirne raised no objection and even signed the council's meeting minutes—a controversial act that precipitated his resignation. A group of Jewish merchants then sought help from the chief rabbi of the Ottoman Empire in Istanbul.[188] He must have convinced the authorities to reverse the decision of the administrative council, because the topic disappeared from the Jewish press for the next two years.

The second act in the *pazar* drama would occur in 1911, but only after another boycott disrupted the region. In 1910, nominally Ottoman Crete escalated its efforts to unite with Greece, triggering protests and boycotts throughout the Ottoman Empire. On a spring day in Edirne, thousands of protestors gathered in the courtyard of Selimiye Mosque, and a local boycott committee was established. It included a Bulgarian teacher, the secretary of the local chief rabbi, and a Greek Orthodox grocer.[189] Officially, the boycott targeted merchants and goods from the Kingdom of Greece, but the scope quickly widened to include Greek-speaking citizens of the empire. For example, the Greek Orthodox owner of a mill in Dedeağaç found that customers in Gümülcine were refusing to buy his flour.[190] Surely, this campaign against the group that dominated local commerce—Orthodox Greeks—sprung from a convenient combination of nascent Ottoman-Muslim nationalism and economic self-interest.[191]

But by September 1911, the main victims of "economic marginalization" in Edirne Province were no longer Greeks but rather Jews.[192] That month, *La Boz de la Verdad* reported bad news from Dimetoka. After two years of failed attempts, "the Greeks and the Turks" had united to successfully move the livestock fair to Saturday. Jewish merchants now faced the impossible choice of desecrating the sabbath or committing commercial suicide.[193] The

Dimetoka community persuaded Jewish leaders in Istanbul to petition the Ottoman government on the grounds that rescheduling the fair constituted an illegal act perpetrated by "enemies of the Jewish merchants."[194] Meanwhile, prodded by the (new) chief rabbi of Edirne, the governor and the administrative council of the province issued orders stating that the fair should continue to occur on Thursdays. They also had Edirne's police director open an investigation in Dimetoka, and they removed "some functionaries who seem to be pushing the people to hold the fair on Saturdays."[195]

However, these actions were not immediately effective. *La Boz de la Verdad* reported that villagers (*kazalinos*) continued to bring their livestock to Dimetoka on Saturdays. "We again call out to the chief rabbi of Turkey and the communal council of the capital," it wrote. "This is a mortal blow to the Jewish merchant."[196] A few weeks later, the newspaper declared that "our brothers in Demotika [Dimetoka] are victims of antisemitism."[197] In October and again in December, the chief rabbi in Istanbul asked the Interior Ministry to intervene, but the latter continued to punt the issue to the provincial government.[198] In a frontpage article published on January 1, 1912, *La Boz de la Verdad* urged a certain "Hakim Efendi" and leaders of the local Armenian, Greek, and Bulgarian Orthodox communities to stop the fair from occurring on Saturdays.[199]

At this point, local authorities began to take the matter more seriously. The treasurer (*defterdar*) of Edirne Province sent a memorandum to the Interior Ministry stating that the situation was being investigated.[200] After that, the local Ladino press stopped writing about the matter, but later articles suggest that the administrative council's ruling was finally enforced. At some point in early 1912, the fair stopped occurring on Saturdays.[201]

Later that year, the center of anti-Jewish animus shifted to Silivri, just east of Edirne Province. There, some Greek Orthodox residents organized a boycott against local Jewish merchants. Though the Greek Orthodox patriarch and the chief rabbi of the Ottoman Empire tried to pacify the situation by sending delegates, violence soon erupted. The Ottoman authorities were compelled to intervene, but, once again, the wheels of justice turned slowly. Months passed before the *kaymakam* (district governor) of Silivri finally promised a reporter for *La Boz de la Verdad* that the boycott would end within three days.[202]

Only with this background established can we turn to the third and final act in the drama of the Dimetoka livestock fair. In 1914, *La Boz de la Verdad* reported that Jewish peddlers had been "expelled" from villages around Dimetoka and, a few months later, that certain actors were *again* trying to move the livestock fair to Saturday.[203] This final attempt to reschedule the *pazar* was probably led by Muslims, as local Christians were themselves being subjected to boycotts and other forms of persecution at this time.[204] Though the authorities eventually had the Jewish peddlers return to the villages and the *pazar* return to Thursdays, the episode rattled Dimetoka's Jewish community.[205]

Eyal Ginio puts this mischief in the context of a "culture of defeat" that weighed on the empire and the ruling Committee of Union and Progress (CUP) after the Balkan Wars. According to Ginio, this attempt to reschedule the fair was motivated by anxiety, resentment, and other factors specific to a certain group (Ottoman Muslims) and a certain time (the period immediately after the Balkan Wars).[206] But if economic warfare was also waged against the Jews (and Christians) of Edirne *by Christians* and *before the Balkan Wars*, then Ginio fails to explain the larger phenomenon.[207]

As mentioned above, boycotts in Edirne Province were first waged by Orthodox Greeks—against Bulgarians and then, to a lesser extent, Jews. Next, Muslims used the tactic to call for Ottoman solidarity in the face of foreign aggression. After that, Jews suffered from the first attempt to move the Dimetoka livestock fair to Saturday. Soon, Muslims led boycotts that initially targeted citizens of Greece but spread to affect local Orthodox Greeks. Enemies became allies when Muslim and Greek Orthodox merchants collaborated in a second attempt to move the livestock fair to the Jewish day of rest.[208] Then it was Greeks boycotting Jews in Silivri followed by the CUP's economic war against non-Muslims. The fact that alliances kept shifting seems to argue against the notion that economic warfare was inherently cultural, ideological, or nationalistic. Practical and material motivations must be considered.

The material goals seem clear. The removal of Jewish buyers from the fair would have pushed down the demand curve and lowered the price of livestock—an outcome that would benefit gentile merchants/buyers and perhaps some colluding officials. In one of the largest livestock centers in the empire, at a time when the price of agricultural goods was rising sharply, the conspirators had much to gain.[209] (Conversely, the herdsmen—probably Bulgarian-Christians—had much to lose if Jewish buyers were excluded from the fair.[210]) Surely it was no coincidence that Dimetoka was the only town in the province where Jewish merchants had the upper hand vis-à-vis their Greek Orthodox competitors, a situation that must have bred resentment among the latter.[211]

Boycotts and other forms of economic warfare would eventually become associated with Turkish nationalism and attempts to build a Muslim bourgeoisie. But before the Balkan Wars—and sometimes after—these tactics were used in Edirne by various groups, targeting various victims, and toward various ends. To be sure, these early boycotts strengthened ethno-religious boundaries and reinforced "imagined communities of shared material interest."[212] But they were tactical responses to specific economic challenges more than self-conscious, ideological projects of nationalism.[213] Of course, the latter could conveniently build on the former.

CONCLUSION

In the late nineteenth and early twentieth centuries, various developments strengthened ties between Jewish communities across Edirne Province and loosened ties between Jewish communities on opposite sides of the *vilayet*'s northern border. And yet, for many Edirnelis, this border remained relatively easy to cross and did not feel inherently different from the provincial border between Edirne and Salonica (for example). Meanwhile, a tendency for economic blocks to map onto ethno-religious categories ensured that communal boundaries remained strong into the twentieth century. Bound and bounded by myriad forces from within and beyond the community, the Jews of Edirne Province deepened a network and a corresponding identity that had more to do with Ottoman legacies and Jewish institutions than modern nationalism and new borders. As we will see, the events of 1908 would complicate this situation.

TWO

Liberty and Limits

Public Spheres on the Imperial Border, 1908–1912

FROM 1878 TO 1908, SULTAN Abdülhamid II ruled the Ottoman Empire as an absolute monarch. For Edirne's Jewish community, this was a complicated period. Ladino and Hebrew newspapers appeared in the 1880s but vanished by 1891. Jewish societies were founded, but fear of secret police soon deterred club members from discussing all but the most anodyne of topics (openly, at least). A stately Jewish school was built in 1904, and a grandiose synagogue project was commissioned in 1906. But in between, a fire ravaged Edirne's Jewish and Christian quarters, destroying the chief rabbinate and its library, the hall of the kosher butcher's guild, the office of the Bikur Holim (society for visiting the sick), the Talmud Torah, the thirteen wooden synagogues, and hundreds of Jewish-owned homes and shops.[1]

Though some historians associate the Hamidian era with reaction and stagnation, it was certainly a dynamic period for the Jews of Edirne.[2] The school built in 1904 would soon boast the largest enrollment in the intercontinental network of the Alliance Israélite Universelle.[3] A few blocks away, the Jewish community's school for girls became the third largest of its kind in the Alliance system.[4] Upon completion in April 1909—the month Abdülhamid was deposed—Edirne's synagogue was the third largest in Europe.[5] These architectural and institutional achievements culminated a thirty-year period in which the province's Jewish population nearly doubled (see Chapter 1).

But what the Jews of Edirne lacked during these years was a robust political life. Throughout the empire, the Hamidian regime quashed attempts to create an Ottoman public sphere and, even more so, "national" public spheres in the Armenian, Greek Orthodox, Bulgarian Orthodox, and Jewish communities (among others).[6] Located at the de facto border with Bulgaria, Edirne Province was certainly no exception to this policy. In fact, it was Bulgaria's (unofficial) secession from the empire that had prompted Abdülhamid to suspend the constitution and prorogue parliament in 1878.

Thirty years later, two events brought modern politics into the lives of Edirnelis and inaugurated a period of vigorous public debate about the meaning of modern citizenship and the function of a line that suddenly separated two constitutional monarchies (Bulgaria and the Ottoman Empire). The first event was the Young Turk Revolution, which swept the empire in July 1908 after a group of officers and bureaucrats forced Abdülhamid to restore the Ottoman constitution and reconvene parliament. As a result, the Committee of Union and Progress (CUP) quickly came to dominate Ottoman politics. The second event was Bulgaria's declaration of independence. In October 1908, Bulgarian leaders ended the legal fiction that their country was a principality of the Ottoman Empire—a diplomatic pretense they had maintained through the Hamidian era. Previously a boundary between two Ottoman provinces—Edirne and autonomous Eastern Rumelia—the northern limit of Edirne Vilayet became an official state border.

In a sense, the Young Turk Revolution and the firming of the border were countervailing forces. The former called for a "union" (*ittihad*) of the empire's religious communities, while the latter entailed political separation along ethno-religious lines (by some interpretations). What these events shared, however, was their tendency to spark political vitality in Edirne.[7] The very tension between these two developments generated political discussion and unprecedented forms of activity. In the Jewish community, specifically, debates about cultural and political identity in a world of parliamentary systems intersected with intracommunal conflicts involving gender, class, and power. In terms of political energy—and population size—Edirne Jewry reached its peak between 1908 and 1912.

This energy was directed toward several projects. One was an Ottoman nationalism pioneered by the Young Ottomans in the 1870s but revived and intensified by the Young Turks after 1908.[8] Another was a Jewish nationalism that attached itself to Zionist organizations. But the Jews of Edirne were especially drawn to a middle path that called for Ottoman patriotism and intercommunal friendship without sacrificing Jewish "national dignity" or communal autonomy. In a region where state borders were local realities more than nationalist abstractions, everyday obstacles more than sacred representations, Jews remained wary of ideologies that romanticized territory and caused "tension between what borders appear to be and what they actually perform or do in real time."[9] While the revolution led to rich, even dangerous debates—and a very bold demand for Jewish equality—the community gravitated toward a style of politics that would keep it safe in a geopolitically sensitive borderland.

The first section of this chapter summarizes intercommunal relations in Edirne Province after 1908. Special attention is paid to political issues that, accruing over economic issues, exacerbated intercommunal conflict at a time of hardening borders, liberal-democratic reform, and nascent modern nationalism. The second section discusses how the Jewish community's leadership changed in the wake of the revolution, especially with the arrival of a new chief rabbi and a new girls' school director. The third section turns to Jewish associational life, which was revived in Edirne and could not be isolated from Jewish political currents in Bulgaria (despite the efforts of some community leaders). The fourth section focuses on the local Ladino press, which led the community into the age of popular politics—as both a record and a weapon. Moving from figurative weapons to literal ones, the last section describes how a shootout with police in Edirne's Jewish quarter sparked a controversy with few parallels in Ottoman-Jewish history.

NATIONS AND PEOPLES AT BORDER

In 1907, the invisible line cutting the plains near the city of Edirne was still subject to interpretation. Some considered it a boundary between two Ottoman provinces, others a border between two countries. For merchants, it was primarily a site of taxation. For governors, it could be a dam against inflows or outflows of certain populations, as seen in the case of Edirne Province's *vali* and his (Jewish) director of political affairs (see Chapter 1). In contrast, Edirne's British consul saw the frontier less as a tool for preserving the demographic status quo and more as a normative guideline for where certain groups should live: "It must be the natural desire of those [Bulgarian Christians] at present residing in Turkey to be with their relations," he told the *vali*.[10] Yet another interpretation was expressed by Edhem Ruhi, a leader of the Young Turk opposition who had fled the Hamidian police by becoming a Bulgarian citizen and settling in Plovdiv (the capital of Eastern Rumelia or a city in southern Bulgaria, depending on one's view).[11] Writing in his Turkish-language newspaper (*Balkan*), he portrayed the border as primarily a line separating two systems of government—one constitutional, the other absolutist.[12]

In part, the border's ambiguity stemmed from the fact that, in the Ottoman Empire, the idea of nations had never been closely linked to territory. The Turkish word *millet*, the Greek word *ethnos*, and the Ladino word *nasyon* were interchangeable terms for the empire's ethnoreligious communities—groups that had distinct cultural identities and long histories of (limited) autonomy.[13] However, these words were *not* meant to imply any right to self-determination in a given territory.[14] An Edirne resident could be a member of the Bulgarian Orthodox *millet*, for example, without desiring to live in or be a citizen of Bulgaria. Indeed, members of the various *millets* often emphasized that national pride was fully compatible with Ottoman patriotism.[15]

With that said, it did not take much imagination to link the old, imperial understanding of nations with the modern understanding that had swept Europe in the nineteenth century. As modern nationalism became an organizing political principle in much of the world, the CUP tried to disassociate the word *millet* from the non-Muslim communities of the empire. As early as the 1890s, Young Turk emigres in Paris had written about a *"millet-i Osmaniye"* (Ottoman nation) that included Ottoman citizens of all religions.[16] Once in power, the CUP literati described the empire's ethnoreligious communities as *"unsurlar"* or *"anasır"* (elements) and called for a "union of the elements" (*ittihad-ı anasır*).[17] This echoed the words of the Young Ottoman writer Namık Kemal, who, three decades prior, had proposed a "fusion of the peoples" (*imtizac-ı akvam*).[18] CUP leaders, however, would seek a level of assimilation in Ottoman society not imagined by their nineteenth-century predecessors.

In Edirne Vilayet, debates about the meaning of the nation were anything but theoretical. The province was home to the empire's largest population of Orthodox Greeks, fourth-largest population of Bulgarian Christians, and fifth-largest population of Jews. Of the 1.1 million people who inhabited the *vilayet*, only about half were Muslim.[19] In addition to having a highly diverse population, Edirne bordered a country whose (brief) history demonstrated how *millet* status could morph into modern, territorial nationalism: Eight years after the creation of the *Bulgar milleti* (in 1870), Bulgaria effectively seceded from the empire.[20] In this historical and geographic context, talk of "nations" was highly charged.

Downplaying the idea of a state with multiple nations, CUP leaders spoke constantly of "the people." In the wake of the revolution, this term indicated the diverse body of citizens for whom leaders governed, in a parliamentary system. While the old concept of nations was inherently linked to cultural identity (and alterity), the new idea of the people was primarily about political legitimacy. À la John Locke, the CUP literati claimed that a government representing the people was more legitimate than an autocratic regime.[21] They also coined the phrase *hâkimiyet-i milliye*, meaning national/popular sovereignty.[22] While the CUP grew increasingly authoritarian after its first year in power, it did manage to oversee parliamentary elections in 1908, 1912, and 1914—albeit problematically. This at least gave it "the appearance of the sanction of the people."[23] Genuine or not, CUP rhetoric about "the people" would be imitated and reappropriated in Edirne's Ladino press—as we will see.[24]

Even when effective, liberal reforms and parliamentary democracy could put local Jewish leaders in difficult situations. What were they to do when a parliamentary deputy from Gümülcine turned out to be a "raving antisemite"?[25] How were they to react when a philosemitic deputy from Edirne asked Ottoman Jews to be a "counterweight" to Orthodox Greeks who possessed dangerous levels of "capital and influence"?[26] Should a Jewish member of parliament speak out against "antisemitic" articles in Turkish newspapers published beyond his district?[27] Or was that the job of local Jewish newspapers and community leaders? As discussed in the following sections, these issues sparked anxious debate among Edirne Jews in the years after 1908.

On the morrow of the revolution, however, the mood in Edirne was decidedly upbeat. This is reflected in a report from Sara Ungar, director of the Alliance girls' school:

> Our school year finished in an epic resounding with events that created a general enthusiasm and a beautiful spectacle of sincere, perfect union among the heterogeneous elements of our city's population. Turks, Jews, Greeks, Armenians, and Bulgarians greeted each other with the beautiful name of "brother." It is truly touching to see people forgive each other for past wrongs in their joy at witnessing the rebirth of the patria under a new regime of liberty and justice.[28]

For his part, the British consul described "the unwonted spectacle of Greeks and Bulgarians, Moslems and Armenians embracing one another in the streets." Using the popular European term for the Ottoman Empire, he added that "the keynote of the new policy thus inaugurated was announced to be 'Turkey for the Ottomans without distinction of race and creed.'"[29]

Especially interesting was the consul's focus on relations between the city's Muslim and Bulgarian Christian communities. "The most noticeable feature" of the summer, he claimed, was the "rapprochement" between these two groups—a phenomenon that reflected the initially good relations between the CUP and Sofia.[30] For its part, the local Young Turk newspaper *Yeni Edirne* dismissed rumors of war with Bulgaria as "absurd." The new Ottoman government was only interested in "uniting the Balkan elements [*unsurlar*] and working hand-in-hand to advance knowledge, trade, and industry."[31]

But this happy picture was about to be marred. In October, Bulgaria's declaration of independence from the Ottoman Empire brought the two countries to the brink of war. New trade barriers were enacted, and the border was militarized on both sides.[32] Young Turk promises to grant Ottoman citizens freedom of mobility (*serbest-i seyr-u seyahat*) now amounted to little in Edirne.[33] Across the province, elation turned to fear.

In the city of Edirne, the declaration of independence was heralded by Bulgarian-language posters that appeared on buildings in the dead of night. Several local Christians were arrested in conjunction with this political crime. Meanwhile, the mayor convoked a public meeting where attendees passed a resolution protesting Bulgaria's declaration of independence, its seizure of the Oriental Railway, and its official annexation of Eastern Rumelia—"an integral part of the Ottoman Empire."[34] The CUP also made sure that no Bulgarian Orthodox candidates from Edirne Vilayet were elected to parliament at the end of 1908.[35]

In the smaller towns and villages, tensions ran even higher. The Ottomans responded to the declaration of independence by performing military maneuvers near the border, while Muslim and Bulgarian Orthodox peasants were given arms by Ottoman authorities and revolutionary organizations based in Bulgaria, respectively.[36] Breaking with the policy of prior *valis*, CUP governors began to encourage the immigration of Muslims from Bulgaria and to settle them near villages with large Bulgarian Orthodox populations. Predictably, the ensuing competition over pasture and forest land prompted Bulgarian Orthodox peasants to consider emigration.[37] While this was not the first case of Ottoman authorities indirectly pushing Christian citizens across an imperial border, it marked an expansion of such policies.[38]

In the immediate border zone, conflicts continued after 1909 (when relations were normalized between Bulgaria and the Ottoman Empire). To calm the situation, three Bulgarian officers visited the city of Edirne in May 1910, where they joined three Ottoman officers in forming a "Frontier Delimitation Commission."[39] Its task was to travel the length of the Ottoman-Bulgarian border and mark a clear boundary line by erecting pillars—work that had been started and abandoned in 1886.[40] Despite the efforts of the commission, "affairs," "collisions," and "encounters" continued to occur near border outposts. For example, in late 1910, guards on opposite sides of the boundary skirmished near the town of Mustafapaşa after cattle thieves drove Bulgarian stock into Ottoman territory.[41] The following month, the director of Edirne's Alliance boys' school took the train to Mustafapaşa and observed great "enmity" between Muslim and Bulgarian Orthodox villagers. (Though he claimed that "the Jews live on excellent terms with both of these elements.")[42]

Other factors, too, made locals feel the presence of the border more than ever. For example, a trade deal between Bulgaria and the Ottoman Empire expired in 1911.[43] Representatives of the two states tried to renew the arrangement, but talks were interrupted by the outbreak of war between Italy and the Ottoman Empire in what is now Libya. In October, Edirne's Ladino newspaper quoted a Bulgarian publication that had claimed the following: "If the Ottoman government refuses to restart the negotiations, a tariff war will again arise between the two countries after November 15."[44] The quote says much about the Ottoman-Bulgarian borderland between the promise of the Young Turk Revolution and the horrors of the Balkan Wars (1912–1913): While political developments brought unprecedented challenges, it seems almost quaint, in hindsight, that a chief concern at the time was a tariff war.

COMMUNITY LEADERSHIP

While the CUP employed the idea of "the people" to merge the empire's ethno-religious communities into a monolithic source of sovereignty, this discourse facilitated a second development: the creation of a public sphere (or public spheres). By definition, a public sphere emerges in relation to a government.[45] Therefore, before we discuss the Jewish and Ottoman public spheres that appeared in Edirne after 1908, I will review the place of local Jews in Ottoman and especially communal governance. Unlike the Ottoman government, Jewish communal institutions in Edirne did not radically change in 1908.[46] But the suddenly liberal climate and the arrival of new personalities both marked major breaks with the Hamidian era.

On the imperial level, it is important to note that no Jews from Edirne Vilayet were ever elected to the Ottoman parliament. This was the largest Ottoman-Jewish community to lack a Jewish deputy, in both constitutional eras (1876–1878 and 1908–1920). Ottoman elections were arranged so that every district sent to the chamber of deputies a cohort whose ethno-religious makeup reflected that of the electorate.[47] And in Edirne Province, Jews only constituted 2 percent of the population.[48] A handful of Jews continued to sit on the municipal and provincial councils that had existed since 1867 (the *belediye meclisi*, the *vilayet idare meclisleri*, and the annual *meclis-i umumi*).[49] Also, in 1908, the mayor of Kırklareli and the chief physician of the *vilayet* were both Jews.[50] But the lack of a Jewish deputy from Edirne would complicate how community members understood parliamentary politics.

After the revolution, the city of Edirne's Jewish communal council continued to be dominated by merchants. Circa 1910–1912, for example, it was led by Jacob Pappo—one of the silk magnates mentioned in

Chapter 1.⁵¹ At the same time, the council began to include members who were less traditional, in multiple senses. One was the lawyer "Haim Efendi" Behmoiras. In 1910, he scandalized certain community members by giving a secular lecture in the Italian Synagogue (the only one of the thirteen wooden synagogues restored after the fire).⁵²

From 1896 to 1909, the chief rabbi of Edirne Province was Abraham Semah, a renowned composer of *maftirim* music. As proven by the two monumental building projects he oversaw—the Great Synagogue and the school—Semah was a skilled operator under the reign of Abdülhamid.⁵³ But in the brave new world of the Second Constitutional Era, Jews from various political camps found him "feeble."⁵⁴ In 1909, after allegedly failing to defend the interests of Jewish merchants at a session of the *vilayet idare meclisi*, the rabbi faced calls to resign.⁵⁵ He was not alone: From the Balkans to the Arab lands, local chief rabbis across the empire were rejected by their flocks in the year following the revolution.⁵⁶

In early 1910, Semah was replaced by Haim Moshe Bejarano. Today, Bejarano is mostly known as the Turkish Republic's first chief rabbi, a complicated tenure that lasted from 1923 to 1931.⁵⁷ But from 1910 to 1920, he led the Jews of Edirne through a period that was, arguably, even more fraught. An advocate of Jewish integration who could propitiate self-described Zionists in Istanbul, Bejarano's politics might seem enigmatic, at first.⁵⁸ But studying his career reveals a coherent worldview that was likely shaped in Edirne—a region that endured four changes in sovereignty during his time there. In short, Bejarano was a realist with a keen understanding of modern politics. Like leaders of the Alliance, he urged Jews to cultivate civic virtues and invest in the project of equal citizenship. But he also acquired a dispassionate awareness of the growing power of nationalism—Jewish, Turkish, or otherwise.

Bejarano was born in Eski Zağra and began his career as a Hebrew teacher at the Alliance school in Rusçuk. Both places had been Ottoman until Bejarano was in his thirties, at which point they became the Bulgarian cities of Stara Zagora and Ruse. In 1878, fleeing the latest Russo-Ottoman War, Bejarano crossed the Danube into Bucharest. There, he became chief rabbi of the local Sephardi community.⁵⁹ He also became a model Romanian by frequenting the court of the royal family, teaching Hebrew at the

University of Bucharest's theology school, and contributing to a history of the "Romanian War of Independence"—that is, the Russo-Ottoman War of 1877–1878.[60]

As chief rabbi of Edirne Province, Bejarano immediately applied his integrationist philosophy to the Ottoman context and heeded the government's call for a "union of the elements." A polyglot who could gloss passages from the Quran and Gospels, he moved easily between Jewish, Christian, and Muslim circles.[61] When Sultan Mehmed V visited Edirne in 1910, Bejarano made a strong impression on the sovereign and his entourage, which included War Minister Mahmud Şevket Paşa, war "hero" Enver Bey, and Interior Minister Talat Bey (who was also a deputy from the Edirne district).[62] While Bejarano's CUP commitments were probably weaker than those of Haim Nahum, chief rabbi of the Ottoman Empire, the Edirne rabbi did not hesitate to criticize the old regime and praise the new one.[63] He did exactly that during his first sermon in Edirne's Great Synagogue, speaking in "Judeo-Spanish garnished with the finest Castilian" and closing with an Arabic prayer he had composed himself. (According to one attendee, "Everyone admired it fervently, though no one understood it.")[64]

Throughout the Ottoman Empire, Alliance school directors tended to become unofficial leaders of local Jewish communities—largely because of their European connections and their control of large budgets.[65] In the Hamidian era, this applied mostly to the men who led the boys' schools. For example, Moise Mitrani became director of Edirne's Alliance boys' school in 1904 and quickly established himself as a local personage, in the eyes of community members and Ottoman authorities.[66] But after the Young Turk Revolution, the female director of Edirne's Jewish girls' school assumed a similar role.

Born in Istanbul, Angèle Guéron (née Cohen) became director of Edirne's Alliance girls' school in 1909. Though she was only twenty-three, Guéron had experience directing the Alliance girls' school in Ottoman Haifa (today in Israel).[67] She immediately worked with Ottoman authorities to hire the Edirne school's first Turkish-language teacher—a woman named Ramzi Hanım. These efforts were praised by the *vali*, the regional director of public education, and one of Edirne's parliamentary deputies.[68] In 1910, Guéron's female students welcomed the sultan to Edirne by

Figure 3. Haim Bejarano, Chief Rabbi of Edirne, circa 1910.
Source: Archive of the Alliance Israélite Universelle.

singing a Turkish song and presenting him with an embroidery they had made of Selimiye Mosque. Mehmet V expressed his gratitude with a ten-lira gift.[69] As discussed in the next chapter, Guéron's patriotic work during the Bulgarian Siege of Edirne (1912–1913) would again earn the praise of Edirne Province's *vali*.

In fact, the young educator had a different surname when she arrived in Edirne. But in 1910, she separated from her mentally unstable husband—one Dr. Algranti—and the man committed suicide.[70] At this point, she described being forced to "suffer that absurd and cruel formality known as *halitzah*"—a degrading ritual by which a childless widow and a brother of the deceased avoid the religious duty to marry.[71] Rabbi Bejarano must have been involved, as he was an international expert on this ritual.[72]

When she married the Ottoman Bank employee Isaiah Guéron eighteen months later, community members whispered that it was too soon.[73] Guéron also ruffled feathers by eliminating a home economics course, publicly desecrating the Jewish sabbath, refusing to favor the daughters of notable families, and jealously guarding her school's financial records. In 1911, Guéron led efforts to create a local Jewish orphanage, but she was soon kicked off the steering committee. A year later, the editor of Edirne's Ladino newspaper started a campaign to remove her from the school—an effort that was only stopped by the outbreak of the Balkan Wars.[74] An Alliance investigator from Paris concluded that Guéron's chief adversaries were a group of notable women who found the young educator "arrogant." (Though he acknowledged that he had only been allowed to interview men.)[75]

In most of her writing, Guéron framed her educational mission in terms of integration, liberalism, progress, and Ottoman patriotism. But in at least one case, she linked these values to women's rights. When the chief rabbi of the empire visited Edirne in 1910, she delivered an address to him that included the following lines:

> Of all the peoples living in the Ottoman Empire, Israel [i.e., the Jewish community] is the best prepared to receive this ideal, this difficult hostess called liberty. We happily embraced the end of tyranny, the nomination of modern and enlightened religious chiefs, and the serious attention that is finally being paid to women, who were previously neglected.[76]

This connection between liberal government and women's rights could also be found in CUP rhetoric.⁷⁷ In attempting—with some success—to achieve a level of influence previously unheard of for a female community member, Guéron was likely driven by a combination of personal idiosyncrasy and revolutionary promise.

ASSOCIATIONAL LIFE: NEW DISCOURSES, OLD FOUNDATIONS

The second half of Abdülhamid's reign cast a chill on the clubs and societies of most Ottoman cities, Edirne included. For local Jewish associational life, the Young Turk Revolution marked a rebirth.⁷⁸ While a narrow definition of the public sphere might exclude clubs and associations—which are technically private—many of the societies that emerged in Edirne after 1908 were relatively accessible to local Jews and facilitated the sorts of political discussions that are the subject of this chapter.⁷⁹ For all intents and purposes, they formed a part of the growing Jewish and Ottoman public spheres.

On one end of the spectrum, clubs promoted the CUP ideology of centralization, integrationism, and—to an extent—acculturation. Obviously, this applied to the handful of religiously mixed societies that appeared in Edirne. For the most part, it also applied to the Jewish clubs affiliated with the Alliance.⁸⁰ On the other end of the spectrum, a small number of local Jews used new freedoms of association to promote Zionism, though understandings of that term were highly contested. The most successful clubs, however, promoted an older sort of Jewish nationalism in a framework of Ottoman patriotism—all while building on Sephardi networks and intellectual legacies that had existed in Edirne for decades.

First, let us review associational life during the Hamidian era. Counterintuitively, that period opened with a Jewish cultural boom in Edirne. In 1879, the rabbi, educator, and publicist Abraham Danon founded a society called Dorshei Haskalah (Seekers of Enlightenment). It propagated the ideals of the Jewish Enlightenment among Edirne's youth through various means, including lectures on Ottoman-Jewish history. By 1889, the society had two hundred members and a reading room filled with Hebrew and Ladino periodicals.⁸¹ Decades later, an Edirne-born Jew recalled the 1880s as a time when "everyone was talking about reforms, learning, progress," and "enlightened" rabbis were "lovingly teaching Hebrew in a rational and grammatical fashion."[82] Surely this "renaissance" was influenced by Edirne's proximity to centers of the European Haskalah—such as Austria—and of ascendant nationalism—such as Bulgaria.[83]

In 1889, as this era was drawing to a close, the director of Edirne's Alliance boys' school founded the Cercle Israélite—a philanthropic and literary society for Edirne's Jewish elite. Embodying the genteel, nineteenth-century style of Ottomanism, its galas attracted notables from all religious communities.[84] In 1900, Edirne Jews founded the Fraternité Scolaire, an association that offered moral and financial support to graduates of the Alliance boys' school while they sought work. Two years later, a group of young men formed the Cercle de la Bienfaisance, which was a less stuffy, more leisurely version of Cercle Israélite that would eventually merge with the latter.[85] While Dorshei Haskalah championed the reading of modern Hebrew and received newspapers from Eastern Europe, the Alliance-affiliated organizations kept their libraries stocked with French classics that arrived from Paris via the Aegean port of Dedeağaç.[86]

The Young Turk Revolution changed Edirne's associational landscape in several ways. To a limited extent, it inspired the creation of religiously mixed clubs. In 1908, two Jewish women became founding members of an association called Hizmet-i Nisvan (Women's Service). It was led by the writer and CUP activist Emine Semiye, who was also the wife of Edirne's new *vali*. The club's mission was to help local women enter the workforce.[87] In 1910, Angèle Guéron founded an association for alumni of the Alliance girls' school, which went by the name La Fourmi (The Ant).[88] As Orthodox Christians formed a sizeable minority in the school's student body, it seems likely that local Greek women joined this society.[89] In 1911, Ottoman officials invited twenty notables from various religious communities to start an Edirne branch of the Ottoman Red Crescent Society (Hilal-i Ahmer Cemiyeti), and among them was the above-mentioned lawyer "Haim Efendi" Behmoiras.[90]

These mixed societies notwithstanding, most Edirne Jews experienced the Young Turk Revolution as the revival and expansion of a specifically Jewish associational life. Bedross Der Matossian argues that the Young Turk Revolution produced a "multiplicity of public spheres" in the empire, including an Armenian sphere and a Jewish sphere.[91] In a similar vein, Scott Ury describes how, after the 1905 Russian Revolution, the Jews of Warsaw created their own "national public sphere."[92] But at least one factor distinguished the associational life of Ladino-speaking Ottoman Jews from that of their Armenian neighbors and their coreligionists in Warsaw: the marginal place of the vernacular language.[93] In the Jewish clubs of Edirne, talks were given in French, Turkish, and sometimes Hebrew—but rarely Ladino. This helps explain why the Armenian public sphere in the Ottoman Empire and the Jewish/Yiddish public sphere in Warsaw both bore traits of modern nationalism that were less pronounced in the Ottoman-Jewish public sphere.[94]

The language politics of Ottoman-Jewish communities led to some ironic situations. For example, Edirne's Alliance-affiliated clubs preached integrationism to exclusively Jewish audiences, often in French.[95] One such club was the Cercle Israélite, composed of wealthier community members who often had ties to European financial interests.[96] Another was Fraternité Scolaire, whose lectures echoed the CUP's call for a "union of the elements" and were often given by government officials themselves.[97] In 1909—when the Ottoman Empire extended military conscription to non-Muslims—the above-mentioned Moise Mitrani spoke about a new gymnastics class that was preparing his students to become "robust soldiers who will show everyone that Jews are true patriots who sacrifice everything for the patria." He added that the Alliance schools were boosting the Turkish-language curriculum and would soon become official preparatory schools for the state institutions of higher learning. But his remarks about the importance of teaching Turkish ("the national language") were made in French ("the universal language").[98]

In contrast, the unpretentious Cercle de la Bienfaisance was less constrained by Eurocentrism. In 1911, it hosted a young Jewish man named Haim Mades who spoke about "the patria and modern patriotism"—in Turkish. Mades, who had grown up in Edirne but was studying law in the capital, vocally supported Turkish-language education in Jewish schools.[99] In 1911, Cercle de la Bienfaisance members founded a second institution called Halutzei Tzavah (from a Hebrew term meaning "Pioneers of the Military"). It gave money to women whose husbands were doing military service, especially during Jewish holidays. Donations immediately came in from the kosher butchers' and firefighters' guilds.[100]

Figure 4. Gym class at Edirne's Alliance Israélite Universelle school for boys, circa 1912.
Source: Archive of the Alliance Israélite Universelle.

Also advocating Jewish integration was a group called Tamim-i Lisan-ı Osmani Cemiyeti (Society for the Propagation of the Ottoman-Turkish Language), whose Edirne branch appeared in 1909.[101] In addition to promoting Turkish-language instruction in Jewish schools, it provided scholarships to help graduates of local Alliance institutions continue their studies in Edirne's government high school and Istanbul's government colleges (the medical, military, and law schools). In 1910, Edirne Province's Ministry of Public Education began to send the club a monthly subsidy, and the Alliance in Paris soon did the same.[102] Around this time, a (presumably Muslim) lawyer named Şeref Bey helped organize an event that raised money for both the Jewish club and a local government school. The fundraiser entailed a dance and film-screening at an outdoor venue called Reşadiye Bahçesi—which, ironically, had recently been the site of a violent clash between Jews and police (see below).[103]

After a failed counterrevolution in April 1909, the Ottoman parliament passed a "Law of Association" designed to curb some of the freedoms that citizens had been enjoying for the past nine months.[104] The law technically banned political associations based on ethnic or religious identity, though in practice it was used toward the narrower goal of fighting separatist movements.[105] It was *after* the passage of this law that attempts were made to form Zionist societies in Edirne. This reflects the CUP's relative tolerance for Zionism and, relatedly, the flexible interpretation of that movement offered by Ottoman Jews. Such clubs had already appeared in Salonica and especially Istanbul, where the World Zionist Organization had quietly opened an Ottoman office in 1908.[106] In Ottoman lands, self-described "Zionists" did not promote the creation of a Jewish state but rather the maintenance of a strong Jewish identity—and body—considered fit for twentieth-century politics.[107] Despite their careful messaging, Zionists clashed with Alliance school directors who saw the movement as an ideological rival, a dangerous vehicle for populism, and a competitor in the field of Jewish education.[108]

If Zionism was an ambiguous idea throughout the empire, this was especially true in Edirne. In 1909, one of the region's Muslim deputies—Rıza Tevfik Bey—told an Anglo-Jewish newspaper: "I am a Zionist myself."[109] Tevfik, who had attended Edirne's Alliance school as a boy and maintained a knowledge of Hebrew and Ladino, immediately qualified his statement.[110] By his understanding, Zionism entailed improving conditions for "the lower classes of the Jewish nation" and encouraging Ashkenazim to settle throughout the empire—without concentrating in a particular territory and seeking "Jewish autonomy." Any push for Jewish separatism in Palestine would create a "Jewish question" in the Ottoman Empire and lead to "intense animosity between the Jews and Turks [i.e., Muslims?], leading perhaps to mutual slaughter."[111]

Such language set boundaries for discussion among local Jews. In June 1910—eleven months after Tevfik's interview—the city of Edirne was visited by Lucien Sciuto, editor of the Istanbul-based Zionist newspaper *L'Aurore* (The Dawn). He gave a lecture on "Jewish national dignity" at the Fraternité Scolaire—an organization of which he was a member.[112] According to Angèle Guéron, he "poorly hid his Zionist message."[113] A Ladino newspaper in Izmir was more specific: "Sciuto implied that Jerusalem will go to the Jews and Palestine will become a Jewish principality."[114] The story created an uproar. In a statement printed by *L'Aurore*, fifty-five men who had attended the talk declared the Izmir newspaper's depiction to be "absolutely false."[115]

While it seems impossible to learn the exact content of Sciuto's talk, we know something about its effect. On June 10, 1910, *L'Aurore* published a letter from an Edirne Jew called "M.S." The writer claimed that the day after the lecture, "all of Edirne" watched thirteen Jewish girls join their Catholic-school classmates in a procession marking the Feast of Corpus Christi. Apparently, Jewish students at the local convent schools had always participated in these annual "religious processions," which involved "all the de rigueur insignia." But this year, for the first time, the participation of Jewish girls sparked an outcry from their coreligionists. This was thanks to Sciuto's talk, which had turned "M.S." and many others into "fervent adepts" of Zionism. In a rhetorical move that "M.S." found highly inspiring, Sciuto's definition of Zionism had emphasized national dignity—a value that "could only be rejected by someone who was not a Jew, not a man."[116]

While Sciuto and other Istanbul Zionists caused their share of controversy in Edirne, the Ottoman capital was not the region's strongest center of modern Jewish nationalism. That honor went to Bulgaria. While thousands of Sephardi Jews had left that country when it achieved de facto independence in 1878, those who stayed often became Zionists. Inspired by Bulgarian nationalism, they "projected this example onto Palestine"—another Ottoman territory that seemed ripe for secession. For its part, the Bulgarian state saw Zionism as anti-Ottoman more than anti-Bulgarian, and therefore encouraged it. Furthermore, Bulgaria was relatively close to Zionist centers in Europe (such as Vienna), and antisemitism was more prevalent in this country than it was in Ottoman lands.[117] By 1909, Bulgaria had a thriving Zionist Organization that was headquartered in Plovdiv—one hundred miles from the city of Edirne.[118]

The most effective way that Plovdiv Zionists exerted influence on the Edirne community was through an international sports institution called Makabi. The first athletic organizations to (eventually) go by that name were founded in Istanbul (1895) and Plovdiv (1897).[119] In 1909, some young men in Edirne attempted to establish a similar organization that would be the Plovdiv club's "sister."[120] The group was led by Yehuda Kahn, the son of an accomplished Hebrew teacher. Members included a dentist named Michel Benbassat, a leader of the Bikur Holim named Haim Levi, a certain "Doctor" Benaroya, and one "Sinyor" Kaneti.[121]

In July 1909, the group invited gymnasts from the Plovdiv Makabi club to perform an exhibition in the vast courtyard of Edirne's Alliance boys' school. But when he learned of these plans, Moise Mitrani refused to make his venue available. (The school committee remained "undecided" on the matter.) In a letter to Paris, he lamented that this was one of many attempts made by budding Zionist societies to meet or propagandize in his school. "As a result of the freedoms of speech and press granted by the constitution," he wrote, "Zionism is invading our community and embarrassing us."[122] The gymnasts cancelled their visit to Edirne (and instead went to Istanbul and Salonica). As an alternative, the organizers in Edirne arranged for a lecture to be given by Behor Azaria, secretary of Bulgaria's Zionist Organization and editor of its Ladino organ, *HaShofar*.[123]

Azaria took the train from Plovdiv to Karaağaç, where he was greeted at the station by his hosts. In an article he would soon write for *HaShofar*, Azaria described these men as "young Zionists" who were "taking all necessary preparations for the founding of a Zionist society" (an area in which the Edirne community "had yet to show any signs of life"). After speaking to the group for only a few minutes, Azaria quickly concluded the following:

> The heart of the Jews of Edirne is not sad, has not hardened in the face of the insufferable persecutions, horrible mistreatment, and unimaginable misery experienced by our brothers in Russia, Morocco, Romania, Galicia, et cetera. But [in Edirne] there are anti-Zionists who terrorize the Jews with the fear that if they become Zionists, they will be slaughtered like the Armenians. Naturally, this mass cannot make use of the constitution when it does not even understand it.[124]

The "slaughter" was a reference to the massacre of Ottoman Armenians committed in the 1890s, under the reign of Abdülhamid. And by "anti-Zionists," Azaria surely meant Moise Mitrani and others who subscribed to the Alliance view that excessive Jewish nationalism hindered the projects of integrationism and republican citizenship.

The next morning—Saturday—Azaria toured Edirne's Jewish societies to promote the talk he would give that afternoon. First, he visited the Bikur Holim medical clinic, where the cantor Behor Pappo was giving an impromptu "Zionist speech" to fellow members of the society. Next, Azaria visited Dorshei Haskalah, whose members were "all good nationalists" and had offered to cover the costs associated with his lecture. From there, he headed to the "more influential" Cercle Israélite, whose offer to make its hall available for the talk he politely declined because the space could only hold sixty people. The last stops on this promotional tour were the Cercle de la Bienfaisance and, finally, the Fraternité Scolaire. There, Azaria sparred with an Alliance teacher who insisted that Ottoman Jewry should be recognized not as a "nation" but as a "religious sect."[125]

Azaria gave his talk that afternoon in the modest courtyard of the former Alliance boys' school. Though the building's tenant was the local Cercle Israélite, its owner was the Alliance in Paris. Therefore, it fell under Mitrani's remit.[126] The latter claimed that he did not learn of the event until it was about to begin, at which point he hurried over and broke up the gathering. To his dismay, Rabbi Semah was among the attendees.[127] In Azaria's account, Mitrani's interruption prompted someone to shout, "The people [*el puevlo*] want the orator to speak!" Mitrani supposedly replied, "What people? I don't know of any 'people.' This building belongs to the Alliance, not the people." The lecture reconvened elsewhere and was so well received that Azaria was asked to give another one the following day (according to him).

Azaria claimed that some attendees promptly formed a Zionist organization called Or Zion (Light of Zion), but no other sources mention such a club.[128] In any case, it is clear that an Edirne branch of Makabi opened in November 1910, one year after the society had been officially registered with the Ottoman government in Istanbul.[129] Held in a hall "decked with Ottoman flags," the inauguration was attended by various Jewish notables, including Rabbi Bejarano, Lucien Sciuto, and the president of Makabi in Istanbul, Maurice Abramowitz.[130] In his opening remarks, Abramowitz described Makabi's dual commitment to "the health of the [Jewish] nation and the honor of the [Ottoman] patria." He continued: "Until we have shown that we, as a people, prioritize national dignity, we will be disdained and deserving of the epithets with which we are all too often bestowed." Stating that Makabi made no distinction between Ashkenazim and Sephardim, Abramowitz made it clear that his "Jewish nation" was larger than the Ottoman-Jewish *millet*.[131]

In its brief existence, Edirne's Makabi club hosted a series of talks that had little to do with a Jewish state in Palestine (or anywhere else). In January 1911, a Jewish student at Edirne's government high school (*idadi*) gave a Turkish-language talk at the club, urging audience members to emulate the ancient Maccabees by serving bravely in the Ottoman army.[132] (While Bulgaria was home to several Makabi branches for women, it seems that no such clubs appeared in Edirne.[133]) A few months later, Makabi members performed an exhibition in the local Fevaid Theater to an audience that included Rabbi Bejarano, the Austro-Hungarian consul, and various Ottoman officials.[134] In August 1911, Nissim Catalan gave a talk titled "Radical Support for our Schools." Director of the Talmud Torah in Mustafapaşa, Catalan had once published a Ladino translation of a Zionist play in his hometown of Kazanlak, Bulgaria (previously Kazanlık, Ottoman Empire).[135] Moise Mitrani called him a "covert Zionist."[136]

Despite its location between the Zionist centers of Istanbul, Salonica, and Plovdiv, Edirne saw a relatively weak manifestation of Zionism at this time. According to the British consul, the local Makabi club's fifty members were "drawn from the lowest classes of the Jewish population," and community leaders tolerated the society only because it had been approved by the Ottoman authorities.[137] In late 1911, flagging membership forced the club to close its doors and sell its furniture.[138] By then, the British consul had already concluded that Edirne was not fertile ground for Zionism, as the movement was "unfavorably viewed by the general body of Jews . . . particularly by the more prosperous amongst them who fear lest it may disturb the good relations at present existing between themselves and the Turkish authorities."[139] But even if the movement struggled to gain a foothold, the reinstatement of the Ottoman constitution and the location of Edirne Province combined to ensure that Zionism would be a perpetual menace to its opponents. This is reflected in Angèle Guéron's rhetorical question about Zionist agitators: "Must they all try to corrupt our good *Andrinopolitains*?"[140]

For Edirne Jews, associational life after the revolution was initially dominated by Alliancists and Zionists ("covert" or otherwise). But a third international Jewish organization would soon arrive. B'nai B'rith (Sons of the Covenant) was founded in New York in 1843 as a Jewish aid society and soon expanded into Europe. In 1911, delegates from the Grand Lodge in

Chicago toured the Middle East and Balkans to establish an "Eastern District" (District XI). The latter soon consisted of eighteen lodges throughout the Ottoman Empire and its successor states. The district headquarters in Istanbul was run by Joseph Niego, an Edirne native with experience working for international Jewish organizations. (He had directed the Alliance's agricultural school in Jaffa and advised the Paris-based Jewish Colonization Association on settlements in Anatolia).[141]

Like the Zionists, B'nai B'rith operated in a relatively decentralized manner that respected the autonomy of Ottoman-Jewish communities and contrasted with the Alliance's Eurocentric paternalism.[142] However, Niego and other B'nai B'rith leaders maintained close ties with the Alliance and—at least before World War I—avoided Zionist language that could alienate Ottoman Muslims. This middle path bore certain resemblances to the Haskalah culture fostered by Danon and others in the 1880s. The strategy would lead B'nai B'rith to great success in the region.

The Jews of Edirne founded their chapter in February 1911—after their coreligionists in Bulgaria and Serbia, but before those in other Ottoman cities. Therefore, it was simply called the "Ottoman Lodge."[143] Its first president, Jacques Behmoiras, died in 1912 and was replaced by Nissim Benbassat. The fact that both men had also served as president of Cercle Israélite suggests that B'nai B'rith was replacing the former club as *the* elite association of Jewish Edirne.

One of the lodge's first initiatives was to help fund the modest Bikur Holim clinic. It also announced ambitious plans to build a proper Jewish hospital in Edirne. While the Bikur Holim clinic and pharmacy would serve the community into the 1930s, a modern Jewish hospital would, in fact, never be built. Circa 1911, the community was more interested in expanding the Alliance girls' school.[144]

B'nai B'rith was also active in the electoral politics of the Second Constitutional Era. According to a report published after the 1912 parliamentary elections, the Edirne lodge rectified the "electoral lists" that had long been "prejudicial to the interests of Judaism in the province." As a result, local Jews "achieve[d] representation in parliament equivalent to the importance of their votes."[145] As mentioned above, Edirne never sent a Jew to Ottoman parliament. What the report seems to describe is an increase in the number of Edirne's Jewish *electors*. (Ottoman parliamentary elections used an indirect voting system in which local authorities granted each religious community a set number of electoral votes.) As was the case in Istanbul, Izmir, and Salonica, Jewish electors in Edirne generally voted for CUP candidates.[146]

Finally, B'nai B'rith influenced Jewish life in Edirne through the very structure of the international organization. The "Eastern District" had three lodges in British Egypt and one in Serbia. More importantly, it had nine lodges in the Ottoman Empire (Edirne, Istanbul, Salonica, Izmir, Jaffa, Safed, Jerusalem, Zikhron Ya'akov, and Beirut) and six in Bulgaria (Plovdiv, Sliven, Varna, Sofia, Ruse, and Burgas).[147] The district was remarkable for the way it ignored the Ottoman-Bulgarian border and continued to delimit the region's Jewish community according to Edirne Province's shape before 1878.[148] Networks of Makabi clubs and Alliance schools were also intensely international and facilitated Jewish cooperation that crossed the Ottoman-Bulgarian border.[149] But B'nai B'rith's rising popularity—in both countries—and the particular shape of its "Eastern District" made it especially effective, on that score.

If CUP leaders hoped that freedom of association would somehow relax the intensity of national identities, the case of Edirne's Jewish community might represent a failure. At the same time, if Zionists like Abramowitz hoped to convince Ottoman Jews that they were, first and foremost, members of a worldwide Jewish community, this notion also fell flat in Edirne. B'nai B'rith's success in Southeast Europe reflected the persistence of a Ladino cultural zone that had spanned the Ottoman Balkans for centuries. In Edirne, freedom of association was supposed to bring Jews toward a new type of Ottoman identity. But mostly it helped them revive an old one.

THE PRESS: POPULAR SOVEREIGNTY AND NATIONAL DIGNITY

Edirne's first Jewish newspapers appeared in the 1880s, when rabbis Barukh Mitrani and Abraham Danon published Ladino-Hebrew periodicals imbued with the spirit of Haskalah. Mitrani's *Karmi* (1881–1882) explored various shades of nationalism, while Danon's *Yosef Da'at/El Progreso* (1888–1889) has been called "the first journal devoted to the Sephardi past."[150] Though their newspapers quickly became casualties of Hamidian censorship, these two publicists inspired a future generation through their medium and message. That is, their use of the press and their brand of Jewish nationalism would both influence the Jewish public sphere that appeared in Edirne after 1908.[151]

In this context, Danon and Mitrani's most important protégé was a man named Josef Barishac (Bar-Yitzhak). Born in 1867, Barishac grew up in the shadow of these local *maskilim*. He attended and then taught at Edirne's Alliance boys' school before directing Talmud Torahs in Dimetoka (1883–1890, 1897–1901), Mustafapaşa (1890–1897), and Gümülcine (1901–1904). In all three places, Barishac tried to prepare his schools to join the Alliance network.[152] But in 1904, he lost his job in Gümülcine, returned to the city of Edirne, and begged the Alliance to help him feed his wife and seven children.[153] After the 1905 fire, the Barishacs were among the Jewish families who moved to the suburb of Karaağaç, where they remained for some time.[154] The fact that Barishac had children in Alliance schools did not stop him from criticizing the organization in an editorial published by *El Tiempo*, the largest Ladino newspaper in Istanbul (and the Ottoman Empire).[155]

Barishac soon decided that instead of submitting pieces to other people's newspapers, he would start his own. Early in 1910, he launched *La Boz de Verdad* (The Voice of Truth), a Ladino publication that was the only Jewish periodical in Edirne at the time. Barishac was sole proprietor and editor-in-chief, while his (Jewish) printers were Yaakov Levi and Yuda Razon.[156] The semiweekly paper reported mostly on the Jewish communities of Edirne Vilayet and the neighboring provinces of Salonica and Istanbul. To a lesser extent, it covered Jewish communities in Bulgaria, Western Europe, and beyond. The fact that it would survive—with intermittent closures—for seventeen years suggests that it maintained a large subscription base. It was also read beyond the Ottoman Empire. For example, the writer Elias Canetti (1905–1994) recalled that his grandfather in Ruse, Bulgaria, was a subscriber.[157] Guéron's claim that the newspaper "deceives many of the ignorant and credulous" only supports the notion that it was popular.[158]

La Boz de la Verdad served many functions. But five of them were especially important for Barishac: to help him increase his own power; to spread democratic ideals and a discourse of popular sovereignty; to support modern education; to fight "antisemitism," broadly defined; and to promote the continued autonomy of Ottoman-Jewish institutions and culture. The first three functions can be grouped under the rubric of an "intellectual" agenda, while the last two represented the dual prongs of what Barishac and Sciuto called "national dignity" (*dinyita nasyonala*).[159]

Almost immediately, *La Boz de la Verdad* launched an attack campaign on Edirne's new chief rabbi, Haim Bejarano. Echoing CUP criticism of Sultan Abdülhamid, Barishac portrayed the rabbi as a despot who treated community members "with violence" and lived a lavish lifestyle at the expense of "the people."[160] In an article that unfavorably compared the situation in Edirne to that in Salonica—where the Jewish community had better financial oversight—Barishac listed the various benefits and income streams received by Bejarano:

> (1) We pay him 5,000 francs per year. (2) We pay for his house and furniture. (3) We pay for his newspapers. (4) We pay for his firewood, water, etc. (5) We pay loads of money for his coach-rides. (6) We pay for countless quantities of coffee, tobacco, and other things. (7) Revenues from *lulavs* go to the chief rabbi. (8) Payments from the communities of the interior go to the rabbi. (9) At every wedding and celebration, one must pay the rabbi to attend. (10) He demands 20 Napoleons from the congregation to give a sermon. (This is what he charged last year.)[161]

These claims were not completely baseless. According to Moise Mitrani, the new rabbi's salary was five times that of his predecessor.[162] And, as mentioned in Chapter 1, chief rabbis had long enjoyed the prerogative of receiving payments from subcommunities throughout the province, in the form of special taxes and the exclusive right to sell the ritual *lulav*.[163] *La Boz de la Verdad* explained that Bejarano was breaking "popular traditions" and "conventions" (*haskamot*) by regularly officiating weddings—a service for which people felt pressured to pay dearly.[164]

Within a year of launching his paper, Barishac had already gained enough clout to join the Jewish delegations that met with Chief Rabbi Nahum and Sultan Mehmed V during their respective visits to Edirne (in May 1910 and November 1910).[165] The editor's influence only grew as *La Boz de la Verdad* continued to attack certain personages in the community. After two years of this, Cercle Israélite members invited leaders from every Jewish organization in the city of Edirne to attend a "reconciliation" meeting. On the understanding that Barishac would stop his hatchet jobs, community leaders agreed to put him in charge of a new financial oversight committee that would review the activities of the chief rabbinate and communal council.[166] Soon, Barishac also became secretary of the communal council, a member of the steering committees for the Alliance boys' and girls' schools, and a member of the Jewish general assembly. He also became a confidant of Rabbi Bejarano, his erstwhile foe.[167] In short, Barishac leveraged his control of the Jewish press to make himself one of the most powerful people in the community.

La Boz de la Verdad never accused Bejarano of wronging the nation of Ottoman Jews. Rather, the chief rabbi's alleged crime was offending "the people."[168] If Barishac believed that the Jewish *nasyon* needed to protect itself from other nations, he also felt that the Jewish *puevlo* needed protection from its own leadership—just as the *"puevlo Otomano"* needed a constitution to protect it from the imperial government.[169] While an individual could only be a member of one nation, he or she could be a member of multiple peoples. For example, an Edirne Jew was part of the local Jewish people as well as the larger Ottoman people, which was united not through religion or ethnicity but through a shared right to be represented by the Ottoman government. *La Boz de la Verdad* also spoke of a *"puevlo Bulgaro"* united by these same rights vis-à-vis the Bulgarian government.[170]

Barishac's understanding of the people was probably influenced by several sources. One was his Alliance education, which promoted a republicanism rooted in the ideals of the French Revolution. Another was the CUP, which justified its revolutionary actions by claiming to rule in the name of the people. Equally important, I think, was Barishac's firsthand knowledge of Bulgaria—a state that legitimated its existence on the premise that it represented the Bulgarian people in a way that the Ottoman state did not. All three influences were reflected in articles Barishac published in September 1912, weeks before the outbreak of the Balkan Wars.

In what reads like a response to Azaria's *HaShofar* articles from 1909, Barishac visited Plovdiv and published his observations. First, he described how much prettier the city had become since his last visit. The wide streets and attractive storefronts made a strong impression on "that traveler who, a few hours earlier, had left the city of Edirne where, except for one street, everything is but a mass of miserable-looking buildings." Why, he asked, were the Ottomans so far behind the Bulgarians?

> Is it that the Ottoman people . . . do not want to sacrifice the money to beautify and clean up the city in which they dwell? . . . Why have we Ottomans let ourselves fall behind a people that, not long ago, was still an integral part of our great empire? What is the cause of this inertia, this apathy of ours? Are we not made of the same clay? Do we not have the same sentiments?[171]

Barishac's logic echoed that of Edhem Ruhi, the above-mentioned editor in Plovdiv.[172] Only thirty-four years prior, Edirne and Plovdiv had been part of the same empire, and many families continued to count members in both towns. The differences between these two cities simply reflected the different political regimes under which they had come to exist. In Bulgaria, "the entire population—even in the villages—has received a civic education, which allows people to assess current events and exercise their right of popular sovereignty." This last phrase was not understood in the Ottoman Empire, where it was commonly believed that "paying taxes to the country, in money or blood, provides only for the needs of state functionaries, never for the needs of the people." In Bulgaria, civic education among the general "Bulgarian people" had taught the Jews to become active, responsible citizens. This had alleviated antisemitism and caused everyone to regard the Jews as "true Bulgarians." While the reinstatement of the constitution had been a step in the right direction for the Ottoman Empire, there was still much progress to be made.[173]

Education was central to Barishac's agenda. Despite his complicated relationship with the Alliance, he remained, for the time being, an advocate of its work in Edirne. Barishac criticized school directors for dedicating too many hours to French-language instruction at the expense of teaching modern Hebrew. But he shared their zeal for fighting "backward" attitudes regarding science and modern politics.[174] His newspaper supported the Alliance's expansion in the province and praised people who made donations to the cause.[175] Jewish schools were to play an important role in the larger project of cultivating civic virtues in the empire. Ottoman citizens of all religions would become civically engaged "to the extent that new generations will be formed on the benches of modern schools."[176]

Barishac—whose education did not exceed the contemporary equivalent of junior high school—was a peculiar sort of "intellectual." Historical sociologist Charles Kurzman claims that the Dreyfus Affair (1894–1906) and other events of the early twentieth century inspired self-described "intellectuals" throughout the world to develop a class consciousness based on their shared interest in promoting democracy and education. This new "global class," which included many CUP members, believed that its "superior qualifications to rule" would become apparent to the masses if only the latter became educated. Therefore, democracy and universal education formed the core of the intellectual class's "self-interested ideology."[177] In this sense, Barishac shared with intellectuals around the globe—including other Sephardi publicists—a vested interest in both of these modern institutions.[178]

If Barishac's support for democracy and education was driven by rational self-interest and a certain type of class consciousness, his call for "national dignity" was largely a matter of sentiment. Here, he was motivated by his feelings about the Ottoman-Jewish collective and his sense of Jewish identity. In *La Boz de la Verdad*'s prospectus, he promised to "raise the prestige of the name 'Jew' that we carry with pride."[179] He believed that "Ottomanism" was fully compatible with Jewish "nationalism," and that Jews who sacrificed the latter in pursuit of CUP ideals were "more royalist than the king."[180] This stance, plus his flirtation with the Liberal Entente opposition party, put Barishac on a collision course with Chief Rabbi Nahum, who became *La Boz de la Verdad*'s new favorite target.[181] In short, Barishac believed that the Second Constitutional Era demanded not a relaxation of communal identity but rather a newly assertive role for the Jewish collective in Ottoman politics.[182]

Often, this view prompted him to urge Jewish deputies to fight "*antisemitismo*" (instead of practicing the "cowardly" policy of "*kayades*"—a Ladino word meaning silence or discretion).[183] The four Jews in the Third Chamber of Deputies (1908–1912) represented Salonica, Istanbul, Izmir, and Baghdad. Though none of them represented Barishac's district, he excoriated these deputies for failing to "raise their voices" after Edirne's chief of police mistreated the Jewish community. (The so-called "Edirne Incident" is discussed below.) *La Boz de la Verdad* suggested that if something similar had happened to local Greeks, Armenians, or Bulgarians, these Christians would have been helped by "their representatives in the chamber," regardless of what district the deputies officially represented.[184]

Jewish members of parliament were also accused of failing to fight antisemitism in the chamber itself. In 1911, a series of parliamentary debates about Zionism elicited comments from some deputies that, for Barishac, amounted to a "new antisemitism." He claimed that "this poisonous microbe had been hidden underground before the [1908] constitution. But with [the reinstatement of] the constitution and freedom of the press, many people felt it was time to unearth it." He even wondered if there would soon be "an antisemitic party" in the chamber.[185] A year later, *La Boz de la Verdad* shamed "our deputies" for failing to condemn "the raving antisemite" İsmail Hakkı Bey, deputy from Gümülcine and member of the Liberal Entente opposition party.[186] Apparently Barishac believed that every Jewish deputy represented the entire nation of Ottoman Jews.

In addition to prodding Jewish deputies in the capital, *La Boz de la Verdad* also fought "antisemitism" by appealing directly to local Christians and Muslims. On this score, Barishac had experience. In the 1890s, when he was director of the Talmud Torah in Mustafapaşa, some local Bulgarian Christians had accused their Jewish neighbors of killing a Christian boy and using his blood to bake Passover matzah—a centuries-old accusation known as a ritual murder allegation (or "blood libel"). Barishac prevented an outbreak of violence by "battling against the Bulgarian notables in the newspapers," as he was the only local Jew "able to voice dissent in the [Bulgarian-language] publications that ran these crazy accusations." He was also a part-time French teacher in Mustafapaşa's Bulgarian school, where he managed to "calm the spirits of the seventeen Bulgarian teachers, who then calmed their students."[187] (In this, he was following the example of his predecessor Barukh Mitrani, who had refuted a ritual murder allegation among locals Christians back in 1874.[188])

As editor of *La Boz de la Verdad*, Barishac would continue to fight blood libels on the Bulgarian side of the border—such as one that occurred in Asenovgrad in 1912.[189] But he no longer witnessed this problem on the Ottoman side of the line. There, he had to deal with inflammatory articles published by *Yeni Edirne*, the city's main Turkish-language newspaper. This was especially so during the Italo-Ottoman War (1911–1912).

After Italy attacked the Ottoman province of Tripolitania in September 1911, anti-Italian sentiment gripped the empire.[190] *Yeni Edirne* quickly published a list of Italian citizens living in the city, some of whom were Jewish.[191] Later, it ran a piece titled "The Jews" that questioned Jewish loyalties in both Tripoli (today in Libya) and Edirne. The article also claimed that during the Russo-Ottoman War of 1877–1878, local Jews with Italian citizenship had cooperated with the occupying Russian soldiers. The writer now wanted Edirne's "Italian-Jewish families" to prove their loyalty by applying for Ottoman citizenship. "The true sources of danger to the Ottoman Empire," he warned, "are the foreign citizens with their privileges."[192]

La Boz de la Verdad published a strong response, claiming that the *Yeni Edirne* article contained "a whiff of antisemitism."[193] In Barishac's corner were two Salonican Jews—Moise Cohen and Izak (Izakino) de Boton. The former edited a Turkish-language newspaper called *Yeni Asır* (New Century) and would later become an ideologue of Turkish nationalism under the name Munis Tekinalp. The latter would eventually run a Zionist Ladino-language newspaper in Xanthi, Greece (see Chapter 4). In December 1911, both men wrote letters, in Turkish, to the editor of *Yeni Edirne*, complaining about its anti-Jewish coverage.[194] While he never apologized, the editor did agree to publish Boton's letter, which said that Jews across the empire "are attached to the Ottoman patria as much as the Turks are."[195]

Though it was a major event, *La Boz de la Verdad*'s skirmish with *Yeni Edirne* seems to have been a gentlemen's dispute. Barishac made a point of saying that the newspaper's editor, Mustafa Şevket, was not an antisemite.[196] In fact, until the month of their journalistic dustup, the two men had used the same Jewish publisher and rented next-door offices in the sixteenth-century Rüstempaşa Kervansarayı.[197] Also, by 1910, both editors supported parties that opposed the CUP.[198] What was more, when Barishac had taught at the local Alliance school in the 1880s, one of his students was a young Mehmet Şeref—*Yeni Edirne*'s chief writer in the years following the Young Turk Revolution.[199] I think that Barishac's relationship with these Turkish journalists embodied the sort of Jewish-Muslim relations that he envisioned for a liberal Ottoman Empire, where Jews would continue to form a distinct interest group that could strengthen Ottoman society through constructive debates with other communities.²⁰⁰

In the name of national dignity, Barishac called for Jewish children to learn conversational Hebrew, for the community to handle its issues without involving the police, for local clubs to give political lectures in Ladino, and for Jewish leaders in the capital to unapologetically defend the interests of Ottoman Jewry.²⁰¹ All this made Barishac a Jewish nationalist, in the contemporary Ottoman sense of the word. But did his newspaper cross the threshold into what we can call Zionism?

Though Barishac frequently referenced or picked up stories from Zionist newspapers in Istanbul—such as *L'Aurore* and *El Djudyo* (The Jew)—he refused to be identified with this movement. In 1912, after *El Tiempo* repeatedly accused *La Boz de la Verdad* of being a "Zionist" paper, Barishac denied the charge and insisted that his publication received no money from Zionist organizations.²⁰² (In contrast, *L'Aurore*, *El Djudyo*, and even *El Tiempo* received Zionist funding.²⁰³) In an article on the tenth Zionist Congress in Basel (1911), Barishac wrote that while "no one can totally condemn this movement," its leaders would do better to settle Russian and Romanian Jews in Ottoman lands *outside of* Syria and Palestine. In the latter region, he claimed, the presence of Ashkenazi settlers was beginning to inflame local Arabs.²⁰⁴ (Rıza Tevfik Bey had a similar stance.²⁰⁵) It is also telling that, after his above-mentioned trip to Plovdiv, Barishac ran damaging gossip about Presidio Romano, the "autocratic" president of the Central Committee of Bulgarian Zionism.²⁰⁶

Barishac seems to have aligned most closely with local proponents of Hebrew language and culture. Known as the *ebraizantes* (Ladino for "Hebraizers"), members of this loose teachers' collective wrote open letters to *La Boz de la Verdad* supporting the revival of Hebrew and better pay for Hebrew teachers. Some members, such as the above-mentioned Nissim Catalan, gave talks that were clearly Zionist. Others, such as Solomon (Shlomo) Mitrani, seem to have avoided any association with that movement.²⁰⁷ The spirit of the *ebraizantes* is captured in an editorial he wrote for *La Boz de la Verdad*, in which he cited Genesis 11—the Tower of Babel story—as proof that "over four thousand years ago, the force of a language in the national domain had already been remarked upon."²⁰⁸

Perhaps more interesting than *La Boz de la Verdad*'s place on the political spectrum was its place in the journalistic scene of Southeast Europe. In addition to having subscribers in Bulgaria, Barishac's paper was in conversation with at least two Plovdiv periodicals: one published in Ladino (*HaShofar*), the other in Ottoman-Turkish (*Balkan*). Surely, this interstate conversation was facilitated by the Young Turk Revolution, which made it easier for Bulgarian publications to enter the empire.[209] Also, all three editors—Josef Barishac, Behor Azaria, and Edhem Ruhi—made trips across the Ottoman-Bulgarian border, a relatively new line that only appeared in their youth and did not become an official state boundary until they were middle-aged.[210] These trips allowed them to make firsthand comparisons between two constitutional monarchies. Biased as these accounts may have been, they were very much products of the borderland milieu, where one could hardly imagine the state without considering its neighbors.

PUSHING THE LIMIT: "THE EDIRNE INCIDENT"

In cities throughout the Ottoman Empire, the period 1908–1912 was characterized not only by new freedoms but also by a flurry of patriotic protests. In response to Bulgaria's declaration of independence and Austria-Hungary's annexation of Bosnia and Herzegovina, both of which occurred in October 1908, popular demonstrations swept the empire. In 1910, a second wave of protests erupted when nominally Ottoman Crete declared itself part of Greece. As discussed in Chapter 1, Edirne's Jews and Christians sometimes joined their Muslim compatriots at these events.

Against this backdrop, an event occurred in the city of Edirne that had few precedents in Ottoman history: Jews started a spontaneous demonstration that devolved into a shootout with police.[211] The event and its aftermath posed a serious test to the professed liberalism of the CUP and the integrationist style of politics some Jews were promoting. While the protestors claimed to want nothing more than equal treatment for Jews, as promised by the constitution, Ottoman and Jewish leaders alike feared that the event would be perceived as a form of nationalism akin to what some Ottoman Christians were advancing. The audacious expression of Jewish discontent was immediately followed by conciliatory action—or inaction—on the part of Jewish leaders, to the dismay of some community members.

In the spring of 1910, the municipality of Edirne opened a small park in the Kaleiçi neighborhood. As mentioned above, it was called Reşadiye Bahçesi (in honor of the current sultan, Mehmed V Reşad). On warm evenings, the park served as an outdoor "brasserie," concert venue, and open-air cinema. Later that season, a Jew named Moise (Moshe) Behar opened a "cabaret" on the ground floor of the residential building that he owned, directly across from the park.[212] Apparently, Edirne's Jewish Quarter was becoming a nightlife destination.

But before long, municipal authorities told Behar that his building lacked permits and was structurally unsound.[213] Though a French architect found no problems with the building, Behar told the authorities that he would make all required repairs. The president of the Jewish communal council even offered to cover the cost. Nevertheless, on the evening of June 20, 1910, the municipality demolished the building. Several commentators believed that the authorities simply wanted to eliminate competition for the venue in the park.[214]

The British consul wrote that Cemal Bey, chief of police, demolished the building "at an hour when he knew that the Jewish workmen would be returning to their homes and would pass the spot."[215] Indeed, a large crowd of Jews eventually "stopped before the rubble to protest," in Moise Mitrani's words.[216] Edirne's police headquarters was nearby, and Cemal Bey had decided to watch the demolition while enjoying a beer—or two, or three—in Reşadiye Bahçesi.[217] At some point, he confronted the crowd and used "language highly insulting to the Jewish community and to their religion." Next—according to the British consul—the crowd "attacked" Cemal Bey, police fired on the crowd, and some Jews fired back.[218] Mitrani's narrative differed slightly: "The chief of police, who has previously shown himself to be malevolent toward Jews, ordered the crowd to disperse. It was about to do so when the police chief, his agents, and some officers rushed the Jews, who would have been crushed like flies had they not defended themselves bravely."[219]

In his official report, Cemal Bey claimed that the crowd had been cursing and threatening the municipal engineer overseeing the demolition. When Cemal Bey and his men arrived, the crowd started pelting them with stones, one of which struck an artillery officer in the head. The police chief telephoned for reinforcements, gathered his men in the park, and closed the gates for protection. At this point he claimed that "revolvers started to fire" from the Jewish crowd and surrounding houses.[220] Believing that the mob was about to storm the gates of the park, Cemal Bey ordered his men to fire into the air and affix bayonets to their rifles.[221]

All accounts agree that the gendarmerie soon arrived and finally dispersed the crowd (after firing additional rounds, according to Mitrani).[222] A handful of Jews were immediately arrested. No one was killed in the altercation and only a few people were wounded, which led the British consul to conclude that "neither mob nor police were at all expert in the use of their weapons."[223] Alternatively, it may be that neither side was shooting to kill.

That night, gendarmes roamed the neighborhood to maintain order and round up those responsible for the disturbance. According to Angèle Guéron, they searched the Cercle Israélite building and tried to enter the synagogue, though this was prevented by Rabbi Bejarano. She claimed that fifteen Jews were arrested, while Mitrani and others put the number at thirty.[224] "Homes were stormed, people were dragged out at night," wrote *La Boz de la Verdad*, which also claimed that at least one Jew was beaten by police.[225] Most suspects were released in the coming days, and ultimately the judicial authorities decided to try only eight men (including the secretary of the chief rabbinate). Meanwhile, Cemal Bey was transferred to Beirut.[226] Defended in court by the above-mentioned Şeref Bey, the eight Jews were acquitted in July. Meanwhile, Cemal Bey was issued a court summons "for using insulting language."[227]

Perhaps the most interesting part of the story is what transpired after the arrests but before the acquittals. For both Jewish and Ottoman authorities, the crux of the issue was to what extent the disturbance was a political act with a "national" character. Four days after the clash, Mitrani assessed the situation as follows:

> What is most troubling to the Jewish community is that the authorities would cover up these unjust acts of the municipality and the police by trying to portray the event as a premeditated riot [*émuete*] instead of a spontaneous expression of outrage against the acts of the police chief. They want to paint it as a criminal plot against the government hatched by the entire community—something that could meet with a very severe punishment.[228]

Similarly, the British consul wrote that the authorities were straining to give the event "a political complexion" by disingenuously charging the Jews with "creating a revolution."[229] In the words of *La Boz de la Verdad*: "The most saddening part was to see almost all the officials, first and foremost the *vali*, get carried away by the current of false insinuations . . . to see enlightened Turkish notables believe in this comedy of a conspiracy hatched by Jews."[230]

Soon, fuel was thrown on the fire. The events were covered with an anti-Jewish slant by the Turkish-language press in Edirne and even Plovdiv.[231] After someone posted a bill to the façade of a church "inviting the Jewish people to revolt," the *vali* summoned Rabbi Bejarano for questioning.[232] The lawyer "Haim Efendi" Behmoiras and the editor Josef Barishac visited the local mufti in an attempt to deescalate matters.[233] Apparently, what troubled the authorities most about the affair was the possibility that the Jews' newfound boldness might inspire local Greeks, Armenians, or Bulgarians. This anxiety was reflected in the closing lines of Cemal Bey's report: "Such displays of audacity in which [the Jews] went so far as to attack the police and even army officers can influence others and open the door to regrettable situations."[234]

Community leaders faced something of a catch-22: any demands they might make for government redress could tie them to the protestors and give the scandal "the character of a national affair." According to Guéron, the rabbinate and the communal council therefore decided to proceed "*en douceur.*" (One wonders if she was translating the Ladino word "*kayades*" for her readers in Paris.) Jewish leaders refrained from contacting the capital and demanding an investigation, opting instead to leave matters with the local justice system. When local Christians and Muslims stopped patronizing Reşadiye Bahçesi to show solidarity with their Jewish neighbors, members of the communal council visited the garden to break the boycott. "I do not know how to judge this act!" wrote Guéron.[235] Less ambivalent, *L'Aurore* in Istanbul claimed that "the weakness shown by our leaders in Edirne" did a disservice to all Ottoman Jewry.[236]

Notably, even Alliance personnel seemed to invoke a sense of "Jewish dignity." In his reports to Paris, Moise Mitrani suggested that he was losing patience with community leaders and their "*en douceur*" diplomacy. While the combative approach of the Christian communities often earned results from the government, official attitudes toward the Jews seemed to follow the dictum "no ceremony between friends." As for the initial demolition of the building, he cynically concluded that "one can afford such liberties with a Jew."[237]

Despite the conciliatory response of the communal council, the protest itself shattered the picture of the Jewish community as a "model *millet*" (at least momentarily). This public image had been cultivated for decades by Ottoman-Jewish leaders who wanted to distinguish their community from the supposedly troublesome Christian *millets*.[238] Ten days after the shootout, the British consul said that, for the moment, the Jews "must be reckoned as strong opponents of the Government."[239] Even if he was exaggerating, the protest and its aftermath revealed a growing divide in Edirne's Jewish community about the style of politics that was appropriate for the Second Constitutional Era.

It seems that Behar was never compensated for the loss of his building. His wife went so far as to approach Talat Bey in the street and beg the interior minister to help her family. In a conversation that occurred entirely in Ladino—Talat had been both a student and a teacher at Edirne's Alliance school—he promised the woman his assistance.[240] But apparently nothing came of it.[241]

"The Edirne incident"—as the Jewish press in Istanbul called it—was disheartening for many local Jews. At the same time, it was a somewhat successful test of the era's allegedly liberal climate and enlarged public sphere(s). After a group of Jews staged a public protest and shot at the police (!), no Jews were convicted, and the police chief was transferred to Beirut (later Istanbul).[242] In his condescending way, the British consul drew an optimistic conclusion: "In view of the bad state of all the legal tribunals here, it is satisfactory to be able to report one instance at least when justice has been done, even at the expense of a Turkish official."[243] In choosing a response to injustice, the community was torn between delicate conciliation and assertive national politics. The communal council ultimately went with the former, but the latter was championed through the summer by other Jewish leaders. If caution won the day, boldness certainly had its moment.

CONCLUSION

Commenting on the "Edirne Incident" in his newspaper, Lucien Sciuto wrote the following: "We know the Jews of Edirne. They are the most peaceful people in the world. Among all the Jewish communities of [the Ottoman Empire], the one in Edirne is distinguished by its bonhomie and, let us admit, its tranquil insouciance."[244] Echoed in Guéron's rhetorical question about Zionists—"Must they all try to corrupt our good *Andrinopolitains*?—the claim might contain a germ of truth. Compared to their coreligionists in Salonica and Istanbul, where Jewish politics were becoming highly polarized, the Jews of Edirne tended to resist the two extremes of CUP-style integrationism and overt Zionism, opting instead to use new constitutional liberties in pursuit of a middle way that borrowed from the local Haskalah tradition.

Sciuto's comment, however, obscures the fact that a vociferously modern Jewish politics emerged in Edirne after the Young Turk Revolution. Jews debated a range of political options in a somewhat liberal public sphere—even if they ultimately gravitated toward safer choices. It is tempting to wonder how these choices might have changed, had this period of liberalism and stability continued. However, subsequent events would force the Jews of Edirne to find even more conservative survival strategies and to abandon the spirit of political experimentation that marked the period 1908–1912.

THREE

The Eye of the Storm

Borderland Violence and the Jews, 1912–1918

"THE 1912–13 SCHOOL YEAR BEGAN most auspiciously," wrote Moise Mitrani, director of the Alliance Israélite Universelle boys' school in the city of Edirne. His enrollments had been growing, the Alliance had been opening schools throughout the province, local Jews had been enjoying a robust associational life, and intercommunal relations had been mostly civil, certain tensions notwithstanding.[1] But by the summer—when Mitrani wrote these lines—the outlook for Edirne's Jewish community had drastically darkened. This was because the 1912–1913 school year turned out to be coterminous with a conflict known as the Balkan Wars.

Hardly "auspicious," the fall of 1912 marked the beginning of an extremely violent period that would permanently alter Edirne's physical and demographic landscapes. By the close of World War I (1914–1918), both the Jewish and general populations in the city of Edirne would be half of what they had been in 1912, an interstate border would separate the city from its western suburbs (including Karaağaç), and the countryside would lie in ruin.[22] Of the six hundred thousand Christians who had lived in Edirne Province before these wars, only seventy thousand would remain when the dust settled.[3] The departing refugees would largely be replaced by Muslims fleeing violence and persecution in the Balkans.[4]

For Edirne's Jewish community, the Balkan Wars marked the start of a downturn. But this decline narrative contains surprises and ironies that help us understand two related processes at the core of this story: the development of what is today the northwestern border of Turkey, and the ethnoreligious homogenization of a borderland. From 1912 to 1918, hundreds of thousands of Muslims and Christians in Southeast Europe were forced across borders, an experience that must have shaped popular conceptions of these lines. The Ottoman-Bulgarian border morphed from a mundane site of coercion and taxation into a symbol that helped refugees and migrants make sense of their plight.[5]

But the Jewish experience was different. Contemporary documents written by local Sephardim suggest that the border failed to produce this symbolic effect on the Jews of Edirne Province. Unlike many of their neighbors, they rarely faced violent deportation at this time. Far from reimagining the border as an essential, ethnoreligious divide, many local Jews maintained and even strengthened ties with coreligionists in Bulgaria and beyond. In this, they demonstrated a growing sense of Sephardi solidarity and a refusal to interpret the border as anything more than a physical hindrance in an arbitrary place. What holds today was also true in the last Ottoman decade: A border can be perceived and experienced differently by different groups of people.

For the Jews of Edirne, what changed during and after the Balkan Wars was not the meaning of the border but the meaning of the border*land*. According to the map, Edirne became a border province in the late nineteenth century. But local Jews did not immediately see this as cause for alarm.[6] As Pieter M. Judson says of the contemporary Habsburg borderlands: "There was nothing intrinsic about such regions, not even their inhabitants' use of more than one language, that caused them later to become the settings for ethnic cleansing or genocidal violence."[7]

Tragically, however, Edirne experienced that "later" scenario in the years covered by this chapter. As ethnic cleansing campaigns swept the region, leaders of Edirne's Jewish community anxiously sought survival strategies. Notably, they chose to abandon some of the civic ventures they had undertaken before the wars; to again separate their Sephardi cultural identity from their Ottoman political loyalty; and to strengthen bonds of solidarity and mutual support with Bulgarian Jewry in ways that confound nationalist historiographies. The Jews of Edirne adapted to life in the borderland by defying the very logic of territorial nationalism that was transforming the region.[8]

This chapter begins with the First Balkan War and the Siege of Edirne, focusing on some Jews' attempts to demonstrate and document their loyalty to the empire. The next section covers the Bulgarian occupation of Edirne Province, an overlooked episode that reveals the limits of what patriotism could accomplish in a contested borderland. After that, the discussion turns to the expulsions of the *vilayet*'s Christian populations, a chilling process that began during the Balkan Wars and continued into World War I. Jewish reactions to these expulsions are discussed in the fourth section, which goes on to study how the community avoided this sort of mass displacement. Finally, the chapter looks at some ostensible ironies that emerged between 1915 and 1918, a period that presented the Jews of Edirne with new hardships and threats but also new ways to serve the empire and connect with coreligionists across the border.

DOCUMENTING LOYALTY: THE FIRST BALKAN WAR AND THE SIEGE OF EDIRNE

In her study of Ottoman Macedonia from 1878 to 1908, İpek Yosmaoğlu claims that violence caused nationalism more than nationalism caused violence. Far from being "incidental to nation-making and imperial disintegration," violence was "an independent variable in creating the differences and animosities that were purportedly its cause."[9] The same can be said for Edirne Province in the period 1912–1918. Ultimately, it was war itself—specifically, a new sort of "total war"[10]—that killed the multicultural project known as "civic Ottomanism" and spurred people to accept certain connections between ethnoreligious identity and political affiliation.[11] But for several reasons, many Jews managed to keep those two realms separate. This is reflected in various accounts produced by Jewish elites, documents that may not represent the entire community but provide, nonetheless, a suggestive picture of people eager to demonstrate their Ottoman loyalty while maintaining their Sephardi identity.

The First Balkan War began when Greece, Bulgaria, Serbia, and Montenegro attacked the Ottoman Empire in October 1912. Within weeks, the empire lost 83 percent of its European territory.¹² People across the Balkans were astonished. In the words of novelist Ivo Andrić, who was a student in Sarajevo at the time, "Not even in dreams did frontiers change so quickly."¹³

The war allowed Bulgarian forces to immediately occupy most of Edirne Province. The main exception was the city of Edirne, which endured a grueling siege before capitulating in March 1913. When the Second Balkan War pitted Bulgaria against its former allies, the Ottomans retook the city of Edirne and the eastern half of the *vilayet*—now known as Eastern Thrace— but Bulgaria retained the western half of the *vilayet*—now known as Western Thrace. When the final peace treaty was signed in September, the city of Edirne found itself nearly surrounded by Bulgaria—suddenly the empire's only European neighbor.¹⁴

During the first weeks of war, some Edirne denizens sensed that their Christian neighbors were sympathetic to Bulgaria and Greece. Anxieties were heightened by the fact that, in the suburb of Karaağaç, many employees of the Oriental Railway Company were Bulgarian or Greek Orthodox Christians.¹⁵ While some local Christians fought bravely in the Ottoman army, others did align with Greece and Bulgaria.¹⁶ Writing in 1979, Dimitar Voinikov described his childhood near the Ottoman town of Pınarhisar and how, as a teenager, he helped the Bulgarian army in its 1912 invasion of Thrace.¹⁷ Several accounts describe Christian soldiers deserting the Ottoman army and Christian civilians warmly welcoming the Balkan Alliance soldiers who entered their towns.¹⁸

Such behaviors were rarely attributed to Ottoman Jews, whose loyalty was claimed by no foreign state. (However, this lack of a connection to an enemy state hardly helped the Ottoman Armenians, who were eventually accused of treachery during the Balkan Wars.¹⁹) At worst, Jews were sometimes accused of draft dodging and demonstrating cowardice on the battlefield.²⁰ At best, some Ottoman officials lauded Jewish wartime sacrifices while extolling Ottoman Jewry as proof that non-Muslims could maintain warm relations with the state.²¹

When the Bulgarian army entered Thrace in October 1912, it set off a series of population displacements. In Western Thrace, massacres spurred thousands of Muslims to flee toward Istanbul, though most local Jews were spared such violence and stayed put.²² In the city of Edirne, Jews and Muslims of means fled for the Ottoman capital while they could.²³ Meanwhile, Jews and Muslims from the villages of Eastern Thrace fled *into* the city of Edirne, which was safer than the countryside.²⁴ In Çorlu and Tekirdağ, many Jews and Muslims left for nearby Istanbul.²⁵ In short, the First Balkan War forced many Muslims and a smaller number of Jews to flee Thrace's towns and, in some cases, its principal city.

As Eyal Ginio has shown, this turmoil prompted the Jews of Ottoman Europe to emphasize that they shared the plight of their Muslim compatriots. For example, the "Refugees' Haggadah" (Haggadah de los Muhadjires) was printed in spring 1913 by a Jew who had fled to Istanbul from Silivri.²⁶ This Ladino document is a parody of the text read by Jews at the Passover Seder, and its author describes himself and other Jewish refugees as *muhadjires*—the Ladino version of an Arabic/Turkish word usually associated with *Muslim* refugees.²⁷ As Ginio also notes, however, the sense of a shared Muslim-Jewish experience was limited by certain factors. For instance, Muslim and Jewish war refugees were usually assisted by religiously distinct aid societies in Istanbul.²⁸

Another partially shared experience was military service. On the one hand, Ottoman Jews in Edirne and beyond largely heeded the call to enlist in 1909 and to fight in 1912.²⁹ In 1911, a young man from Kırklareli became the first Jewish officer in the Ottoman army.³⁰ In 1912, enough Jewish soldiers were stationed in Edirne for the local chief rabbi to get them eight days' leave during Passover.³¹ The Ladino press—and even Ladino ballads—reflect Jewish sacrifice on the battlefields of Edirne Province, places where both the Ottoman and Bulgarian armies counted Jews among their ranks.³² On the other hand, Ladino newspapers reported that many Jews left the empire around this time to avoid conscription. And anecdotal accounts suggest that Jews deserted the Ottoman army in higher proportions than Muslims (but in lower proportions than Christians).³³

It was in this context that Angèle Guéron, director of the Alliance girls' school in Edirne, documented her Ottoman loyalty more successfully than any other Edirne Jew at this time. The French-language journal that she kept during the Bulgarian siege of Edirne remains the best source available regarding Jewish life in the city during this ordeal, which lasted from

November 1912 to March 1913. As Avigdor Levy notes, it also reflects how this twenty-six-year-old woman struggled against the patriarchy of her own community.[34]

The journal begins during the first weeks of war, when Guéron's mother, sister, and Alliance colleague (Moise Mitrani) all fled for Istanbul. Meanwhile, Guéron dutifully stayed at her post, joined the local Red Crescent Society (Hilâl-i Ahmer Cemiyeti), and volunteered at the Sultaniye military hospital. She also had her students sew bandages for wounded Ottoman soldiers. Guéron was often assisted by Rosa Avigdor, who directed the Alliance girls' school in Kırklareli but had gotten stuck in Edirne. (Rosa's surname would later become "Mitrani.") In a letter he sent in November, the *vali* thanked the two Jewish women for their "true Ottoman patriotism."[35]

Guéron had to contend not only with Bulgarian shelling—which killed twenty Jews during the siege[36]—but also with two of the most powerful people in Edirne's Jewish community: the local chief rabbi (Haim Bejarano) and the editor of Edirne's Ladino newspaper (Josef Barishac). When she moved her students' sewing workshop from the school to the military hospital, both men objected, implying that it was neither safe nor seemly for Jewish girls to work so close to male soldiers (most of whom were Muslim). Three months later, when much of the Jewish community had crowded into a few large buildings serving as bomb shelters (including the Alliance boys' school), Guéron proposed that long-awaited donations from international Jewish organizations be disbursed to community members as foodstuffs, because cash would feed the gambling that was rampant in the shelters. Her proposal was rejected by the rabbi and the editor, both of whom are harshly criticized in the journal.[37] Guéron's project of documenting Jewish loyalty to the empire did not presuppose a monolithic community.

The journal ends on March 27, 1913, the day after Bulgarian troops entered the city. For the Ottoman public, the loss of Edirne—former Ottoman capital, site of the empire's largest mosque, buffer between Istanbul and the Balkan nation-states—was nothing short of traumatic.[38] In Guéron's words, "so many brave men have fallen without saving Turkey from this painful amputation.... The wound will long continue to bleed."[39] For the moment, Ottoman Edirne had become Bulgarian Odrin.

JEWISH LIFE IN NEW BULGARIA

Bulgaria's occupation of Edirne Province began in October 1912, and the city of Edirne capitulated five months later. Except for the Gallipoli (Gelibolu) peninsula, which Bulgaria never occupied, the entire province would stay under Bulgarian rule until July 1913, when the Ottomans reclaimed Eastern Thrace. During this period, Jews from İskeçe (today Xanthi, Greece) in the West to Çorlu in the East found themselves in a region called "New Bulgaria."

One of the few historians to cover this episode in Ottoman-Jewish history is Abraham Galante (1873–1961), a Sephardi Jew and Turkish patriot whose work often "[idealizes] good relations between Jews and Turks."[40] Like other figures in this chapter, Galante was concerned with documenting loyalty to the Ottoman Empire (and Turkey), so it is not surprising that he paints a picture of Jewish-Muslim friendship through the Bulgarian occupation. He claims that when the Bulgarians implemented a hat law to make Muslims discernable from Jews, the latter thwarted the system by sharing their headgear with "Turks." Jewish children, he says, did their part to frustrate and confuse the occupiers by speaking Turkish whenever Bulgarian soldiers were near. And when "the Muslims of India" sent relief money to their coreligionists in Edirne, Rabbi Bejarano's daughter, Sévère, collected the funds from the local British consulate, purchased food staples, and tirelessly distributed them in the city's "Turkish quarters."[41]

Galante's account resonates with many of the primary sources. However, his tale of Ottoman patriotism is not the whole story. Notably, it obscures the extent to which Jews were subject to the political contingencies of the borderland—regardless of their patriotic sentiments. Exploring this dynamic provides a more nuanced picture of life in an occupied zone.

When the Balkan Wars started, thousands of Jews in Edirne Province inhabited those towns and villages that quickly fell to Bulgaria.[42] Generally speaking, their experience of the occupation was painful. With that said, local Jewish leaders were somewhat successful in adapting to the new reality, and their efforts were often aided by Jewish networks that extended into Bulgaria (and beyond). While many Jews shared with their Muslim neighbors the hardships of persecution, dispossession, and displacement, the plight of the Jews was usually less severe. Furthermore, Jews faced fewer obstacles when it came to integrating their institutions into the Bulgarian system. All this is evident in the reports of local Alliance school directors and in documents describing the work of international Jewish organizations.

One glimpse of Jewish life in New Bulgaria comes from Çorlu, a town in the district of Tekirdağ with a prewar Jewish population of about one thousand.[43] When the Bulgarian army approached, most Muslims and some Jews fled for Istanbul. Among the Jews who stayed put was the director of the local Alliance school, who said that Bulgarian troops received a warm welcome in Çorlu. He claimed that women cheered from their windows and toasts were made in the local Greek club. "You could have believed we were in Sofia," he wrote.[44]

But by late November, the mood in Çorlu had soured. Bulgarian soldiers underpaid local shopkeepers, seized goods left behind by Muslim merchants, requisitioned mills, and savagely beat people who tried to file complaints with higher-ups. The occupiers also turned a blind eye to looting, which emboldened some Greek Orthodox and Armenian residents to raid the homes of departed Muslims and steal their livestock. The Alliance school director noted with embarrassment that, despite the admonishments of the local rabbi, some of his coreligionists had participated in these thefts. At the same time, some Jewish merchants who were "associated with Muslims" had their goods seized by Bulgarian authorities. Many of these Jews had been doing business in Istanbul when the First Balkan War erupted and found themselves stuck in the capital.[45] From Jewish merchants to Christian owners of requisitioned mills, the propertied class had much to lose under military rule—and opportunists of all religions had much to gain.

Twenty miles southwest of Çorlu, the port city of Tekirdağ experienced a far more violent occupation, in part because the Bulgarians were anxious about the proximity of the Ottoman fleet.[46] Clearly, Muslims suffered most. According to David Levy, director of Tekirdağ's Alliance school, the "nouveaux Huns" who occupied the region wanted to "exterminate the Turks in order to seize their land." The Bulgarians committed "systematic massacres," especially in the countryside, where "the entire population of certain villages was exterminated, the goods looted, and the homes reduced to ash." Within the city limits, soldiers were content to terrorize the Muslim population so that "its only means of salvation would be expatriation." Toward that end, the Bulgarians executed hundreds of men who had been convicted of trumped-up spying charges.[47]

About half of Tekirdağ's Jewish population fled to Istanbul during the war, but mostly because of factors that affected the city in general (as opposed to persecution that targeted Jews).[48] For example, all residents were prohibited from traveling and using the postal and telegraph services—restrictions that devastated all merchants, regardless of religion. During the occupation, Bulgarian troops were billeted in most of Tekirdağ's schools, including Levy's.[49] The Alliance building was damaged and eventually looted by the new tenants, who took the additional liberty of turning some classrooms into stables.[50]

But in Tekirdağ, "no home left behind by Jewish emigrants was pillaged or destroyed"—a sharp contrast to the scene in Çorlu. Levy also reported no cases of Bulgarians killing Jews. He attributed this relatively mild treatment to "the presence of 5,000–6,000 Jewish men in the Bulgarian army and their desire to attach themselves to the Jewish population of the conquered country."[51] We might add that the strategically sensitive location of Tekirdağ gave rise to violence that was brutal but carefully targeted (toward Muslims), while the more secure region of Çorlu experienced an occupation that lacked ferocity as well as discipline.

Even more interesting, perhaps, are factors that facilitated the Tekirdağ community's transition back to Ottoman rule in July 1913. One was Levy's extraordinary web of connections. Born in Ottoman Şumla[52]—shortly before it became Bulgarian Shumen—Levy had family members who continued to live in that region, including a nephew who served in the Bulgarian army. During the war, this relative had been a guard at a prisoner-of-war camp in Yambol (Bulgaria), where he kindly treated inmates from Tekirdağ.[53] This would make Levy popular among his Muslim neighbors in the summer of 1913. Furthermore, at the Alliance school in Edirne, Levy had once taught none other than Mehmed Talat—now known as Talat Paşa, de facto leader of the Ottoman Empire (arguably). This greatly impressed the local Ottoman officials who resumed power in July.[54]

According to Levy, another conciliatory factor was the kindness that Jews had shown their Muslim neighbors during the Bulgarian occupation.

Jews hid persecuted Muslims in their homes and sometimes gave them money. Levy himself admitted Muslim children to the Alliance school at no cost, and, with approval from the Bulgarian authorities, created two courses taught by Muslim teachers. Many of these students remained in the school after Tekirdağ returned to Ottoman rule.[55]

This account does not seem implausible. However, it is worth noting that Levy, Guéron, and other Jews had an interest in documenting loyalty at this time: Ottoman military tribunals were harshly sentencing people convicted of mistreating local Muslims during the occupation.[56] Perhaps the fairest thing we can say is that loyalty and self-interest were not mutually exclusive.

In Dedeağaç, Gümülcine, İskeçe, and other towns in Western Thrace, most Jews stayed put through the war.[57] Their distance from Istanbul and disruptions in train and boat service made it difficult to move to the Ottoman capital. While many Muslims fled this region during the first weeks of war, those who owned valuable tobacco farms tended to stay, and Western Thrace maintained a large Muslim population through the period of Bulgarian rule (and after).[58] During the Second Balkan War, it was mostly Orthodox Greeks who fled Bulgarian persecution in this region. In fact, many of the "atrocities" committed against civilians in the Balkan Wars—to quote a word that fills contemporary reports—were entirely Christian affairs.[59]

Remaining in Western Thrace was hardly an indicator of pro-Bulgarian sentiment. In August 1913, representatives of the Muslim, Armenian, Greek Orthodox, and Jewish communities of Dedeağaç petitioned Britain to oust the Bulgarians and put the town under Greek administration.[60] In the fall, when a group of Muslim and Greek Orthodox leaders rejected Bulgarian rule and declared Gümülcine capital of the Provisional Government of Western Thrace (Garbi Trakya Hükümet-i Muvak-katası), their press agency was run by a Jew named Samuel Karaso, who printed a propaganda organ in French and Turkish.[61] But when these efforts failed, locals resigned themselves to Bulgarian rule.

This brings us to the city of Edirne. Its capitulation was followed by three days of violence and looting in which Bulgarian soldiers and Greek Orthodox civilians were usually the preparators, while local Jews and Muslims were usually the victims.[62] One Jewish merchant returned from Istanbul to find that Bulgarian soldiers had cleared out his home: "Everything had disappeared, having been sent to Sofia, even the piano." According to a widely circulated story, a Jewish civilian died while trying to stop a Bulgarian soldier from killing an Ottoman officer in the street. Reportedly, Bulgarian soldiers committed rape with no regard for the religious affiliation of victims.[63]

But after a few days of lawlessness, Bulgarian administration in the city of Edirne became relatively orderly, compared to the situation in other towns.[64] The occupiers quickly reinstated the municipal council, which included three Bulgarian Christians, three Orthodox Greeks, three Muslims, two Jews, and one Armenian.[65] Rebutting the claims of French author Pierre Loti, an international commission concluded that Bulgarian authorities "took every reasonable precaution for safeguarding the [Selimiye] mosque."[66] The day after Edirne capitulated, Guéron wrote that a group of Bulgarian soldiers and local Greeks had targeted Jewish homes for looting and vandalism. But twelve culprits were quickly arrested.[67] It is not surprising that the occupying army was serious about bringing order to Edirne, which was now one of the largest cities in Bulgaria.[68]

The day after Edirne capitulated, a Jewish relief committee in Sofia obtained permission from the Bulgarian government to send aid workers to the conquered city. Shabat Avraam David, Bekhor Samuelov, and Josephine Koen promptly boarded an overnight train provided by Bulgaria's railway minister. They were joined by three Jews from Plovdiv, one Jew from Silistra, and two Catholic nuns from Berlin. When the team arrived in Edirne, it began delivering aid to locals of all religions.[69]

Starting in May, Bulgarian-Jewish committees also assisted in "repatriating" many of the 3,500 Jews who had fled Edirne Province for Istanbul during the First Balkan War.[70] These committees coordinated with local Jewish leaders, who were eager to help the refugees return to their homes in New Bulgaria. Because the new (and ultimately short-lived) border just west of Istanbul was closed, Jewish leaders in the Ottoman capital worked with the Berlin-based Hilfsverein der Deutschen Juden to have the refugees take steamers, at discounted rates, to the Black Sea town of Burgas, Bulgaria. From there, a "Jewish Reception Committee" helped them reach their hometowns.[71] Other Jews took ships from Istanbul to the Black Sea port of Constanța (Bulgarian at the time but now Romanian), from where they traveled up the Danube to Ruse and then boarded trains for the city of Edirne.[72]

Adaptation to life in New Bulgaria was facilitated by Jewish organizations based in Sofia but also in Paris, Berlin, London, and New York. Jewish suffering in the Balkan Wars prompted the Alliance, the Hilfsverein, the Anglo-Jewish Association, and B'nai B'rith to create a Union des Associations Israélites (based in Brussels).[73] The Union allocated today's equivalent of US$2 million for "relief" and "repatriation" of Jewish refugees in Istanbul. It also gave the equivalent of about US$1 million, in today's values, to the Jews of urban Edirne "during and after the siege" (including the funds that Guéron wanted to distribute as foodstuffs.)[74] Representatives of the Union also met with Tsar Ferdinand of Bulgaria to discuss the fate of New Bulgaria's Jewish population. The tsar assured his guests that "the Jews in his dominion could count upon his good-will, that they had hitherto enjoyed all rights of citizenship, and that they would so continue."[75]

Considering its history in Southeast Europe, it is not surprising that the Alliance quickly involved itself with the Jews of New Bulgaria. In May, a

Figure 5. Edirne during the Bulgarian occupation of spring 1913. Selimiye Mosque is in the background.
Photograph: Samson Chernov. Source: Balkansi Rat 1912–1913, Puric (Bozidar) Papers, Box 19, Hoover Institution Library & Archives.

senior functionary traveled from Sofia to Edirne in an effort to reorganize the region's Jewish schools. These were to become vehicles for helping local Jews "fulfill their duties as Bulgarian citizens" and exercise their "facility for assimilation." In the past decade, the Alliance had lost control of Bulgaria's Jewish schools to the Zionists. Now, the latter were to be stopped at all costs from advancing onto "the Edirne turf."[76] When the director of Edirne's Alliance boys' school finally returned from Istanbul, one of his first moves was to hire two Bulgarian-language teachers.[77] Perhaps they utilized a new Ladino-Bulgarian dictionary that a Jew in Sofia had published for his coreligionists in New Bulgaria.[78] Forced to deal with the new reality, even Guéron lobbied to ensure that the girls' school, badly damaged during the war, would be included in the reconstruction effort.[79]

Guéron embodied the fact that, for the Jews of Edirne, Ottoman patriotism coexisted with a level of political flexibility that was necessary to survive in a contested borderland. This comes into focus if we compare her journal in the Alliance archive with a slightly different version from the 1914 yearbook of a Jewish organization in Salonica (which had recently become Thessaloniki, Greece). Published under the pseudonym "Ben Israel" (son of Israel/the Jewish people), it is unclear who submitted it to the yearbook and why a pen name was used. This version of the journal is especially interesting because, unlike the Alliance document, it continues into the (brief) period when Edirne was a Bulgarian city.

In an undated entry, the author describes joining a Bulgarian lieutenant and his sister on a tour of the city's fortifications, where the officer visited the graves of his fallen comrades.[80] Another entry, dated July 22, 1913, was written shortly after the Ottomans retook Edirne. It reveals the author's thoughts on the departing Bulgarians:

> During their short stay in the conquered city, our neighbors succeeded in giving it a frankly Bulgarian appearance, more so than the Ottomans after several centuries of possession [had given it an Ottoman appearance]. No more Turkish, no more Greek, no more French. Bulgarian everywhere, in the streets, in the government offices, on the storefronts. Not even the smallest object could be purchased without using the language of the Slavs. Everyone was willing to learn it. The Turks are more tolerant, but—at least regarding language—I believe they are wrong. Their citizens of

foreign religion [i.e., non-Muslim citizens] would be more attached to the Ottoman nation if they spoke the language of the Ottomans.[81]

Assuming that Guéron wrote these "Ben Israel" entries—which seems likely, though it is not certain—her attitude toward Bulgaria is striking for the way it mixes outrage with admiration. In this, Guéron resembled contemporary Ottoman-Muslim writers who reflected on the empire's defeat in the First Balkan War and concluded that it urgently needed to change.[82] It is not even so strange that these comments, very much in line with the brand of Turkish nationalism that would dominate after 1922, were written by a Jew (whose mother-tongue was Ladino). After all, Guéron's Jewish contemporary Moise Cohen—better known as Munis Tekinalp—would become a chief ideologue of Turkish nationalism.[83] However, no other woman in Edirne's Jewish community left a record of such thoughts. In this sense, Guéron was unique.

Ultimately, Guéron's personality was better suited for the rigors of the siege than the subtle politics that followed. In 1915, she had a dispute with Alliance leadership over a potential transfer. Meanwhile, her enemies in the local Jewish community resumed their campaign to have her fired. Unable to surmount this combined hostility, she lost her job.[84] By 1919, Guéron, her husband, and their three children were living in Istanbul (which was under Allied occupation).[85] According to one of her living relatives, Guéron's "short life" came to an unceremonious end when she died of cholera on a sea voyage and her body was thrown into the Mediterranean.[86] Chief rabbis, Ladino journalists, notable Jewish women, military bombardment, occupying armies, cholera—an ambitious woman in an early twentieth-century borderland faced many obstacles.

CHRISTIAN DEPARTURES

After the Ottomans entered the city of Edirne in July 1913, some European commentators called for the Great Powers to intervene and restore the region to Bulgarian rule. In response, Ottoman leaders selected fourteen local men to form the Edirne Delegation (Edirne Heyeti). Its mission came straight from Interior Minister Talat Paşa: tour the European capitals and convince politicians that Edirne would be better governed by the tolerant Ottoman Empire than the intolerant Tsardom of Bulgaria. The ethnoreligious makeup of the delegation—six Muslims, three Orthodox Greeks, three Armenians, and two Jews (namely, Josef Barishac and Haim Behmoiras)—was meant to embody Ottoman pluralism.[87]

However, the notion that Edirne was a place of coexistence was becoming less true by the day. First, conspicuously absent from the deputation was a representative of Edirne's Bulgarian Christian population. This is hardly surprising. When Ottoman forces returned to Eastern Thrace during the Second Balkan War, they strove to push Bulgarian Christians out of the region. In part, this was to avenge attacks on Muslim civilians committed by the Bulgarian army during the First Balkan War; in part, it was to weaken Bulgaria's claims on the region (which often cited demographic statistics). In the summer of 1913, most of Eastern Thrace's Bulgarian Christian population was either killed or, more often, forced to seek refuge in Bulgaria.[88]

In September, Ottoman and Bulgarian leaders signed the Treaty of Istanbul, which officially ended their conflict and clarified the new border. It also included a protocol by which both governments agreed "to facilitate the optional and mutual exchange of Bulgarian and Muslim populations and of their properties," in villages located within fifteen kilometers of the border.[89] But Hacı Adil Bey, the *vali* of Edirne and a CUP stalwart, soon extended the policy to the entire province (save for Tekirdağ, Gelibolu, and the city of Edirne). He also made the departure of Bulgarian Christians compulsory, for all intents and purposes.[90]

In November, a commission of six Ottoman and nine Bulgarian delegates met in Edirne to sign a standalone "convention concerning the exchange of populations." In conversations with the Bulgarian delegates, Hacı Adil Bey "justified the wholesale expulsion of the Bulgarians" on the grounds that "their presence might lead to disturbances" in a province that was receiving an influx of dispossessed Muslims from the Balkans.[91] The convention was primarily a mutual acceptance of (forced) migrations that had already occurred. But it also incentivized the emigration of those villagers still living on the "wrong" side of the border by promising compensation for their real estate.[92] By 1914, Edirne Province's Bulgarian Christian population had

Figure 6. A portion of the Edirne Delegation in Rome, August 1913. One of these men is Josef Barishac, editor of *La Boz de la Verdad*. Source: Bıyıklıoğlu, *Trakya'da millî mücadele* Vol. II, Image 7.

been reduced from fifty thousand to about one thousand people, most of whom lived in the city of Edirne.[93]

The presence of Orthodox Greeks in the 1913 Edirne Delegation is no more surprising than the absence of Bulgarians. At that moment, relations between Orthodox Greeks and regional Ottoman authorities were relatively good. While not immune to the depredations of the Ottoman army in the summer of 1913, local Greeks often preferred the returning Ottomans to the departing Bulgarians.[94] This mirrored the political alliances of the Second Balkan War, in which Greece joined the Ottoman Empire to fight Bulgaria. That summer, the Greek Orthodox community still seemed to have a future in the truncated province of Edirne.

But the situation quickly deteriorated. By the end of the year, anti-Greek boycotts and a massive resettlement of Muslims from the Balkans combined to spur Orthodox Christians to leave Edirne for Greece. CUP machinations and a deterioration of intercommunal relations rooted in the First Balkan War served to fan the flames.[95] By the spring of 1914, efforts to expel local Greeks "began to take on a more systematic form," in the words of Taner Akçam.[96] His analysis is consistent with what Edirne's British consul wrote on March 31:

> It is clear that the Government has recently adopted the policy of establishing in this Vilayet a population as far as possible purely Moslem.... A general exodus of the Bulgarian population from this Vilayet was one of the chief features of the last quarter of 1913. The authorities have now turned their attention to the Greek element who have been made the object of a minor system of persecution.... The exodus of Greeks which commenced at the end of last year has increased in volume during the past quarter.

The consul claimed that this Ottoman policy was based on two fears regarding the Christians of Edirne Province: First, that they would serve as a pretext for meddling on the part of neighboring states; and second, that they would turn treacherous in the event of future military conflicts.[97]

Increasingly, Orthodox Greeks in Eastern Thrace—and the Aegean littoral—suffered sporadic attacks at the hands of their Muslim neighbors. Attributing the violence to unruly Muslim immigrants, the authorities condemned the lawlessness in their official statements.[98] Responding to complaints from Athens, Talat Paşa toured Eastern Thrace in April, ostensibly to stop the persecutions.[99] But only a few weeks prior, he had sent a cable to the district governor of Tekirdağ stating that a mass of Greek Orthodox villagers assembled on the coast should "emigrate by boarding steamships, but without any indication being given that [the emigration] is the result of a directive."[100] European diplomats were not fooled by official Ottoman rhetoric. On June 30, the British consul in Edirne wrote of an "expulsion campaign." He claimed that Şükrü Kaya, civil inspector of the province, had said that "it was the intention of his Government to establish a purely Moslem population between the Frontier and the capital."[101]

In the summer of 1914, leaders of Greece and the Ottoman Empire agreed, in principle, on the "voluntary" exchange of Muslims in Macedonia for Orthodox Greeks in Eastern Thrace and Western Asia Minor. The two governments assembled a mixed commission to help migrants receive properties in their new countries, and subcommissions were formed in Izmir and Edirne.¹⁰² But as the statesmen conferred, the persecution of Orthodox Greeks continued.¹⁰³ In 1914, over one hundred thousand of them were exiled from Edirne Province, especially the coastal regions. Some went to Greece while others were sent to the Anatolian interior, where authorities believed they would pose less of a security threat.¹⁰⁴

When the Ottoman Empire entered World War I in October 1914, talks of a population exchange were interrupted and the persecution of Ottoman Greeks was paused. But after British forces landed at Gallipoli and Greece hinted at joining the Entente, Ottoman authorities again sent tens of thousands of Orthodox Greeks from Edirne Province to inner Anatolia.¹⁰⁵ As late as March 1916, the acting US consul in Edirne claimed that the authorities were "expelling the Greek villagers from their homes, installing mussulmans in their stead, sending [the Greeks] to Adrianople, and permitting them to depart thence into Greece."¹⁰⁶ By the end of the war, the province's Greek Orthodox population had dropped from about 250,000 to just over 50,000.¹⁰⁷

The most surprising section of the Edirne Delegation would have to be the three Armenian members. A few weeks before the delegation embarked for Vienna, Armenians in Tekirdağ and nearby Malkara suffered extreme violence at the hands of the returning Ottoman army, which tended to view them as Bulgarian collaborators.¹⁰⁸ Three years later, in the midst of World War I, Talat Paşa and other members of the CUP resolved to send Armenians from all corners of the empire to the Syrian desert, where it was known and intended that they would die en masse.¹⁰⁹ Despite its distance from the Russian front in Eastern Anatolia, Edirne Province was included in the Armenian genocide.¹¹⁰

Early in October 1915, a few dozen Armenian men were expelled from Karaağaç and sent to nearby Babaeski.¹¹¹ On October 27, "in compliance with an order from the central government," the authorities began deporting the roughly five hundred Armenian families who lived in the city of Edirne. According to the acting US consul, every night about fifty-five families were removed from the city by carriage and made to proceed on foot, presumably to a train station on the way to Istanbul.[112] In the course of a week, most of the wealthier Armenians were deported, their possessions seized and their stalls in the bazaar ransacked.[113]

Raymond Kévorkian claims that in Tekirdağ, up to thirteen thousand Armenians were deported. Armenians from both Tekirdağ and Edirne were sent to Syria in cattle cars, via Istanbul, Konya, and Pozantı. Meanwhile, the Armenians of Çorlu were sent by ship to Izmit, from where they were put on trains that took the Konya–Pozantı route. In the city of Edirne, a second round of deportations occurred in February 1916, ensnaring poorer Armenians who had been spared until that point.[114] After World War I, Edirne Province saw the return of about six thousand Armenians—less than one-fourth of its Armenian population circa 1912.[115]

By and large, the Christians discussed so far were citizens of the Ottoman Empire. But during World War I, authorities in Edirne Province also forcibly displaced hundreds of citizens of Entente states. Some were local Orthodox Greeks and Armenians who had obtained Russian citizenship from local consulates (or inherited it from parents who had done so). Others were natives of France, Britain, and Italy who had moved to the empire for work purposes. Most of these foreign citizens were sent to the Anatolian interior, where they were monitored for the duration of the war or else slated to be "exchanged" with Ottoman citizens detained in Allied countries.[116] But a smaller number were transferred within the province. For example, dozens of "Russians and Italians" were interned in Kırklareli and Hayrabolu.[117] In general, authorities feared that foreign citizens might aid and abet Entente forces fighting in the Gallipoli Campaign, which was raging on the southern coast of Edirne Province.

"We learned the practice of deportation from our neighbors," said an Edirne deputy on the floor of Ottoman parliament in 1918.[118] While it is not so clear who started this vicious cycle, the period 1912–1918 saw Greece, Bulgaria, and the Ottoman Empire fall into a three-way project of ethnic cleansing centered on the borderlands. Meanwhile, the deportation of local Armenians was a chilling reminder that ethnic cleansing and even genocide could target minority groups that lacked any connection to a neighboring state. Less dramatically, about half of Edirne Province's Jewish population left during these years. Those who remained eventually found their presence to be more conspicuous and less secure than it had been before the wars. What place did Jews have in a borderland where the population was decreasing and diversity was coming to be seen as a geopolitical weakness?[119] The community was beginning to grapple with this question.

THE EYE OF THE STORM

From 1912 to 1918, perhaps twelve thousand Jews left Edirne Province for Istanbul, Paris, the Americas, and elsewhere.[120] Their motivations were largely economic, as the new Bulgarian border severed the city of Edirne from its agricultural hinterland and the port of Dedeağaç. It also separated the Jews of Eastern Thrace from two thousand coreligionists in Western Thrace, many of whom were their business partners and/or family members.[121] For locals of all religions—and on both sides of the new border—the Balkan Wars shattered a socioeconomic world that had existed for decades, perhaps centuries.[122]

Less of a shared experience, however, was borderland violence. Ethnic cleansing targeted local Muslims in 1912, Bulgarians in 1913, Greeks in 1914, and Armenians in 1915–1916 (the last case crossing the threshold into genocide). But it largely spared the Jews of Edirne Province. These Edirnelis lived in the eye of the storm.

This experience was hardly passive or peaceful. Small numbers of Jews were ensnared in the persecutions of non-Muslims, and a climate of fear descended on towns across the province. Leaders actively pursued strategies to protect the community, even if these were regressive compared to the political experimentation of 1908–1912. Specifically, Rabbi Bejarano and others sought vertical alliances with the most powerful members of the CUP—namely, the *vali* and the ruling triumvirate in Istanbul.[123] Another characteristic of life in the eye of the storm was flexibility, especially in the realm of political rhetoric. That flexibility was on display by 1914, when both the local population and the dominant political discourse were becoming more "Muslim"—a claim I will unpack at the end of this section.

Jewish reactions to Christian departures were rarely recorded, as community members hesitated to write about such politically sensitive issues. But some sources reflect the tensions that were surely growing in the city of

Edirne between Jews and the small number of Christians who had managed to stay. One case involved the Sisters of Agram school, a German-language institution attended mostly by Bulgarian Catholics but also by one hundred Jewish girls.[124] Months after Jews and Muslims celebrated the end of the Bulgarian occupation, it emerged that one of the nuns had been calling her Jewish students "*çıfıt*"—a Turkish slur for "Jew." When parents complained, "the interim directress received their complaints poorly and acted with such arrogance that the Jewish girls quit the school en bloc." Ultimately, about fifty Jewish students left the institution and enrolled in the Alliance girls' school down the street.[125]

We know slightly more about Jewish reactions to Greek departures. This is thanks to *La Boz de la Verdad*, Josef Barishac's Ladino newspaper. (For its origins, see Chapter 2.) Though it ceased publication during the Balkan Wars, the paper reappeared in 1914. That year, it referred to the flight of local Greeks as an "emigration," and it reprinted official Ottoman press releases denying a government role.[126] Only when a local Jew was threatened did *La Boz de la Verdad* sound the alarm.

In May 1914, about forty citizens of Greece who lived in the Ottoman border town of Uzunköprü were sent to Tekirdağ and scheduled for deportation. Among them was a Sephardi Jew named Albert Alfassa. When the chief rabbi of Edirne approached the governor to vouch for this "honest merchant," Hacı Adil Bey replied that the deportation was only meant to protect Greek citizens from "the excited masses"—a reference to Muslim refugees who had recently arrived from Macedonia. Nevertheless, the *vali* agreed to temporarily hold Alfassa in Tekirdağ.[127] Meanwhile in Istanbul, the chief rabbi of the Ottoman Empire asked Talat Paşa to let Alfassa return home.[128] Soon, the chief rabbi of Edirne was granted an audience with none other than Enver Paşa. The minister of war was "very much interested in the situation of the Jews of Edirne and gave assurances that better times were coming for that city."[129] Alfassa was transferred to Istanbul, from where he awaited a decision on his case.[130] A few weeks later, Talat Paşa told Hacı Adil Bey that the Greek citizen could return to Uzunköprü.[131]

When Ottoman authorities began deporting Orthodox Greeks from Edirne Province to Anatolia, *La Boz de la Verdad* kept silent on the matter. But it chose to cover something similar that was happening in the Russian Empire. Under the (exaggerated) headline "1,200,000 Jews Expelled," the newspaper reported that all Jews in the governorates of Grodno, Vilna, and Warsaw had been forced from the Pale of Settlement to the Russian interior, in a massive wartime evacuation.[132] Surely, the Jews of Edirne feared that they, too, could be moved from the imperial borderland to the interior. In fact, this would soon happen to a small number of them.

Publication of *La Boz de la Verdad* paused just before the authorities deported local Armenians to the Syrian desert. But diplomatic reports suggest that the Jewish reaction was one of fear. In fact, the Bulgarian and Austrian consuls of Edirne wrote that the deportation of Armenians "frightens not only the Jews and the other Christians living here, but also the overwhelming majority of the Muslim population."[133] While previous violence had targeted people who spoke the language and/or practiced the religion of a rival state, the deportation of Armenians represented a creep in scope that had a chilling effect on local Jewish life.

Nevertheless, only on three occasions were sizeable groups of Jews actually displaced.[134] The first—and largest—case involved about sixty Jewish families from Mustafapaşa. After changing hands several times during the Balkan Wars, this historically Ottoman town was definitively taken by Bulgaria in 1913. Local Jews were prevented from returning to their homes, and many wound up in and around the city of Edirne.[135] In January 1914, Moise Mitrani told the Alliance Central Committee that he had admitted to his school forty-eight children from Mustafapaşa, free of charge, and that their families needed clothing and heating fuel.[136] A few months later, *La Boz de la Verdad* reported that many Jews from Mustafapaşa were "dying of hunger" and living in unsanitary conditions as an outbreak of cholera swept the city.[137]

For the modest Jewish community of Edirne, this was a veritable refugee crisis. A delegation visited Sofia to seek help from the leaders of Bulgarian Jewry, and the latter donated 560 francs.[138] In June 1914, the Edirne community was visited by Joseph Niego, the Istanbul-based director of B'nai B'rith's "Eastern District" (and a native of Edirne). He interviewed the refugees and catalogued the properties they had abandoned in Mustafapaşa. Presumably, he was going to seek reimbursement from Bulgaria in accordance with the above-mentioned "convention concerning the exchange of populations" signed by Ottoman and Bulgarian leaders. But this initiative was cut short by the outbreak of World War I.¹³⁹

A portion of the Jewish community from Mustafapaşa took refuge in Uzunköprü, where the situation was especially dire. Weeks after the Greek citizens of Uzunköprü were deported, local police gave the Jewish refugees twenty-four hours to pack their bags and move to an Ottoman settlement called "New Mustafapaşa." *La Boz de la Verdad* found this order "very strange," as the *Muslim* refugees from Mustafapaşa were left in peace. But after the chief rabbi of the Ottoman Empire intervened, the *kaymakam* of Uzunköprü was dismissed and the Jewish refugees were allowed to stay.¹⁴⁰ *La Boz de le Verdad* concluded that the central government never failed to "rectify wrongs committed by a few [local] functionaries."¹⁴¹

The second case of Jewish displacement occurred the following year. The Battle of Gallipoli had prompted the Ottomans to evacuate much of that district.¹⁴² But it also inspired them to deport Orthodox Greeks from a zone that extended well into the center of Edirne Province, many miles from the Dardanelles. Overzealous local officials sometimes failed to discriminate between Greeks and Jews. For example, a small number of Jews in Vize, Saray, and Silivri were forcibly relocated in November 1915. However, Talat Paşa intervened once again, and most of these people managed to return home.¹⁴³

Meanwhile, a third case of Jewish displacement was underway. The victims were not the residents of a particular town but rather Jews across the province who were citizens of Entente states. As discussed above, Christian citizens of Entente states were also forced to move, so we cannot say that the policy targeted Jews, specifically. Still, the incident profoundly affected Edirne's Jewish community.

In the fall of 1915, the acting US consul in Edirne reported that Kırklareli had become an internment site for dozens of Russian citizens from the Tekirdağ region. The names on his list appear to be Ashkenazi-Jewish, Russian (Christian), and Greek (Christian).¹⁴⁴ People in the last category were probably locals who had acquired Russian citizenship through a consulate, but people in the first two categories were presumably born in the Russian Empire and had migrated to agricultural colonies near Tekirdağ (see Chapter 1). As early as November 1914, officials had spoken of making these immigrants choose between becoming Ottoman citizens or leaving this geopolitically sensitive zone.¹⁴⁵ For his part, the US consul said little about the background of these people.¹⁴⁶

Most of his reporting concerned another group of foreign citizens: the "Italians." On October 11, 1915, the Ottomans ceded the suburb of Karaağaç to Bulgaria in a bid for the latter to join the Central Powers. Muslim residents fled the suburb for Edirne, but most Christians and Jews stayed put.¹⁴⁷ In fact, the town would soon see the creation of its first official Jewish community, independent of the one in Edirne.¹⁴⁸

But the Ottomans added a last-minute term to the deal with Bulgaria: all citizens of Entente states had to leave Karaağaç for internment in the empire. Most people who fell into this category were citizens of Italy, and among them were some Sephardi Jews.¹⁴⁹ This small group of people—probably locals who had obtained Italian citizenship from a consulate—faced a difficult decision. Some quickly became Ottoman citizens and thereby managed to stay in Karaağaç as it was ceded to Bulgaria (ironically).¹⁵⁰ Others hesitated to surrender their Italian nationality and were interned in the city of Edirne.¹⁵¹

But in November, Ottoman authorities made a dizzying reversal: now the place where "Italians" posed the biggest threat, they decided, was the city of Edirne. According to the US consul, "persons of Italian race"—that is, Catholics from Italy—were promptly sent *back* to Bulgarian Karaağaç.¹⁵² Meanwhile, the chief of police told Rabbi Bejarano that no Jews with Italian citizenship could remain in the city (or even Karaağaç, it seems).

At this point, most of the twenty "Italian" Jewish families in Edirne chose to become Ottoman citizens. But eight people held fast to their Italian nationality.¹⁵³ Of these, three were interned in the town of Hayrabolu (in the Tekirdağ district). The other five were ultimately allowed to stay in Edirne, perhaps because of their pitiable situations. "Mrs. Simone Levy" and her two young children were without Mr. Simone Levy, who was stuck in Plovdiv on account of his Italian citizenship. The sisters Sarah and Anna Alfassa were elderly and in no condition for deportation and internment.¹⁵⁴

The dearth of Jewish sources from this phase of the war makes it hard to understand the community's response to the persecution of "Italian" Jews. But a letter from the US consul contains a clue. In February 1916, he was asked by Italy's foreign minister for information on those Edirne Jews who had recently changed their nationality. The consul contacted Rabbi Bejarano, but the latter claimed that "the records of the Grand Rabbinat [*sic*] contain only very meagre information relative to these people, in most cases only their names."[155] This seems unlikely. A core role of the local chief rabbinate was to hold vital records—such as marriage and divorce documents—for all local Jews, regardless of citizenship. I suspect that the rabbinate *did* have additional information on these ex-Italians, but Bejarano was loath to cooperate with leaders of enemy states or to work at cross purposes with the authorities (who wanted these Jews to become Ottoman citizens). In other words, this was no time for assertive Jewish politics.

Before the Balkan Wars, some local Jews had called for a "union" of the empire's Muslim, Christian, and Jewish citizens, while others had evoked "national" dignity to censure Jewish leaders for mindlessly supporting the CUP.[156] But by 1914, political options had narrowed in Edirne. Leaders were distancing the community from Ottoman Christians and doubling down on the old Jewish survival strategy of "royal alliance." That is, they decided that the best way to protect Jews was to go directly to the highest authority in the land, even at the cost of resentment from Christian neighbors and local authorities.[157]

This was a logical response to depressing events. The coup d'état carried out by the CUP in January 1913 effectively spelled the end of multiparty politics in the empire, and the subsequent removal of most Christians from the province was the nail in the coffin of civic Ottomanism. Now, horizontal alliances and parliamentary politics made little sense.[158] The Jewish community's successful appeals to the central government point to a pair of conclusions: First, the nature of Jewish politics changed drastically after 1912; and second, Ottoman leaders such as Talat Paşa pursued a clear and focused policy of expelling *Christians* from the borderland and coast.

As Edirne Province became demographically more Muslim, a parallel development occurred in the realm of political discourse. Ottoman military defeat and the ingathering of Balkan Muslims prompted the rise of what Erik Zürcher calls "Ottoman Muslim nationalism."[159] Also known as "Islamic Ottomanism," this style of politics saw Islam and its symbols as necessary components in building an Ottoman nation that could do battle, figuratively and literally, with the self-described nations that had routed the empire in the First Balkan War. This new discourse was especially prominent in Edirne, whose annexation to Bulgaria had shocked the public and whose subsequent return to the empire made it a symbol of hope and redemption.[160]

While the previous version of Ottomanism had called for a "union of the elements," the new iteration seemed, in theory, to exclude Jews from the imagined community of the Ottoman nation.[161] However, this abstract premise rarely translated into anti-Jewish practices on a day-to-day level, and local Jews seemed perfectly comfortable with this discursive style. For example, when a ceremony was held to mark the anniversary of Edirne's fall to the Bulgarians (March 26, 1913), attendees included the leaders of all religious communities and a reporter for *La Boz de la Verdad* (presumably Barishac.) The entire ceremony was tinged with Islamic rhetoric, from the fiery speech given by Edirne's commanding officer to the mufti's closing prayer, which called for "the repose of the martyrs, the long life of his majesty the sultan, and the prosperity of [the Ottoman Empire]."[162] But the proceedings raised no concerns for the Jewish reporter who, in his own commentary, used language echoing that of the mufti.

Already during the reign of Abdülhamid II (1876–1909), Ottoman Jews had demonstrated a "willingness to work within a framework of politicized Islam," as Julia Phillips Cohen puts it. Claiming a special affinity with Muslims and even adorning Jewish ritual objects with the star-and-crescent motif had been among "the different options Jews debated" in the late nineteenth century, during an earlier attempt by the state to combine Islam and politics.[163] Immediately after the Balkan Wars, Edirne Jews returned to some of these strategies.

Ironically, the very resistance to merging cultural and political identity that had inhibited many Jews from fully embracing civic Ottomanism also made them relatively comfortable with Islamic political discourse, including the Ottoman Muslim nationalism that emerged after 1912. At the same time, the rise of this discourse must have prompted Edirne Jews to further separate their cultural identity from their civic life. While it was a very old theme in Ottoman-Jewish history, the gap between culture and politics was not static.[164] Rather, it was liable to widen or narrow, depending on the context. From 1914 to 1918, that gap was widening.

NEW ALLIANCES, OLD *VILAYET*

More than those of 1878, 1885, or 1908, the Ottoman-Bulgarian border developments of 1913 devastated Edirne's economy, to the extent that many Jewish merchants began to leave the province. Nevertheless, subsequent events would allow some Jews to move with a freedom that summoned the *vilayet* of Edirne as it had existed at its largest expanse (from 1826 to 1877). As we will see, interstate Sephardi networks both facilitated this phenomenon and grew stronger from it.

For Edirne's Jewish community, World War I was characterized by some ostensible contradictions: The border disrupted economic life in Edirne more than ever, but Jews on both sides of the boundary maintained and sometimes strengthened their Sephardi networks; Jews faced new forms of discrimination during the rise of Ottoman Muslim and/or Turkish nationalism, but the form of interstate Jewish solidarity that emerged sometimes served the needs of the Ottoman Empire and its allies. Untangling these statements requires us to suspend some modern notions regarding borders and nationalism. For people like Josef Barishac, Jewish "nationalism" and Ottoman patriotism were fully compatible.[165] He was one of many Ladino publicists who did not see nationalism as "primarily a political principle, which holds that the political and the national unit should be congruent" (as Ernest Gellner has it).[166]

With that said, Barishac was a dynamic character whose political stance shifted slightly between the first and second runs of his newspaper (1910–1912 and 1914–1915). *La Boz de la Verdad* had always championed a certain form of Jewish "nationalism."[167] But before the Balkan Wars, the paper had virtually ignored Edirne's short-lived Makabi branch, and it had announced the club's closing in a neutral tone.[168] In contrast, *La Boz de la Verdad* praised the Zionist athletic organization in 1914 for "bringing together the sons of bankers and fishmongers," and it called for the "persecuted" Edirne branch to reopen.[169] The newspaper also commemorated the tenth anniversary of Theodore Herzl's death, claiming that the man "belongs to all Jewry."[170] *La Boz de la Verdad* even gave free advertising to one Yitzhak Chiprut from Edirne, in the form of short articles praising his new hotel in Ottoman Jaffa ("*Or Hadash* Balkan Hotel").[171] Still, Barishac did not go so far as to champion a Jewish state or call himself a Zionist (at least in print). Only during the Greek occupation of Edirne (1920–1922) would the issue of Zionism publicly divide the community.[172]

La Boz de la Verdad can be read as a political mouthpiece but also as a record of socioeconomic patterns that continued to link Sephardim on both sides of the border. For example, the newspaper announced numerous marriages between members of the Edirne community and members of Jewish communities in Plovdiv, Burgas, Yambol, and Stara Zagora. These Ottoman-Bulgarian weddings became especially common after 1913, probably because the pool of Jewish brides and grooms was shrinking in Edirne.[173] The paper also alerted Edirnelis about Jewish job openings in Bulgaria, such as the Shumen community's need for a cantor who could double as a mohel.[174] Additionally, some Edirne Jews sent their daughters to work as domestics in the homes of their Bulgarian coreligionists.[175] In June 1915—before Bulgaria had joined the Central Powers—a Jew from Pazardzhik "passed through" Edirne and made a small donation to the Halutzei Tzavah society, which supported the families of Jewish soldiers in the Ottoman army.[176] Such charity from Bulgarian Jews resembled earlier cases and was probably not unusual.[177]

International Jewish organizations only strengthened these regional Jewish bonds. This was especially true for B'nai B'rith, whose "Eastern District" now consisted of twenty-one lodges located mostly in the Ottoman Empire and Bulgaria.[178] In June 1914, all lodges sent delegates—the Edirne lodge sent five—to district headquarters in Istanbul for a weeklong conference organized by the above-mentioned Joseph Niego.[179] In the words of a Jewish contemporary from Sofia, this landmark conference of "Oriental Jewry" facilitated "the organization of hundreds of Jewish communities separated [from each other] by different states and distant borders."[180] Laws enacted during World War I "suppressed all freedom of association" and forced Edirne's B'nai B'rith lodge to close its doors from October 1915 to January 1919. But communal welfare organizations continued to receive donations from B'nai B'rith centers in Germany and the United States, distributed via district headquarters in Istanbul.[181]

After the Ottomans entered World War I on the side of Germany and Austria-Hungary, life became harder for Edirnelis. Locals of all religions suffered from rampant inflation, aerial bombardment, and travel restrictions.[182] Meanwhile, many Jews fought and died alongside Muslims in the Ottoman army.[183] To an extent, the suffering was general.

Some hardships, however, fell squarely on non-Muslims. "Almost without exception," Christian conscripts throughout the empire were placed in unarmed labor battalions where they were forced to repair roads and railways, carry supplies to the front, and do other forms of work that were grueling and humiliating.[184] Hundreds of Jews from Edirne Province faced a similar fate—though the work gangs contained far more Christians than Jews.[185] In December 1915, military authorities requisitioned Edirne's Alliance boys' school and used it as a hospital, despite a recent ruling from Istanbul declaring Alliance schools to be communal institutions (as opposed to French institutions).[186] And in 1916, local authorities levied an emergency tax designed to be paid mostly by leaders of the Jewish and Greek Orthodox communities.[187] Small wonder that most of the Jewish community's merchant class departed during the war years.

But if World War I prompted the authorities to discriminate Jews from Muslims in new and unsettling ways, it also created opportunities for Edirne Jews to serve the state and connect with coreligionists across the border—simultaneously, in some cases. This was largely a result of Bulgaria's decision to join the Central Powers in October 1915. To secure Bulgaria's entry into the war, Ottoman leaders gave that country the sliver of land on the west bank of the Meriç (Maritsa) River and the railway that ran along it. This meant that Edirne Province lost the towns of Dimetoka and Karaağaç.[188] But it also meant that, for the first time since 1877, the larger region of Thrace was not divided between rival states. The Bulgarian-Ottoman border still existed, of course, but the wartime alliance between these two countries allowed certain people to operate in a zone that encompassed (Ottoman) Eastern Thrace, (Bulgarian) Western Thrace, and (Bulgarian) Northern Thrace. Sephardi Jews, it turned out, were especially useful in this alliance, and many found themselves working across an entity that mirrored Edirne Province as it had existed at its largest expanse.[189]

One way that Jews proved useful to the Ottoman-Bulgarian alliance was through their work in the Red Cross and Red Crescent societies. During the war, Jews made donations to the Edirne branch of the Red Crescent, and two daughters of the local chief rabbi worked as nurses in Edirne's military hospital. Just across the Meriç River, five young Jewish women worked for the Red Cross in Bulgarian Karaağaç.[190]

Jews became increasingly useful to these organizations as the war progressed. In February 1918, the Ottomans established a Red Crescent branch in Sofia and staffed it with local "Turkish subjects, the vast majority of whom were Jews."[191] The quote comes from a member of Sofia's Jewish community who seems to reference the Ottoman policy of recognizing Sephardim in Bulgaria as Ottoman subjects. (In fact, many Bulgarian Jews continued using their old Ottoman passports until the empire dissolved.[192]) The president of this new Red Crescent branch was Albert Pipano, a notable in Sofia's Jewish community. Though he worked closely with the Bulgarian Red Cross, officially he answered to the Ottoman sultan. Among other things, his team cared for wounded Ottoman soldiers and brought in a full Ottoman orchestra for a fundraising concert.[193]

Another Jew who served the Ottoman-Bulgarian alliance was Barishac. Shortly after Bulgaria acquired Karaağaç, he left the newspaper business to become dragoman in that town's new Ottoman consulate.[194] Barishac was well qualified for the job: He had diplomatic experience (even if the Edirne Delegation's tour of Europe had been decidedly *anti*-Bulgarian); he knew Turkish, Bulgarian, and French (not to mention Ladino and Hebrew); he had lived in Karaağaç; and he had spent considerable time in Bulgaria.[195] It is also worth recalling that Karaağaç had been emptied of its Muslim population when the town became Bulgarian. That process involved transporting a mosque across the river and banning the fez.[196] In choosing a dragoman for the new consulate, the Ottomans might have felt that a Jew would be less conspicuous than a Muslim (but more trustworthy than a Christian).

In any case, the first two years of Barishac's consular service seem to have passed without incident. But in spring 1918, Ottoman officers told the Foreign Ministry in Istanbul that they suspected Barishac of participating in a Jewish spy ring involving Hasköy (Haskovo, Bulgaria), Uzunköprü, and the Edirne branch of Deutsche Orientbank. According to their memorandum, Barishac was exploiting "the freedom to cross the border that comes with his official position." Though he doubted the accusations, an official at the Ottoman consulate in Dedeağaç, Bulgaria agreed to investigate the matter. After all, it was "impossible to trust non-Muslims." But after six weeks of surveillance, he concluded that Barishac was "a trustworthy man [and] spying is not to be expected from him."[197] His name cleared, Barishac was sent on a mission to Sofia.[198] Ultimately, there was no reason to doubt that a self-styled champion of "Jewish nationalism" with many connections in Bulgaria could be a loyal servant of the Ottoman Empire. In fact, these qualities probably made him the right man for the job.

Naturally, the Ottoman-Bulgarian alliance also created opportunities for illicit business, and Jews were not necessarily above this sort of work. In 1915, the Bulgarian consulate in Edirne became the center of a "highly organized" gold-smuggling operation. Because the war wreaked havoc on rates of inflation and currency exchange, there was a moment when gold fetched a far higher price in Bulgaria than it did in the Ottoman Empire. Capitalizing on this opportunity, guards and couriers (*kavasses*) at the consulate began to purchase gold from local Jewish moneychangers (*sarrafs*) and smuggle it across the river into Karaağaç. At least this is what the Ottoman ambassador in Sofia communicated to the Ottoman foreign minister in Istanbul, with great annoyance.[199] The tendency among Ladino speakers to work in interstate networks—Jewish or otherwise—aligned with the interests of the Ottoman state in many but not all cases. For the Jews of Edirne, the proclivity to participate in networks that spanned Southeast Europe was deeper than Ottoman patriotism, which was a popular but relatively new concept.

Whether economic, familial, institutional, or diplomatic, the Jewish networks discussed in this section might be called "international." However, it is unlikely that the Jews involved would have used this word, and historians might find more accurate adjectives. For one thing, the Jews of Edirne must have experienced these networks as *Ottoman*, first and foremost. Edirnelis of Barishac's generation could remember the days when their province had encompassed all of Thrace, and when Sofia—in the adjacent Tuna (Danube) Province—had been an Ottoman city.[200] Both psychologically and physically, Edirne Jews had never ceased to inhabit this space. After all, their friends, relatives, and business partners continued to live in regions to the North and West, long after those became Bulgarian. To describe these networks as international is to imply the transcending of national limits. But during World War I, Jews in Edirne—and maybe Bulgaria, though that is another story—had yet to fully identify with the nation that borders purported to represent. For people like Barishac, the most significant "national" entity was the interstate network itself, in the sense that it embodied the *nasyon Djudya* (to use the Ladino term). By employing Barishac's older definition of the nation instead of the modern one—which holds that nations and borders are inherently linked—we begin to understand why the Ottoman-Bulgarian border failed to produce a symbolic, organizing effect on Sephardim in Southeast Europe.

CONCLUSION

"Borders are not the same for everybody," writes Manlio Graziano.[201] While he is referring here to the vastly different experiences that people have when trying to enter a given country, the statement can also be applied to the historical processes by which borders are created. For example, the Ottoman-Bulgarian border that emerged in 1913 produced multiple meanings and experiences. More specifically, I argue, the border meant one thing to Jews and another to almost everyone else. For local Muslims and Christians, a new conception of the border was forged by a series of violent expulsions and the rise of a discourse linking nations with territory. In contrast, the Jews of Edirne had not been affected by these processes to the same degree. But they lived through the violence and dealt with its consequences, namely, the shrinking of the province and the beginning of its ethno-religious homogenization. These developments tended to reinforce networks and feelings of Jewish solidarity that extended beyond the border. As stated above, what changed for the Jews of Edirne was not the meaning of the border but the experience of living in the borderland. Over the next two decades, that experience would become increasingly difficult.

FOUR

Days of Blue and White

Hellenism and Zionism in Northeastern Greece, 1919–1922[1]

AFTER WORLD WAR I, EDIRNE'S Jewish institutions developed in ways that reflected the bleak situation in what remained of Ottoman Europe. The local orphanage was expanded to accommodate the sixty-five Jewish children who had lost parents during the war.[2] B'nai B'rith started a small loan fund for workers and peddlers who had depended on the Jewish merchant class that departed during the period 1912–1918.[3] So many Jews had moved from Edirne to Istanbul that Passover matzah was sent each spring from the former city to the latter, where it was sold from a hotel called Yeni Edirne (New Edirne).[4] Meanwhile, Edirne's famous *maftirim* singers relocated to the Ottoman capital, where their Saturday morning concerts at the Italian Synagogue became the pride and joy of the Galata community.[5] After four centuries, Edirne no longer held a position of economic and cultural prominence in the Ladino-speaking world.

But if this is a story of decline, it is also one of adaptation and survival. Perhaps no event demonstrates this better than Greece's annexation of the Edirne region, a two-and-a-half-year episode that is largely overlooked in Greek and Turkish historiographies.[6] From 1920 to 1922, the towns and cities of Eastern Thrace were part of Greece, and their Jewish communities were reunited with those of Athens (Greek since 1827); Ioannina, Thessaloniki, and Kavala (Greek since 1913); and Xanthi, Komotini, and Soufli (newly Greek).[7] In the port of Kavala, a ceremony was held in August 1920 to celebrate Greece's eastward expansion, and a local Jewish tobacco merchant spoke these words to the crowd: "From Epirus to Edirne, over 300,000 Jews wildly applauded the victories of this valiant and heroic [Greek] people.... Today in Thrace, the sun is shining brighter.... Over the entire region flies this blue-and-white striped flag."[8]

The Greek flag, however, was not the only blue-and-white banner to appear in Eastern Thrace around this time. Zionism, which had been slow to take hold in Edirne Province during the late Ottoman period, quickly gained popularity among local Jewish communities—only to vanish from public life two years later. In part, the emergence of Zionism and the "Jewish flag" stemmed from factors affecting Sephardi communities across the Balkans.[9] Leaders in Bulgaria and Greece, for example, tended to tolerate a movement that harmonized with the project of dividing Ottoman lands into religiously tinged nation-states. Meanwhile, diplomatic developments on the world stage buoyed Zionists everywhere. Changing social conditions within Sephardi communities—where the Francophile elite faced a popular revolt—also provided fertile ground for this movement.[10]

At the same time, Zionism in Eastern Thrace developed from factors related to the region's recent history as a borderland. Between 1912 and 1922, Eastern Thrace changed hands five times. Constant political flux and a sense of uncertainty about the future pushed many Jews to identify with a local version of Zionism that, ironically, provided a neutral path in treacherous political landscapes.[11] Furthermore, internal conflicts tended to push the Jewish community of Eastern Thrace toward a largely symbolic form of Zionism that most parties could agree on. Here, Zionism was not an ideological rejection of the status quo so much as a survival strategy and a middle ground.

This chapter begins with the immediate consequences of the Ottoman surrender in World War I (which was effected by the Mudros Armistice on October 30, 1918). From there, it moves to the official Greek annexation that began in 1920 amid great fanfare—including several performances of Greco-Jewish friendship. The third section looks at the perils faced by local Jews during the difficult middle phase of the occupation, when the community was challenged from within and without. In contrast, the fourth section shows how, by 1922, the Jewish communities of Eastern Thrace were adapting to the new political situation and finding internal equilibrium. But this was accomplished just as Greece began to lose its war with the Turkish National Movement (Millî Hareket). The final section describes the collapse of Greek rule in the fall of 1922, which triggered another mass departure of Christians from Eastern Thrace and permanently changed the region's demographic landscape. Contrary to historians who treat this period as an interlude—if they treat it at all—this chapter shows that the Greek annexation of Eastern Thrace was a central episode in the history of this borderland and its Jewish community.

BETWEEN ARMISTICE AND OCCUPATION

French forces reached Thrace at the close of World War I and stayed until the summer of 1920. Though some historians describe this period as a "French occupation," military authorities allowed Ottoman officials to continue governing.[12] Meanwhile, a third party entered the scene. At the request of Eleftherios Venizelos, prime minister of Greece, France permitted Greek troops to occupy the train stations of Eastern Thrace in January 1919. From there, Greek military units entered towns located on the railway, including Uzunköprü, Lüleburgaz, and Çorlu.[13]

In Istanbul—which was also occupied by Allied forces—local Greek organizations did their part to bring Greece closer to the irredentist Megali Idea.[14] This included helping Orthodox Greeks who had fled Eastern Thrace five years prior return to their old homes.[15] Soon, the Ottoman foreign minister was telling British officials that Christians who had "emigrated" to Greece in 1914 were now "arriving at the Ottoman frontier from Salonica and Bulgaria with a permit issued by the French military authorities and settling in their former villages with assistance from Greek troops."[16] Already, the situation in Eastern Thrace was beginning to resemble a Greek occupation. This perception only grew stronger when the Hellenic Army landed at Izmir (Smyrna) in May 1919, thereby starting the Greco-Turkish War (1919–1922).

By and large, the new military presence in Eastern Thrace produced celebration among Orthodox Greeks and vexation among Muslims. As had been the case during the Bulgarian occupation (1912–1913), the Jewish experience was somewhere in the middle. For most Jews, this period was marked by suspense and anxiety, as opposed to oppression or celebration. But it is hard to make general statements for a period in which Jewish life was characterized by an increasingly divergent set of experiences and growing fissures in the community. If suspense and anxiety were characteristics of Jewish life at this time, so were intracommunal conflict and discord.

During the unofficial Greek occupation, the worst place for Jews was the town of Lüleburgaz, where Greece had established its military headquarters for Eastern Thrace. In spring 1919, local Orthodox Greeks told their Jewish neighbors that an Allied Commission from Istanbul would soon tour the region and ask residents whether they preferred Greek or "Turkish" rule. How, asked the Greeks, would local Jews vote? "Perplexed," Jewish leaders deferred to the newly formed Jewish National Council in Istanbul. The latter learned from a British general that "the Allies had no intention of sending such a Commission." This was relayed to the communities of Eastern Thrace—but not quickly enough.[17] After the president of Lüleburgaz's Jewish community refused to say how he would vote in the supposed commission, Greek soldiers raided his home. By one account, he was jailed, tortured, and brought to the Greek consulate in Istanbul for further abuse.[18] Another source claims that he was arrested along with three Muslim neighbors, all of whom were charged with "political crimes" and dragged before an Allied military tribunal in Istanbul.[19] In any case, the Lüleburgaz community president is a rare example of a Jewish leader who was violently persecuted by the Greek occupiers.

More typical of the Jewish experience at this time was the complicated case of Conorté Canetti, director of Kırklareli's Alliance Israélite Universelle school. Local Jews, he wrote, had to "adopt a line of conduct that precludes any accusation of partiality on the part of the Muslim or the Christian element."[20] For example, when local Orthodox Greeks invited their Jewish neighbors to join them in celebrating the Mudros Armistice, Canetti saw little choice but to accept. After all, Kırklareli's Jewish and Greek Orthodox communities had recently been instructed by their respective religious chiefs in Istanbul to maintain friendly relations. At the same time, Canetti tried to limit his participation in the celebrations, leaving one ceremony early to avoid the part in the program where he would be expected to manifest his "supposed Greek sympathies."

Despite his diplomatic efforts, Canetti began to acquire "a poor standing among the Turks."[21] In October 1919, the local Jewish community abstained from participating in municipal and parliamentary elections (what would turn out to be the last Ottoman elections). Soon after, Canetti declined an invitation for his students to join an event supporting "Ottoman independence"—by which he surely meant the Turkish National Movement of Mustafa Kemal (Atatürk).[22] Though Canetti denied responsibility for both decisions—the first had been made in accordance with orders from the Istanbul community, while the second had been forced on him by local Jewish leaders—his Muslim neighbors held him accountable.[23] The last straw came in June 1920, when French officers convened a meeting with Muslim, Jewish, and Christian educators in Kırklareli to discuss the region's political future. According to Canetti, the Muslim representatives "mistook" his words as being pro-Greek. He fled to Istanbul and did not return until the Greek occupation of Eastern Thrace had been firmly established.[24]

Meanwhile, some Jews saw the waning of Ottoman sovereignty and the waxing of Greek power as an opportunity to express new forms of nationalism. This was especially true after March 1919, when the Zionist Federation of the East was founded in Istanbul and the Zionist Federation of Greece appeared in Thessaloniki.[25] Later that spring, the Jews of Kırklareli invited the local British control officer to a ceremony honoring his country, as they had heard that "Palestine had been declared an Independent State under the mandate of Great Britain."[26] (In fact, the British Foreign Office had merely been conferring with the Zionist Organization about drafts of the Mandate for Palestine.[27]) Later, when a British representative visited Kırklareli to discuss the region's political future, the Greek Orthodox community organized a performance in his honor and invited local Jews. The latter "wanted to imitate the Greeks by making a Jewish flag—the first of its kind in [the] community—which they secretly brought to the celebration [before] unfurling it next to the Greek flag." A Jewish girl opened the event by reading "some lines recalling the strong Greco-Jewish rapport of the [ancient] Alexandrian period and the common collaboration [between Greeks and Jews] in the project of civilization." In Canetti's words, this "profoundly offended the Turks."[28]

A few months later, Zionist agitators began to arrive from Istanbul. David Elnekave worked for the Zionist Federation of the East and edited its newspaper, *El Djudyo*. In October 1919, he left Istanbul and toured Eastern Thrace, determined to establish Shivat Tzion (Return to Zion) societies throughout the region. Bearing letters of introduction from the Greek Orthodox patriarchate—which he presented to local metropolitans—Elnekave visited Edirne, Kırklareli, Uzunköprü, Lüleburgaz, and Tekirdağ. He also received assistance from the Greek military commander.[29] Elnekave's mission was somewhat successful, as Shivat Tzion societies soon appeared in several towns of Eastern Thrace.[30] However, at least one Jew complained that these new clubs stoked "antisemitism" among local Muslims.[31]

In the spring of 1920, the chief rabbi of the Ottoman Empire was ousted by Istanbul Zionists and replaced by Haim Bejarano, the chief rabbi of Edirne.[32] When Meir Behmoiras became acting chief rabbi of Edirne, he quickly ordered local Jews to celebrate the recent San Remo Resolution, in which the Allied Supreme Council had restated the Balfour Declaration's commitment to "a national home for the Jewish people" in Palestine. A Çorlu resident described how his community received the rabbi's order "with great pleasure" and how, in preparation for the event, the synagogue was adorned with "plants, flowers, and—shining in the center—the national flag." The ceremony began with the singing of "Hatikvah," the unofficial anthem of the Zionist movement, and ended with the collection of donations (presumably for the Jewish National Fund).[33] While there was nothing explicitly pro-Greek about the celebration, surely people knew that the San Remo Conference had also laid the groundwork for Greece's annexation of Thrace.[34]

All these cases suggest that Zionist activity was correlated with the waxing of Greek power in the region. The point is not that Zionist ideas came from Greece, but that Greek and Jewish nationalism enjoyed something of a symbiosis during the final months of (nominal) Ottoman rule in Eastern Thrace. This would continue to be the case after Greece's annexation of the region.

Surely there was some truth to Canetti's claim that "the inquietude among the Jewish community only grows at the prospect of a Greek occupation of Eastern Thrace."[35] Still, he did not speak for all local Jews. (In fact, Canetti himself returned to the region once Greek rule was consummated.) The period 1917–1919 brought a flurry of events on the world stage that would create a new political climate for the Jews of Eastern Thrace (and beyond). These included the Balfour Declaration (1917), the outlining of Woodrow Wilson's Fourteen Points (1918), the founding of Zionist Federations in Thessaloniki and Istanbul (1919), and devastating pogroms in Ukraine (1918–1921).[36] As international developments intensified, new divisions formed within the Jewish community of Thrace along the lines of gender, class, and political alignment. These rifts would deepen over the next two years.

CEREMONY BETWEEN FRIENDS?

The director of the Alliance boys' school in Edirne had once claimed, archly, that the Ottomans' brusque treatment of local Jews followed the dictum "No ceremony between friends."[37] This dynamic reached extremes in 1920, when Turkish nationalist fighters treated local Jews in ways that were decidedly unceremonious. In contrast, early relations between Jews and the new Greek government consisted of much pomp and circumstance but little else.

The Trakya-Paşaeli Müdâfaa-i Hukuk Cemiyeti (Association for the Defense of Rights in Thrace) was founded immediately after World War I. Based in Edirne, its mission was to contest territorial claims on Thrace made by Bulgaria and, later, Greece.[38] The group's organ, *Trakya Paşaeli,* was run by Mehmet Şeref (Aykut) and printed by Yuda Razon (both of whom appear in Chapter 2).[39] Delegates of the association attended the Paris Peace Conference, where they emphasized that Turkish-speaking Muslims constituted the majority in Thrace and deserved self-determination.[40]

Tevfik Bıyıklıoğlu, historian and veteran of the Greco-Turkish War, sees the 1913 Edirne Delegation (see Chapter 3) as a precursor to the Association for the Defense of Rights in Thrace. He notes that both groups evoked self-determination and demographic statistics to convince the Great Powers that Eastern Thrace should remain Ottoman/Turkish.[41] What he does not say, however, is that the 1913 delegation was religiously mixed, while the 1920 association was entirely Turkish-Muslim. This was an important difference that reflected two major developments in the period 1913–1920: the changing demographics of the Edirne region, and the international community's embrace of ethnonationalist principles.

When the Great Powers indicated that they would authorize the Greek occupation of Thrace, the Association for the Defense of Rights in Thrace traded diplomacy for armed resistance.[42] In May 1920, it demanded that Edirne Jews support the Turkish National Movement, through either fighting or funding. At least five young men from the local community took up arms and shipped out to Samsun.[43] But they were somewhat exceptional. After going to war for the Ottomans twice in the past eight years, most Jewish men were loath to risk their lives again—especially when the official cause was no longer the Ottoman Empire but rather the Turkish-Muslim population.[44] For all intents and purposes, the Turkish resistance fighters were telling local Jews to pay up.

What was more, the categories of "resistance fighter" and "bandit" often overlapped.[45] Self-described nationalist fighters kidnapped Jewish merchants and demanded enormous ransoms from the community, in the name of Ottoman/Turkish patriotism. In Kırklareli, Jews had their livestock requisitioned, and some of those who resisted were killed. In Çorlu, where "brigands roamed the street," the impoverished Jewish community was told to hand over the equivalent of US$170,000, in today's values. In the city of Edirne, the community was told to pay US$42,000 in late June, as nationalist fighters prepared to fend off a Greek invasion from Western Thrace (just across the Meriç River).[46] Echoing what had happened during World War I, this harassment spurred many Jewish merchants to leave Eastern Thrace for Istanbul and, to a lesser extent, Bulgaria.[47]

After a four-day siege that must have reminded locals of the First Balkan War (see Chapter 3), the city of Edirne capitulated to the Hellenic Army on July 25, 1920.[48] The next day, King Alexander of Greece and his generals made a triumphal procession in their automobiles. Delegations from the Jewish, Muslim, Armenian, and Greek Orthodox communities cheered the twenty-seven-year-old monarch as he passed. Exiting a ceremony in Edirne's main Greek Orthodox church, Alexander was handed a blue-and-white wreath by a student from the Alliance girls' school. At a reception later that day, leaders from each religious community "paid homage" to the king, which presumably entailed the giving of symbolic gifts. For his part, Alexander donated one thousand Ottoman lira to the local Muslim community and five hundred lira each to the Jewish and Armenian communities.[49]

On August 1, the king visited Edirne's Great Synagogue, where he was welcomed by Rabbi Behmoiras. The scene recalled "the High Priest of Jerusalem receiving Alexander the Great," wrote the director of Edirne's Alliance boys' school. (His letter to Paris must have been penned with Greek censors in mind, as this was a grandiose way to describe a locum tenens chief rabbi and a king widely regarded as Venizelos's puppet.) A religious service was given in Alexander's honor, during which Rabbi Behmoiras gave a speech in Hebrew, and the boys' school director gave one in French. The Hebrew speech was simultaneously translated into Greek by one Solomon Mitrani, a former director of the Alliance school in Kırklareli and soon-to-be member of Greek parliament.[50] The event greatly impressed the king, his entourage, and the entire audience, which included notables from the local Jewish and Greek Orthodox communities.[51]

The Treaty of Sèvres—drafted by the Entente powers and signed by representatives of the Ottoman Empire in August 1920—officially put Eastern Thrace under Greek sovereignty. Edirne became the capital of the General Government of Thrace, an administrative region of Greece under provisional military rule.[52] Also included in the Sèvres Treaty was the text of the Balfour Declaration, almost verbatim.[53] The treaty was accompanied by a separate agreement between the Entente powers and Greece that guaranteed group rights and protections for "racial, religious, or linguistic minorities" throughout that country, including Jews and Muslims in the newly annexed territories.[54] This document resembled the recently passed Greek Law 2456—largely the result of lobbying by Thessaloniki Jews—which gave the Jewish communities of Greece corporate statuses that combined elements of the Ottoman *millet* system with the League of Nations principle of minority rights.[55] And in September 1920, Greek Law 2493 officially gave Greek citizenship to residents of Thrace.[56] This flurry of laws and treaties made it a good summer for Greek citizens who supported territorial expansion and/or some shade of Jewish nationalism.

The Greco-Jewish honeymoon continued into the fall, when Rabbi Behmoiras accompanied religious leaders from the local Armenian, Greek Orthodox, and Muslim communities on a visit to Athens. There, they paid "the respects of the population of the newly acquired territories to M. Venizelos."[57] While in the Greek capital, Behmoiras met with Moshe Cofinas, a Jewish member of parliament representing Thessaloniki. Together, they convinced the Greek government to send, free of charge, two male and two female teachers of Greek to the Alliance schools in Edirne. The government also agreed to remove a regional ban on peddling, with the result that "50 Jews [were] again able to make a living" in Edirne.[58] Additionally, the minister of the interior promised Cofinas that all Greek towns with significant Jewish communities—including Edirne and Alexandroupoli (Dedeağaç)—would receive a mass mailing of pamphlets meant to teach people about "important Jewish figures" such as Max Nordau, cofounder of the World Zionist Organization.[59] (In 1921, the municipality of Edirne would even name a street after Nordau.[60]) When Behmoiras passed through Thessaloniki on his way home, he proudly told a local journalist about his rapport with Aristeidis Stergiadis, high commissioner of occupied Izmir.[61]

Subsequent developments would reveal the superficial nature of this initial friendship between Greek administrators and local Jews. The turning point for residents of Thrace was the Greek legislative election of November 1920. In the wake of that debacle, the pompous inauguration of Greek rule gave way to a period of conflict in which all parties would show their true colors—blue and white or otherwise.

DISCORD: NOVEMBER 1920 TO DECEMBER 1921

Even during the darkest days of the occupation, the Jews of Eastern Thrace rarely faced deadly violence—something that cannot be said of their Muslim and Bulgarian-Christian neighbors.[62] But their relationship with the military government was sorely tested, and the community was riven by internal conflicts related to the larger political situation. In 1921, anything seemed possible. This was exciting for some community members, horrifying for others.

In the summer of 1920, the approaching legislative election had been considered a mere formality by Venizelos and his Liberal Party. But in October,

King Alexander was bitten by a domesticated monkey and died of sepsis. Venizelos lost his puppet king, and people spoke of reinstating the exiled Constantine I—father of Alexander and nemesis of Venizelos. Suddenly, the republican Liberals faced serious competition from the royalist United Opposition.

In Thrace, military leaders and the local Greek population were firmly Venizelist.[63] General Emmanouil Zymvrakakis, the region's supreme military commander, warned Muslim notables against running on the United Opposition ticket and made it clear to residents of all religions that Thrace was to go to the Liberals. Ultimately, it did. But this was not enough to offset the United Opposition's strong showing in "Old Greece" and Macedonia.[64] The anti-Venizelists secured 246 out of 370 seats in the legislature, and Venizelos lost his own parliamentary race.[65]

After suffering "the biggest shock in Greek political history," Venizelists lashed out at various targets.[66] General Zymvrakakis riled up his troops by claiming that Jews and Muslims were celebrating in the streets of Edirne and hoping for a Greek civil war. *El Pueblo*, the largest Ladino newspaper in Thessaloniki, immediately condemned the general's remarks as patently false and wildly inflammatory, accusing him of "following the disgraceful tactics of the Polish generals and other pillars of reaction" by diverting antipathy between political parties toward the Jews.[67] Thessaloniki's Jewish members of parliament sought redress from both the minister of war and Dimitrios Gounaris—the United Opposition leader who would soon become prime minister.[68]

On the surface, the response of the new Greek government seemed encouraging. Zymvrakakis was quickly replaced, and Gounaris condemned the general's remarks. The new prime minister affirmed his government's "absolute confidence . . . in the Jewish community of Greece."[69] With that said, Zymvrakakis's departure was probably a fait accompli, as many Venizelist officers in the newly annexed territories resigned or deserted after the elections.[70] On a tour of Thrace, Gounaris again offered encouraging words—this time in the form of a promise to grant twenty-five thousand drachmas to the Jews of Edirne for communal welfare institutions.[71] But in Athens, bureaucratic red tape delayed the disbursement of funds.[72] While their coreligionists in Thessaloniki largely supported the royalists, the Jews of Eastern Thrace remained ambivalent about the new administration.[73]

If the elections in Thrace had been rigged to go to the Venizelists, they had also been designed to send a religiously mixed cohort to Athens.⁷⁴ This was probably meant to show the League of Nations that Greece was fit to govern a diverse population. In the General Government of Thrace—where all elected deputies ran on the Venizelist ticket—thirty deputies were Greek Orthodox, twenty were Muslim, one was Armenian, and one was Jewish.⁷⁵ This last was the above-mentioned Solomon Mitrani, who represented the Edirne prefecture.⁷⁶ Ironically, the 1920 elections sent to Athens a Jewish deputy from the party opposed by most Greek Jews (the Liberals). They also brought to power the party that would become most associated with the persecution of minorities in Thrace (the Royalists).⁷⁷

Despite its reputation for religious tolerance, the Ottoman era had not seen a single Jew from Edirne/Eastern Thrace enter parliament. Solomon Mitrani was the first (and last) person from this community to serve in the legislature of the ruling state. The son of a Kırklareli cantor who arranged *maftirim* music, Mitrani began his adult life by studying at Abraham Danon's rabbinical seminary in Edirne.⁷⁸ After that, he directed the Talmud Torah in Mustafapaşa (1896–1900) and the Alliance boys' school in Kırklareli (1900–1912) before taking a job at a local "Turkish" school.⁷⁹ A vocal proponent of modern Hebrew, he also knew French, Turkish, and Greek (as well as Ladino, of course). Mitrani's taste for Jewish nationalism distinguished him from the handful of local Jews who had reached high positions in the Ottoman administration of Edirne.⁸⁰ By 1920, this "diaspora" brand of nationalism had become popular among the new communal elite who filled Edirne's B'nai B'rith lodge (of which Mitrani was a member).⁸¹

When he arrived in Athens, Mitrani's political acumen was quickly put to the test. In March 1921, a Greek girl in Edirne claimed that some Jewish men had tried to plunge her into a barrel of needles, drain her blood, and use it to bake Passover matzah. This ritual murder allegation led to several Jewish men being dragged to an Edirne police station and subjected to "tortures reminiscent of the Middle Ages or the Inquisition" (according to a Jewish source).⁸² The case quickly caused a sensation throughout (Greek) Eastern Thrace and was even covered by the Ladino press in (Ottoman) Istanbul.⁸³

Deputy Mitrani returned to Edirne to combat the allegation and contain its fallout. He received support from Charilaos Vouzikis, the new Royalist governor of Thrace.⁸⁴ Vouzikis released the Jewish prisoners and punished some policemen. Not satisfied, Jewish community leaders sought the dismissal of the police commissioner and all officers involved in the incident. A letter to this effect was sent by the president of Edirne's Jewish community to the interior minister of Greece. Soon, Governor Vouzikis fired the police commissioner and several officers. Additionally, the Prefecture of Edirne distributed a circular condemning the blood libel as a fabrication and a threat to public order.⁸⁵

Describing the incident to his superiors in Paris, Edirne's Alliance school director claimed that, in his eighteen years of local service, this was the first ritual murder allegation he had witnessed. "So," he wondered, "did Thrace have to return to a Christian government—an enlightened and civilized government, in both ancient and modern times—for these dark, ridiculous fables to emerge and find credibility among fanatics and the ignorant . . . ?"⁸⁶ But after musing on the nature of Christian antisemitism, he ended his letter by praising the response of Deputy Mitrani and the new governor—a man who was "at the height of his high mission."⁸⁷ The writer seemed to grasp the paradoxes of Greek rule: the regime brought new problems (ritual murder allegations) but also new solutions (a local Jew in the legislature). The Ottoman system of having the chief rabbi of the empire intercede with leaders in the capital seemed to be a thing of the past.⁸⁸

The blood libel occurred during a year of mounting tension between the Jews of Thrace and the new administration. When France began supporting the Turkish National Movement in Anatolia, Greek authorities in Thrace grew wary of the Francophone Alliance schools. At one point, the director of the school in Kırklareli was imprisoned for five days. The authorities also made travel to and from Istanbul extremely difficult. Among other things, they wanted to prevent Jewish emigration and to reorient Jewish merchants toward Thessaloniki. Violators of the travel laws were heavily fined and sometimes jailed. Meanwhile, in their efforts to replace the Ottoman lira with the drachma, Greek authorities required anyone entering Thrace from Istanbul to immediately convert their liras to the Greek currency. Reportedly, Jews more than any other group frustrated this effort by clinging to the lira.⁸⁹ All this occurred as Muslims endured violent persecution at the hands of local Orthodox Greeks and the dreaded Horofilaki (gendarmerie).⁹⁰

If relations between local Jews and the occupying power recalled the Bulgarian occupation of eight years prior, the intracommunal strife that developed at this time was strikingly new. Greek rule and the departure of the Jewish mercantile elite shifted the community's power center and created new dynamics along the lines of class and gender. These developments often manifested as clashes between Zionists and anti-Zionists, but other issues existed below the surface.

In theory, the Greek annexation reunited the Jews of Edirne with their coreligionists in Thessaloniki, for the first time since 1912. However, from 1919 to 1922, the Zionist center that played the largest role in Eastern Thrace was Istanbul, across a state border. Occasionally, the Zionist Federation of Greece ordered Jewish communities throughout the country—including Thrace—to protest or celebrate certain developments in Palestine.[91] But most Zionist agitators who appeared in Edirne during these years came from Istanbul or, to a lesser extent, Bulgaria.[92] Thessaloniki's Jewish leaders—Zionist or otherwise—showed little interest in their coreligionists to the east.[93]

In Eastern Thrace, one of the most influential Zionists was Shlomo Goldmann. A "former Hebrew teacher in Bulgaria," he eventually found work with the Zionist Federation of the East in Istanbul.[94] In May 1921, he toured the communities of Eastern Thrace to raise money for the Jewish National Fund. In Edirne, Goldmann and other Zionist agents collected "sizeable" donations, to the chagrin of those who felt that the community had better things to do with its scarce resources than send them to Palestine.[95] He also visited Uzunköprü and Babaeski, where the communities made respectable contributions, considering their small size. Reportedly, a newborn baby in Babaeski was named Herzl, in commemoration of Goldmann's visit. When the Zionist orator arrived in Kırklareli, "the entire Jewish population . . . gathered in the assembly hall of the Jewish school, which was nicely decorated in the national colors." Toward the end of his speech, the crowd burst into applause when he proclaimed, "Palestine is ours if we want it! It depends only on us."[96]

Another important agitator was the above-mentioned David Elnekave. After his 1919 tour of Eastern Thrace, Elnekave began sending issues of his Zionist paper to the region's Jewish communities. In the summer of 1921, he obtained special permission from the Greek authorities to take the train from Istanbul to Eastern Thrace. There, he hoped to collect payment for the newspapers that he had sent, unsolicited.

Though he claimed the trip was "exclusively for business purposes," Elnekave was also checking on the progress of local Zionist clubs. On that score, results were mixed. Especially in the Jewish communities of Tekirdağ, Lüleburgaz, and Uzunköprü, Elnekave encountered nothing but "egoism," "materialism," and people whose "only God is money." Çorlu alone received high marks, as that town led the region in contributions to the Jewish National Fund. Edirne ranked somewhere in the middle. The community was "in decline" and riven by disputes, including a debate over the proposed hiring of two "well-paid" Hebrew teachers (one of whom was Goldmann). But it maintained a moderate level of Zionist activity and was "well-treated" by the Greek administration.[97]

Compared to Elnekave's travelogues, reports from Moise Mitrani, director of the Alliance boys' school in Edirne, convey an opposite opinion but similar facts. Mitrani—who was not closely related to Solomon—complained that the city of Edirne was home to chapters of Shivat Tzion, Tzeirei Tzion (Youth of Zion), B'nai Tzion (Sons of Zion), and B'not Tzion (Daughters of Zion).[98] These clubs were "not very active or effective," as they merely convened "two or three times a year" for fundraising soirees followed by meetings where attendees "saturate themselves with Zionist ideas and phrases." By and large, Mitrani was opposed to Zionist activity for reasons that were "material" (i.e., financial) more than "moral" (i.e., ideological). In July 1921, he wrote that the community had sent to Palestine nearly twenty-five thousand francs—money that should have been used to support the school and other communal institutions.[99]

Mitrani also opposed the two Jewish newspapers that appeared in Edirne during the winter of 1921, for reasons that combined ideological, economic, and personal factors. One paper was Nissim Behar's *L'Écho d'Andrinople*, which appeared in French. The other was Josef Barishac's *La Boz de la Verdad*, a Ladino periodical that had been published intermittently between 1910 and 1915 (see Chapter 2 and Chapter 3). Both used the printing press of the above-mentioned Yuda Razon, one of the few cultural institutions in Edirne to ride out the wars and occupations of 1912–1922.[100] Both tended to be pro-Greek, pro-Zionist, and critical of the Alliance—though *L'Écho d'Andrinople* was more extreme, at least on the first two counts. And both editors collaborated—allegedly—with a woman named Julie Beja, director of Edirne's Alliance girls' school from 1915 to 1920.

Behar was twenty-four years old when he started what was, at the time, the only Jewish newspaper in Edirne. With money from his "nouveau riche" father and approval from the Greek authorities (presumably), he launched his weekly in January 1921.[101] Like many Sephardi opponents of the Alliance, Behar had been educated in its schools. In 1917, he was sent to teach at the Alliance school in Safi, Morocco, but he found his boss "insufferable" and quit after a few months. The Alliance secretary in Paris derided his histrionic letters and attributed Behar's "excès de plume" to his youth.[102] Three years later, Behar's younger sister was expelled from the Alliance girls' school in Edirne after an altercation with her teacher, Rosa Mitrani (née Avigdor). Determined to have his sister reinstated, Behar complained to the Jewish communal council and even the Greek authorities (including the director of public education and the governor).[103] It was in this context that he launched *L'Écho d'Andrinople*.

The first series of this newspaper ran from January 1921 through January 1922, at which point Behar was "expelled from Thrace." At least nineteen issues of a second series were printed elsewhere, in 1922.[104] While only two issues of *L'Écho d'Andrinople* are available today (both from the first series), they give an idea of the newspaper's political stance. For example, on May 20, 1921, under the headline "The Arabs are Thirsty," a front-page article decried the killing of Jews in the recent Jaffa riots: "If the Jews have escaped the fury of Kishinev's antisemites," the Palestinian Arabs "are there to remind them that humanity is still not sufficiently saturated with Jewish blood."[105]

In that same issue, a page-two article reported that the Jews of Edirne had recently filled the Great Synagogue to "protest" the riots.[106] Rabbi Behmoiras gave the opening remarks, and Aron Danon, a local dentist who led Edirne's B'nai Tzion society, recounted "the history of pogroms against Jews in Palestine."[107] Next, Josef Barishac explained that donating to the Zionist cause in Palestine was among "the obligations of a good Jew." Finally, the communal council and the Zionist societies passed a set of resolutions that were radioed to the Zionist Federation in London and the "British minister" in Athens.[108]

Changing its target from Palestinian Arabs to local Jewish educators, this issue of *L'Écho d'Andrinople* proceeded to update readers on Behar's campaign to reinstate his sister at the Alliance school. The article impugned Rosa Mitrani, who co-ran Edirne's Alliance schools with her husband, Moise. The latter summarized the situation as follows: "After putting the Turks on trial—in order to please the new masters of Thrace—[Behar's] newspaper is now doing the same to us"[109]

While local newspapers had little choice but to support Greek rule, Behar's flattery could be excessive. In an article from October 1921, he reflected on the arrival of governor Vouzikis and his deputy: "After the valiant army's brilliant liberation of the land, the [Greek] government sent two of its best organizing minds and administrators to give Thrace a prosperity and justice it had never known before."[110] Statements like this caused an outcry among Ladino journalists in Istanbul, who feared that Behar's articles would strain Jewish-Muslim relations on the Ottoman side of the border.[111]

La Boz de La Verdad was revived a few weeks after the launch of *L'Écho d'Andrinople*.[112] The fact that one newspaper appeared in French and the other in Ladino suggests that the two editors were targeting separate audiences. (Jews with an Alliance education could have read the French newspaper, while Jews without one would have read—or listened to someone read—the Ladino publication.) Barishac had a way of achieving positions of influence under almost any regime (see Chapter 2 and Chapter 3). Eight months into the Greek occupation, he revived his Ladino newspaper, and soon he was elected to the Jewish community's general assembly. According to Moise Mitrani, Barishac pursued a dangerous four-point agenda: to turn the Alliance schools into communal schools, to cut communal taxes for the middle class, to intensify the teaching of modern Hebrew, and to promote "excessive nationalism."[113]

This program was reflected in Barishac's newspaper, which had grown increasingly Zionist over the years. Now in its third iteration, *La Boz de la Verdad* gave regular updates on Jewish settlements in Palestine, local fundraisers for Jerusalem, and the activities of Zionist organizations worldwide.[114] But compared to his younger colleague, Barishac displayed more political tact. The Ladino paper's coverage of the Greek administration stopped short of the adulation expressed by *L'Écho d'Andrinople*, and in the (admittedly few) issues available from this period, *La Boz de la Verdad* avoided criticizing Muslims—in Palestine or elsewhere. This might explain how Barishac managed to continue playing an active role in Edirne's intercommunal affairs after Turkish rule was established in the fall of 1922.[115]

When it came to attacking the Alliance, however, Barishac was no less aggressive than Behar. Previous runs of *La Boz de la Verdad* had combined criticism of the Alliance with a degree of praise. But by 1922, Barishac was pushing for the Paris-based association to relinquish control of the local schools—something it had recently done in nearby Komotini.[116] Barishac lambasted the Alliance schools for charging high tuition, overpaying staff, and employing young, female teachers in the boys' school. Even worse, the Alliance neglected modern Hebrew, gymnastics, and "national and religious education."[117] If this critique contained elements of Jewish nationalism and religious conservatism, it also reflected the rejection of Franco-Jewish paternalism that was occurring throughout the Sephardi world at this time. Among other things, this rejection entailed B'nai B'rith supplanting the Alliance as the most important international Jewish organization in the Eastern Mediterranean.[118] Edirne was no exception to this trend.

In addition to Behar and Barishac, Edirne's anti-Alliance clique allegedly had two more members. These were Julie Beja and her husband, Joseph. Born in Ottoman Salonica in 1878, Julie Beja (née Naar) directed the Alliance girls' school in Edirne from 1915 until the eve of the Greek occupation, when repeated complaints from Moise Mitrani and others led to her firing. Beja's replacement was Rosa Mitrani, former director of the Alliance girls' school in Kırklareli.[119] According to Moise Mitrani, the Bejas started attacking the Alliance through editorials in *L'Écho d'Andrinople* published under a pseudonym.[120] However, Julie Beja denied that she or her husband wrote the articles in question.[121]

In a sense, this conflict pitted the married directors of Edirne's Alliance schools (the Mitranis) against those they had offended (the Bejas, along with Behar and Barishac). But wrapped up in this family feud were other issues. Both of Edirne's Jewish newspapers had nationalist leanings, and this gave the anti-Alliance campaign a Zionist veneer.[122] Meanwhile, "ignorant intriguers of Josef Barishac's mindset" were being elected to the community's general assembly, thanks to support from local Zionist associations, the workers' corporation, the butchers' corporation, and the porters, all of whom gravitated toward the "demagogic and Zionist" program of *La Boz de la Verdad*.[123] Like Alliance school directors in other Sephardi communities, the Mitranis were confronted by a concatenation of factors—social and political, local and international—that made their job increasingly difficult.[124]

It is the (alleged) role of Julie Beja that makes the Edirne situation especially interesting. Though Beja denied any involvement in the affair, it is hard to imagine why Moise Mitrani would have falsely accused someone who no longer held an official position in the community or its schools. But even if his accusations were false, the very fact that he made them reveals a telling intersection of gender and politics in the community. Beja was the second consecutive director of the Alliance girls' school in Edirne to cause a scandal and lose her job. Her predecessor, Angèle Guéron, had made enemies of Barishac and the wives of Jewish notables by refusing to take their advice on how to run the school and by publicly breaking the sabbath (see Chapter 2). Moise Mitrani had defended her, albeit unsuccessfully.[125] With Beja, the alliances were flipped: the boys' school director was her enemy, while the editor was her friend. In Guéron's case, conservative elements in the community had attacked a woman for violating local Jewish norms. But Beja's case was different.

For Moise Mitrani, Beja had come to embody the "demagogic and Zionist" opposition gaining power in the community. From the spring of 1919 through the spring of 1921, he complained about her more than any other adversary—including Barishac, Behar, and the Greek occupiers. In this campaign he was joined by the president of Edirne's Jewish community.[126]

It hardly seems coincidental that war and emigration had recently lowered the community's male population, forcing Jewish women to work as store clerks, peddlers, field workers, porters at the train station, and typists and stenographers in banks and public administrations. "Desperate for bread," wrote Moise Mitrani, "these women and children do not shrink from any task, no matter how rude."[127] The male-to-female ratio had also dropped in local Jewish schools. In almost every town in Thrace, girls' enrollment was similar to or greater than that of boys. Furthermore, a general decline in population forced the boys' and girls' schools in the city of Edirne to merge.[128] For Moise Mitrani, the community president, and other men,

Beja may have embodied various forces that were distressing them, namely, Zionism, Ottoman decline, a popular rejection of Alliance paternalism, and changing gender dynamics. This combination of forces was a new phenomenon in Edirne.

Admittedly, Mitrani's accusations are the only documents linking Beja with Zionism. But it is also true that, unlike the girls' school directors who immediately preceded and followed her, Beja never condemned this political movement in her reports.[129] Most likely, Mitrani's negative obsession with this woman was the result of new fears prevalent among Jewish leaders in his camp, as well as some degree of pro-Zionist, anti-Alliance sentiment actually held by Beja.

ACCOMMODATION: JANUARY TO SEPTEMBER 1922

Greece's Anatolian adventure was widely regarded as a blunder by the start of 1922, and things only deteriorated from there.[130] But in Eastern Thrace, that year was characterized by an improvement in Greco-Jewish relations and the resolution of some intracommunal conflicts. Ironically, Greece's retreat from Eastern Thrace (and Anatolia) in the fall of 1922 came just as local Jews were adjusting to Hellenic rule. As had been the case during the Bulgarian occupation, longstanding sentiments of Ottoman loyalty did not prevent Jewish leaders from adapting to a new government. Nor did internal conflicts stop the community from eventually finding a new equilibrium. On both levels, adaptation was the general tendency.

The new modus vivendi between Greek administrators and Jewish leaders was on display by January 1922. Greece was facing military resistance in Anatolia and diplomatic resistance in Western Europe.[131] Meanwhile, some denizens of Thrace had taken the bold step of staging anti-Greek protests in the fall of 1921.[132] In response to this growing tide of opposition, Greek authorities in Edirne organized a rally at city hall to demonstrate that locals of all religions supported the Greek administration. Jewish, Muslim, Armenian, and Greek Orthodox speakers took the podium, and a mixed committee—including Rabbi Behmoiras and Deputy Solomon Mitrani—passed a resolution opposing any modification of the Sèvres Treaty. The signed resolution was sent to local representatives of the Great Powers and to Greek parliament in Athens.[133]

The rabbi and the deputy probably had little choice but to sign the resolution, as failure to do so would have been detrimental to the Jewish community (and themselves). Still, their participation was more than ceremonial. What differentiated this event from the ceremonies described above was that the Jews involved were now integral parts of the General Government of Thrace. As one of Edirne's eleven deputies in parliament, Mitrani was a representative of the entire prefecture, not just the Jewish community (at least in theory). Meanwhile, Behmoiras and other religious leaders were crucial components in the administrative machinery. In a way that recalled the Ottoman *millet* system, they made their communities "legible" to the Greek state by translating—literally and figuratively—the needs of their coreligionists.[134]

Behmoiras must have been pleased by the revival of another Ottoman legacy: namely, an administrative unit that covered both Eastern and Western Thrace. Like the old Ottoman province of Edirne, the General Government of Thrace stretched as far west as Komotini (Gümülcine) and Xanthi (İskeçe). Behmoiras' jurisdiction now resembled that of his late relative, Raphael "the Angel," who had been chief rabbi of Edirne in the nineteenth century. Behmoiras did not hesitate to exercise his authority over the old family fief. By December 1921, he was writing to the president of the Xanthi community, requesting payment for the ritual *lulav* and reminding him about taxes owed to the chief rabbinate.[135] Four months later, Behmoiras asked him to prepare, in Greek, a budget for Xanthi's Jewish school. Apparently, the government of Thrace was planning to cover the deficits of all Jewish schools in the region.[136]

In addition to rabbis, merchants in Edirne's Jewish community benefited from the reunification of Western and Eastern Thrace. Edirne's western hinterland had always been an important region for the city's agricultural merchants, and the splitting of Thrace that occurred after the Balkan Wars (1912–1913) had devastated this group. From 1920 to 1922, the General Government of Thrace allowed Edirne merchants to again conduct business in the silk center of Soufli (Sofulu), the tobacco towns of Xanthi and Komotini, and the Aegean port of Alexandroupoli—without paying interstate tariffs.

One example involved an especially Jewish business: the production and sale of matzah. In March 1922, shortly before the Passover holiday, the Jewish community of Edirne offered to sell the Xanthi community a quantity of matzah flour that was milled in Edirne from Bulgarian grains.[137] In other words, the raw goods came from Northern Thrace (southern Bulgaria), the mill was in Eastern Thrace (Edirne), and the potential customers were in Western Thrace (Xanthi). The arrangement neatly illustrates the persistence of Sephardi networks that had spanned greater Thrace for decades, if not centuries, during the time of Ottoman rule in the Balkans.

While it is not the focus of this chapter, it is worth saying a few more words about Western Thrace. That region, which had long been part of Edirne Province, was ruled by Bulgaria from 1913 to 1919. During that time, local Jews were exposed to Zionist currents from Plovdiv and Sofia. Western Thrace was also close to Thessaloniki, another center of Zionism in the Balkans. These factors might explain why the small Jewish community of Xanthi—about 700 people—managed to maintain a B'nai Tzion society and a Zionist Ladino newspaper, both of which were launched in 1922 by the dentist Izak (Izakino) de Boton (see Chapter 2).[138] Once again, Zionism seemed to facilitate good relations between local Jews and Greek authorities. When the League of Nations approved the Mandate for Palestine—a document that repeatedly mentioned a "Jewish national home"—the mayor of Xanthi submitted a congratulatory letter to Boton's newspaper. "We Greeks," he wrote, "feel a cordial joy over this success for a sister people."[139]

Though the modus vivendi that emerged between Greek administrators and Jewish residents often entailed the reinstatement of Ottoman institutions,[140] this rule had some important exceptions. Healthcare, banking, and education where three sectors in which the Greek state was more apt than its imperial predecessor to intervene in "minority" affairs. While the Ottomans had left the Jewish communities of Eastern Thrace to run their own healthcare institutions, the Greek hospital in Edirne treated 51 Jewish inpatients and 365 Jewish outpatients in the period 1920–1921.[141] The ancient Bikur Holim societies did not disappear, but they were diminished.[142] While the misleadingly named Ottoman Bank had been run by French shareholders, the National Bank of Greece was that country's main bank of issue, and, after 1919, it quickly opened five branches in Eastern Thrace and Asia Minor.[143] As late as July 1922, Thrace's Ladino press was announcing branch openings in the Edirne region.[144] Finally, while the Ottomans had paid the salaries of three Turkish teachers at the Alliance boys' school in Edirne, the Greeks went so far as to cover the school's deficit (in addition to supplying five teachers of Greek).[145] Compared to the Ottoman Empire, the Greek state was more adamant about minorities learning the majority language.[146]

The topic of education brings us to a final case in which relations between the Jewish community and the Greek government were linked to intracommunal affairs. As mentioned above, the Hellenic administration had been wary of connections between the Alliance schools and France. According to Moise Mitrani, this was partly because the masters of the local Jewish press were intentionally fueling the governments' paranoia. But Behar's departure from Thrace in 1922 marked a turning point.[147] Seizing the opportunity, Deputy Mitrani organized a meeting between the prefect of Edirne and the main Alliance school director. Barishac, always more circumspect than Behar, saw which way the wind was blowing and quieted his paper's attacks on the Alliance. From then on, the authorities wrote glowing reports about the progress of Alliance students in learning Greek.[148]

In Edirne, the two Jewish newspaper editors had championed a strong form of Jewish nationalism, while the leading Alliance educator had railed against those who wanted to give Hebrew instruction a Zionist flavor.[149] But underneath this rhetoric, Barishac, at least, was a realist more than an ideologue, and Moise Mitrani was not categorically against the teaching of Hebrew (or the establishment of a "Jewish national home" in Palestine).[150] Mitrani did not even complain to Paris when Jews in Edirne and nearby Didymoteicho (Dimetoka) celebrated the ratification of the British mandate for Palestine. Reportedly, three thousand people—including members of the Alliance associations—filled the Great Synagogue of Edirne. Aron Danon gave another speech, young members of the Makabi sports club wore their blue and white uniforms, and the orphanage brass band played the Greek national anthem followed by "Hatikvah." "It was a happy day," wrote the organ of the Zionist Federation of Greece, "when the Alliance alumni association Fraternité [Scolaire] conversed with Tzeirei Tzion about the latter's work."[151]

After months of fierce dispute, the community found a middle ground between the patronizing elitism that had characterized its leadership for years and the bombastic populism that had exploded in 1921. So-called *Alliancistes* and so-called Zionists had reached a compromise. In the end, most parties were relatively uninterested in official Zionist ideology and somewhat committed to what has been called an "autochthonous social and cultural Jewish nationalism."[152] If Greek rule and international developments encouraged Zionist expressions, the need for communal solidarity in the face of political uncertainty pushed local Jews toward common ground.

COLLAPSE: SEPTEMBER TO NOVEMBER 1922

Well after the Greek campaign in Asia Minor had begun to collapse, Hellenic rule in Thrace remained stable. In fact, Greek leaders were so confident about their position in this region that they began its transition from military to civilian administration in June 1922.[153] Meanwhile, Moise Mitrani reported that the 1921–1922 school year had marked a return to normalcy for the Jewish community. He predicted that many "tranquil and prosperous" years were likely to follow, "especially if the political situation in Thrace becomes stable."[154]

But as he wrote these words, the Greek catastrophe unfolding in Anatolia was beginning to cast a shadow across the Marmara Sea. In Eastern Thrace, angry and demoralized Horofilaki intensified their attacks on Muslim villagers in ways that recalled "the Inquisition," according to the Alliance school director in Kırklareli.[155] In September, members of the Association for the Defense of Rights in Thrace—who had regrouped in Bulgaria and Istanbul—sneaked into Eastern Thrace and attacked Greek troops.[156] In response, the Greek authorities court-martialed Muslims and even a few Jews, in a bid to exile them to Aegean islands.[157] Thrace found itself between two regions in which Greek leaders struggled: In Anatolia, the army was losing the war; and in Athens, the Royalist government was overthrown (in September). As the Great Powers debated where to place the new Greco-Turkish border, the political future of Eastern Thrace was again up in the air.

Though it is known for triggering a Christian exodus, the collapse of Greek rule in Eastern Thrace was preceded by a brief *influx* of Orthodox Greeks to the region. After the burning of Izmir (September 13) but before the Mudanya Armistice (October 11), "hundreds" of Anatolian Greeks and a smaller number of Armenians took refuge in Edirne each day. In what would turn out to be its swan song, the General Government of Thrace established a commission to provide housing and other services to the refugees. As schools throughout the city were converted to shelters, Moise Mitrani—whose school had repeatedly been used as a shelter or barracks over the past decade—urged the authorities not to requisition his building and instead use another one that the Jewish community would provide. Meanwhile, the population influx caused a surge in prices.[158] In this moment, Edirne resembled Greek refugee destinations, such as Thessaloniki, more than the Anatolian cities being evacuated, such as Izmir.

This changed after October 11, when the Mudanya Armistice ended the Greco-Turkish War and signaled the Greek army's retreat from Eastern Thrace.[159] Over the next few weeks, most of the region's Armenian and Greek Orthodox residents fled across the new border to Greece.[160] Michael Llewellyn-Smith claims that "a primitive, communal instinct of panic fear told the Greeks that it was time to leave at once."[161] But at least one Jewish observer believed that the emigrants were obeying orders from Venizelist leaders.[162] In any case, this event would retroactively become part of the "Greek-Turkish Population Exchange"—a massive, two-way ethnic cleansing blessed by the League of Nations in 1923.

The Christian departures from Eastern Thrace entailed utter misery for the Greeks and sleepless nights for everyone else.[163] After the signing of the Mudanya Armistice, over a week passed before British, French, and Italian troops reached the region.[164] During these nine precarious days, the Alliance school in Edirne remained closed, and Jewish parents forbade their children from walking in the streets.[165] In Kırklareli, rumors spread that the Greeks would burn down the city as they left. According to Moise Mitrani, emigrants "poured their gall" onto the Jews and Bulgarians for disloyally staying put.[166] Near Çorlu, two Jewish merchants were killed by Orthodox Greeks from the Caucasus—so-called Circassians who had been "armed to the teeth" by Greek military authorities during the occupation.[167] "Anything seemed possible," wrote the Alliance school director in Kırklareli.[168]

In the end, neither the departing Greeks nor the arriving Turkish soldiers started new rounds of violence, and at no point in this transition did local Jews become victims of pogroms. This was consistent with their experiences during previous changes of sovereignty—in 1912, 1913, and 1920—but in marked contrast to what had recently befallen their coreligionists in today's Ukraine (and Western Anatolia, to a much lesser extent).[169] As the Russian Empire collapsed, soldiers and sometimes civilians repeatedly attacked unarmed Jews in a series of pogroms that, after 1918, devolved into what has

Figure 7. Orthodox Greeks prepare to leave Edirne in November 1922. Photograph: Frédéric Gadmer. Source: Albert-Kahn Museum/Archives of the Planet, Inventory # A 36 427 S. CC BY-SA 4.0.

been called a "holocaust."[170] In contrast, the ethnic cleansing campaigns that plagued Eastern Thrace during the last decade of Ottoman rule never targeted Jews en masse.

The striking difference between these two experiences was probably connected to several factors. First, the Russian borderland in Europe—the so-called Pale of Settlement, more or less—had far more Jews than did the Ottoman Balkans. In fact, many of its towns had Jewish majorities, in part because of laws restricting Jewish settlement.[171] After World War I, when Poland, the Soviet Union, and short-lived Ukrainian states fought for the southern half of this zone, its apparent Jewishness threatened to belie their claims (which often involved demographic arguments). This inconvenience intersected disastrously with another regional trait: antisemitism. Over the centuries, various economic, cultural, and legal factors had fed popular notions of the Jew as alien and antipathetic—especially among the ranks of the Russian army.[172] A third factor was the ideological component of the fighting in Eastern Europe. During World War I, when Russian soldiers terrorized the Jews of Austrian Galicia, the latter were portrayed as ruthless capitalists who exploited Hapsburg liberalism to dominate Christian peasants.[173] During the pogroms of 1918–1921, village Jews who knew nothing about modern political ideologies were murdered for their supposed Bolshevik sympathies.[174] Tragically, Ashkenazim in what is now Ukraine could be equated with almost any force whose destruction was desired.

The Ottoman borderland in Europe presented a different picture. In the towns and cities of Thrace, Jews were typically the fourth- or fifth-largest ethno-religious group. There was no special link—legal or demographic—between Jews and the borderland. Furthermore, the Ottoman state and local Muslim society had historically shown no special antipathy toward Jews—certainly nothing that resembled the antisemitism of Christian Europe. And compared to the situation some six hundred miles to the north, the conflicts that roiled Thrace from 1912 to 1922 lacked a strong ideological component. Residents of Thrace were usually mobilized along ethno-religious lines, and it was difficult (though not impossible) to equate Bulgarian, Greek, or Turkish nationalism with local Ladino speakers.

CONCLUSION

By November 25, 1922, all of Eastern Thrace had fallen to the Grand National Assembly of Turkey (founded in Ankara two years prior).[175] Unlike their Christian neighbors, the Jews of Edirne and nearby towns managed to ride out yet another change in sovereignty. A combination of external factors and communal strategies—conscious or not—had allowed the Jewish communities of this region to survive a decade of ethnic cleansing, albeit in a diminished form. During the Greek annexation, one of those strategies entailed the formation of Zionist organizations and the deployment of Zionist representations—actions that satisfied the Greek authorities without prompting violent backlash from the Turkish government after 1922.

However, the era in which minorities could publicly express loyalty to the state *and* sentiments of communal nationalism was coming to an end. Simultaneous expressions of this sort would become highly problematic throughout Turkey and especially in the borderlands. In some cases, so would the mere existence of religious minorities.

FIVE

Peacetime Violence

Completing Borderland Intolerance, 1923–1934

WHEN THE DUST SETTLED IN 1923, Eastern Thrace was almost unrecognizable from the place it had been ten years prior. War and ethnic cleansing had reduced the population almost by half, and the city of Edirne had come to look more like a town.[1] There, the Muslim population had dropped to about twenty-eight thousand, the Jewish population to around six thousand, and the Christian population to a few hundred.[2] The regional economy had been devastated by the exodus of Christian merchants, the physical damage of war, and the redrawing of a border around Edirne (yet again). What had happened in Eastern Thrace was an extreme version of what had happened in Turkey as a whole: in a span of ten years, the place had become poorer, less populated, and less diverse (in terms of religious affiliation).[3]

The Lausanne Treaty was signed in the summer of 1923 by Turkey, on the one hand, and Britain, France, Italy, Japan, Greece, Romania, and Yugoslavia, on the other. The treaty recognized the new Republic of Turkey, whose capital (Ankara) was 430 miles from Edirne. (Istanbul, the old Ottoman capital, was only 150 miles away). It also established that Eastern Thrace would be included in this new state, that Western Thrace would remain Greek, and that Northern Thrace would remain Bulgarian.[4] Additionally, the treaty classified non-Muslim citizens of Turkey as minorities entitled to certain communal rights. For the Jews of Eastern Thrace, Lausanne furthered two ominous processes: Edirne's demotion from a regional center to a border town, and the Jewish community's transition "from *millet* to minority."⁵

All Jews in the early Turkish Republic underwent a process of minoritization as it became increasingly clear that non-Muslim citizens existed on or beyond the boundary of the "Turkish nation"—an entity that was gradually being constructed through legal and discursive means.⁶ But for the Jews of Edirne, the danger of living at the margins of Turkish society was heightened by the fact that they lived on the edge of Turkish territory. Ultimately, this combination would distinguish the fate of Eastern Thrace's Jewish community from its counterparts in Istanbul and Izmir. For one week in the summer of 1934, mobs across Eastern Thrace attacked their Jewish neighbors, killing no one but spurring an exodus that spelled the end of this very old community. In Turkish, the episode is euphemistically known as the Trakya Olayları (Thrace Events).

Scholars have shown that the proximate cause of the attacks was probably the behavior of a government official known as the general inspector of Thrace, who toured the region shortly before violence erupted.⁷ But this leaves us with several questions. What worldviews and concerns prompted Turkish officials to create the General Inspectorate of Thrace and send this official to the European borderland? How important were recent developments, as opposed to long-term history? And why were denizens of Turkish Thrace receptive to calls to attack their Jewish neighbors? The answers entail local dynamics, international anxieties about minorities near borders, and a long Ottoman tradition of population management in the Balkans—three factors that mixed disastrously in 1934. What ultimately drove Jews out of Eastern Thrace was not chauvinistic nationalism or antisemitism per se, but rather a combination of factors involving the recent history of the region, the changing nature of Balkan borderlands, and certain legacies of the Ottoman Empire.

This chapter begins by summarizing the "events" of 1934 and the state's role in them. Next, it discusses local Jewish life during the first ten years of the Turkish Republic. From there, it sketches a culture of economic resentment that was growing among certain Turkish Muslims in the region. With that accomplished, the chapter moves from the local to the international by situating the Thrace Events in a broader phenomenon that was sweeping Southeast Europe in the interwar period. Finally, the discussion shifts from similarities across borderlands to particularities of Turkish Thrace by exploring continuities between the Ottoman state and its Turkish successor. The local and the international, the interwar moment and the *longue durée*—all intersected in the summer of 1934, with tragic results. In a place where Turkey bordered two European countries and at a time when empire had recently given way to nation-states, such coincidences were not so remote.

THE "EVENTS"

In the history of the Turkish Republic, the only case of mob violence directed specifically against Jews occurred in Eastern Thrace and Çanakkale in the summer of 1934. Throughout the affected towns, trouble for Jews usually started with boycotts, threats, and exhortations to leave, before escalating to physical attacks and looting. If the goal was to evict Jews from the region and take their property, the attacks were moderately successful, in the short run: At least one third of the Jewish population of Eastern Thrace fled for Istanbul and beyond.[8] Meanwhile, official efforts to return Jewish property were half-hearted.[9] In the long run, the Thrace Events combined with other factors to precipitate the end of Jewish life in Eastern Thrace, a region that today has no permanent Jewish residents.

Almost certainly, what triggered the "events" was a visit from a government official named İbrahim Tali (Öngören). Tali and his boss, Interior Minister Şükrü Kaya, had both done secretive work for the Ottoman government in eastern Anatolia during the Armenian genocide (1915–1917).[10] From 1928 to 1933, Tali led the First General Inspectorate—a special administrative area created by the government of Mustafa Kemal (Atatürk). With its seat in Diyarbakır, it sought to secure Turkey's southeastern borderland and prevent the formation of a Kurdish state that could be backed by imperialist powers and their proxies in northern Syria and Iraq.[11]

In February 1934, as tensions mounted with Bulgaria and Italy, Ankara created the Second General Inspectorate (the General Inspectorate of Thrace) in Turkey's northwestern borderland. Its mission was to improve public works and facilitate the settlement of Muslim immigrants in the provinces of Edirne, Kırklareli, Tekirdağ, and Çanakkale—a region roughly congruent with Edirne Vilayet as it had existed before World War I.[12] Tali was tapped to leave Diyarbakır and come to the city of Edirne, from where he would lead this new inspectorate.[13]

From May 6 to June 7, Tali conducted a tour of Eastern Thrace and Çanakkale, visiting offices of the Republican People's Party (Cumhuriyet Halk Fırkası, CHF) in all towns that would soon see anti-Jewish attacks. The consensus among historians is that Tali encouraged local leaders to spur a Jewish exodus, though it is unclear to what extent he prescribed violence and to what extent his actions had been sanctioned by the Interior Ministry.[14] If Tali's bosses were displeased, they hardly showed it: The man continued to run the Second General Inspectorate until the beginning of 1935, at which point he was elected member of parliament for Diyarbakır.[15]

On June 16, Tali sent the CHF general secretary a confidential report on the region. It included a flagrantly antisemitic section called "The Jewish Problem in Thrace" (Trakya'da Yahudi Meselesi), and it ranted about Jews in sections ostensibly on other topics (such as the economy, public safety, and agriculture). Among other things, the Jews of Eastern Thrace were accused of controlling capital in the region, promoting communism, spying for foreign countries, and spreading pro-Bulgarian propaganda in anticipation of an invasion by that country. Tali wrote that it was "of crucial importance—for Turkish life, the Turkish economy, Turkish security, the Turkish regime, and the [Kemalist] revolution—to abolish Jewry" in Eastern Thrace.[16] The report ended with an unannotated map that divided Eastern Thrace into three zones.[17]

Two days before Tali submitted his report, Turkish Parliament passed Law 2510, also known as the İskan Kanunu (Settlement Law). While the legislation had first been drafted in 1932 with the goal of assimilating Kurds in eastern Anatolia, the final version was probably more concerned with Thrace.[18] The legislation called for Turkey to be divided into three zones. In Zone 1, the plan was to increase the percentage of the population that was "attached to Turkish culture." Zone 2 was supposed to receive people—immigrants as well as longstanding citizens—who were "not attached to Turkish culture" and eventually become the site of their assimilation. Zone 3 was not appropriate for settling immigrants and could, at any time, be totally evacuated for security or public health purposes.[19] The law did not include a map or specify the locations of these zones.[20] And, at least in the context of Thrace, it was never implemented. Subsequent developments would make it unnecessary.

The Thrace Events began on June 21, 1934, in Çanakkale—on the Anatolian side of the Dardanelles. There, the Jewish community of about 1,800 people had recently been subjected to a boycott. But now they endured several days of physical attacks and looting that spurred many to flee to Istanbul.[21] Violence in Çanakkale erupted the day that Law 2510 was published, and some observers began to connect the dots. On June 29, the American ambassador to Turkey cabled Washington: "The interesting fact has come to light that the entire Jewish population of Thrace is in the process of being expelled. . . . A decision [has been made] in high places to evacuate the Jews." He concluded that "They will probably all, or at least the majority, come to Istanbul."[22] The next day, Edirne's CHF-affiliated Halk Evi (People's House) added fuel to the fire when its organ ran a piece titled "Economic War" about unnamed parties who "suck our blood" and enjoy a "mastery of capital."[23]

From July 3 to July 5, anti-Jewish attacks spread across the municipalities of Eastern Thrace—the cities of Edirne, Kırklareli, and Tekirdağ as well as the towns of Uzunköprü, Keşan, Çorlu, Lüleburgaz, and Babaeski. Local authorities permitted and sometimes participated in the lawlessness, which mostly entailed the looting of Jewish homes and stores.[24] However, at least one Jewish witness claimed that the mob vandalized his local synagogue, destroying Torah scrolls and other religious books.[25] The worst violence occurred in Kırklareli, where crowds had gathered for a traditional oil wrestling competition on July 3. Witnesses recalled stabbings, the pulling of gold teeth, attacks on the local rabbi, and at least one woman beaten into a state of unconsciousness. Some claimed that attackers raped Jewish women and girls, though at least one Jewish writer denies this.[26] All sources agree that no Jews were killed in the affair, which seems to indicate economic motives as opposed to a deep-seated culture of antisemitism.[27]

Thousands of Jews immediately fled the region, and possessions that had not been stolen were sold to neighbors for a song.[28] A relatively small number of Jews—along with some Christians—fled to Bulgaria.[29] A slightly larger contingent of Jews crossed into Greece, either to the border town of Nea Orestiada or as far as Thessaloniki.[30] However, the vast majority of people headed to Istanbul, fleeing the borderland but not the country (for the time being). Over one thousand Jews packed the train stations of Alpullu, Lüleburgaz, and Çorlu, where conditions were "indescribable."[31]

The Turkish government eventually condemned the attacks and encouraged Jews to return to their homes. Several officials in Kırklareli were arrested, including the mayor, the police commissioner, and the president of the chamber of commerce. However, they were released within a few days. Only six men without titles of distinction were convicted of participating in the attacks and given (short) prison sentences. On July 14, the government claimed that 75 percent of the property looted in Kırklareli had been returned to its rightful owners, but this report is suspect. For example, it omitted the fact that the goods had been found in the home of the local police commissioner.[32] The overall lack of accountability was hardly reassuring for Jews who had fled the region.

If the authorities' immediate response (or lack thereof) was telling, so were subsequent developments. Ninety thousand Muslim immigrants settled in Eastern Thrace and Çanakkale in 1935.[33] From Bulgaria alone, immigration to Turkey quadrupled between 1934 and 1935.[34] At a party convention in May 1935, Şükrü Kaya stated that "the upper echelons of the government" had made a policy of settling as many Balkan immigrants as possible in Çanakkale and Thrace, where "the land is bountiful and open."[35] Meanwhile, Ankara began to remilitarize Turkey in Europe, a project that accelerated in 1936 when the Montreux Convention ended international restrictions on Turkish military activity near the Bosporus and Dardanelles.[36] Though Mustafa Kemal and his inner circle might have disapproved of the lawless way in which Jews were expelled from Eastern Thrace, historians have noted that "the end result fitted the overall policy of Ankara to diminish the presence of Non-Muslims in frontier areas."[37]

JEWISH LIFE IN A TURKISH BORDERLAND

To get from 1923 to 1934, we must understand the concerns of Ankara but also the local scene in Eastern Thrace. Toward that end, the next section follows the development of anti-Jewish attitudes among some local notables, and the present section studies Jewish life in the Edirne region during the first years of the Turkish Republic. In addition to bringing Jewish agency into the picture, this discussion responds to İbrahim Tali's report, which claimed that Jews dominated the local economy and supported Turkey's rival, Bulgaria. While the first claim was an unfair exaggeration and the second was completely baseless, such misconceptions were highly consequential and must be addressed when analyzing the violence of 1934.

In the period 1923–1933, it was not obvious that Eastern Thrace was becoming uninhabitable for Jews. After ten years of war and ethnic cleansing, the region enjoyed a relatively peaceful era, and antisemitism was less prevalent here than in much of interwar Europe (an admittedly low standard). As late as 1930, the Jewish community of Edirne was still "known among Eastern Jewry for its fine administration and the excellence of its institutions," according to a contemporary observer. These institutions included the communal council, the chief rabbinate, the schools, an orphanage, two charities, a workers' syndicate, and the Bikur Holim society, which opened a so-called "hospital" in 1930.[38] (In fact, it was a newly expanded clinic.) Between 1922 and 1934, about two thousand Jews left Eastern Thrace for greener pastures, a figure that is substantial but still smaller than the number of Jews who left immediately before and after this period.[39]

As the Ottoman Empire transformed into a nation-state, Jewish associational life was sorely challenged. As early as World War I, the Cercle Israélite—which had ties to the Paris-based Alliance Israélite Universelle—had been ordered to accept non-Jews and change its name to Cercle d'Andrinople. It reverted to being a Jewish society during the Armistice period, but in 1925 Turkish officials again forced the club to change its name and membership criteria.[40] In 1923, a Zionist society established during the Greek occupation had its office vandalized in a night raid, at which point local Zionist activity was forced underground.[41] In the early Turkish Republic, there was little tolerance for associations that could be linked to other states, actual or potential.

But Jewish associational life soon adapted to the nation-state paradigm and regained its footing. This was largely thanks to the international Jewish organization B'nai B'rith, which operated in a relatively decentralized manner (compared to the Alliance) and was careful about mentioning a Jewish state (compared to Zionist organizations). As mentioned in Chapter 2, the Edirne chapter had been founded in 1911 as the "Ottoman Lodge."

But sometime between 1918 and 1921, it changed its name to HaSharon, in reference to the region of Palestine mentioned in the biblical Song of Songs.[42] Lodge members funded cultural institutions, dominated the communal council, and ran the Jewish orphanage. In 1921, they started a fund that made small loans to local Jews, using capital from international Jewish organizations (as mentioned in Chapter 4). In 1923, the fund merged with a similar one in Istanbul and officially registered with the Turkish government, at which point it became an indispensable institution for the Jews of Eastern Thrace.[43]

In 1925, wives, sisters, and daughters of HaSharon members founded the lodge's female counterpart and named it HaVatzeleth ("The Rose"—a reference to the "Rose of Sharon" in the Song of Songs). Largely a charitable association, the lodge revived a program that helped poor girls prepare their dowry trousseaus (*ashugar*, in Ladino).[44] The club's first president was Rosa Mitrani (née Avigdor), who also codirected Edirne's Alliance school with her husband, Moise. The HaVatzeleth lodge would continue to operate after the 1934 attacks.[45]

In addition to supporting local communal life, B'nai B'rith allowed the Jews of northwestern Turkey to maintain old social networks with coreligionists in other post-Ottoman states. Headquartered in Istanbul, B'nai B'rith's "Eastern District" covered Turkey, Greece, Bulgaria, Yugoslavia, Egypt, Palestine (under British Mandate), Syria (under French Mandate), and Rhodes (annexed by Italy)—all of which contained territory that had been Ottoman circa 1908 (nominally, at least). The Balkan lodges helped Jews in Edirne maintain ties with fellow Ladino speakers in Southeast Europe, and the district's French-language organ printed a portion of its articles in Ladino or Turkish. Into the 1930s, the Edirne lodge had members from nearby towns in Turkey (such as Kırklareli) but also Greece (such as Didymoteicho).[46] Even on the local level, B'nai B'rith helped Jews overcome borders.

In maintaining ties with Ladino speakers in Greece, Bulgaria, and Yugoslavia, Edirne Jews were hardly expressing solidarity with those countries. Rather, they were preserving a supercommunity of Sephardim through networks that were Ottoman more than "international," imperial legacies more than challenges to the Turkish nation-state. It was disingenuous, to say the least, for Tali and his ilk to claim otherwise. Commenting on the Thrace Events a few weeks after they happened, a Bulgarian newspaper put it this way:

> What could be the pretext for the sudden persecution of Jewish masses ... peaceful and loyal people who are not suspected of any sort of irredentism? One cannot say that they sing the [Bulgarian] hymn of St. Sophia, even in spirit. One cannot claim that they have links to some nonextant Thracian organization that threatens the territorial integrity of the Turkish Republic by giving speeches in a [Bulgarian] Strandzha village populated by refugees from [Greek and Turkish] Thrace.[47]

In other words, if Bulgarian speakers in Turkish Thrace had been unfairly accused of harboring foreign sympathies, such claims were even more chimerical when it came to local Jews.

Here it is worth touching on Zionism and migration to Palestine. While Tali's report made the vague claim that local Jews were "in the process of turning Thrace into a counterpart to Palestine," migration to Mandate Palestine was not a common itinerary, and whatever Zionist activity existed was carried out quietly. A 1924 article in the *JTA News Bulletin* reported that Istanbul's Palestine office was handling "many" visa applications from "agricultural workers from Thrace," and that fifteen Jewish families from Edirne had recently requested "facilities to enable them to proceed to Palestine." But these claims must be balanced against the fact that the vast majority of the two thousand Jews who left Eastern Thrace between 1922 and 1933 went to Istanbul, Paris, and the Americas. Perhaps a few hundred people migrated to Palestine during the first decade of the Turkish Republic, most of whom were young men.[48]

If it is hard to find traces of Zionist—and even assertively Jewish—activity during the presidency of Mustafa Kemal (1923–1938), it is easier to find documents related to Jewish economic life. Business directories, community ledgers, balance sheets of Jewish loan funds, and records from municipal chambers of commerce all provide a sense of the work Jews did in the Thracian economy. When read together, these mundane documents tell a story that can be contrasted with the bombastic claims of Tali and certain local leaders.

One of the most helpful sources is the *Annuaire oriental* commercial directory. Unlike the other documents I discuss, it was not created in Eastern Thrace but rather in Istanbul (by a private concern). The *Annuaire oriental* purported to list the prominent merchants, retailers, professionals, manufacturers, and financial institutions of every province in Turkey. While people were not identified by religion, their names usually betrayed this data point. The directories show that in 1925, about 55 percent of commercial firms in Edirne Province were run by Muslims, 39 percent were run by Jews, and 6 percent were run by Christians.[49] By 1934, about 24 percent of such firms were run by Muslims, 68 percent were run by Jews, and 8 percent by Christians.[50] These numbers suggest that Jews were already overrepresented in local commerce circa 1925 (when only 4 percent of Edirne Province's population was Jewish), and that the phenomenon grew even more pronounced over the next nine years. This situation was unique to Eastern Thrace. In Istanbul, the continued presence of Greek and Armenian merchants prevented such a lopsided occupational profile, and in Izmir, the goal of replacing the Christian bourgeoisie with a Muslim one was quickly achieved.[51]

Similar conclusions emerge from old directories of Edirne's Chamber of Commerce (now the Chamber of Commerce and Industry). One document, which simply lists the names of members in the order they joined the chamber, shows that 556 Muslims, 337 Jews, and 14 Christians joined between 1930 and 1935.[52] A more official—yet less comprehensive—directory records 20 Muslims, 17 Jews, and no Christians joining the chamber between 1929 and 1934.[53] Together, these documents suggest that between 37 and 46 percent of the chamber was Jewish on the eve of the 1934 Trakya Olayları.

When this is considered alongside the *Annuaire oriental* numbers, it seems that the Jews of Eastern Thrace did, in fact, enjoy a commercial presence that exceeded their demographic presence. And apparently the opposite was true for Muslims. When Edirne's Greek consul and British ambassador claimed, respectively, that local Jews were "relatively prosperous" and "comparatively wealthy," they were not exactly wrong.[54]

But this fact must be balanced against others. First, the local economy contained sectors other than commerce, and these tended to have a stronger Muslim presence. The 1934 *Annuaire oriental* listed six "manufacturing" concerns in Edirne: a Jew who made soda, a Jew who made oil, a Jewish distiller, a Muslim distiller, and—the only two things in Edirne that could properly be called factories—a cannery and a flour mill run by well-connected local Muslims. The 1929 *Annuaire oriental* listed two Jewish "bankers," but the only financial institutions that appeared in the 1934 edition were the Ottoman Bank and the Agricultural Bank (Ziraat Bankası), both of which were partly controlled by the state.[55] While Jewish commercial firms were certainly *numerous*, no Jewish-owned company could approach the size and influence of the banks in downtown Edirne, the beet sugar factory in the town of Alpullu, or the cannery nearby.[56]

Second, in the evaluations of the Greek and British diplomats, one should stress the words "relatively" and "comparatively." The Jewish community of Eastern Thrace, which had lost much of its merchant class between 1912 and 1923, was poor by Western standards. This is evidenced by the continued involvement of Jewish aid organizations such as the American Jewish Joint Distribution Committee (JDC). Balance sheets for the above-mentioned small-loan fund—which was capitalized by the JDC—reveal the modest livelihoods pursued by most community members. For example, from March to August 1924, 98 loans went to small shopkeepers, 34 went to artisans, 31 were for commercial use, 6 were for "employees," 6 were for peddlers, and 1 was for a "free professional." Most loans were for amounts lower than US$54 dollars (converted to today's values).[57]

Another glimpse of the community's occupational profile comes from its own records. A loan ledger for the years 1932–1933 listed the occupations of about 1,500 Jewish men and 30 Jewish women—probably most of the working Jews in the city of Edirne. Based on my analysis of the first half of this massive document, the most common occupation was grocer, a job held by about 11 percent of the people in my sample. Sellers of textiles and other dry goods made up the second-largest group, composing 7 percent of the entries, followed by people in the dairy business (6 percent). From there, the most common jobs were: "merchants" (5 percent), cereals merchants (4 percent), wagoners (4 percent), shoemakers (4 percent), tailors (3 percent), market vendors (3 percent), peddlers (3 percent), butchers (3 percent), sellers of dried fruit and nuts (2 percent), stove repairmen (2 percent), tinsmiths (2 percent), timber merchants (2 percent), vegetable sellers (2 percent) and brokers/agents (2 percent).[58]

Figure 8. Jewish cheesemakers in the Edirne region, circa 1930.
Source: Archive of the Alliance Israélite Universelle.

On the one hand, it is remarkable that such a large portion of the community worked in retail and commerce—a phenomenon that distinguished Jews from their Muslim neighbors and frustrated those who wanted to build a "Muslim bourgeoisie."[59] On the other hand, a community of grocers, drapers, and cheesemakers was hardly headed for "domination" of the economy, especially as Ankara moved toward a policy of statism that promoted industrial factories and agricultural cooperatives (in which Jews were not prominent). Even by the standards of Istanbul's Jewish community, the Jews of Eastern Thrace were poor.[60] Only in such a depopulated, underdeveloped region could a group like this be so conspicuous.

A CULTURE OF ECONOMIC RESENTMENT: JEWISH-MUSLIM RELATIONS IN TURKISH THRACE

Having established the state's role in the Thrace Events and the contours of Jewish life after 1922, we still must address the following question: In the summer of 1934, why were so many Turkish Muslims willing to attack Jews, steal their property, and scare them out of Eastern Thrace? The answer can only be reached through "a micro-structural approach that enables insights into local conditions, local actors, and situational factors," in the words of Berna Pekesen.⁶¹ In that spirit, this section will trace a culture of economic resentment that developed among certain Muslims in Edirne as attempts to create a Muslim bourgeoisie were repeatedly frustrated.⁶² Sometimes, resentment of Jews in commerce was clearly expressed as such. Other times, it came out in complaints that were ostensibly about language, culture, or politics. But most cases, I argue, were related to widespread anxieties about economic scarcity in this war-torn borderland.

To understand 1934, we must begin with 1922 (at the latest). That fall, as the army of the Turkish National Movement pushed Greek soldiers and civilians from the region, Edirne's new *vali* made it clear that Jews would continue to have a place in Turkish Thrace. At a ceremony in Çorlu, Mehmet Şakir (Kesebir) promised local Jews the full support of the new government in Ankara. For his part, the president of Çorlu's Jewish community hailed the end of the "oppressive" Greek regime.⁶³ A few weeks later, the *vali* visited Edirne's Great Synagogue and had a friendly exchange with the local chief rabbi.⁶⁴ Interviewed by a Ladino newspaper in Istanbul, the governor predicted that Jews who had moved to that city from Edirne would soon return to their hometown, "where they will continue their progress that was temporarily interrupted" by wars.⁶⁵

But while the *vali* was publicly praising the region's Jewish community, his comrades in the army were subjecting Jews, specifically, to wartime taxes and "extensive requisitioning" that prompted another small wave of Jewish emigration.⁶⁶ This echoed similar taxes that had been levied at the start of the Greco-Turkish War (see Chapter 4). Many leaders of the local branch of the nationalist army—the Association for the Defense of Rights in Thrace— would go on to become the political fixtures and industrial captains of the region.⁶⁷ Speculatively, we might connect these wartime requisitions to subsequent hostility that Jewish merchants faced from local notables. At very least, we can say that the wartime taxes revealed a lasting tendency among this set to see the Jewish community as a concentration of capital more than a group of devoted Turkish citizens.⁶⁸

One of the four founders of the Association for the Defense of Rights in Thrace was Kasım Yolageldili. Already a successful grain merchant in the late Ottoman era, he served as Edirne's first mayor in the Republican period and went on to become the region's leading industrialist.⁶⁹ Edirne's Ladino newspaper described him as "the richest businessman in all of Thrace."⁷⁰ By 1923, he was producing flour and sesame oil. In 1924, he cofounded a coal mining operation near Uzunköprü and joined two members of parliament in building the region's first cannery. A year later, he was among the ten people tapped by President Mustafa Kemal to run the region's first beet sugar factory. Yolageldili also helped found Edirne's commodities exchange and chamber of commerce, serving as president of both until 1933.⁷¹

Kasım Yolageldili often worked with his sons, Cevat and Mustafa Kasım.⁷² With the latter he launched the Edirne-based newspaper *Paşaeli*. Officially edited by young Mustafa Kasım, this Ottoman-Turkish publication ran from 1923 to 1925 and repeatedly portrayed local Jews as foreigners and economic enemies.⁷³ The fact that it was printed by a Jew (Yuda Razon) is telling: to the extent that an anti-Jewish discourse existed in Edirne, it was often perpetuated by people who interacted with Jews on a regular basis.

As noted by historian Avner Levi, *Paşaeli* began its attacks in the summer of 1923.⁷⁴ While an Istanbul paper had run some anti-Jewish pieces at the end of 1922, the articles in *Paşaeli* probably represent the first extended press campaign against Jews in modern Turkey.⁷⁵ In stories that were often picked up by papers in other Turkish cities, *Paşaeli* accused local Jews of various offenses, including collaboration with the Greeks during the recent occupation.⁷⁶ But the most common charge was that, in Thrace over the past few years, Jews had grown wealthy while Muslims suffered, and now the former were economically exploiting the latter.⁷⁷ In particular, Jews were accused of duping Muslim peasants. For example, one story claimed that a Jew in Tekirdağ had tricked a grain farmer into cancelling a contract with a Muslim merchant and selling the grain to him, the Jew, at a lower price.⁷⁸

Paşaeli's claims were constantly refuted by Edirne's Ladino newspaper, *La Boz de la Verdad*. As discussed in previous chapters, this paper had already defended Jews from allegations of ritual murder (made by Christians) and treason (made by Muslims). Editor Josef Barishac now strove to fight the latest round of libel. After *Paşaeli* ran the story about the Tekirdağ incident, Barishac published the Jewish merchant's side of the story: Indeed, the grain farmer had arranged to sell barley to a certain Muslim, but when the latter failed to appear at the commodities exchange, the farmer wheeled his cart to another stall and successfully "implored" the Jewish merchant to buy his goods.[79] After *Paşaeli* reported that the Edirne branch of Türk Ocakları (Turkish Hearths) had accused local Jews of economic exploitation, Barishac had the branch's president deny the claim, on the record.[80]

Despite these efforts, *Paşaeli*'s campaign had grave consequences for the Jews of Eastern Thrace. Barishac blamed the newspaper for an anti-Jewish boycott in Uzunköprü that nearly turned violent, rising tensions in Babaeski that were forcing Jews to leave town, and a general climate of hostility toward Jewish merchants that was sweeping the province.[81] This last claim may have alluded to an incident in which Muslim merchants had temporarily blocked their Jewish competitors from attending a silk cocoon fair near the city of Edirne.[82] Describing the damage done by *Paşaeli*, Barishac added that even in the city of Edirne, "not a day goes by without Turkish children and uneducated adults insulting and menacing" Jewish vendors at their stalls, saying things like, "Your turn, too, will come to leave the country."[83]

The situation hit its nadir when three Jewish merchants were killed in the Thracian countryside, an incident that Jews and Muslims alike blamed on *Paşaeli*'s provocations. These murders—almost the only case of local Muslims killing local Jews that I encountered in my research on the period 1908–1934—had a profound effect on the community.[84] In the late-Ottoman period, Edirne Province had been exceptional for the large number of Jews who lived and worked in the countryside (compared to other provinces). But now, Jewish merchants began to think twice about doing business in remote villages. Even midsized towns like Uzunköprü and Babaeski no longer seemed safe for Jews.[85]

The murders finally prompted the authorities to intervene. In September 1923, after a Jewish delegation visited the *vali*, the state opened a libel case against *Paşaeli*.[86] After hearing from witnesses including Barishac, the chief rabbi of Edirne, and a local Muslim merchant, the court acquitted Kasım and Mustafa Kasım Yolageldili of all criminal charges—a verdict that was criticized by the Ladino press. But in a related civil suit brought by one Fethi Bey (which is a Muslim name), the Yolageldilis were ordered to pay four hundred liras in restitution. Meanwhile, *Paşaeli* published a pseudo-apology, explaining that a recent piece had only been meant to describe "a limited number of Jews of narrow character." Most local Jews, it continued, were "patriotically committed to the good of the country through their economic activities."[87] While these responses hardly satisfied the local Jewish community, it is notable that men of such stature—Kasım Yolageldili had just finished his term as Edirne's mayor—were at least brought to trial.[88]

When *Paşaeli* published another spate of anti-Jewish articles the following year, the Ladino press suggested that these campaigns were economically motivated. According to *La Boz de la Verdad*, the Yolageldilis timed their attacks to coincide with the busy season for agricultural commerce (late spring through early fall).[89] Indeed, commercial yearbooks show that most of the merchants who competed with the Yolageldilis in the grain trade were Jews.[90] It seems that the Yolageldilis used their newspaper to advance the general interest of the budding Muslim bourgeoisie and the particular interests of their own family business.

The Yolageldilis' anti-Jewish vitriol was not always directed at merchants. In June 1923, for instance, *Paşaeli* published a warped account of a dispute that had occurred between a Jewish woman (Rosa Mitrani) and a Muslim man, in their capacity as teachers at Edirne's Alliance school. The inflammatory piece demonized Mitrani and the Alliance to the extent that members of the Turkish Hearths club vowed to occupy the school, which had to be guarded by police. The Jewish community sought help from leaders in Ankara—including Mustafa Kemal himself—but this only aggravated local authorities.[91]

A second example occurred in July 1924. According to *La Boz de la Verdad*—which would close in a few years[92]—"an editor of *Paşaeli*" made a scene at an outdoor concert in Edirne's Reşadiye Bahçesi. (For an earlier incident involving this venue, see Chapter 2.) When the orchestra concluded its set with a "customary" Ladino *kantika*, the editor—either Kasım Yolageldili or his son—rose from his seat and ordered the band to stop. Ignored, he left the concert and returned with an entourage. After shouting, "This isn't Palestine!" he lashed out at the venue's Jewish manager. Days later, *Paşaeli* recounted the incident in a piece titled, "Are We in Palestine?" It also called for a boycott of the venue. However, the editor withdrew his call upon learning that some co-owners were Muslim.[93]

These two cases of anti-Jewish hostility involved many factors, including gender anxieties, Francophobia, disapproval of the British Mandate for

Palestine, and chauvinistic Turkish nationalism. But even here, economic resentment was just below the surface. It is revealing that the editor of *Paşaeli* expressed his anger over the concert by quickly calling for a boycott of the venue (too quickly, in fact). Also, it is not hard to imagine that, for people like the Yolageldilis, every Jewish teacher in Edirne occupied a job that could go to a Muslim.

Another local notable who lambasted Jewish merchants was Mehmet Şeref (Aykut). Though he was a lawyer and not a businessman, Şeref Bey (as he was known) had much in common with Kasım Yolageldili: both had been founders of the local Turkish resistance movement in 1918, both ran newspapers, and both entered politics. In 1918 and 1919, Şeref Bey had been editor-in-chief of the Turkish newspaper *Trakya Paşaeli*, a predecessor to Yolageldili's similarly named publication. Şeref Bey represented Edirne in the last parliament of the Ottoman Empire (1920) and the first parliament of the Turkish Republic (1921–1923). After an eight-year hiatus, he returned to the Grand National Assembly of Turkey for the 1931–1934 term, which coincided with the 1934 Thrace Events.[94]

Şeref Bey's relationship with the local Jewish community was complicated. As a boy, many of his friends were members of notable Jewish families. He even attended Edirne's Alliance school, where a fifteen-year-old Josef Barishac taught him Ladino.[95] As editor of *Trakya Paşaeli*, Şeref Bey used the above-mentioned printer Yuda Razon.[96] And throughout his political career, Şeref Bey seems to have maintained friendships with both Moise Cohen (also known as Munis Tekinalp) and Abraham Galante, two prominent Turkish Jews who urged their coreligionists to dissolve the linguistic and social barriers that separated them from Turkish Muslims.[97] So, it is hardly surprising that in May 1923—at the end of his first term in parliament—Şeref Bey praised the loyalty of local Jews in an open letter to *La Boz de la Verdad* (which was run by his former Ladino teacher). He said that unlike their Christian counterparts, "the Jews of Turkey remained our friends through hard times."[98]

Ten years later, however, Şeref Bey would sing a different tune. In 1933—while once again deputy for Edirne—he wrote a series of anti-Jewish articles in the Turkish newspaper *Edirne Milli Gazete* (which had ties to the ruling party).[99] One piece, which portrayed Jews as parasites feeding on Turkish peasants, was harsh enough to prompt a rebuttal from Edirne's other Turkish newspaper, *Edirne Postası*. Dated August 17, 1933, the rebuttal accused Şeref Bey of making "an inept imitation of Hitlerism" and called his theories "unscientific": Turkish peasants suffered not because of Jews but because of low crop prices.[100] A few weeks later, Şeref Bey wrote an article on local Jewish history. After reading the complete works of his "very old, very beloved friend" Abraham Galante, Şeref Bey concluded that Jews had been loyal Ottoman subjects until the twentieth century, when the Balkan Wars, World War I, and the Armistice had brought out the worst in Edirne's Jewish population—thanks in part to the influence of French institutions (read: the Alliance).[101]

These themes would reappear in a letter that Şeref Bey wrote to Moise Cohen just two months before the outbreak of the Thrace Events.[102] In this twenty-five-page rant, Şeref Bey complained to his friend about the slow speed of assimilation among Turkish Jews. He claimed that certain Jewish merchants in late Ottoman Edirne had "robbed" the people, only to move "with their millions" to Italy and France where they started silk factories, hotels, and banks in the 1910s. He also claimed that the Greek occupation of Eastern Thrace had allowed Jewish traders to establish themselves in the town of Uzunköprü, where suddenly "the market and the bazaar were stuffed with Jews."[103]

Why did Şeref Bey's opinion—and even memory—of Jews change between 1923 and 1933? Likely it had something to do with how, over the course of that decade, local Jews filled the commercial void that had been left by departing Christians. While merchants like the Yolageldilis may have resented Jewish competition from the inception of the Turkish Republic (or earlier), Şeref Bey had no reason to feel threatened by the presence of Jews in 1923. But ten years later, he must have been frustrated by the fact that efforts to create a Muslim bourgeoisie in Thrace had largely failed. In fact, the presence of Muslims in the commercial sector probably *declined* during this period (as discussed in the previous section).

While they cannot be traced to a particular notable like Kasım Yolageldili or Şeref Bey, three more episodes are central to the story of intercommunal relations and economic resentment in early Republican Thrace. The first involved the Alliance schools, which did not fare well in the nationalistic climate of the era. In 1923, just as Ankara ruled that all primary-school teachers in the country had to be Turkish citizens, Edirne's director of education instituted an additional requirement: classes related to Turkish language and culture could only be taught by "Turks"—that is, Turkish Muslims.[104] Furthermore, the Alliance schools—and therefore the Jewish communities that funded them—had to pay these Turkish teachers very high salaries. Because classes dedicated to Turkish language and Turkish culture were mandatory in all schools, the new hiring requirement amounted to a form of wealth transfer. And the rule was enforced: when the Jews of Lüleburgaz delayed hiring a "Turk," their school was shuttered by the authorities.[105]

The second episode involved a campaign known as "Citizen, Speak Turkish!" (Vatandaş Türkçe Konuş!). Launched in January 1928 by law students at Istanbul University, the campaign urged minorities to use Turkish instead of the traditional languages of their respective communities.[106] Immediately, *Edirne Milli Gazete* ran an article urging "minorities who trade and profit here" to form clubs that promote the speaking of Turkish. In March, addressing "Armenians, Orthodox Greeks, and especially Jews," *Edirne Postası* said the following: "You are obligated to speak Turkish; anyone who fails to speak it is not one of us and cannot live in this country."[107] In April, matters escalated: overzealous students tried to stop the Jewish communal ovens from baking matzah for the Passover holiday, and at least one local imam urged mosque worshippers to ostracize and boycott their Jewish neighbors.[108] After an initial attempt to reign in the movement spurred three hundred students to protest, the *vali* of Edirne finally managed to quash the campaign.[109] Language initiatives would reappear in the 1930s, but these were generally tamer and sometimes led by local Jews.[110]

Following Senem Aslan, I would argue that this eruption of cultural nationalism was largely about "the creation of a Muslim-Turkish bourgeoisie by curbing the power of non-Muslims in the economy."[111] Whatever the intentions of the movement's founders in Istanbul, the "Citizen, Speak Turkish!" campaign in Edirne became a vehicle for marginalizing Jewish shopkeepers and merchants.[112] One obvious link between language politics and economic warfare was the imam's call for a boycott. Another was the above-mentioned boycott in Çanakkale, which immediately preceded the 1934 Thrace Events. The full name of that campaign was "Citizen, Speak Turkish; Citizen, Buy from Turks" (Vatandaş, Türkçe Konuş; Vatandaş, Türkten Alış-Veriş Yap).[113] In this context, there is no doubt that "Turk" meant "Turkish Muslim." In theory, language campaigns were part of a national assimilation program. In practice, they were often used as vehicles of exclusion.[114]

The third episode involved a highly fraught municipal election. In 1930, at the request of President Mustafa Kemal, Fethi Okyar created the Free Republican Party (Serbest Cumhuriyet Fırkası, SCF) to oppose the ruling CHF in upcoming elections. Reportedly, 180 Jews joined the party in Kırklareli, and in Edirne five Jewish candidates ran on the SCF ticket (unsuccessfully). In Eastern Thrace and across Turkey, the opposition had only modest success at the polls. But this was enough to alarm the CHF and its literati. The Turkish press in Edirne claimed that the Jews of Thrace had voted overwhelmingly for the SCF, and the party was described as "Jewish."[115] The opposition was disbanded at the end of the year, but the experiment in multiparty democracy permanently strained relations between the ruling party and the Jews of Eastern Thrace.

Attempts to paint the SCF as a "Jewish" party played off the fact that its brand of economic liberalism was popular among members of the non-Muslim bourgeoisie in Istanbul and Thrace. However, almost all leaders of the party were Muslim, and Kasım Yolageldili himself was reportedly asked to cofound the Edirne branch. (Though it seems he declined the offer.)[116] In Edirne, certain publicists disingenuously used the elections to draw a triangle connecting Jews, opposition to the CHF, and free-market capitalism—at a time when statism was the ruling party's official economic policy.[117] Even in this ostensibly political conflict, a discourse of economic nationalism was at work.

Why was it that in Eastern Thrace—more so than in other parts of Turkey—Jews maintained such a large presence in these retail and commercial positions, despite the efforts of local notables to build a Muslim bourgeoisie? First, the wars and ethnic cleansings that raged in this region during the last Ottoman decade took a devastating toll on the economy. While not unique to Eastern Thrace, this factor was more intense here than in many other parts of Turkey. Second, Eastern Thrace in the Republican era found itself on the periphery of an Anatolian nation-state—and cut off from its former markets in the Balkans. Combined, these two factors led to an underdeveloped, largely agricultural economy with few opportunities for Muslims to enter the bourgeoisie.[118] Partly because of the region's position near the border, the economic pie was small in Eastern Thrace—and a noticeable portion was held by Jews.

"LET'S IMITATE OUR NEIGHBOR": DEMOGRAPHIC ENGINEERING ACROSS BORDERLANDS

To the extent that international factors appear in studies of the Thrace Events, discussions tend to focus on the influence of Nazi Germany.[119] Teaching in Edirne High School around this time was one Nihal Atsız, an ideologue of Turkish racism who was known to imitate the hair and clothing style of Adolph Hitler. Eight months before the Thrace Events, he launched an ultranationalist publication called *Orhun*.[120] Meanwhile, an antisemitic tabloid was published in Istanbul by a Turkish man who had recently returned from Germany and was clearly inspired by *Der Stürmer*.[121] While it is tempting to link these publications to the 1934 attacks, it seems unlikely that European antisemitism could have taken root so quickly in Thrace (where low literacy rates were an additional impediment).[122] While Nazism may have had a small influence on some well-read people in Edirne and Ankara, it was not the most important international trend in this story.

For that, we must turn to a disturbing chain of events that swept Southeast Europe in the interwar period. As leaders began to challenge the borders—and minority clauses[123]—that the Great Powers had imposed on much of Europe after World War I, the states of Southeast Europe entered a grim competition in which each one tried to alter its borderland demography by replacing minority citizens with immigrants thought to resemble the national majority.[124] The idea was to put supposedly reliable populations in the borderlands at a time when irredentism was becoming an international trend.[125]

In a sense, this dark contest in demographic engineering was rooted in the ethnic cleansings of the last Ottoman decade (see Chapter 3).[126] More proximately, however, this process began with the so-called Population Exchange between Greece and Turkey that was sanctioned by the League of Nations in 1923.[127] From Turkey's standpoint, this two-way ethnic cleansing was especially consequential in Eastern Thrace, where about 190,000 Orthodox

Christians followed the Greek army in its westward retreat during the fall of 1922, and about 116,000 Muslims arrived from Greece, per the Population Exchange agreement.[128] Local Jews quickly became collateral damage. In December 1923, the police commissioner of Çatalca "expelled" the local Jewish population to make room for incoming *mübadiller* (Muslim exchangees), and a similar measure in Çorlu was only stopped at the last minute, "in response to urgent representations" from the Jewish community.[129]

The Greek-Turkish Population Exchange set off a domino effect of displacement that turned minorities across the Balkans into refugees and migrants. Bulgarian speakers in Greek Thrace (Western Thrace) were effectively deported as authorities tried to accommodate Orthodox Greeks streaming in from Turkey. When the refugees from Western Thrace arrived in Bulgaria, popular outrage was directed at local Greek speakers. The latter, by and large, fled to Greece.[130] That country was home to thousands of Aromanians—Orthodox Christians speaking a language related to Romanian—who also found their lifeways threatened by the Greek refugee crisis. They asked the Romanian state for land in Southern Dobruja, which had recently been annexed from Bulgaria. When Bulgarian bands intensified their cross-border raids on that region, Romanian leaders agreed to fortify it by establishing colonies of Aromanians.[131] Local Turkish-speaking Muslims were not expelled outright, but they found life in the Romanian borderland increasingly uncomfortable and moved to Turkey in droves.[132] Between 1923 and 1933, over one hundred thousand Muslims moved from Bulgaria to Turkey, in part because Sofia had been settling Christian refugees from Western Thrace in predominantly Muslim regions of southern Bulgaria. This Muslim migration was facilitated by a 1925 agreement between Bulgaria and Turkey that was probably inspired by the Greek-Turkish Population Exchange.[133]

In a parallel development, Bulgaria's territorial aspirations became so alarming that all four of its neighbors—Turkey, Romania, Yugoslavia, and Greece—signed a mutual-defense agreement in February 1934.[134] It was against this backdrop of Bulgarian irredentism and borderland demographic engineering that the Istanbul newspaper *Cumhuriyet* urged Turkish leaders to build a demographic "wall in Europe" by settling Muslim immigrants from the Balkans near the border with Bulgaria.[135] Months later, the government heeded this call by establishing the General Inspectorate of Thrace and passing Law 2510. Soon, impatient mobs took it upon themselves to make room for this "wall" by forcing Jews out of Eastern Thrace—and stealing their property in the process.

The intensification of hostility toward borderland minorities was very much an international trend. This becomes especially clear if we focus on dynamics between Turkey and its two European neighbors. While each country faced unique circumstances, Turkey, Greece, and Bulgaria all witnessed remarkably similar discussions about demographic engineering in the borderlands.

Greece normalized relations with Turkey in 1930, when the Treaty of Ankara affirmed the border between those two countries.[136] Shortly before, Greek journalists in the Prefecture of Evros—which borders Turkey and Edirne Province—had started slandering local minorities. In 1928, the Alexandroupolis newspaper *Vima tis Thraki* (Thrace Tribune) questioned the loyalty of Jews in the border towns of Didymoteicho and Nea Orestiada. Echoing the Turkish press in Edirne, it also claimed that "the Greek farmer is the slave of the Jewish usurer." Elsewhere, *Vima tis Thraki* called for Jews, Muslims, and Armenians to be removed from Greece's northeastern borderland because they supported the Communist Party of Greece (among other reasons). Consistent with its intimations that the local Jewish community harbored pro-Turkish sympathies, the paper also complained about a group of Jews who had moved from Edirne to Didymoteicho, where they now ran an international smuggling operation (allegedly).[137]

Próodos (Progress), another Alexandroupolis newspaper, also expressed attitudes that were common to the Greek and Turkish borderlands. Aligned with the Liberal party of Eleftherios Venizelos, this paper wrote about Turkish Law 2510 on June 17, 1934. Under the headline "Let's Imitate Our Neighbor," the writer urged Athens to follow Ankara's example by passing legislation that would facilitate the removal of Jews from the borderland. When pogrom-like attacks swept Turkish Thrace two weeks later, *Próodos* complained not about the violence but about the influx of Jews it had caused. The newspaper claimed that Nea Orestiada had been "overrun" by Turkish Jews to the point that "today it looks like a Jewish town." It urged the police to prevent further settlement there and to monitor Jews in the Kastanies market, a weekly event attended by many residents of Edirne (just across the border).¹³⁸ *Próodos* probably exaggerated the number of Jews who fled from Turkey to Greece that summer. But its coverage shows how one state's borderland anxieties could stoke those of its neighbor, even when diplomatic relations were friendly.

Unlike Greece and Turkey, Bulgaria did not have a large Jewish community near its Thracian border.¹³⁹ It also lacked an ally in the region. Combined, these factors may have colored Bulgarian press coverage of the 1934 Thrace Events, which was relatively sympathetic toward the Jewish victims. One Sofia newspaper condemned the attacks as an act of Turkish intolerance and suggested that a right of return should be granted to Ladino-speaking Jews *and* Bulgarian-speaking Christians who had fled Eastern Thrace over the past few decades.¹⁴⁰ Promoting multiple stereotypes, another paper predicted that Turkey's scheme to replace local Jews with Balkan Muslims would be an economic disaster.¹⁴¹

For Bulgarian leaders, the most worrisome minorities in the southern borderland were Muslims. As mentioned above, Turkey and Bulgaria established a bilateral policy in 1925 that helped Turkish-speaking Muslims leave Bulgaria for Turkey and Bulgarian-speaking Christians leave Turkey for Bulgaria. Both Ankara and Sofia desired something of a gradual, unofficial population exchange—for the most part.

Complicating matters were the Muslims of southern Bulgaria, a borderland that had been part of Edirne Province until 1912 and today includes Kurdzhali, Smolyan, and Haskovo provinces (roughly). It soon became clear that Turkish immigration authorities, while eager to accept Muslims from northern Bulgaria, hesitated to accept those from the south. Sofia feared an irredentist scheme whereby Turkey would call for a plebiscite in this region. Therefore, Bulgarian officials tried to prioritize the emigration of Muslims from the south and to settle this region with Bulgarian-speaking Christians. Meanwhile, Muslims entering Bulgaria from Turkey were closely monitored as potential agents of Kemalist propaganda.¹⁴²

In short, Sofia wanted to settle the borderland with Bulgarian-speaking Christians—including immigrants—who would replace local Muslims or at least tip the balance toward the desired demography. This was analogous to Ankara's designs for Eastern Thrace. In both cases, government leaders sought to do three things at once: settle immigrants, secure a borderland, and assimilate minorities. Demographically, the Greek, Bulgarian, and Turkish borderlands were becoming increasingly distinct from each other. Regarding the treatment of immigrants and minorities, however, the three borderlands of Thrace were starting to look alike.

OTTOMAN LEGACIES

With that said, Jews were not attacked in the borderlands of Greece or Bulgaria during this period. In 1931, Jews in the Campbell quarter of Thessaloniki were the victims of a pogrom led by refugees from Asia Minor, but this occurred far from the border.[143] The Bulgarian state's gradual nationalization of the economy largely excluded Jews from "the new managerial order," but anti-Jewish violence in interwar Bulgaria was rare.[144] If the Thracian borderlands of three adjacent countries were coming to resemble each other, why did mass violence against minorities only occur in one of them?

Unlike its Greek and Bulgarian counterparts, the Turkish state was the direct successor to a six-hundred-year-old empire. In the words of Aron Rodrigue, "The Ottoman Empire, like the Russian Empire to its north and many similar polities in the past, had long and established models of population management and relocation," especially vis-à-vis the borderlands. The demographic engineering polices of the late Ottoman Empire were part of this "long imperial state tradition."[145] When leaders in Ankara and notables in Edirne resolved to move Jews from the borderland, they were not only reacting to an interwar dynamic but also utilizing a set of population management techniques that had accumulated over centuries of Ottoman rule. Furthermore, everyday denizens of Eastern Thrace were, on some level, aware of this history. If not quite normalized, the practice of moving certain populations to and from the borderland had a historical resonance.

The practice of settling Muslims near the northwestern edge of the state dated to the fourteenth century, when the Ottomans moved Turkic peoples from Anatolia to newly conquered territory in the Balkans (where local Christian populations needed to be counterbalanced). In the nineteenth century, when Tatars fled Russian persecution in Crimea, Ottoman authorities mostly settled them in the empire's Balkan domains, including Edirne Vilayet. And when the Balkan Wars forced Muslims to flee Bulgaria, Serbia, and Greece for Ottoman lands, the Committee of Union and Progress settled most of these refugees in Eastern Thrace (and western Asia Minor, to a lesser extent).[146] Regardless of whether the empire was expanding or contracting, the constant goal was to settle and secure the European borderland with Muslims. (It also bears repeating that when the Ottomans conquered Istanbul in 1453, the Jews of Edirne were moved en masse to the new imperial capital, in a type of forced relocation known as *sürgün*.[147])

Often, it was supposedly troublesome Muslims who were moved to the borderland. In the fourteenth and fifteenth centuries, the Ottomans sent to the Balkans precisely those Anatolian Muslims who "were seen as unreliable either because of their unruly nomadic existence or their rebelliousness and loyalty to rivals of the Ottoman dynasty."[148] The idea was that a change of scenery and a breaking up of tribes would bring these people into line. Meanwhile, the state would achieve its additional goal of establishing a Muslim bulwark in Europe. Similarly, the nineteenth century saw at least one powerful Shia "Kızılbaş" family exiled from Lebanon to Edirne.[149] And after the 1930 Ağrı Rebellion in eastern Turkey, Ankara strategically broke up some notable Kurdish clans by settling certain people in Thrace, many of whom arrived around the time of the 1934 attacks.[150] In the European borderlands, alleged rebels who identified as Muslim were better than quiet taxpayers who did not (in the eyes of the state).

It seems impossible to prove that Muslims made the northwestern borderland more secure or—this part deserves emphasis—that Jews somehow made it less so. What we *can* trace is the development of this perception among writers and officials in Edirne through the early twentieth century. In 1911, Edirne's main Turkish newspaper claimed that Jews holding Italian citizenship had cooperated with Russian troops during the Russo-Turkish War of 1877–1878 (see Chapter 2). During World War I, some Jews in Eastern Thrace suffered forced relocation to the interior, conscription into labor battalions, and other discriminatory policies reflecting mistrust of non-Muslims. Meanwhile, paranoid Ottoman officers suspected the existence of a Jewish spy ring with nodes in Edirne, Uzunköprü, and nearby Bulgarian towns (see Chapter 3). After the Greek occupation of Eastern Thrace ended in 1922, some writers impugned the behavior of Jews during that episode. For example, an Edirne newspaper claimed that Jewish families in Kırklareli had attended a ball where their daughters flirted with Greek officers, the Ottoman/Turkish flag was disrespected, and everyone cheered "Zito Venizelos!"[151] In his above-mentioned letter from 1934, Mehmet Şeref repeated a similar anecdote, only his version was set in Uzunköprü.[152]

Together, the six-hundred-year history of imperial population management and the fifty-year history of vilifying borderland minorities supplied a reservoir of ideas for Edirne denizens to draw on. This, as opposed to a deep-seated culture of antisemitism, was the historical legacy that facilitated the 1934 Thrace Events. Writing about a German town that experienced a ritual murder accusation in 1900, Helmut Walser Smith says that "The vengeful anti-Semitic heart had behind it the full force of nearly a millennium of historical experience. . . . The people had come to know a series of stories, a collection of murderous tales, which served as alibis for aggression. The stories also came with a familiar script."[153] Residents of Eastern Thrace had a different "script" to turn to in socially fraught moments, one that traded antisemitic tropes for insidious questions about the place of non-Muslims in the borderland.

CONCLUSION

Looking back in time from 1934, we see a host of historical factors that explain the Thrace Events. This includes local resentment of Jewish merchants that developed after 1922, anxieties about borderland minorities that spread across Southeast Europe in the interwar years, and harsh Ottoman legacies that went back decades or even centuries.

But it is equally revealing to look *forward* from 1934. Just as ethnic cleansing policies tested in Thrace during the Balkan Wars were soon applied throughout Anatolia, methods of intimidation and wealth transfer tested during the 1934 Thrace Events were later used in other parts of Turkey.[154] One of these later uses was the 1942 Varlık Vergisi (Wealth Tax), a punitive measure that was especially devastating for Turkey's Jews (and Christians, to a lesser extent).[155] Another was the 1955 Istanbul Pogrom—also known as the "September Events" (6–7 Eylül Olayları)—which mainly targeted Orthodox Greeks but also ensnared Jews and Armenians.[156] In hindsight, we can say that the Thrace Events were both a culmination of developments that had begun in the Ottoman era *and* a rehearsal for subsequent acts of displacement and dispossession that would occur in Istanbul and beyond. By 1955, the population center of Turkey had come to resemble the borderland. The latter—in the worst way—always seemed to be ahead of its time.

Conclusion

"SPENDING THE PAST FIFTEEN YEARS in this region of constant unrest has caused me to develop a nervous condition whose only cure is peace and a sense of certainty about the future." This self-diagnosis was made in 1922 by the director of a Jewish school in Eastern Thrace. Indeed, he had watched his region endure three wars, two foreign occupations, one revolution, and a string of ethnic cleansings. To fill his prescription for "peace and a sense of certainty about the future," he would have to move elsewhere (namely, Istanbul).[1]

Meanwhile, thousands of his coreligionists managed to tolerate the region's chronic uncertainty—for the time being. But in 1934, one-third of these people fled a spate of anti-Jewish violence in Eastern Thrace. Six years later, only 3,500 Jews lived in the city of Edirne, the region's Jewish center.[2] In 1944, only 2,500 Jews remained.[3] By 1949, the number had dropped to 1,650.[4] While no single event immediately ended Jewish life in northwestern Turkey, the attacks of 1934 mark the moment when the community lost its critical mass. By 1971, when the provincial government expropriated Edirne's Jewish cemetery and sold the gravestones to a construction company, one thing had become certain: a large Jewish community could not exist in the European borderland of Turkey.[5]

Throughout this book, I have strived to capture the agency of Jewish men and women who lived in the Edirne region during the early twentieth century. The preceding chapters are largely about Jews adapting to rapid changes and surviving near a border whose position and meaning kept shifting, often amid tremendous violence. The Jews of Eastern Thrace approached new political options with caution, exploring the possibilities of an allegedly liberal era in a way that balanced Jewish "nationalism" with integrationist Ottomanism, time-tested methods with bold experimentation.[6] As the region descended into war, local Jews only grew more circumspect and conservative, resisting the relatively new idea that state borders in Southeast Europe had assumed the role once played by Ottoman communal boundaries.[7] And, in certain contexts, Edirne Jews actively pursued their own form of Zionism—which combined old notions of communal autonomy with contemporary Zionist representations—to save the community from external threats and internal strife.

But as the middle of my narrative begins to intimate and the ending makes clear, the agency of Jews was limited in this borderland. Or, to repeat Jeremy Adelman and Stephen Aron's term, Jewish agency decreased precisely as the region morphed from a diverse, interstate borderland to "bordered lands" that were homogenous and closed.[8] Ultimately, a combination of factors forced community members away from the edge of the country and toward its largest city. This was one of many places in the world where borders shaped Jewish life far more than Jews shaped borders (a dynamic that political Zionism aimed to change).

Why did Edirne Jews eventually lose their fight against forces that were pushing minorities out of the region? One answer has to do with how the functions of a given border can change and accrue over time. The (roughly) longitudinal line between Turkey and Greece has largely held steady since 1915, while the (roughly) latitudinal line between Turkey and Bulgaria has an even longer history. Far from constant, however, are the entities that these lines have delimited. Today's Turkish-Bulgarian border grew out of ancient conflicts between Bulgarian speakers (to the North) and *Greek* speakers (to the South).[9] By 1913, that same line—more or less—was separating Bulgarian speakers from *Turkish* speakers. During World War II, it took on the additional task of separating neutral Turkey from Axis Europe. In the Cold

War, it was part of the Iron Curtain, and, since 2007, it has formed the southeast limit of the European Union (EU).[10] In a similar fashion, today's Turkish-Greek border has separated Bulgaria from the Ottoman Empire (1913–1919), Turkey from Nazi-occupied territory (1941–1944), and the EU from whatever we call the zone beyond it (1981–present).

Borders that developed to separate Christians from Muslims or one group of Christians from another tended to spare Jews the agonies of ethnic cleansing and demographic engineering—at first. But once these borders had produced the initial rounds of population displacement—or once those displacements had produced the borders—other groups were liable to become targets. The Jews of Eastern Thrace were one such group. The ease with which old borders can be put to new uses suggests the following: Borders and borderlands are not necessarily inimical to Jewish communities, but they are always liable to become so, in the modern era.[11]

Another reason why the Jews of Eastern Thrace lost their battle with the border has to do with the latter's special role in modern nation-states. For centuries, Ottoman control of Southeast Europe (Rumeli) had allowed Sephardi Jews to move (or send letters and literature) across the Balkans without encountering a state border. Members of this expansive Ladino-speaking community—which extended to Western Anatolia—were not expected to identify with the culture of their Muslim or Christian neighbors, and their difference vis-à-vis these neighbors was neither celebrated nor problematized.[12] Cultural and social life played out mostly in Jewish milieus, on the local and imperial levels.

This paradigm began to crumble in the nineteenth century. Serbian and Greek Revolutions (in the period 1804–1835) followed by Romanian independence and Bulgarian autonomy (in 1878) all created new dynamics between the Jews of these young countries and their non-Jewish neighbors (most of whom were Christian, as the formation of these states often involved Muslim expulsions). As Jews were cut off from coreligionists by new state borders, their cultural distinctiveness became a problem to be solved by assimilation or else marginalization.[13] In regions that had—or were beginning to have—Muslim majorities, the nation-state paradigm emerged after 1908, in the Turkish-speaking realms of Anatolia and Thrace. Soon after, it spread to the post-Ottoman Arab world, where Jews from Egypt to Iraq tried to embrace the nationalism of the country in which they lived. In these places, the issue of Jewish otherness became much more pressing after the creation of the State of Israel in 1948.[14]

Compared to Sephardim in other post-Ottoman regions, the Jews of Eastern Thrace were especially affected by the nation-state paradigm (in the interwar period). Edirne was severed from its immediate hinterland in a way that Izmir, Istanbul, and even Thessaloniki, Greece, were not. Despite efforts to maintain cultural and economic networks across the Balkans—another recurring theme of this book—Edirne Jews generally led more circumscribed lives in the interwar years than they had in the early twentieth century, an ironic development considering the technological advances that occurred between 1900 and 1940. And while Jews throughout Central/Eastern Europe and Southwest Asia struggled to situate themselves in societies that were now structured around notions of "majority" and "minority," the problem was especially acute in Eastern Thrace.[15] This was because leaders in Ankara worried that non-Muslims near the border could aid and abet foreign countries, and because local notables saw Jews as obstacles in the effort to build a "Muslim bourgeoisie" in this war-torn economy.[16] If much of Turkey came to acquire traits of the borderland, the differences between the borderland and the rest of the country were not erased entirely. After all, there must be reasons why about twelve thousand Jews live in Istanbul today, while about zero live in Eastern Thrace.

By making a conceptual distinction between the two factors that ended Jewish life in this region—the border's ability to serve many functions over time, and the rise of the nation-state paradigm—I am not suggesting that these phenomena were totally separate. In fact, they often emerged together. Consider the way in which Ottoman-era networks were dissolved. This development followed the rise of nation-states in Southeast Europe but was also related to the multifunctionality of the border. In the years 1912–1923, disrupting Sephardi networks was surely not the most pressing issue for Bulgarian, Greek, and Ottoman/Turkish leaders. But once the border between their countries was solidified, it proved useful in accomplishing this task, too.

The modern history of the Jews of Edirne—people who lived with the devastating consequences of ethnic cleansing while shedding very little blood—challenges two popular notions. One is that in late nineteenth- and early twentieth-century Europe, imperial borderlands became inherently deadly places for Jews (and especially for Jews). The other is that Sephardim in the late Ottoman Empire and early Turkish Republic enjoyed a happy experience that was insulated from what befell their coreligionists in Eastern Europe and their Christian neighbors down the street. While such notions may not always be stated explicitly, they creep into scholarship more often than we acknowledge. By tracing a history less "lachrymose" than that of Eastern European Jewry but more violent than that of other Ladino-speaking communities (in the period 1908–1934), this book should prompt scholars to overcome simplistic dichotomies and probe the many shades of Jewish experience reflected in historical documents from disparate places.

I will close by suggesting some new avenues of research that this book might open for historians of Ottoman Jews and of Jews in Eastern Europe (especially in the modern era). Those who look at Jewish communities in the late Ottoman Empire might turn their attention from colorful port cities and Francophone intellectuals toward overland Sephardi networks, physical mobility between (and within) states, and the fate of both in the late nineteenth and early twentieth centuries.[17] While the dissolution of the Sephardi world has been painted in broad strokes by several scholars, the details—on the ground, so to speak—of how this process played out for Jewish merchants, migrants, and war refugees have yet to be understood.[18]

As for historians of Central and Eastern European Jewry, they might hear this conclusion as a call for a comparative study of Jews and borders. Without meaningful categories of analysis, the act of comparing distant communities can misleadingly feed notions of an essential Jewishness. But borders are just the sort of analytical tool we need. They also represent a topic that is all too relevant in today's political moment. By comparing and connecting the experiences of distant Jewish communities that exist (or existed) near modern borders (or modern borders in the making), scholars might expand our notions of Jewish history while contributing to a wider discussion about borders that begs for depth and nuance.

EPILOGUE

Bordering the Holocaust

AFTER 1934, THE DISSOLUTION OF Thrace's Jewish community was not particularly dramatic. The community lost its critical mass, while the region became provincial—an economic backwater that lacked the kinds of commercial, educational, and cultural institutions associated with urban life. Proximity to Istanbul—Turkey's largest Jewish center—made migration to that city relatively easy. And after 1948, the State of Israel became another pull factor for some Edirne Jews, albeit a complicated one.

With that said, there would be one last drama in the story of this community: the World War II years, especially 1939 to 1943. While Turkey remained neutral in that conflict, its European border assumed two roles that reveal much about the themes of this book and the Holocaust in the Sephardi world. First, in late 1939 and early 1940, the border became the center of a crisis in which dozens of Jewish families were sent back and forth between Bulgaria and Turkey. Some of these stateless people literally resided *at* the border for a time. Three years later, the boundary between Greece and Turkey became the eastern limit of the European Shoah. Jewish communities on one side of the line were annihilated by the Nazi apparatus of genocide, while those on the other side stayed just beyond its reach.

The Jewish refugee crisis began in the summer of 1939. On September 8, one week after Germany invaded Poland, the president of Edirne's Jewish community informed his counterpart in Istanbul of some "saddening facts." For the past two months, Sephardi Jews in Bulgaria were being deported "back" to the city of Edirne and stripped of their property.[1] This group of around 130 people had moved from Edirne to Bulgaria in the period 1920–1925.[2] Some may have fled the Greek invasion of Eastern Thrace in the summer of 1920, while others may have joined a wider Jewish migration out of Turkey during the first years of the republic.[3] In any case, they were not Bulgarian citizens. In 1939, Bulgaria was deepening its friendship with the Axis Powers, and suddenly its population of four thousand foreign Jews—including many from Central Europe—"became an embarrassment." The director of police was charged with expelling them all. The first step was to "[dispose] of Turkish and Greek Jews by escorting them across the border," in the words of Frederick Chary.[4]

The first expellees to reach Edirne mostly carried valid Turkish nationality certificates. When they stepped off the train, they were "received as brothers by the [Turkish] authorities and the [Jewish] community."[5] Because they had not been allowed to bring or even sell their possessions, they arrived in a state of destitution and became a drain on the local Jewish community, which was already poor. Still, they faced few legal hurdles in migrating to Turkey.

But later that summer, a second wave of Sephardi Jews arrived. Unable to afford train fare, deportees from Bulgaria began traveling to Edirne on foot.[6] Many came from Plovdiv, 110 miles away.[7] Most importantly, these people were stateless. According to the president of Edirne's Jewish community, they had "lost" their Turkish nationality certificates while living in Bulgaria, and they reached Edirne to discover that their "citizenship had been annulled" (*tabiyeten ıskat*).[8]

Yuda Romano, secretary of the Edirne community, claimed that "these people cannot be recognized as Turkish citizens according to the laws of our government because, during their sojourn in Bulgaria, they failed to do their duty and register with the Turkish consulate in their city."[9] Similarly, a letter from the Edirne Chief Rabbinate said that "the fault" of these deportees was "not applying to the Turkish consulate during their residency in Bulgaria."

This letter cited Turkish laws 1041 and 1312 as the legislation working against the refugees.[10] The stateless Jews themselves told a slightly different story. For example, one of them included the following detail in a letter to the Foreign Ministry in Ankara: "The reason we did not apply [for renewed citizenship] at the consulate of the [Turkish] Republic was that we were unaware of the law that was published."[11]

These statements refer to an interwar policy that Turkey pursued on an "unofficial" and "semilegal" basis.[12] Especially after 1926, the Turkish government took various measures to annul the citizenship of non-Muslims who had left the Ottoman Empire or the Republic of Turkey for other European countries. The above-mentioned Law 1041 was passed in 1927. It empowered the Council of Ministers to strip Turkish citizenship from people (read: non-Muslims) who had failed to fight in the Greco-Turkish War (1919–1922) and were abroad at the time of the law's passage. This described those Jews who had fled Edirne for Bulgaria in 1920. Citizenship Law 1312 was passed in 1928. Among other things, it said that Turkish citizens who had lived abroad for more than five years were required to immediately register at their nearest consulate or risk losing their citizenship. But the law was passed quietly, and many of those affected—almost always Christians or Jews—learned of it too late.[13] Finally, a Passport Law from 1938 stated that anyone who had lost their citizenship due to the above-mentioned legislation was prohibited from even stepping foot in Turkey. In the words of Corry Guttstadt, "Jews of Turkish descent who had lost or changed their citizenship were thus denied even temporary exile as refugees in Turkey."[14]

This broader policy explains the statelessness of the second wave of Jewish refugees. When these people reached the Turkish-Bulgarian border in 1939, they entered a Kafkaesque cycle. In a game of human ping-pong, Turkish and Bulgarian authorities sent these displaced persons back and forth across the boundary line, basically "shuttling them between the two border stations."[15] Some people made five roundtrips in a single week.[16] In at least one case, women and girls were "savagely violated at gunpoint" while crossing the border.[17] Temperatures plummeted as the crisis dragged into winter. While some of the refugees managed to receive provisional housing in Edirne, others "had to crawl around on trains" parked at Karaağaç station, a stone's throw from the border (on the Turkish side).[18]

The Jewish community of Edirne scrambled to help. It provided food, shelter, heating fuel, and money, when possible.[19] It paid the train fares each time the stateless people were sent back to Bulgaria, lest they be forced to walk along a dirt road in weather that "could lead to their death."[20] They begged Jewish leaders in Istanbul to send funds for the "unfortunate *muhadjires*," the latter word being the Ladino version of an Arabic/Turkish term for "refugee."[21] (For more on this word, see Chapter 3.)

The Edirne community also petitioned the central government in Ankara. It sent telegrams to the Ministry of Foreign Affairs listing the deportees and begging for "pity and salvation."[22] As mentioned above, desperate pleas from stateless people in Edirne were forwarded to the Interior and Foreign Ministries. The president of the Edirne community even asked his counterpart in Istanbul to telegraph Sami Ginsburg, an Ashkenazi Jew who was the dentist of President İsmet İnönü (and had been the dentist of Mustafa Kemal Atatürk until the latter's death in 1938).[23]

A breakthrough came in February 1940. On a "deadly cold" night, a group of Jewish refugees returned to Edirne from the Bulgarian side of the border—and were not sent back. Ankara had decreed that the stateless people could remain in Turkey. Yuda Romano rushed to the train station, made some "necessary payments" to officials, and arranged for cars to bring the refugees from the suburb of Karaağaç to the city of Edirne. It is unclear what, exactly, swayed Ankara to suddenly take pity. The president of Edirne's Jewish community told his counterpart in Istanbul to thank Sami Ginsburg "for all the pains he took toward achieving this good result," but also to call off an appeals process that the dentist had suggested.[24] Perhaps Turkish leaders simply resigned themselves to what Hannah Arendt would write eleven years later: "It would seem that the very undeportability of the stateless person should have prevented a government's expelling him."[25] Regardless, the "martyrs of *Hitlerismo*" were saved.[26]

Did these people remain in Edirne? Or did they join the hundreds of local Jews who moved to Istanbul each year? Or perhaps they took the advice of Jewish leaders in Sofia to "do all they can to leave for Palestine?"[27] The documents do not say. Wherever they wound up, most of them must have lived to see the end of World War II. This cannot be said of their fellow Sephardim on the Greek side of the border.

EPILOGUE

In the spring of 1941, Greece was occupied by the Axis Powers. Bulgaria took most of Western Thrace, including Komotini, Xanthi, and Alexandroupoli. German forces occupied the strip of territory along the border with Turkey, which included Didymoteicho. Some residents of that town—Muslims, Christians, and Jews—immediately crossed the riverine border into "free" Turkey. But most of them were promptly sent to the port of Tekirdağ by Turkish authorities, from where they were shipped to the Greek island of Lesbos (also occupied by Germany).[28]

In the spring of 1943, the Jews of Western Thrace were deported to death camps and exterminated. In the Bulgarian zone, Jewish residents were sent by train to northwestern Bulgaria, where the Germans put them on barges that went up the Danube to Vienna. Trains took them from Vienna to Treblinka, where the new arrivals were immediately killed.[29] In Didymoteicho and nearby towns, the Germans rounded up Jewish residents and put them on trains bound for Thessaloniki. From there, they were sent to Auschwitz-Birkenau. The vast majority were killed.[30] A small number of Jews managed to escape the German-occupied zone by crossing the border into Edirne Province, thanks to sympathetic Turkish border guards. But these cases were exceptional and violated Turkey's wartime policy of sealing the border.[31]

In the city of Edirne and the suburb of Karaağaç, Jews could see the German-occupied zone. They suffered as the wartime economy went from bad to worse. They fretted about the safety of friends and family members across the border.[32] And they were devastated by the 1942 Varlık Vergisi that transferred wealth from non-Muslim to Muslim citizens, throughout Turkey.[33] Nevertheless, this Jewish community stayed beyond the clutches of the Shoah.

For decades, the Jews of Thrace had resisted the trend of attaching new meanings to the border that was breaking up their region. That resistance was tested in 1934, when Jews in Turkish Thrace were attacked for living too close to the boundary line (among other reasons). It was worn down further in 1939 and 1940, when Bulgarian and Turkish authorities used the border to justify their inhumane treatment of the many Sephardi families who found themselves in limbo. By 1943, any remaining resistance had surely come to an end. The border separated life from death. There was no room for interpretation.

Notes

Introduction

1. In Turkish, the name of the mountain range is Istranca.

2. Gülru Necipoğlu, *The Age of Sinan: Architectural Culture in the Ottoman Empire* (London, 2005), 241–42.

3. Steffen Wippel, "Edirne as a Secondary City: Global Reconfiguration of the Urban," in *The Heritage of Edirne in Ottoman and Turkish Times: Continuities, Disruptions and Reconnections*, ed. Brigit Krawietz and Florian Riedler (Berlin, 2020), 484–533.

4. AAIU, Turquie, XI E, Moise Mitrani, April 19, 1910.

5. *Ethnic cleansing* is an imperfect term. But ethnicity and religion in the late-Ottoman Balkans were not totally distinct categories. Also, while the term was not popularized until the Yugoslav Wars of the 1990s, Russian officials spoke of "cleansing" certain ethno-religious groups from disputed territory as early as the 1850s: Mara Kozelsky, "The Crimean War and the Tatar Exodus," in *Russian-Ottoman Borderlands: The Eastern Question Reconsidered*, ed. Lucien J. Frary and Mara Kozelsky (Madison, 2014), 165–83.

6. The photograph can be found online, in the Alliance Israélite Universelle digital library: https://www.bibliotheque-numerique-aiu.org/records/item/13211-le-personnel-du-service-sanitaire-et-de-l-administration-de-l-hopital-militaire-sultanie-d-andrinople-assiege-pendant-la-guerre-balkanique

7. Rosa's maiden name was Avigdor. See the historical database of personnel of the Alliance Israélite Universelle: http://www.archives-aiu.org/aiu/index.htm.

8. AAIU, Turquie, XII E, Rosa Mitrani, August 16, 1935, and November 20, 1935.

9. A. C. S. Peacock, "Introduction: The Ottoman Empire and its Frontiers," in *The Frontiers of the Ottoman World*, ed. A. C. S. Peacock (Oxford, 2009), 24. Peacock paraphrases Zürcher, who is cited below.

10. Omer Bartov and Eric D. Weitz, "Introduction: Coexistence and Violence in the German, Habsburg, Russian, and Ottoman Borderlands," in *Shatterzone of Empires: Coexistence and Violence in the German, Habsburg, Russian, and Ottoman Borderlands*, ed. Omer Bartov and Eric D. Weitz (Bloomington, 2013), 8.

11. Jordi Tejel and Ramazan Hakkı Öztan, "Introduction: Regimes of Mobility in Middle Eastern Borderlands, 1918–46," in *Regimes of Mobility: Borders and State Formation in the Middle East, 1918–1946*, ed. Jordi Tejel and Ramazon Hakkı Öztan (Edinburgh, 2022), 6.

12. It should now go without saying that "conservative" is not the opposite of "modern." Furthermore, I mean "conservative" in the broadest sense. For more on "broad versus narrow sense conservatism," see *Stanford Encyclopedia of Philosophy*, s.v. "Conservatism," October 29, 2019, https://plato.stanford.edu/entries/conservatism.

13. Kenneth B. Moss, *An Unchosen People: Jewish Political Reckoning in Interwar Poland* (Cambridge, MA, 2021), 6.

14. For more on demographic engineering in the late Ottoman Empire, see Fuat Dündar, *Modern Türkiye'nin Şifresi: İttihat ve Terakki'nin Etnisite Mühendisliği, 1913–1918* (Istanbul, 2008).

15. AAIU, Turquie, I C 3, Angèle Guéron: journal entry dated October 30, 1912.

16. Journal entry written under the pseudonym "Ben Israel," dated July 22, 1913, in *Almanach national au profit de l'hôpital de Hirsch* (Thessaloniki, Greece: 1914).

17. Renée Hirschon, "'Unmixing Peoples' in the Aegean Region," in *Crossing the Aegean: An Appraisal of the 1923 Compulsory Population Exchange between Greece and Turkey*, ed. Renée Hirschon (New York, 2003), 3–12.

18. TNA, FO 195/2304, No. 78, Samson to Lowther, December 31, 1909.

19. TNA, FO 195/2239, Nos. 61–62, Samson to O'Conor, December 31, 1907.

20. Dimitris Livanios argues that, ironically, ethnic identity among Balkan Christians was often forged by ethnic cleansing: "Beyond 'Ethnic cleansing': Aspects of the Functioning of Violence in the Ottoman and Post-Ottoman Balkans," *Southeast European and Black Sea Studies* 8, no. 3 (2008): 189–203. See also: İpek Yosmaoğlu, *Blood Ties: Religion, Violence, and the Politics of Nationhood in Ottoman Macedonia, 1878–1908* (Ithaca, 2014).

21. For a study of Thracian refugees in Bulgaria—and their descendants—see: Valentina Ganeva-Raycheva, "Migration, Territories, Heritage: Discourses and Practices in Constructing the Bulgarian-Turkish Border," in *Migration, Memory, Heritage: Socio-cultural Approaches to the Bulgarian-Turkish Border*, ed. Valentina Ganeva-Raycheva and Meglena Zlatkova (Sofia, 2012), 29–64.

22. Joel S. Migdal, "Mental Maps and Virtual Checkpoints: Struggles to Construct and Maintain State and Social Boundaries," in *Boundaries and Belonging: States and Societies in the Struggle to Shape Identities and Local Practices*, ed. Joel S. Migdal (Cambridge, 2004), 3–23.

23. AAIU, Turquie II. C., David Levy, July 22, 1913.

24. "Albert Alfassa," *La Boz de la Verdad*, July 27, 1914, 1.

25. For additional problems with the term "bystanders," see Bartov and Weitz, "Introduction: Coexistence and Violence," 12.

26. For just one example of historians using the phrase, see Stephan H. Astourian and Raymond H. Kévorkian, eds., *Collective and State Violence in Turkey: The Construction of a National Identity from Empire to Nation-state* (New York, 2021).

27. For a survey of Tukish Jewish during the first decades of the Republican period, see Rıfat N. Bali, *Cumhuriyet Yıllarında Türkiye Yahudileri: Bir Türkleştirme Serüveni, 1923–1945* (Istanbul, 1999).

28. The specific documents are cited throughout this book, but the general files are: AAIU, Turquie, XI E, Moise Mitrani; and AAIU, Turquie, XII E, Moise Mitrani.

29. Hasan Adnan Önelçin, *Trakya Basını* (Tekirdağ, Turkey, 1972), 26; Ender Bilar, *Edirne'nin Basın-Yayın Tarihi, 1361–2006*, Vol. 1 (Edirne, 2006), 105; Also see the mastheads of these newspapers. Initially, Razon printed *La Boz de la Verdad* with one Yaakov Levi: Gad Nassi, *Jewish Journalism and Printing Houses in the Ottoman Empire and Modern Turkey* (Istanbul, 2001), 32.

30. I am guided by Salo Baron's critique of the "lachrymose conception of Jewish history," but also by Adam Teller's call for the "balanced re-insertion of hatred, persecution, and violence as factors in the way 'normal' Jewish life is understood in its various historical settings": "Revisiting Baron's 'Lachrymose Conception': The Meanings of Violence in Jewish History," *AJS Review* 38, no. 2 (November 2014): 439. For a critical history of friendship narratives coproduced by Sephardi Jews and the late-Ottoman state, see Julia Phillips Cohen, *Becoming Ottomans: Sephardi Jews and Imperial Citizenship in the Modern Era* (Oxford, 2014).

31. For the purposes of this book, borderlands must be near *state* borders. Domestic frontiers that were "pockets of transformation within the Ottoman provinces" and the "internal borders" of modern Turkey are both fascinating topics, but they are inherently different from what I am studying. For those themes, see Chris Gratien, *The Unsettled Plain: An Environmental History of the Late Ottoman Frontier* (Stanford, 2022), 14; and Zeynep Kezer, "Spatializing Difference: The Making of an Internal Border in Early Republican Elazığ, Turkey," *Journal of the Society of Architectural Historians* 73, no. 4 (December 2014): 507–27.

32. In 1986, the Association for Borderlands Studies began publishing the *Journal of Borderland Studies*. One year later, Gloria Anzaldúa's landmark book was published: *Borderlands/La Frontera: The New Mestiza* (San Francisco, 1987). Another key text is Oscar J. Martinez, *Border People: Life and Society in the U.S.-Mexico Borderlands* (Tucson, 1994). While these works all deal with the modern period, an important study of early-modern borderlands is Peter Sahlins, *Boundaries: The Making of France and Spain in the Pyrenees* (Berkeley, 1989).

33. For the early-modern period, see Maria Baramova et al., eds., *Bordering Early Modern Europe* (Wiesbaden, 2015); and Jovan Pešalj et al., eds., *Borders and Mobility Control in and*

between Empires and Nation-States, ed. Jovan Pešalj (Leiden, 2023). For the modern period, see Bartov and Weitz, eds., *Shatterzone of Empires*; Matthew H. Ellis, "Over the Borderline? Rethinking Territoriality at the Margins of Empire and Nation in the Modern Middle East (Parts I and II)," *History Compass* 13, no. 8 (2015): 411–34; Tejel and Öztan, eds., *Regimes of Mobility*; and Ebru Boyar and Kate Fleet, eds., *Borders, Boundaries and Belonging in Post-Ottoman Space in the Interwar Period* (Leiden, 2023).

34. Furthermore, European borderlands often had large Christian populations marked by ethno-linguistic diversity and ambiguity: Philipp Ther, "Caught in Between: Border Regions in Modern Europe," in *Shatterzone of Empires,* 485–502.

35. Ussama Makdisi, *Age of Coexistence: The Ecumenical Frame and the Making of the Modern Arab World* (Oakland, 2019); and Sara Pursley, "'Lines Drawn on an Empty Map': Iraq's Borders and the Legend of the Artificial State" (Parts 1 and 2), *Jadaliyya* https://www.jadaliyya.com/Details/32140.

36. Oscar J. Martinez, *Border People,* 5. Martinez himself recognizes this on page xviii.

37. Ther, "Caught in Between," 487. Ther also uses the term "lands in between."

38. Linda T. Darling, "The Mediterranean as a Borderland," *Review of Middle East Studies* 46, no. 1 (Summer 2012): 58. Darling paraphrases Martinez.

39. Martinez, *Border People,* xvii.

40. Tejel and Öztan, "Borders of Mobility? Crime and Punishment along the Syrian-Turkish Border, 1921–1939," in *Borders, Boundaries and Belonging,* 211; Anzaldúa, *Borderlands,* 3.

41. The quote is from BOA. HR. SYS., 2267/87, April 12, 1918. All other examples are discussed and cited in subsequent chapters.

42. Martinez, *Border People,* xix.

43. Michiel Baud and Willem Van Schendel, "Toward a Comparative History of Borderlands," *Journal of World History* 8, no. 2 (Fall, 1997): 211–42. See also Bogdan G. Popescu, *Imperial Borderlands: Institutions and Legacies of the Habsburg Military Frontier* (Cambridge, 2024).

44. Kemal H. Karpat, "Comments on Contributions and the Borderlands," in *Ottoman Borderlands: Issues, Personalities and Political Changes,* ed. Kemal H. Karpat and Robert W. Zens (Madison, 2003), 1–12.

45. Technically, between the provinces of Edirne and Istanbul was the independent *sancak* of Çatalca. But this tiny district often functioned as an extension of Istanbul.

46. Hans-Lukas Kiesler, *Talaat Pasha: Father of Modern Turkey, Architect of Genocide* (Princeton, 2018), 32–33, 47, 108, 193, 321; Erik-Jan Zürcher, "The Young Turks: Children of the Borderlands?" in *Ottoman Borderlands,* 275–85.

47. In the wake of World War I, British diplomat George Curzon (Lord Curzon) euphemistically called for the "unmixing of peoples" across Ottoman domains. Such projects began in Edirne as early as 1912.

48. Eyal Ginio, "Constructing a Symbol of Defeat and National Rejuvenation: Edirne (Adrianople) in Ottoman Propaganda and Writing during the Balkan Wars," in *Cities into*

Battlefields: Metropolitan Scenarios, Experiences and Commemorations of Total War, ed. Goebel and Keene (Burlington, 2011), 83–99.

49. Oscar J. Martinez, "The Dynamics of Border Interaction: New Approaches to Border Analysis" in *Global Boundaries*, vol. 1, ed. Clive H. Schofield (New York, 1994), 6.

50. Anzaldúa, *Borderlands/La Frontera*, 77.

51. More broadly, I agree with Sarah Abrevaya Stein's claim: "At its core, Ottoman Jewish identity was not plural but self-consciously 'Jewish.'": "The Permeable Boundaries of Ottoman Jewry," in *Boundaries and Belonging*, 49–70, 51–52.

52. Compare Paul Nugent's claim that, in contrast to North America, "European border regions have generally combined dense settlement with the lack of a well-defined borderland identity": "Border Towns and Cities in Comparative Perspective," in *A Companion to Border Studies*, ed. Thomas M. Wilson and Hastings Donnan (Malden, 2012), 564.

53. For example: "Un Kapitan Bulgaro Pasos [sic] en Frontyera," *La Boz de la Verdad*, January 11, 1912, 3. In his Ladino-French dictionary, Joseph Nehama simply defines *frontéra/frontyéra* as "frontière." More interestingly, he notes the Ladino expression "meterse a la frontera," meaning "s'exposer au danger": *Dictionnaire du Judéo-Espagnol* (Madrid, 1977), 218.

54. In the early twentieth century, there was ambiguity in the villages of Edirne Province regarding Greek versus Bulgarian identity: Paraskevas Konortas, "Nationalism vs Millets: Building Collective Identities in Ottoman Thrace," in *Spatial Conceptions of the Nation: Modernizing Geographies in Greece and Turkey*, ed. P. Nikiforos Diamandouros et al. (London, 2010), 170, 177; and Vemund Aarbakke, "Urban Space and Bulgarian-Greek Antagonism in Thrace, 1870–1912," in *Balkan Heritages: Negotiating History and Culture*, ed. Maria Couroucli and Tchavdar Marinov (Burlington, 2015) 29–44. Bartov and Weitz note that levels of ethno-religious ambiguity varied greatly across different borderlands: *Shatterzone of Empires*, 7–8.

55. Anzaldúa, *Borderlands/La Frontera*, 3.

56. Zürcher argues that, for the dozens of Balkan Muslims who went on to lead the Young Turk movement, the experience of borderland violence hardened their Muslim identity (even if it failed to increase their religiosity): Zürcher, "The Young Turks," 275–85.

57. For articles published in Edirne about the Muslims of Bulgaria, see "Bulgaristan Havâdisi," *Yeni Edirne*, February 8, 1909, 2; "Bulgaristan Müslümanlarının Ahvali," *Âfitab*, July 25, 1910, 4; and "Bulgaristan Müslümanlarının Ahvali," *Âfitab* August 1, 1910, 3. After the Balkan Wars, Turkish writers in Istanbul and other cities would (unfavorably) compare the Ottoman Empire to Bulgaria: Eyal Ginio, *The Ottoman Culture of Defeat*. This is yet another trait that eventually came to characterize Istanbul and Anatolia but appeared first in Edirne.

58. Jeremy Adelman and Stephen Aron, "From Borderlands to Borders: Empires, Nation-States, and the Peoples in between in North American History," *American Historical Review* 104, no. 3 (June, 1999): 814–41.

59. Until the early twentieth century, empires tended to be more concerned with the demographics of the capital than the demographics of the borderland. For example, Sultan Abdülhamid II prohibited certain categories of people from entering Istanbul, and the Russian tsars restricted Jewish access to Saint Petersburg (and other cities). For more on the Hamidian restrictions, see İlkay Yılmaz, *Ottoman Passports: Security and Geographic Mobility, 1876–1908* (Syracuse, 2023), 168–72.

60. Ebru Boyar and Kate Fleet, "Introduction," in *Borders, Boundaries and Belonging in Post-Ottoman Space in the Interwar Period*, ed. Ebru Boyar and Kate Fleet (Leiden, 2023), 2.

61. Bartov and Weitz, "Introduction," *Shatterzone of Empires*.

62. In the Russian border town of Vilna, *maskilim* writing in Hebrew for *HaCarmel* (1860–1880) compared Jewish life on the Russian and Prussian sides of the border. In Lyck, Prussia (today Elk, Poland) *maskilim* writing for *HaMagid* (1856–1890) did the same. In both newspapers, Prussia was usually compared favorably to Russia. I am grateful to Gabriella Safran for pointing this out to me. Also, Derek Penslar notes that *HaMagid* was "intended for a Russian market," even though it was published in Prussia: "Introduction: The Press and the Jewish Public Sphere," *Jewish History* 14, no. 1 (2000): 4.

63. I exclude Western Europe from this discussion, as that region had a unique set of dynamics. For a study of a borderland community in Western Europe, see Vicki Caron, *Between France and Germany: The Jews of Alsace-Lorraine, 1871–1918* (Stanford, 1988).

64. Grodno was another city in Russian *Lite* that became part of Poland after World War I. In Vilna and Grodno, Jewish merchants suddenly had to survive without the Russian market—and with a slew of discriminatory laws. Shmuel Spector and Bracha Freundlich, *Lost Jewish Worlds: The Communities of Grodno, Lida, Olkieniki, Vishay* (Jerusalem, 1996), 37–46. For more on the disintegration of *Lite*, see Bemporad, *Becoming Soviet Jews*, 21, 50.

65. Habsburg Czernowitz became Romanian Chernivtsi in 1918, but many local Jews continued to speak German and identify with Viennese high culture. Marianne Hirsch and Leo Spitzer, *Ghosts of Home: The Afterlife of Czernowitz in Jewish Memory* (Berkeley, 2010), 72–98; In addition to a pro-Austrian bourgeoisie, the Jewish community of Trieste also included pro-Italian irredentists. John McCourt, *The Years of Bloom: James Joyce in Trieste, 1904–1920* (Madison, 2000), 217–38; and Ira B. Nadel, *Joyce and the Jews: Culture and Texts* (Iowa City, 1989), 198–207.

66. Halina Dudala, "Jews in Upper-Silesian Grammar Schools in the Second Half of the Nineteenth and Early Twentieth Century," in *Jews in Silesia*, ed. Marcin Wodinski and Janusz Spyra (Krakow, 2001), 79–97. The Jewish Theological Seminary in Breslau was established in 1854, and the Higher Institute for Jewish Studies in Berlin was founded in 1870. Also see Aleksandra Namyslo, "The Religious Life of Katowice Jews in the Inter-War Period," in *Jews in Silesia*, 125–38.

67. The situation was not finalized until the Polish-Soviet War ended in 1921.

68. Nesi Altaras, "The Jews of Van-Urmia: Remembering Borderland Migrations (1914–18)," *Jewish Social Studies: History, Culture, Society* 28, no. 1 (Winter 2023): 79–115.

69. Alexander V. Prusin, "A 'Zone of Violence': The Anti-Jewish Pogroms in Eastern Galicia in 1914–1915 and 1941," in *Shatterzone of Empires*, 362–77; Eric Lohr, "The Russian Army and the Jews: Mass Deportation, Hostages, and Violence during World War I," *Russian Review* 60, no. 3 (July, 2001): 404–19.

70. Jeffrey Veidlinger, *In the Midst of Civilized Europe: The Pogroms of 1918–1921 and the Onset of the Holocaust* (New York, 2021), 9.

71. Bemporad, *Becoming Soviet Jews*, 2–7, 30, 212–13.

72. It was the 1917 Balfour Declaration that spoke of "the establishment in Palestine of a national home for the Jewish people."

73. On Zionist migration as a response to poverty, see Gur Alroey, *An Unpromising Land: Jewish Migration to Palestine in the Early Twentieth Century* (Stanford, 2014).

74. Admittedly, the history of cultural Zionism complicates this statement. Steven J. Zipperstein, *Elusive Prophet: Ahad Ha'am and the Origins of Zionism* (Berkeley, 1993).

75. Esther Benbassa and Aron Rodrigue, *Sephardi Jewry: A History of the Judeo-Spanish Community, 14th–20th Centuries* (Berkeley, 2000), 121–30, 142; and Aron Rodrigue, "From *Millet* to Minority: Turkish Jewry," in *Paths of Emancipation: Jews, States, and Citizenship*, ed. Pierre Birnbaum and Ira Katznelson (Princeton, 2014), 254–55.

76. With that said, similar situations could emerge in other postimperial borderlands. Writing about interwar Czechoslovakia, Tatjana Lichtenstein claims that "Zionism was not an exit strategy for Jews, but a ticket of admission to the societies in which they already lived." *Zionists in Interwar Czechoslovakia: Minority Nationalism and the Politics of Belonging* (Bloomington, 2016), 3.

77. When I speak of a Jewish "community," sometimes I refer to the supercommunity of Edirne province, and other times I refer to one of the subcommunities (for example, the subcommunity of Kırklareli, Dimetoka, or the city of Edirne).

78. Of course, "political" is not synonymous with "state-centered." Bernard Yack argues that even Aristotle understood "politics" to mean not just the affairs of the state but also reasoned discourse (*logos*) on topics related to justice. *The Problems of a Political Animal: Community, Justice, and Conflict in Aristotelian Political Thought* (Berkeley, 1993), 51–85.

79. Pamela Dorn Sezgin, "Maftirim Choir," *Encyclopedia of Jews in the Islamic World Online*.

80. Tamir Karkason, "Printing and Modernity: The Activities of the Dorshei Ha-Haskalah Association ('Seekers of the Enlightenment,' 1879–1889) to Revive Hebrew-Alphabet Printing in Edirne," *Ladinar: Studies in the Literature, Music & the History of the Sephardic Jews* 11 (2020): 131–54; and Tamir Karkason, "Maskilic Families in the Ottoman Empire," *Journal of Jewish Studies* 74, no. 2 (2023): 429–54.

81. For efforts by Turkish elites to securitize and "reborder" Thrace in the interwar years, see Sertaç Şen, "Marshaling Development: Turkish Thrace in the Interwar Years," *Diyâr* 4, no. 2 (2023): 232–61.

82. For more on "Turkification" (*Türkleştirme*), see Rıfat Bali, *Bir Türkleştirme Serüveni*.

83. In Chapter 3, I explain my use of the phrase "eye of the storm."

Chapter 1

1. Serbia was a widely recognized entity at the time, but it did not achieve official independence from the Ottoman Empire until 1878.

2. And in at least one case, the local Ladino press used the adjective *Edirneliya* to describe a Jewish girl from Edirne: "Una Ninya Djudya Edirneliya de 14 Anyos Violada por Dos Mansevos en Tatar-Bazardjik," *La Boz de la Verdad*, July 9, 1914, 1.

3. In his periodization scheme, Erik J. Zürcher includes "The Young Turk Era in Turkish History (1908–50)." *Turkey: A Modern History* (London, 2017), v.

4. While many European countries liberalized domestic mobility after the French Revolution, the Russian and Ottoman Empires enforced internal passport regimes throughout the nineteenth century. From 1841 to 1910, the Ottomans required domestic travelers to carry a document known as a *mürûr tezkeresi*: Christoph Herzog, "Migration and the State: On Ottoman Regulations Concerning Migration since the Age of Mahmud II," in *The City in the Ottoman Empire: Migration and the Making of Urban Modernity*, ed. Ulrike Freitag et al. (London, 2011), 121, 130.

5. For more on migration checks and border controls in the dynastic states of Europe, see Jovan Pešalj et al., "Introduction," in *Borders and Mobility Control in and between Empires and Nation-States*, ed. Jovan Pešalj et al. (Leiden, 2023), 1–9.

6. Like international borders, the boundary between land and sea was also an important site of revenue collection for the state: "In the history of Ottoman customs regimes, the idea of the border referred primarily to the line between two states but secondarily to the line between land and sea": Mehmet Genç, *Osmanlı İmparatorluğu'nda Devlet ve Ekonomi* (Istanbul, 2013), 195.

7. An example of forthcoming work on late-Ottoman Edirne is the following: Pınar Odabaşı, "Ottoman Edirne in the Early 20th Century: War, Diplomacy and Violence in the Western Borderlands of the Empire on the Eve of the Nation-State," PhD diss., (University of Akron, forthcoming).

8. My approach here resonates with the following: Jordi Tejel and Ramazan Hakkı Öztan, "Introduction: Regimes of Mobility in Middle Eastern Borderlands, 1918–46," in *Regimes of Mobility: Borders and State Formation in the Middle East, 1918–1946*, ed. Jordi Tejel and Ramazan Hakkı Öztan (Edinburgh, 2022), 1–25.

9. Similarly, in her study of the Jewish community in late-Ottoman Izmir, Dina Danon sees "socioeconomic factors as primary agents of change": *The Jews of Ottoman Izmir: A Modern History* (Stanford, 2020), 5–6.

10. Today, the term *economic warfare* is usually associated with interstate conflict, but I extend it to include intercommunal conflict. Indeed, the contemporary Ladino press spoke of *"guerra komersyala"* between ethno-religious communities. "Ismirna: El Boykotaje," *El Tiempo*, March 20, 1914.

11. Edward J. Erickson, *Defeat in Detail, The Ottoman Army in the Balkans, 1912–1913* (Westport, 2003), 15–21.

12. Kemal H. Karpat, "Comments on Contributions and the Borderlands," in *Ottoman Borderlands: Issues, Personalities and Political Changes*, ed. Kemal Karpat and Robert W. Zens (Madison, 2003), 1–12.

13. 1906–1907 Ottoman Census, from Kemal H. Karpat, *Ottoman Population, 1830–1914: Demographic and Social Characteristics* (Madison, 1985), 168. Edirne Province was home to 618,604 Muslims, 340,908 Greeks, 119,476 Bulgarians, 26,144 Armenians, 23,839 Jews, 3,386 Romani, and 563 foreign citizens.

14. Yunus Uğur, "Edirne," *Encyclopedia of the Ottoman Empire*, ed. Gábor Ágoston and Bruce Alan Masters (New York, 2009), 195–97.

15. Amy Singer, "Enter, Riding on an Elephant: How to Approach Early Ottoman Edirne," *Journal of the Ottoman and Turkish Studies Association* 3, no. 1 (May 2016): 89–109.

16. Gürer Karagedikli, "In Search of a Jewish Community in the Early Modern Ottoman Empire: The Case of Edirne Jews (c. 1686–1750), master's thesis (Bilkent University, 2011), 65–67, 114–17. The Turkish words *kazzaz*, *bezzaz*, and *çukacı* refer to people who deal in silk, cloth, and broadcloth, respectively.

17. Karagedikli, "In Search of a Jewish Community," 18.

18. Donald Quataert, *Ottoman Manufacturing in the Age of the Industrial Revolution* (Cambridge, 1993), 34; Angelos A. Chotzidis, "The Impact of the Ottoman Public Debt Administration on the Economies of Epirus, Macedonia and Thrace: A Preliminary Approach" (unpublished conference paper), 4. The Meriç River is known as the Evros, in Greek.

19. The month-long fair was drawing fifty thousand visitors by 1849. Kadir Arslanboğa, "Osmanlı Devleti'nde Uluslararası Bir Fuar: Uzuncaabad-Hasköy Panayırı'nın 1769 ile 1818 Yıllarına ait Gümrük Gelirleri," in *Uluslararası Sosyal Araştırmalar Dergisi* 8, no. 36 (February 2015): 774–86. See also Charles Issawi, *The Economic History of Turkey, 1800–1914* (Chicago, 1980), 143–45.

20. Issawi, *The Economic History of Turkey*, 118–20, 178; *Edirne İl Yıllığı: Edirne Vilâyet Sâlnâmesi H.1319-M.1901* 2 (Edirne, 2014), 216.

21. Çağlar Keyder, *State and Class in Turkey: A Study in Capitalist Development* (London, 1987), 32–33; Issawi, *The Economic History of Turkey*, 143–45, 151.

22. Uğur, "Edirne," *Encyclopedia of the Ottoman Empire*.

23. This happened in 1858: Chotzidis, "The Impact of the Ottoman Public Debt Administration," 4–5.

24. AAIU, France, XVI. F. 27, Samuel Loupo, October 24, 1886; Mihail Macarov, "A Pilgrimage Sixty Years Ago." In this 1929 document, the Bulgarian Orthodox author recalls a pilgrimage from Plovdiv to Jerusalem that his family made in 1868. The document was translated from Bulgarian to Turkish and published in *Bulgar Gözüyle Edirne*, ed. Hüseyin Mevsim (Istanbul, 2012), 24.

25. Sam Levy, "Andrinopole," *La Epoka*, August 17, 1900, 5–6.

26. Issawi, *The Economic History of Turkey*, 118–20.

27. Haluk Kayıcı, *Salnamelere Göre İdari, Sosyal ve Ekonomik Yapısıyla Edirne Sancağı* (Edirne, 2013), 224–26; Osman Nuri Peremeci, *Edirne Tarihi* (Edirne, 2011), 316–18. The

Russians won some commercial advantages under the 1829 Treaty of Edirne, but far more significant were the advantages secured by Great Britain in the 1838 Treaty of Baltalimanı. Issawi, *The Economic History of Turkey*, 233.

28. Mehmet Genç, *Osmanlı İmparatorluğu'nda Devlet ve Ekonomi* (Istanbul, 2013), 194–200. The typical Ottoman subject had to pay a domestic tariff equal to 12 percent of the merchandise's value.

29. Joseph G. Rahme, "Namık Kemal's Constitutional Ottomanism and Non-Muslims," *Islam and Christian-Muslim Relations* 10, no. 1 (1999): 23–39; Petko Slaveykov's Bulgarian-language account of Edirne appeared in an Istanbul publication in 1873. A Turkish-language translation is found in Mevism, *Bulgar Gözüyle Edirne*, 32.

30. Karpat, *Ottoman Population*, 117.

31. For a historiographical discussion of this term, see Tom Papademitriou, *Render unto the Sultan: Power, Authority, and the Greek Orthodox Church in the Early Ottoman Centuries* (Oxford, 2015), 19–62.

32. Anthim I, the first holder of this office, was born in Kırklareli in 1816: Mercia MacDermott, *A History of Bulgaria, 1393–1885* (New York, 1962), 166. An English translation of the *firman* is available in Stojan M. Protić, *The Aspirations of Bulgaria* (London, 1915), 245–49.

33. Thomas A. Meininger, *Ignatiev and the Establishment of the Bulgarian Exarchate: 1864–1872* (Madison, 1970), 126–31; Ümit Eser, *Nationalist Schism in the Empire: Tanzimat Reforms and the Establishment of the Bulgarian Exarchate* (Istanbul, 2019), 157–65; Vemund Aarbakke, "Urban Space and Bulgarian-Greek Antagonism in Thrace, 1870–1912," in *Balkan Heritages: Negotiating History and Culture*, ed. Maria Couroucli and Tchavdar Marinov (Burlington, 2015), 36–37.

34. Bulgarian speakers affiliated with the patriarchate were classified by the Ottomans as *Rum*, not *Bulgar*. Paraskevas Konortas, "Nationalist Infiltrations in Ottoman Thrace (ca. 1870–1912): The Case of the *Kaza* of Gumuljina," in *State-Nationalisms in the Ottoman Empire, Greece, and Turkey: Orthodox and Muslims, 1830–1945*, ed. Benjamin C. Fortna et al. (New York, 2013), 73–100.

35. At least one hundred thousand Muslims and a few thousand Jews fled the Principality of Bulgaria and the Province of Eastern Rumelia to settle in the truncated Edirne Vilayet. At least twenty thousand Christians made the opposite migration. Justin McCarthy, *Death and Exile: The Ethnic Cleansing of Ottoman Muslims, 1821–1922* (Princeton, 1995), 86–91. Also see Kemal H. Karpat, "Jewish Population Movements in the Ottoman Empire, 1862–1914," in *Studies on Ottoman Social and Political History: Selected Articles and Essays*, ed. Kemal H. Karpat (Leiden, 2002), 404–9.

36. The Ottomans acknowledged the fait accompli soon after. Raymond Detrez, *Historical Dictionary of Bulgaria* (London, 1997), 173. Interestingly, from 1878 to 1885, Eastern Rumelia's chief trading partner was the Ottoman Empire, *not* Bulgaria. "Trade Notes," *The Economist Monthly Trade Supplement*, October 10, 1885, 8–9.

37. Maps from 1892 depict Eastern Rumelia as a distinct entity. Maps from 1900 depict the region as part of Bulgaria.

38. Before 1885, the Ottomans had no customshouses on the border of Eastern Rumelia. "The Turkish Customs Duties," *The Economist*, May 10, 1884, 6–7. "The border which separated the Ottoman Empire from Eastern Rumelia, especially in the section between Edirne and the Black Sea, was hardly guarded" in the period 1878–1885. Dimitar Voinikov, *The Bulgarians in the Easternmost Part of the Balkan Peninsula—Eastern Thrace* (Sofia, 2014), 100. Also see "The Roumelian Customs Question," *The Economist*, March 20, 1886, 365; Theodore Bent, "Baron Hirsch's Railway," *Fortnightly Review* XLIV, new series, (July 1–December 1, 1888): 229–34; Hasan Ünal, "Ottoman Policy during the Bulgarian Independence Crisis, 1908–9: Ottoman Empire and Bulgaria at the Outset of the Young Turk Revolution," *Middle Eastern Studies* 34, no. 4 (October 1998): 135–76.

39. "Bulgaria, though under the suzerainty of the Sultan, possesses, like Egypt, the right and powers to conclude commercial agreements with foreign Powers." "The Balkan Crisis," *The Economist*, December 12, 1885, 1507–8. The period 1870–1914 is sometimes called the "first globalization." Thomas Piketty, *Capital in the Twenty First Century* (Cambridge, 2014), 36–37.

40. In the early nineteenth century, the city of Edirne's population of about one hundred thousand began to fall. Issawi, *The Economic History of Turkey*. In the late nineteenth century, the population figure began to rise again, returning to one hundred thousand by 1912. From 1893 to 1907, no group in the province grew by a faster rate than the Jewish community (74 percent). Karpat, *Ottoman Population*, 122–69.

41. Chotzidis, "The Impact of the Ottoman Public Debt Administration," 5–6. For a new study of the *Düyun-u Umumiye-i Osmaniye Varidat-ı Muhassasa İdaresi* (as it was called in Turkish), see Emre Can Dağlıoğlu, "Silk-Made Capitalism: Local Networks and Financial Control in the Late Ottoman Empire," PhD diss. (Stanford University, forthcoming).

42. AAIU, Turquie, XI. E., Mitrani, March 5, 1906; AAIU, Turquie, I. H., Cercle Israélite to Paris, May 31, 1908. Only the Italian synagogue survived the fire.

43. Between 1886 and 1889, the Ottoman Empire was the largest purchaser of Bulgarian exports and a significant seller to the Bulgarian market. "The Trade of Bulgaria," *The Economist Monthly Trade Supplement*, December 10, 1886, 6; "The Trade of Bulgaria," *The Economist Monthly Trade Supplement*, August 16, 1890, 5.

44. From 1879 to 1885, certain textiles were traded between the two countries duty-free. Similar terms were established in a trade deal effective 1900–1910. Circa 1900, Bulgaria and the Ottoman Empire charged each other tariffs of 8 percent on textiles and agricultural products. That was the same low rate they applied to imports from the Great Powers. Michael Palairet, *The Balkan Economies c. 1800–1914* (Cambridge, 1997), 196; and George Young, *Corps de droit Ottoman: Recueil des codes, lois, règlements, ordonnances et actes les plus importants du droit intérieur, et d'études sur le droit coutumier de l'Empire Ottoman* 3 (Oxford, 1906), 411–12. In 1907, the Ottomans eliminated an import duty on Bulgarian wheat. TNA, FO 371/581, Inclosure in No. 1, Samson to O'connor, December 31, 1907.

Bulgaria raised its general import tariff in 1906 to protect domestic industry, while the Ottomans raised theirs in 1907 to pay off the Ottoman public debt. John R. Lampe and Marvin R. Jackson, *Balkan Economic History, 1550–1950* (Bloomington, 1982), 265; and Issawi, *The Economic History of Turkey*, 76.

45. Smugglers often used paths in the Strandzha (Istranca) Mountains that straddled the border near the Black Sea. Voinikov claims that Bulgarian Christians were especially familiar with these paths, in *The Bulgarians*, 100–102. For an example of Jewish smuggling, see Erol Haker, *Once Upon a Time Jews Lived in Kırklareli: The Story of the Adato Family, 1800–1934* (Istanbul, 2003), 219.

46. BOA DH.MKT: Yer Bilgisi 842-28, Görüntü Sayısı 42, April 15, 1904; BOA DH.MKT: Yer Bilgisi 1146-5, Görüntü Sayısı 29, February 10, 1907; BOA HR.SFR.04: Kutu 397, Gömlek 56, March 26, 1906. Ottoman documents refer to this tax as the *"zimmet-i emiriye,"* a name that betrays what everyone knew: it was a tax on non-Muslims.

47. "A Los Viajeros para la Bulgarya," *La Boz de la Verdad*, September 14, 1911, 2.

48. These were efforts to combat cholera and Macedonian terrorists, respectively. "Sobre la Linya de Salonika," *La Boz de la Verdad*, September 11, 1911, 1.

49. İlkay Yılmaz, *Ottoman Passports: Security and Geographic Mobility, 1876–1908* (Syracuse, 2023), 168–72.

50. TNA, FO 195/2211, No. 1, Townshend to O'conor, January 1, 1906.

51. Voinikov, *The Bulgarians*, 191. Bulgarians expelled from the empire in 1903 were later granted amnesty and allowed to return to Edirne. TNA, FO 195/2211, No. 4, Townshend to O'conor, January 5, 1906.

52. TNA, FO 195/2239, Nos. 61–62, Samson to O'Conor, December 31, 1907.

53. Anna M. Mirkova, *Muslim Land, Christian Labor: Transforming Ottoman Imperial Subjects into Bulgarian National Citizens, 1878–1939* (Budapest, 2017), 192. Ottoman taxation authorities also applied a guarantor system to Armenians who left Eastern Anatolia for the Russian Empire. Sinan Dinçer, "An Exclusionary Border Regime: The Ottoman Case, 1890–1914," in *Borders and Mobility Control in and Between Empires and Nation-States*, ed. Jovan Pešalj et al. (Leiden, 2023), 184–218.

54. Herzog, "Migration and the State," 129–31.

55. For more on the Oriental Railway (also known as the Chemins de fer Orientaux), see Matthias Lehmann, *The Baron: Maurice de Hirsch and the Jewish Nineteenth Century* (Stanford, 2022); and Kurt Grunwald, *Türkenhirsch: A Study of Baron Maurice de Hirsch, Entrepreneur and Philanthropist* (Jerusalem, 1966).

56. Peter F. Sugar, "Railroad Construction and the Development of the Balkan Village in the Last Quarter of the 19th Century," in *Nationality and Society in Habsburg and Ottoman Europe* (Brookfield, 1997), 485–98. In the Balkans, a weak Ottoman Empire (as opposed to independent nation-states) served the interests of European railroad companies and "other corporations that sought the convenience of a single market with guaranteed low customs tariffs." Şükrü Hanioğlu, *A Brief History of the Late Ottoman Empire* (2008), 206.

57. In January 1907, officials in the Bulgarian State Railways organized a strike to demand higher wages. Inspired, employees of the Oriental Railway soon formed a union. Their counterparts at the Anatolian Railway followed suit in 1908 and, on the heels of the Young Turk Revolution, staged a strike in Istanbul. In turn, this prompted the Oriental Railway strike. Donald Quataert, *Social Disintegration and Popular Resistance in the Ottoman Empire, 1881–1908: Relations to European Economic Penetration* (New York, 1983), 71–93.

58. Bulgaria's declaration of independence had major consequences regarding repayment of the Ottoman public debt. "Corporation of Foreign Bondholders (Great Britain)," *Annual Report of the Council of the Corporation of Foreign Bondholders* 38, Year 1911 (London: Wertheimer, Lea and Co., 1911), 49–50.

59. Charles S. Maier, "Consigning the Twentieth Century to History: Alternative Narratives for the Modern Era," *American Historical Review* 105, no 3 (June 2000): 808.

60. Maier, "Consigning the Twentieth Century to History," 820.

61. Ünal, "Ottoman Policy during the Bulgarian Independence Crisis," 166; R. J. Crampton, *A Concise History of Bulgaria* (Cambridge, 2005), 118–31. By controlling the rail lines, Bulgaria could periodically stop the Ottomans from receiving livestock, grain, and the rolling stock itself. TNA, FO 195/2305, No. 9, Samson to Lowther, February 9, 1909. Bulgaria's declaration of independence also led to stronger enforcement of quarantines at the border. AAIU, Turquie, XI. E., Mitrani, November 3, 1911.

62. Aksel Erbahar, "Edirne (Adrianople)," in *Encyclopedia of Jews in the Islamic World*, ed. Norman A. Stillman (First published online 2010). Also see Esther Benbassa and Aron Rodrigue, *Sephardi Jewry: A History of the Judeo-Spanish Community, 14th–20th Centuries* (Berkeley, 2000), 5–6.

63. Karagedikli, *In Search of a Jewish Community*, 34. These names are my translations. In Ottoman records from 1703, the names were Budin, Alaman, Sisilya, Italya, Polya, Portagal, Küçük Portagal, Katalan, Toledo, Aragon, Mayor, İstanbul, Gerush.

64. Circa 1912, there were 150 Jewish families in Karaağaç. AAIU, Turquie XII. E., Mitrani, July 29, 1912. See also AAIU, Turquie XI. E., Mitrani, June 15, 1910; *Almanach Israelite 5688* (Thessaloniki), 113, from Jewish Museum of Greece Collection, inv.no.1981.091.1.

65. Florian Riedler, "Building Modern Infrastructures on Ancient Routes: Road and Rail Development in 19th-Century Edirne," in *The Heritage of Edirne in Ottoman and Turkish Times: Continuities, Disruptions and Reconnections*, ed. Birgit Krawietz and Riedler (Berlin, 2020), 460–63.

66. Avigdor Levy, "The Siege of Edirne (1912–1913) as Seen by a Jewish Eyewitness: Social, Political, and Cultural Perspectives," in *Jews, Turks, and Ottomans: A Shared History, Fifteenth through the Twentieth Century*, ed. Avigdor Levy (Syracuse, 2002), 156; *Bulletin de l'Alliance Israélite Universelle*, Troisième Série, No. 38 (1913): 131; Bekir Sıtkı Baykal says that the city of Edirne's population circa 1912 was 106,000: *Edirne'nin Uğramış Olduğu İstilâlar* (Ankara, 1965), 187. Rıfat Osman says that "before the Balkan Wars" Edirne was home to 47,289 Muslims, 19,608 Greek Orthodox, 14,469 Jews, 4,000 Armenians, and 2,324 Bulgarian Orthodox, in *Edirne Rehnüması* (Edirne, 2013), 46. The 1901 Salname for Edirne

Province counted the following for the city of Edirne: 26,547 Muslims, 15,952 Greeks, 8,033 Jews, 3,650 Armenians, 2,525 Bulgarians, 63 Protestants, and 43 Bulgarian Catholics, in *Edirne İl Yıllığı* 2, 223. M. Tayyib Gökbilgin says that at the start of the twentieth century, Edirne was home to 47,000 Muslims, 20,000 Greeks, 15,000 Jews, 4,000 Armenians, and 2,000 Bulgarians, in "Edirne," *The Encyclopaedia of Islam*, ed. Bearman et al. (Leiden, 2002).

67. For Salonica, see *A Jewish Voice from Ottoman Salonica: The Ladino Memoir of Sa'adi Besalel a-Levi*, ed. Aron Rodrigue and Sarah Abrevaya Stein (Stanford, CA: Stanford University Press, 2012), xiii-lx. For Izmir, see Dina Danon, *The Jews of Ottoman Izmir: A Modern History* (Stanford, 2020), 35–59.

68. Rifat Osman, *Edirne Rehnüması*, 57–70. Also see https://www.edirne.bel.tr/sayfa/edirne-belediye-binasi

69. The church burnt down in 1907. Aarbakke, "Urban Space and Bulgarian-Greek Antagonism," 33.

70. Eyal Ginio, "Challenging Communal Boundaries in Late Ottoman Thrace: Jews and Muslims in Dimetoka (Didymoteicho)," *Jewish Social Studies* 27, no. 3 (Fall 2022): 110.

71. The fact that the Jewish community did not fit perfectly into the province resonates with Samuel Dolbee's warning against giving too much weight to *vilayet* boundaries, in *Locusts of Power: Borders, Empire, and Environment in the Modern Middle East* (Cambridge, 2023), 12.

72. Sultan Mehmet IV (r. 1648–1687) forcibly moved Ashkenazi Jews from Poland to Kırklareli. Avram Galanté, *Türkler ve Yahudilar: Tarihi, Siyasi araştırma* (Istanbul, 1995), 24. Haker mentions a rabbinic responsum between the Edirne chief rabbi and the rabbi in Kırklareli from about 1760. Haker, *Once Upon a Time*, 277; The Jewish presence in Dimetoka was ancient. Bracha Rivlin, *Pinkas ha-kehillot: Yavan* (Jerusalem, 1998), 86–90. Jews had been in Çorlu since the sixteenth century and in Tekirdağ and Lüleburgaz since the seventeeth. *Almanach Israelite 5688*, 106–18.

73. Around the time of the Napoleonic Wars, many Edirne Jews migrated north and "strengthened" the Jewish communities of Bulgaria and the Danube region. Solomon Abraham Rosanes, *Korot ha-Yehudim b'Turkiya u-b'Artzot ha-Kedem* 6 (Jerusalem, 1930–1945), 109–42. In 1801, a new congregation was formed in Rusçuk (today Ruse, Bulgaria). Many members, including the rabbi, were from Edirne. "Bekemoharar," *Encyclopaedia Judaica*, ed. Michael Berenbaum and Fred Skolnik, vol. 3 (Macmillan Reference USA, 2007), 273–74. For the origins of the Jewish community of Mustafapaşa, see AAIU, Turquie, XI. E., Mitrani, April 19, 1910. For the origins of the Jewish community of Gümülcine, see AAIU, Bulgarie, XXXV. E., Josef Barishac, September September 28, 1901. Even long-established Jewish communities like the one Dimetoka benefited from the arrival of Jewish merchants from the city of Edirne. Ginio, "Challenging Communal Boundaries," 95.

74. AAIU, Turquie XI. E., Mitrani, August 25, 1910.

75. McCarthy, *Death and Exile*, 86–89; Karpat, "Jewish Population Movements," 404–9; *Almanach Israelite 5688*, 117–18.

76. *Almanach Israelite 5688*, 173, 119, 173. The Jewish community in Bulgarian Karaağaç was founded in 1916 under unique circumstances. See Ch. 3 and *Almanach Israelite 5688*, 113–14.

77. Karpat, *Ottoman Population*, 162–69. These statistics downplay the extent to which Jews settled beyond the city of Edirne, because the central *sancak* included smaller towns such as Dimetoka and Mustafapaşa.

78. Nissim Eliezer Djivri, "Korespondensia," *El Tiempo*, May 5, 1904. From Ginio, "Challenging Communal Boundaries," 96.

79. AAIU, Turquie XI. E., Mitrani, April 19, 1910, and September 29, 1910.

80. M. Mitrani, "Correspondencia de Kırklareli," *La Boz de Türkiye*, July 1, 1944, 366–67; *Annuiare Oriental* 29 (1909), 1722–29; and Haker, *Once Upon a Time*, 274.

81. AAIU, Turquie, XI. E., Mitrani, April 19, 1910, and September 29, 1910; Karpat, *Ottoman Population*, 166–67.

82. "Notas de Viaje: Kirkilisse-Demotika," *La Boz de la Verdad*, September 2, 1912, 3. The article also described the communities of Dimetoka and Kırklareli as "model communities."

83. For more on describing Sephardi centers as "mother" cities, see Devin Naar, "The 'Mother of Israel' or the 'Sephardi Metropolis'? Sephardim, Ashkenazim, and Romaniotes in Salonica," *Jewish Social Studies* 22, no. 1 (Fall 2016), 81–129.

84. *Bulletin de l'Alliance Israélite Universelle*, Troisième Série, No. 33 (1908): 168; Karpat, *Ottoman Population*, 166–67.

85. AAIU, Turquie, XI. E., Mitrani, August 25, 1910.

86. "Los Komunidades del Vilayet de Edirne," *La Boz de la Verdad*, September 28, 1911, 1; "Chorlu," *La Boz de la Verdad*, November 16, 1911, 1; "Letra de Chorlu," *La Boz de la Verdad*, September 2, 1912.

87. "Dédéagatch," *Encyclopaedia Britannica* 7 (1911); Riedler, "Building Modern Infrastructures," 460. The fastest route from Salonica to Istanbul was to take a train to Dedeağaç and then proceed by boat. CAHJP, TR/Ed/66: *Istanbul Kalendaryo, 5666–5667* (1906).

88. Karpat, *Ottoman Population*, 166–67.

89. About 82 percent of Gümülcine *sancak*'s population was Muslim. Karpat, *Ottoman Population*, 166–67

90. AAIU, Bulgarie, XXV. E., Josef Barishac, September 28, 1901.

91. Yitzchak Kerem, "Xanthi," *Encyclopaedia Judaica*, 257–59; Yitzchak Kerem, "Serres (Siroz)," *Encyclopedia of Jews in the Islamic World*; Dimitrios N. Kasapidis, "Traces and Memories of the Jewish Presence in Xanthi."

92. *Bulletin de l'Alliance Israélite Universelle*, Troisième Série, No. 33 (1908): 168; Karpat, *Ottoman Population*, 166–67; Leah Bornstein-Makovetsky, "Gallipoli," *Encyclopaedia Judaica*, 350–51.

93. Rosanes, *Korot ha-Yehudim b'Turkiya u-b'Artzot ha-Kedem* 5 (Jerusalem, 1938), 389–410.

94. The first chief rabbi of Bulgaria was elected in 1889. Avraam Moshe Tadjer, *Notas istorikas sovre los djudyos de Bulgaria i la komunita de Sofya* (Sofia, Bulgaria: 1932), 63, in

Amor Ayala, *Los sefardíes de Bulgaria: Estudio y edición crítica de la obra "Notas istorikas" de Avraam Moshe Tadjer* (Berlin, 2017). See also Aksel Erbahar, "Edirne", *Encyclopedia of Jews in the Islamic World*; Leah Bornstein-Makovetsky, "Geron (Gueron) Family," *Encyclopedia of Jews in the Islamic World*; Yaron Ben Naeh, "Bekemoharar Family," *Encyclopedia of Jews in the Islamic World*; Simon Marcus et al., "Edirne," *Encyclopaedia Judaica* 6, 148–50; and Simon Marcus et al., "Bekemoharar," *Encyclopaedia Judaica* 3, 273–74.

95. Karpat, *Ottoman Population*, 166–67.

96. The chief rabbi also oversaw the ritual of *halitzah,* which absolves a childless widow of the obligation to marry her late husband's brother. Rosanes, *Korot ha-Yehudim* 5, 389–91.

97. Haker, *Once Upon a Time*, 295. Haker claims that Jewish merchants sometimes stayed overnight in Turkish-Muslim villages and, in some cases, had romantic relationships with local women.

98. Chotzidis, "The Impact of the Ottoman Public Debt Administration," 4–6. Also, a significant portion of cocoons produced in Edirne Province were sent to Ottoman Bursa.

99. *Annuaire oriental du commerce de l'industrie de l'administration et de la magistrature* 29 (1909): 1710–51. However, at least one Jewish-owned *kozahane* was built in Kaleiçi after the 1905 fire. Cennet Emekci, *Kozahane ve İpek Fabrikaları Üzerine Bir Araştırma: Edirne Kozahane Restorasyonu*, master's thesis (Trakya University, 2011), 1, 72.

100. These three families seem to have rented the filatures from a European owner, at least initially. *Annuaire oriental* 29 (1909): 1714, 1747; Kayıcı, *Salname Göre*, 236; Chotzidis, "The Impact of the Ottoman Public Debt Administration," 10; Issawi, *The Economic History of Turkey*, 254, 313. In 1934, Edirne member of parliament Mehmet Şeref Aykut wrote that the Pappo family "took the millions they made in Turkey over to Italy, where they established a silk factory." He added, "The Azarias, with the waterwheel they turned in the Fındıklıyan mill, nicely fleeced the people during the Balkan Wars and the World War. They brought their stolen money to Florence, Paris, and Rome, where some of them purchased large hotels and others became bankers." This anti-Jewish letter is discussed in Rıfat Bali, *Edirne Mebusu Mehmet Şeref Aykut'un Munis Tekinalp'e Mektubu* (Istanbul, 2023).

101. Chotzidis, "The Impact of the Ottoman Public Debt Administration," 10.

102. Ali Çakır, "Kırklareli/Pavli Panayırından Kakava Şenliklerine Yaşamı Kutlarken," in *Rakı Gastronomisi: Türkiye'nin Cilingir Sofrasi* (Istanbul, 2017).

103. *Edirne İl Yıllığı* 2, 269–329; "Notas de Viaje: Ksanti," *La Boz de la Verdad*, September 7, 1911, 1.

104. *Edirne İl Yıllığı* 2, 330–51; "Notas de Viaje: En Sofuli," *La Boz de la Verdad*, September 4, 1911, 2. Also, twice a year villagers flocked to the port of Tekirdağ, where they sold local agricultural products and purchased "colonial goods." Voinikov, *The Bulgarians*, 6, 55–58. For the situation in 1892, see Kayıcı, *Salname Göre*, 242–47.

105. For Bulgarian-Christians raising livestock, see Voinikov, *The Bulgarians*, 5, 10.

106. "Jewish Enlightenment and Nationalism in the Ottoman Balkans: Barukh Mitrani in Edirne in the Second Half of the Nineteenth Century," in *Minorities in the Ottoman Empire*, ed. Molly Greene (Princeton, 2005), 129–41.

107. *Bulletin de L'Alliance Israélite Universelle*, Troisième Série, No. 37 (1912): 99–128.

108. However, Alliance networks were hardly effective in connecting local Jews to their coreligionists in Bulgaria, a country from which the Franco-Jewish organization had been mostly ousted by Zionists. For an overview of the Alliance's activities in Southeast Europe, see Aron Rodrigue, *French Jews, Turkish Jews: The Alliance Israélite Universelle and the Politics of Jewish Schooling in Turkey, 1860–1925* (Bloomington, 1990).

109. The line to Salonica was completed in 1896 by the Compagnie du Chemin de Fer Ottoman Jonction Salonique-Constantinople. The line to Plovdiv was completed in 1873 by the Chemins de fer Orientaux. The latter was led by Baron Maurice de Hirsch, a German Jew who also founded the Jewish Colonization Association and donated large sums to the Alliance. See Lehmann, *The Baron*.

110. Another consequence of the railroads was economic ruin for peasants in the new Balkan nation-states. Sugar, "Railroad Construction," 492–97.

111. For a historiographical take on the concept of "Balkanization," see Maria Todorova, *Imagining the Balkans* (Oxford, 2009), 21–37.

112. Edirne was underdeveloped even compared to Izmir, Istanbul, and especially Salonica. That city provided thread to the commercial weavers of Edirne. Quataert, *Ottoman Manufacturing*, 45.

113. Most of these facilities were operated by Ottoman Christians and geared toward the domestic market. Quataert, *Ottoman Manufacturing*, 90; *Annuaire oriental* 32 (1912): 1417, 1560, 1622, 1679; Kayıcı, *Salname Göre*, 236–38. Additionally, several towns had tanneries and at least two had small distilleries: *Annuaire oriental* 29 (1909): 1713, 1726, 1728, 1740. A cottage industry for wool cloth—the coarse *aba* and the finer *şayak*—remained strong into the early twentieth century and was mostly geared toward domestic buyers, including the Ottoman army. Quataert, *Ottoman Manufacturing*, 49–50, 85, 97.

114. *Annuaire oriental* 29 (1909): 1710–51; Quataert, *Ottoman Manufacturing*, 85–86; CAHJP, TR/Ed/272: Letter from the chief rabbi of Edirne to the chief rabbi of the Ottoman Empire certifying the kosher status of cheese produced by local Jews, July 1893.

115. Issawi, *The Economic History of Turkey*, 341; *Annuaire oriental* 29 (1909): 1710–51.

116. AAIU, Turquie, VI. E. Report of the School Committee, March 13, 1913.

117. *Annuaire oriental* 29 (1909): 1710–51. More anecdotally, see Haker, *Once Upon a Time*, 112. When Greeks began leaving the province in 1914, European diplomats noted that this "element" had dominated local commerce. TNA, FO 195/2456, No. 17, Samson to Mallet, March 31, 1914, and No. 36, Samson to Mallet, June 30, 1914.

118. In most towns, Greeks outnumbered Jews in categories such as cloth sellers, silk and silk cocoon dealers, wine and rakı makers/vendors, and cheese makers/vendors. For the unusual situation in Dimetoka, see *Annuaire oriental* 29 (1909): 1748–50, and *Annuaire oriental* 32 (1912): 1557–60.

119. My sources for this rough calculation are *Annuaire oriental* 29 (1909): 1710–51; AAIU, Turquie XI. E. Mitrani, December 21, 1908; and Karpat, *Ottoman Population*, 162–69.

120. Literally, *meclis-i cismani* means "lay council." The term was used in contradistinction to *meclis-i ruhani*, meaning "spiritual/religious council." The city of Edirne's "lay council" was created in 1860—five years before Istanbul's, ten years before Salonica's, and twenty-four years before Izmir's. *Almanach Israelite 5688*, 99; Devin Naar, *Jewish Salonica: Between the Ottoman Empire and Modern Greece* (Stanford, 2016), 40; Danon, *The Jews of Ottoman Izmir*, 152.

121. *Annuare Oriental* 33 (1913): 1800; AAIU, Turquie VI. E. 100a, Bidjarano and Papo, September 3, 1912 (signed by Halfon) and August 20, 1912 (signed by Pappo).

122. Merchants Jacques Behmoiras and Nissim Benbassat both served as presidents of both organizations. See Chapter 2.

123. "Los Komunidades del Vilayet de Edirne," *La Boz de la Verdad*, September 28, 1911, 1; *Annuaire oriental* 32 (1912): 1915–18. The president of the communal council in Dedeağaç was a "Sr. Salinas" who worked for the Oriental Railway Company, while his counterpart in Gümülcine was Saltiel Carasso, whose family was prominent in local commerce. *Annuaire oriental* 32 (1912): 1548, 1619–22.

124. In 1911, the Second Army moved its headquarters from Edirne to Salonica, and Edirne Province fell into the zone of the First Army, headquartered in Istanbul. Within the First Army, the 2nd Corps was headquartered in Tekirdağ, the 3rd Corps in Kırklareli, and the 4th Corps in Edirne. Erickson, *Defeat in Detail*, 24–33, 371–75.

125. "Avizos: Kuatren Kol Ordu Imperyal," *La Boz de la Verdad*, November 30, 1911, 2.

126. TNA, FO 195/2364, No. 13, Samson to Lowther, March 2, 1911, and No. 38, Von Hersfeldy to Lowther, June 14, 1911.

127. TNA, FO 371/581, Inclosure in No. 1, Samson to O'connor, December 31, 1907.

128. "Kirklisse," *La Boz de la Verdad*, August 28, 1911, 1; Haker, *Once Upon a Time*, 283; Karpat, *Ottoman Population*, 162–69.

129. AAIU, Turquie, XI. E., Mitrani, April 19, 1910. He added that Jewish merchants in Mustafapaşa "travel to remote Bulgarian Orthodox villages where residents are hostile to outsiders."

130. AAIU, Turquie, XCV. E., Catalan, February 15, 1911; August 6, 1911; and August 28, 1911. Also see Erickson, *Defeat in Detail*, 24–33.

131. AAIU, Turquie, XI. E., Mitrani, August 25, 1910.

132. Locals told the functionary that "you couldn't find a single poor Jew in Çorlu." *Bulletin de la Grande Loge de District XI et de la Loge de Constantinople N. 678 I.O.B.B.*, Report by Dr. Israel Auerbach, delegate of Grand Lodge XI, on the earthquake of August 9, 1912, 36–49. In Gümülcine, the increased military presence seems to have been especially beneficial to Jews who traded in cereals and "colonial foodstuffs," which included sugar, spices, chocolate, and other products imported from European colonies. *Annuaire oriental* 29 (1909): 1717–19.

133. "Andrinopla: Ridikuliz-Evropiado," *La Boz de la Verdad*, September 4, 1911, 1.

134. Dina Danon, "Francos," *Encyclopedia of Jews in the Islamic World*.

135. Dina Danon says that in Izmir and other Ottoman port cities, a modern middle class emerged out of the "deliberate cultivation of discourses and practices meant to reinforce such [a bourgeois] identity," in *The Jews of Ottoman Izmir*, 19.

136. Jews who led a European bourgeois lifestyle tended to live in Karaağaç, where many Jewish children attended Catholic schools. There was talk of building a Jewish school there, affiliated with either the Alliance or the Hilfsverein der deutschen Juden, but the Balkan Wars scuttled those plans. "La Eskula de Kara-Ach," *La Boz de la Verdad*, August 21, 1911, 1; AAIU, Turquie, XII. E., Mitrani, March 25, 1912, and July 29, 1912.

137. AAIU, Turquie, VII. E., Guéron, October 4, 1912 (afternoon).

138. *Annuaire oriental* 29 (1909): 1710–51.

139. AAIU, Turquie XI. E., Mitrani, April 1, 1912. Additionally, 1 graduate was hired by an exporter of eggs, 1 was hired by the Alliance school in Monastir (today Bitola, North Macedonia), 4 boys went on to study at the Alliance teachers' training school in Paris, and 9 of the 25 graduates were unable to find work.

140. *Annuaire oriental* 29 (1909): 1710–51.

141. AAIU, Turquie XI. E., Mitrani, Modiano, and Rabbi Abraham Semach to JCA president, November 15, 1905.

142. For the city of Edirne, the 1909 *Annuaire oriental* lists a total of forty-one *manufactures, merciers*, and *quincailleries*, of whom seven had Jewish names but most had Armenian names. *Annuaire oriental* 29 (1909): 1715–16. Jewish men were more likely to work around the city as cloth dealers (*bezzaz*) than to have stalls in the *pazar*. The occupation of *bezzaz* had been associated with Jews since the seventeenth century. CAHJP, TR/Ed/341; Karagedikli, *In Search of a Jewish Community*, 114–17; Haker, *Once Upon a Time*, 39–44, 168–71. For an anecdote about a Jewish *bezzaz*, see "Tahsildar Model," *La Boz de la Verdad*, August 14, 1911, 2.

143. *American Jewish Yearbook 5674*, ed. Herbert Friedenwald and H. G. Friedman (Philadelphia, 1913), 203–4. The rest of the list is as follows: vegetable dealers (60), grocers (60), blacksmiths (60), colporteurs (50), dealers in grain (50), saloonists and distillers (50), retail dealers in groceries and drugs (50), shoemakers (40), brokers (40), rabbis (40), shoemakers (40), old clothes men (30), "batlanim" (30), wheelwrights (30), dealers in glass and crockery (30), employees in cheese factories (30), money changers (sarafs) (30), cap (fez) dealers (25), laundrymen (25), clothiers (25), wholesale merchants (20), barbers (20), tinners (20), cabinet makers (20), bankers (12), army contractors (10), apothecaries (10), moulders (10), confectioners (10), physicians and dentists (10).

144. Haker, *Once Upon a Time*, 285.

145. AAIU, Bulgarie XXV. E., Josef Barishac, September 28, 1901.

146. AAIU, Turquie, XCIII. E., Aron Halevy, August 22, 1907; AAIU, Turquie, XCIII. E., David Levy, May 12, 1911; *Bulletin de la Grande Loge de District XI*, Report by Dr. Israel Auerbach, August 9, 1912, 36–49.

147. In 1871, a resident of Tekirdağ predicted, rather accurately, that the Oriental Railway would turn his town into a mere "village port" (*kariye iskelesi*). Riedler, "Building Modern Infrastructures on Ancient Routes," 460.

148. AAIU, Turquie, XCIII. E., David Levy, May 12, 1911. Levy claimed that cholera outbreaks hit the Jews harder than any other community.

149. AAIU, France, XVI. F. 27, Mitrani, annual report, September 12, 1911.

150. Haker, *Once Upon a Time*, 284.

151. "Verso la Amerika," *La Boz de la Verdad*, September 2, 1912, 1. The article claimed that economically motivated emigration was most common in Çorlu and other towns, while young Jewish men in the city of Edirne were "timid to the bone" and preferred to stay put.

152. AAIU, Turquie, XCIII. E., David Levy, May 12, 1911.

153. Yavuz Selim Karakışla, "The 1908 Strike Wave in the Ottoman Empire," in *Turkish Studies Association Bulletin* 16, no. 2 (September, 1992): 166–167. In 1909, fifty-nine Bulgarian Christians and three Muslims staged a strike in Xanthi/İskeçe. İbrahim Yalımov, "The Bulgarian Community and the Development of the Socialist Movement in the Ottoman Empire During the Period 1876–1923," in *Socialism and Nationalism in the Ottoman Empire, 1876–1923*, ed. Mete Tunçay and Erik J. Zürcher (London, 1994), 93–94.

154. Stefo Benlisoy, *İstanbul'un Irgatları: II. Meşrutiyet'te Sosyalist Bir İşçi Örgütü* (Istanbul, 2018); Naar, *Jewish Salonica*, 22; Paul Dumont, "A Jewish, Socialist, and Ottoman Organization: The Workers' Federation of Salonica," in *Socialism and Nationalism*, 49–75. Still, compared to the Russian Revolution of 1905 and the Iranian Revolution of 1905–1911, socialism played a relatively small role in the Young Turk Revolution. Houri Berberian, *Roving Revolutionaries: Armenians and the Connected Revolutions in the Russian, Iranian, and Ottoman Worlds* (Oakland, 2019), 29.

155. Yalımov claims that "Bulgarian socialists were . . . active in Macedonia and the vicinity of Edirne," and that "national minorities had formed separate or joint socialist groups in Istanbul, Edirne, Izmir and other industrial cities." He adds that workers in Edirne, Istanbul, Salonica, and Köprülü (today Veles, North Macedonia) all celebrated May Day on May 1, 1911. "The Bulgarian Community," 94–95, 100.

156. AAIU, Turquie, XI. E., Mitrani, January 18, 1910; *Annuaire oriental* 29 (1909): 1710–51; Quataert, *Ottoman Manufacturing*, 131. Attempts were made to create sewing workshops where students from the Alliance girls' school could bring their skills to a more professional level, but by 1910 Alliance leadership in Paris had given up on funding such programs: AAIU, Turquie, XI. E., Mitrani, February 1, 1910; Rodrigue, *French Jews, Turkish Jews*, 108–10.

157. "Konversyon Eskandaloza," *La Boz de la Verdad*, October 19, 1911, 1.

158. For conditions in the silk-reeling factories of Bursa, see Dağlıoğlu, "Silk-Made Capitalism."

159. "Una Ninya Djudya Edirneliya de 14 Anyos Violada por Dos Mansevos en Tatar-Bazardjik," *La Boz de la Verdad*, July 9, 1914, 1.

160. "El Orfilinato," *La Boz de la Verdad*, December 28, 1911, 2; "Orfilinato," *La Boz de la Verdad*, January 1, 1912, 1.

161. Also, the Alliance ran coeducational schools in Dimetoka, Gelibolu, Gümülcine, and Tekirdağ. *Bulletin de L'Alliance Israélite Universelle*, Troisième Série, No. 37 (1912): 99–128.

162. Derek J. Penslar, *Shylock's Children: Economics and Jewish Identity in Modern Europe* (Berkeley, 2001), 6.

163. Danon, *The Jews of Ottoman Izmir*, 17.

164. A society of this nature was founded in 1884, even before the Alliance arrived in Dimetoka. Aron Rodrigue, "Jewish Society and Schooling in a Thracian Town: The *Alliance Israélite Universelle* in Demotica, 1897–1924," *Jewish Social Studies* 45, no. 3/4 (1983): 275.

165. Rodrigue, *French Jews, Turkish Jews,* 100–102, 121; AAIU, Turquie, XI. E., Mitrani, June 28, 1904.

166. The group included joiners, cabinetmakers, turners, house painters, chest makers, blacksmiths, stove makers/tinsmiths, metal casters, mechanics, cartwrights, brush makers, carpenters, and carpetmakers. Rodrigue, *French Jews, Turkish Jews,* 106.

167. AAIU, Turquie XII. E., Mitrani, January 12, 1912.

168. Issawi, *The Economic History of Turkey*, 38, 204. Meanwhile, agricultural wages rose sharply around 1911, prompting landlords in Edirne Province to replace farmhands and sickles with oxen and binders.

169. AAIU, Turquie, X. E., Loupo, September 7, 1902. Presumably these were attempts to form short-term *ortaklık* (partnership) contracts, which were common in Edirne. Issawi, *The Economic History of Turkey*, 208.

170. AAIU, Turquie, X. E., Loupo, March 25, 1901. Indeed, land prices in rural Edirne dropped sharply in the late nineteenth century. Issawi, *The Economic History of Turkey*, 207.

171. AAIU, Réponses, 132, Leven's response to Loupo's letter dated March 25, 1901. Ultimately, the Alliance supported one small Jewish agriculture project in Edirne: In 1906, it lent six thousand francs to Albert Haim Navon and his son, who had graduated from the school in Djedeida. The Navons used the funds to start one asparagus garden in Karaağaç and one in Edirne. In 1910, they sold one of these to Joseph Jacob Pappo. AAIU, Turquie XI. E., Mitrani, April 20, 1906; AAIU, Turquie, XIII. E., A. Haim Navon, May 8, 1909, and November 12, 1910.

172. BOA DH.İD, Yer Bilgisi 8–7, Görüntü Sayısı 21, July 7, 1911.

173. Ginio, "Challenging Communal Boundaries," 92; Taylan Esin, "19; Yüzyılın Sonunda Osmanlı İmparatorlu'nda Kurulan Musevi İskan Birliği (JCA) Çiftlikleri," *Toplumsal Tarih* no. 249 (September 2014): 22–33. The vice-president of the JCA at the time was the Belgian-Jewish banker Franz Philippson.

174. Esin, "19. Yüzyılın Sonunda," 22–33.

175. For apprenticeship programs in the Ottoman Empire, see Rodrigue, *French Jews, Turkish Jews*, 107.

176. Karpat, *Ottoman Population*, 223; Tevfik Güran, ed., *Osmanlı Dönemi Tarım İstatistikleri 1909, 1913 ve 1914* (Ankara, 1997), 25–81.

177. AAIU, Turquie, V. E., Benforado, July 26, 1882.

178. Hafız Rakım Ertür, "Eski Esnaf Loncaları," *Yeni Edirne Gazetesi*, June 1, 1951; AAIU, Turquie, V. E., Benforado, October 28, 1881. In small towns such as Dimetoka, non-Jewish masters hesitated to take on Jewish apprentices. Rodrigue, "Jewish Society and Schooling in a Thracian Town," 275.

179. Compare the situation among German Jews discussed by Penslar in *Shylock's Children*, 1–9, 124–26. For this "materialist" way of thinking among Russian Jews, see Eliyahu Stern, *Jewish Materialism: The Intellectual Revolution of the 1870s* (New Haven, 2018).

180. TNA, FO 195/2239, no. 42, Samson to O'Conor, July 1, 1907.

181. Paraskevas Konortas, "Nationalism vs Millets: Building Collective Identities in Ottoman Thrace," in *Spatial Conceptions of the Nation: Modernizing Geographies in Greece and Turkey*, ed. P. Nikiforos Diamandouros et al. (London, 2010), 170, 177.

182. Aarbakke, "Urban Space and Bulgarian-Greek Antagonism," 35.

183. At least, this was the start date in Edirne. In Izmir, Jews had been boycotted as early as 1897, when war between Greece and the Ottoman Empire prompted some local Orthodox Greeks to shun Jewish businesses: Danon, *The Jews of Ottoman Izmir*, 14.

184. TNA, FO 195/2270, no. 68, Samson to Lowther, September 30, 1908.

185. Aron Rodrigue, *Jews and Muslims: Images of Sephardi and Eastern Jewries in Modern Times* (Seattle, 2003), 234.

186. Y. Doğan Çetinkaya, *The Young Turks and the Boycott Movement: Nationalism, Protest and the Working Classes in the Formation of Modern Turkey* (London, 2014), 39–42, 55–79. Around this time, Muslims were migrating from Bulgaria to Edirne Province because, allegedly, they were being boycotted at village shops and told to leave: TNA, FO 195/2304, no. 22, Samson to Lowther, March 31, 1909.

187. TNA, FO 195/2270, no. 73, Samson, October 22, 1908. Arif Bey, deputy from Gümülcine, and Rıza Tevfik, deputy from Edirne, both signed public proclamations supporting the actions of Ottoman dockworkers. Çetinkaya, *The Young Turks and the Boycott Movement*, 64.

188. "Echos," *L'Aurore*, August 15, 1909, 3. The chief rabbi of Edirne was Abraham Semah.

189. A boycott committee was formed in Edirne, and threatening notices were posted to "the offices and shops of all Greek subjects in the town." TNA, FO 195/2335, no. 25, Samson, May 13, 1910, and no. 33, Samson to Lowther, June 29, 1910. See also Uğur Peçe, *Island and Empire: How Civil War in Crete Mobilized the Ottoman World* (Stanford, 2024).

190. Çetinkaya, *The Young Turks and the Boycott Movement*, 131. Ultimately, the Interior Ministry intervened on behalf of the miller, whose name was "Yani of Kırkkilise." Also see TNA, FO 195/2335, no. 53, Samson, October 17, 1910, and no. 54, Samson, October 20, 1910.

191. The same can be said for a subsequent boycott that targeted Orthodox Greeks after the Balkan Wars. Zafer Toprak, *Türkiye'de Ekonomi ve Toplum (1908–1950): Milli*

İktisat-Milli Burjuvazi (Istanbul, 1995), 107–11. For the term "Ottoman-Muslim nationalism," see Zürcher, *Turkey*, 116.

192. Ginio aptly uses the term "economic marginalization" to describe the incident. Eyal Ginio, *The Ottoman Culture of Defeat: The Balkan Wars and their Aftermath* (London, 2016), 223.

193. "Demotika: A la Atensyon del Gran Rabno de Turkya," *La Boz de la Verdad*, September 14, 1911, 1. Ten days prior, the newspaper had reported that the weekly bazaar in nearby Sofulu had been moved to Saturday and that certain parties were preventing the local Jewish community from buying land on which it hoped to build a school and cemetery. "Notas de Viaje: En Sofuli," September 4, 1911, 2.

194. "Demotika," *La Boz de la Verdad*, September 19, 1911, 2

195. "El Bazar en Demotika," *La Boz de la Verdad*, October 7 [*not* October 15], 1911, 2. The article contains an interview with the chief rabbi of Edirne, whom I quote.

196. "El Bazar de Demotika," *La Boz de la Verdad*, October 19, 1911, 2.

197. "El Bazar en Demotika," *La Boz de la Verdad*, October 29, 1911, 1. In Ladino, the town was called Demotika.

198. "El Bazar en Demotika," *La Boz de la Verdad*, October 29, 1911, 1; "El Bazar en Demotika," *La Boz de la Verdad,* January 1, 1912, 1.

199. "El Bazar en Demotika," *La Boz de la Verdad,* January 1, 1912, 1.

200. "El Bazar en Demotika," *La Boz de la Verdad* January 4, 1912, 1.

201. At some point after August 1909, the normal fair day had changed from Thursday to Tuesday. "En Syudad: El Bazar de Demotika de Nuevo en Shabbat," *La Boz de la Verdad*, July 9, 1914.

202. "Notas de Viaje: En Silivri," *La Boz de la Verdad*, August 26, 1912, 2; AAIU, Turquie, II. C., Catarivas Vitali, May 10, 1912.

203. "En Demotika," *La Boz de la Verdad*, March 12, 1914; "El Gran Rabbino de Turkía i la Komonidad de Demotika," *La Boz de la Verdad*, March 16, 1914; "En Demotika," *La Boz de la Verdad*, March 19, 1914; "El Bazar de Demotika de Nuevo en Shabbat," *La Boz de la Verdad*, July 9, 1914.

204. In January 1914, an Ottoman official urged the Jews of Çorlu to avoid stores owned by Greeks and Armenians. AAIU, Turquie, XCVI E, 1125.01: January 15, 1914. Meanwhile, tens of thousands of Orthodox Greeks were forced to flee Edirne Province in 1914 (see Chapter 3).

205. "En Demotika," *La Boz de la Verdad*, March 19, 1914; "En Syudad: El Bazar de Demotika," *La Boz de la Verdad*, July 13, 1914.

206. Ginio, *The Ottoman Culture of Defeat*, 214–23.

207. Also, when Bulgarian and Greek forces took Ottoman territory during the First Balkan War, they often changed the market day from Monday to Saturday, "to the great injury of the Jews." *American Jewish Yearbook* 5674, 192–93.

208. "El Bazar en Demotika," *La Boz de la Verdad*, January 1, 1912, 1.

209. Issawi, *The Economic History of Turkey*, 334.

210. When Jewish merchants were blocked from a silk cocoon fair in 1923, the results were similar. "Jews Persecuted in Turkey," *Jewish Chronicle*, July 18, 1923, 41.

211. For more on Dimetoka, see AAIU, Grèce, I. E. 12, Attié, January 9. 1912; Ginio, "Challenging Communal Boundaries"; and Rodrigue, "Jewish Society and Schooling in a Thracian Town," 267–68, 278.

212. Stern, *Jewish Materialism*, 7. Stern is describing Jews in the Russian Empire.

213. Compare what Karakışla says about strikes: "Political and nationalist demands and strikes against minorities did not exist in the 1908 Strike Wave; nationalist boycotts were a later development." "The 1908 Strike Wave," 167.

Chapter 2

1. AAIU, Turquie, I. B. 5.08, Rabbi Abraham Semach to Paris, September 4, 1905; AAIU, Turquie XI. E., Moise Mitrani, October 12, 1905. Houses that survived the fire became severely overcrowded, and in at least one case, "10 Jewish families [were] inhabiting the same house." TNA, FO 195/2211, No. 1, January 1, 1906, Townshend to O'Conor.

2. For a review of the literature on this period, see Nadir Özbek, "Modernite, Tarih ve İdeoloji: II. Abdülhamid Dönemi Tarihçiliği Üzerine Bir Değerlendirme," *Türkiye Araştırmaları Literatür Dergisi* 2, no. 1 (2004): 71–90.

3. Opened as a Talmud Torah, the school joined the Alliance network in 1906. By 1910, it enrolled 1,179 students—more than any other Alliance school: *Bulletin de l'Alliance Israélite Universelle*, Troisième Série, No. 35 (1910): 220–48. In 1905, Ottoman authorities used the new school building for an exposition showcasing local agriculture and manufacturing. AAIU, Turquie, XI. E., Mitrani, May 15, 1905, May 30, 1905, and November 8, 1905. For more on the history of the Alliance in Edirne, see Aron Rodrigue, "The *Alliance Israélite Universelle* and the Attempt to Reform Jewish Religious and Rabbinical Instruction in Turkey" in *L'"Alliance" dans les communautés du bassin méditerranéen à la fin du 19ᵉᵐᵉ siècle et son influence sur la situation sociale et culturelle,* ed. Simon Schwarzfuchs (Jerusalem, 1987), 56–61.

4. The girls' school in Edirne enrolled 551 students. Its counterparts in Galata and Tunis counted 671 and 553 students, respectively. *Bulletin de l'Alliance Israélite Universelle*, Troisième Série, No. 33 (1908): 151–76.

5. On the trend of neo-Moorish synagogue architecture, see John M. Efron, *German Jewry and the Allure of the Sephardic* (Princeton, 2016), 112–60. Some Jews continued to worship in improvised house-synagogues organized by occupation, including the Butchers' Congregation and the Tanners' Congregation. "En Siudad," *La Boz de la Verdad*, October 7, 1911, 2; "Djuzdan Askeri," *La Boz de la Verdad*, January 4, 1912, 2; AAIU, Turquie XII. E., Haim Aron Levy et al., March 25, 1912. For more on Edirne's Great Synagogue, see Roysi Ojalvo Kamayor, *Turkey's Jewish Heritage Revisited: Architectural Conservation and the Politics of Memory* (Istanbul, 2018), 97.

6. On the idea of the public sphere, see Jürgen Habermas, *The Structural Transformation of the Public Sphere: An Inquiry into a Category of Bourgeois Society* (Cambridge,

1991). On the idea of a "Jewish" or "national" public sphere, see Scott Ury, *Barricades and Banners: The Revolution of 1905 and the Transformation of Warsaw Jewry* (Stanford, 2012), 1–21, 141–71. For Ottoman public spheres, see Bedross Der Matossian, "Formation of Public Sphere(s) in the Aftermath of the 1908 Revolution among Armenians, Arabs, and Jews," *Faculty Publications, Department of History, University of Nebraska-Lincoln* (2012): 189–219.

7. On a more theoretical level, James J. Sheehan says it was no accident that constitutions and modern borders often appeared together. Both institutions limited state sovereignty, but in a way that ultimately served to validate it. "The Problem of Sovereignty in European History," *American Historical Review* 111, no. 1 (February 2006): 7–8.

8. For the Young Ottomans' "Ottoman territorial nationalism," see Joseph G. Rahme, "Namık Kemal's Constitutional Ottomanism and Non-Muslims," *Islam and Christian-Muslim Relations* 10, no. 1 (1999): 33.

9. Nicole M. Guidotti-Hernandez, "Borderlands Scholarship for the Twenty-First Century," *American Quarterly* 68, no. 2 (June, 2016): 488.

10. TNA, FO/195/2239, No. 62, Samson to O'Conor, December 31, 1907.

11. Milena B. Methodieva, "The Debate on Parliamentarism in the Muslim Press of Bulgaria, 1895–1908," in *The First Ottoman Experiment in Democracy*, ed. Christoph Herzog and Malek Sharif (Würzburg, 2010), 124–25. From his articles, it is clear that Edhem Ruhi saw Plovdiv as part of Bulgaria.

12. Methodieva, "The Debate on Parliamentarism," 126. The articles referenced were published in 1907 and 1908.

13. The Ottoman Constitution of 1876 used the word "*tabaiyet*" to refer to Ottoman citizenship/nationality and "*millet*" to refer to the officially recognized non-Muslim communities of the empire. https://www.anayasa.gov.tr/tr/mevzuat/onceki-anayasalar. As noted in Chapter 1, a historiographical piece on the idea of the *millet* can be found in Tom Papademitriou, *Render unto the Sultan: Power, Authority, and the Greek Orthodox Church in the Early Ottoman Centuries* (Oxford, 2015), 19–62.

14. For a famous articulation of modern nationalism, see Ernest Gellner, *Nations and Nationalism* (Ithaca,1983). For an overview of the literature on modern nationalism and its applicability to late-Ottoman Europe, see İpek Yosmaoğlu, *Blood Ties: Religion, Violence, and the Politics of Nationhood in Ottoman Macedonia, 1878–1908* (Ithaca, 2014), 1–18.

15. For an example from the Jewish community, see "En la Kapitala: El Mejlis Djismani," *La Boz de la Verdad*, September 11, 1911, 1.

16. Alp Eren Topal, "Ottomanism in History and Historiography: Fortunes of a Concept," in *Narrated Empires: Perceptions of Late Habsburg and Ottoman Multinationalism*, ed. Johanna Chovanec and Olof Heilo (Cham, 2021), 84.

17. Eyal Ginio, *The Ottoman Culture of Defeat: The Balkan Wars and their Aftermath* (London, 2016), 103–5.

18. Rahme, "Namık Kemal's Constitutional Ottomanism," 34.

19. Kemal H. Karpat, *Ottoman Population, 1830–1914: Demographic and Social Characteristics* (Madison, 1985), 168. The province was also home to 26,144 Armenians, mostly in the district of Tekirdağ.

20. For more on the creation of the Bulgarian *millet*, see Chapter 1.

21. See John Locke's "Second Treatise of Government," originally published in 1689. John Locke, *Two Treatises of Government*, ed. Peter Laslett (Cambridge, 1988).

22. M. Şükrü Hanioğlu, "The Second Constitutional Period, 1908–1918," in *Cambridge History of Turkey, Vol. 4: Turkey in the Modern World*, ed. Reşat Kasaba (Cambridge, 2008), 82. "The claim to rule on behalf of the people was no innovation, although the term employed, *hakimiyet-i milliye* (national sovereignty), was a new one coined by the CUP." Also see pages 109–10.

23. Hanioğlu, "The Second Constitutional Period," 82.

24. For more on the shortcomings of press freedom under the CUP, see İpek K. Yosmaoğlu, "Chasing the Printed Word: Press Censorship in the Ottoman Empire, 1876–1913," *Turkish Studies Association Journal* 27, no. 1 (2003): 15–49.

25. "En la Kamara: Los Djudyos, Un Chiko Insidente," *La Boz de la Verdad*, January 11, 1912, 2.

26. "Turkey," *The Jewish Chronicle*, November 5, 1909, 10. This deputy was Rıza Tevfik, who also visited both of Edirne's Alliance schools in 1909 and 1910. AAIU, Turquie, IV E., Angèle Algranti, September 15, 1909, and November 2, 1910. I am indebted to Louis Fishman for pointing me to articles about Rıza Tevfik in *The Jewish Chronicle*.

27. "Los Djudyos," *La Boz de la Verdad*, December 4, 1911, 1.

28. AAIU, France, XVI. F. 27., Sara Ungar to Paris, October 6, 1908.

29. TNA, FO 195/2270, No. 65, Samson to O'Conor, September 30, 1908.

30. TNA, FO 195/2270, No. 65, Samson to O'Conor, September 30, 1908.

31. "Bulgaristan'la Harb," *Yeni Edirne*, August 2, 1908, 1.

32. Hasan Ünal, "Ottoman Policy during the Bulgarian Independence Crisis, 1908–9: Ottoman Empire and Bulgaria at the Outset of the Young Turk Revolution," *Middle Eastern Studies* 34, no. 4 (October, 1998): 135–76; TNA, FO 195/2270, No. 70, Samson to Lowther, October 15, 1908, and No. 71, Samson to Lowther, October 17, 1908.

33. Furthermore, a string of wars that began in 1911 would spur the Ottoman Empire—and other states—to keep men of military age in the country by limiting the ability of citizens to travel abroad. David Gutman, "Travel Documents, Mobility Control, and the Ottoman State in an Age of Global Migration, 1880–1915," *Journal of the Ottoman and Turkish Studies Association* 3, no. 2 (November, 2016): 363–67.

34. TNA, FO 195/2270, No. 67, Samson to O'Conor, October 8, 1908, and No. 69, Samson to O'Conor, October 12, 1908. For more on Bulgaria's seizure of part of the Oriental Railway, see Chapter 1.

35. TNA, FO 195/2270, No. 95, Samson to O'Conor, December 31, 1908.

36. TNA, FO 195/2270, No. 72, Samson to O'Conor, October 20, 1908, No. 78, Samson to O'Conor, November 2, 1908, and No. 88, Samson to O'Conor, November 24, 1908.

37. TNA, FO 195/2239, No. 62, Samson to O'Conor, December 31, 1907; TNA, FO 195/2304, No. 22, Samson to Lowther, March 31, 1909; TNA, FO 195/2304, No. 78, Samson to Lowther, December 31, 1909; TNA, FO 195/2335, No. 17, Samson to Lowther, March 31, 1910; TNA, FO 195/2335, No. 34, Samson to Lowther, June 30, 1910. In early 1909, every week about 100 Muslim families from Bulgaria were settled in Gümülcine and Vize. By the end of 1909, local authorities had helped about 130 Muslim families settle in the district of Babaeski. In the first quarter of 1910, an additional 180 Muslim families migrated from Bulgaria to Edirne Province.

38. In the 1890s and early 1900s, "the Hamidian policy against Armenians, whether calculated or not, led to the depopulation" of parts of Eastern Anatolia. The Ottomans then did all they could to prevent the return of those Armenians who had crossed the border into Russia. Sinan Dinçer, "An Exclusionary Border Regime: The Ottoman Case, 1890–1914," in *Borders and Mobility Control in and between Empires and Nation-States*, 211–12.

39. TNA, FO 195/2335, No. 26, Samson to Lowther, May 17, 1910. Edirne's British consul was behind with his language. Around this time, British statemen were beginning to distinguish delimitation—defining a boundary on paper—from demarcation—the physical marking of a boundary on the ground. Dennis Rushworth, "Mapping in Support of Frontier Arbitration: Delimitation and Demarcation," *IBRU Boundary and Security Bulletin* (Spring 1997): 61–64. The word used by the local Ottoman-Turkish press was *tahdid*. "Yağmur," *Yeni Edirne*, May 16, 1910, 3.

40. TNA, FO 195/2335, No. 26, Samson to Lowther, May 17, 1910; Ünal, "Ottoman Policy," 135–76.

41. TNA, FO, 195/2335, No. 16, Samson to Lowther, March 29, 1910, No. 17, Samson to Lowther, March 31, 1910, and No. 67, Samson to Lowther, December 31, 1910.

42. AAIU, Turquie, XI. E., Mitrani, April 19, 1910.

43. The trade deal had been established in 1900. Michael Palairet, *The Balkan Economies c. 1800–1914* (Cambridge, 1997), 196; George Young, *Corps de droit Ottoman: Recueil des codes, lois, règlements, ordonnances et actes les plus importants du droit intérieur, et d'études sur le droit coutumier de l'Empire Ottoman* 3 (Oxford, 1906), 411–12.

44. "Turkiya i Bulgarya," *La Boz de la Verdad*, October 23, 1911, 3. The journalist cited the Bulgarian newspaper *Dnevnik*. Also see "Los Tratados de Komersyo," *La Boz de la Verdad*, September 7, 1911, 3; "En Bulgarya," *La Boz de la Verdad*, September 14, 1911, 3.

45. Habermas, *The Structural Transformation of the Public Sphere*, 51–56, 64.

46. As for the governing bodies of the Jewish *millet* in Istanbul, these saw contentious changes in personnel but not the radical realignment of power that occurred in the Armenian *millet*. Der Matossian, "Formation of Public Sphere(s)."

47. Hasan Kayalı, "Elections and the Electoral Process in the Ottoman Empire, 1876–1919," *International Journal of Middle East Studies* 27, no. 3 (August 1995): 265–86. In the Ottoman Empire, parliamentary elections occurred in 1877, 1908, 1912, 1914, and 1919.

48. The provinces of Istanbul, Salonica, Baghdad, and Aydın all sent Jews to parliament in the Second Constitutional Period. In each of the first four provinces, Jews constituted

more than 2 percent of the total population. In Aydın, Jews only constituted 2 percent of the population. Karpat, *Ottoman Population*, 168–69. More research must be done on why Aydın had a Jewish deputy while Edirne did not.

49. Regarding the municipal councils: the 1901 *Salname* (Yearbook) for Edirne Province shows a "Benaroya Efendi" on the council in Edirne, a "Yuda Efendi" on the council in Mustafapaşa, and a "Salomon Efendi" on the council in Kırklareli. *Edirne İl Yıllığı: Edirne Vilâyet Sâlnâmesi H.1319–M.1901* 2 (Edirne, 2014), 30, 83, 101. Rabbi Abraham Semah was among the 15 members of a 1901 "*İl Genel Meclisi*": *Edirne İl Yıllığı:* 12–14. Semah was also on the *vilayet idare meclisi* in 1909: "Echos," *L'Aurore*, August 15, 1909, 3. Also see Tetsuya Sahara, "The Ottoman City Council and the Beginning of the Modernization of Urban Space in the Balkans," in *The City in the Ottoman Empire: Migration and the Making of Urban Modernity*, ed. Urlike Freitag et al. (London, 2011), 34; and Yonca Köksal, "Local Demands and State Policies: General Councils (Meclis-i Umumi) in the Edirne and Ankara Provinces, 1867–1872," *Middle Eastern Studies* 53, no. 3 (2017): 470–85.

50. A Jew named Çelebi Behar Efendi became mayor of Kırklareli in 1907. Allen Upward, *The East End of Europe: A Report of an Unofficial Mission to the European Provinces of Turkey on the Eve of the Revolution* (New York, 1909), 123. A Jew named Avram Garten became Edirne's chief physician in 1908. Sezai Balcı and Ahmet Yadi, *Osmanlı Bürokrasisinde Yahudiler* (Istanbul, 2013), 84. Jews were also prominent in local chambers of commerce/agriculture. For Dimetoka, Kırklareli, and Çorlu, see *Edirne İl Yıllığı*, 87–88, 100, 161. For Edirne, see *Annuaire oriental du commerce de l'industrie de l'administration et de la magistrature* 29 (1909): 1712; and Haluk Kayıcı, *Salnamelere Göre Idari, Sosyal ve Ekonomik Yapısıyla Edirne Sancağı* (Edirne, 2013), 290.

51. AAIU, Turquie IV. E., Algranti, June 23, 1910; AAIU, Turquie VI. E. 100a, Bidjarano and Papo, August 20, 1912; *Annuaire oriental* 33 (1913): 1800.

52. "Il faute qu'une Synagogue soit ouverte ou fermée," *L'Aurore,* January 28, 1910, 3. He retired from the council at the end of 1911. "Demisyon," *La Boz de la Verdad*, December 11, 1911, 1.

53. AAIU, Turquie, I. B. 5.08, Abraham Semach, July 20, 1903.

54. AAIU, Turquie, XI. E., Moise Mitrani, July 12, 1909.

55. It was alleged that he acquiesced to the rescheduling of the Dimetoka livestock fair. "Echos," *L'Aurore*, August 15, 1909, 3. For more on that affair, see Chapter 1.

56. Der Matossian, "Formation of Public Sphere(s)," 206–7.

57. Rıfat N. Bali, *Cumhuriyet Yıllarında Türkiye Yahudileri: Bir Türkleştirme Serüveni, 1923–1945* (Istanbul, 2000), 95–112.

58. For an early example of Istanbul Zionists writing fondly of Bejarano, see "Communauté ideal," *L'Aurore*, November 18, 1910, 2. In 1920, Istanbul Zionists ousted Haim Nahum and replaced him with Bejarano (see Chapter 5).

59. "Le grand-rabbin Haim Béjarano," *L'Aurore*, August 30. 1918, 1–2; Marie-Cristine Varol-Bornes, "Un erudito entre dos lenguas: el 'castellano' de Hayim Bejarano en el prólogo

a su refranero glosado," in *Los sefardíes ante los retos del mundo contemporáneo: identidad y mentalidades,* ed. Paloma Díaz-Mas and María Sánchez Pérez (Madrid, 2010), 114.

60. Baruch Tercatin and Lucian-Zeev Herşcovivi, *Prezențe rabinice în perimetrul românesc: secolele XVI–XXI* (Bucharest, 2008), 92–94.

61. Joseph Niego, *Cinquante Années de Travail dans les œuvres Juives: Allocutions et Conférences* (Istanbul, 1933), 338–47.

62. "Lettre d'Andrinople," *L'Aurore,* November 11, 1910, 2. In 1913, Talat Bey became known as Talat Paşa.

63. For Ottoman Jews and the CUP, see Feroz Ahmad, "The Special Relationship: The Committee of Union and Progress and the Ottoman-Jewish Political Elite, 1908–1918," in *Jews, Turks, Ottomans: A Shared History,* ed. Avigdor Levy (Syracuse, 2002), 212–30.

64. AAIU, Turquie XI. E., Mitrani, February 8, 1910. When the sultan visited Salonica in 1911, the local chief rabbi also recited an Arabic prayer at an official event. Perhaps he was inspired by Bejarano, who was in Salonica at the time. Julia Phillips Cohen, *Becoming Ottomans: Sephardi Jews and Imperial Citizenship in the Modern Era* (Oxford, 2014), 111n56, 114–15.

65. Regarding *Alliance* school directors' "move toward the center," see Benbassa, "Associational Strategies in Ottoman Jewish Society in the Nineteenth and Twentieth Centuries," in *The Jews of the Ottoman Empire,* 466; and Aron Rodrigue, *French Jews, Turkish Jews: The Alliance Israélite Universelle and the Politics of Jewish Schooling in Turkey, 1860–1925* (Bloomington, 1990).

66. AAIU, Turquie, XI.E., Mitrani, December 22, 1905.

67. Guéron received an Alliance education in Istanbul before attending the Alliance teacher's training school in Paris. In 1904, she was sent to teach at the Alliance girls' school in Tunis, French Tunisia. In 1905, she taught at Alliance schools in Istanbul. She was in Haifa from 1906 to 1907. See the Alliance's historical database of personnel, http://www.archives-aiu.org/aiu/index.htm.

68. AAIU, Turquie, IV. E., Algranti, April 15, 1910; May 5, 1910; August 7, 1910; and November 2, 1910. The deputy was Rıza Tevfik Bey.

69. AAIU, Turquie, IV. E., Algranti, November 27, 1910.

70. AAIU, Turquie, IV. E, (Algranti file), Letter from Mitrani to Paris, March 26, 1910.

71. AAIU, Turquie, IV. E., Algranti, September 23, 1910.

72. *L'Aurore,* August 30. 1918, 2.

73. AAIU, Turquie, IV E, Algranti, March 15, 1910; August 24 and 30, 1911.

74. AAIU, Turquie, VI E 100a, Jacob Halfon to Paris, September 15, 1912; Haim Bejerano to Paris, September 16, 1912.

75. AAIU, Turquie, VII E, Avram Benbenisti, from Edirne to Paris, October 6, 1912. For more on Guéron, see Erol Haker, *Edirne, Its Jewish Community, and Alliance Schools, 1867–1937* (Istanbul, 2006).

76. AAIU, Turquie, IV. E., Algranti, May 11, 1910.

77. Gül Aldıkaçtı Marshall, *Shaping Gender Policy in Turkey* (Albany, 2013), 39–43.

78. While the first Ottoman constitution did not guarantee freedom of association, the 1908 constitution—with the modifications of August 1909—"guaranteed associative rights to Ottoman subjects, despite some restrictions." Esther Benbassa, "Associational Strategies," 463.

79. For an example of this narrow definition, see Ury, *Barricades and Banners*, 145.

80. Historically, Alliance institutions in the Ottoman Empire had "encouraged Jews to emulate not the culture of their region, but the culture of a far-away land," i.e., France. Sarah Abrevaya Stein, "Creating a Taste for News: Historicizing Judeo-Spanish Periodicals of the Ottoman Empire," *Jewish History* 14, no. 1 (2000): 11. But after 1908, some of Edirne's Alliance-affiliated clubs urged Jews to integrate into Turkish-speaking society.

81. Hebrew periodicals included *HaMagid* and *HaTsfira*. Rodrigue, "The *Alliance Israélite Universelle* and the Attempt to Reform," 63–64.

82. Among these rabbis was the proto-Zionist Barukh Mitrani. Niego, *Cinquante Années de Travail*, 346–47.

83. Abraham Danon's teacher was Joseph Halevy, who was probably from Hungary. Rodrigue, "Jewish Enlightenment and Nationalism in the Ottoman Balkans: Barukh Mitrani in Edirne in the Second Half of the Nineteenth Century," in *Minorities in the Ottoman Empire: A Reconsideration*, ed. Molly Greene (Princeton, 2005), 74. The term "renaissance" appears in Niego, *Cinquante Années de Travail*, 346. For more on Edirne's place in Haskalah networks, see Tamir Karkason, "Printing and Modernity: The Activities of the Dorshei Ha-Haskalah Association ('Seekers of the Enlightenment,' 1879–1889) to Revive Hebrew-Alphabet Printing in Edirne," *Ladinar: Studies in the Literature, Music & the History of the Sephardic Jews* 11 (2020): 131–54.

84. As late as 1892, Cercle Israélite was hosting events without fear of Hamidian censors (apparently). That year, Abraham Danon lectured to a mixed Jewish-Greek audience about ancient affinities between those two cultures. Tamir Karkason, "An Ambivalent Coexistence: Jews and Christians in Late Ottoman Edirne," *Jewish History* 38, nos. 1–2 (2024): 1–25. Far less political was the fundraiser Cercle Israélite threw 14 years later, for rebuilding the burnt-out Jewish quarter. But it was attended by a who's who of local society. AAIU, Turquie, XI. E., Mitrani, March 5, 1906. For more on Ottoman Jews and pre-1908 Ottomanism, see Cohen, "A Model *Millet*?," 216.

85. The merger occurred after the Balkan Wars (1912–1913): "Unyon i Fraternite: Konferensya echa por el Joven Sr. Izak Barishak, en la 'Fraternite' el Vyernes 17 Abril," *La Boz de la Verdad*, May 11, 1914, 1.

86. AAIU, Turqiue, XI. E., Mitrani, July 8, 1908, and February 21, 1910.

87. Eleven of the founding members were Muslim, five were Christian, and two were Jewish. Of the latter, one was the (unnamed) wife of a Kırklareli merchant named Bohor Mitrani. The other was Bakira Alguadesh, the wife of an Edirne merchant. *Yeni Harflerle Kadın: II. Meşrutiyet Döneminde bir Jön Türk Dergisi* (1908–1909), ed. Fatma Kılıç Denman (Istanbul, 2010), 228; "En Syudad: Orfilinato—Ha Kadosh Alguadesh Djenerozidad," *La Boz de la Verdad*, January 4, 1912, 1.

88. AAIU, Turquie, IV. E., Algranti, May 11, 1910, January 18, 1911, and March 28, 1911.

89. AAIU, France, XVI. F. 27, Sara Ungar, annual reports for the 1907–1908 and 1908–1909 school years.

90. "En Syudad: El Kresyente Korolado," *La Boz de la Verdad*, November 6, 1911, 1; "Echos," *L'Aurore*, May 23, 1911, 2.

91. Der Matossian, "Formation of Public Sphere(s)."

92. Ury, *Barricades and Banners*, 170–71.

93. Compare Aron Rodrigue, "The Ottoman Diaspora: The Rise and Fall of Ladino Literary Culture," in *Cultures of the Jews: A New History*, ed. David Biale (New York, 2002), 863–85.

94. However, Ottoman-Jewish newspapers mostly used Ladino, and Yiddish would ultimately not be the most important language of modern Jewish nationalism.

95. After its building was destroyed in the 1905 fire, Cercle Israélite eventually moved into a larger venue. AAIU, Turquie, I. H. 1b, Cercle Israélite to JCA Paris, May 31, 1908; AAIU, Turquie, IV. E., Algranti, January 10, 1910; "Provinces," *L'Aurore*, February 21, 1911, 3.

96. The club's president circa 1909 was Jacques Danon, chief accountant at the local branch of the Régie des Tabacs. *Annuaire oriental* 25 (1905): 1426; *Annuaire oriental* 29 (1909): 1711–12. He was succeeded by Jacques Behmoiras, a merchant and philanthropist. "Provinces," *L'Aurore*, February 11, 1910, 3. Two other powerful members were Nissim Behmoiras, a wealthy merchant and banker who led the community's reconstruction effort after the fire, and Robert Mizrahi, director of political affairs for several governors of Edirne. AAIU, Turquie, XI. E., Mitrani, March 5, 1906; AAIU, France, XVI. F. 27, Mitrani, August 15, 1908; TNA, FO 195/2211, No. 1, Townshend to O'Conor, January 1, 1906.

97. For example, the regional inspector of public education gave a lecture. "En la Fraternite," *La Boz de la Verdad*, December 11, 1911, 1.

98. Mitrani also criticized Jews who demonstrated "unreasonable patriotism" by demanding that the Alliance cede control of its schools to the Ottoman government. AAIU, Turquie, XI. E., Mitrani, March 20, 1909.

99. "En El Serkula Byenfizensya," *La Boz de la Verdad*, August 10, 1911, 2; "La Lengua Turka en Nuestra Eskulas," *La Boz de la Verdad*, October 23, 1911, 1.

100. "La Anyada 5671 i Nuestros Ermanos del Vilayet de Edirne," *La Boz de la Verdad*, September 24, 1911, 3; "Pour les familles des soldats," *L'Aurore*, April 7, 1911, 1.

101. It was also known as *İkmal Tahsil* (Educational Provision). AAIU, Turquie, XI. E., Mitrani, January 10 1911.

102. "Provinces: Andrinople," *L'Aurore*, August 12, 1910, 3. The club was led by a Doctor Simon Toledo. AAIU, Turquie, XI. E., Mitrani, December 29, 1911. See also AAIU, Turquie, XI. E., Mitrani, January 10, 1911, and AAIU, France, XVI. F., Mitrani, September 12, 1911.

103. "Andrinople," *L'Aurore*, September 23, 1910, 3.

104. Hasan Kayalı, *Arabs and Young Turks: Ottomanism, Arabism, and Islamism in the Ottoman Empire, 1908–1918* (Berkeley, 1997), 75–76.

105. Carter Vaughn Findley, *Turkey, Islam, Nationalism, and Modernity* (New Haven, 2010), 201–2; Feroz Ahmad, *The Young Turks and the Ottoman Nationalities: Armenians, Greeks, Albanians, Jews, and Arabs, 1908–1918* (Salt Lake City, 2014), 113; and Benbassa, "Associational Strategies," 463.

106. As a front, the office used the newly created Anglo-Levantine Banking Company, which was legally run by "the Mitrani Brothers." Der Matossian, "Formation of Public Sphere(s)," 208. The surname Mitrani strongly suggests roots in the Jewish communities of Edirne and Kırklareli.

107. Rodrigue, *French Jews, Turkish Jews*, 136; Benbassa and Rodrigue, *Sephardi Jewry: A History of the Judeo-Spanish Community, 14th–20th Centuries* (Berkeley, 2000), 118–27.

108. Rodrigue, *French Jews, Turkish Jews*, 220–52.

109. "The Turkish Parliamentary Delegation," *The Jewish Chronicle*, July 23, 1909, 13–14. Rıza Tevfik (Bölükbaşı) is best known in Turkey as one of the four Ottoman signatories of the infamous Treaty of Sèvres (1920). A polyglot and a polymath, he was sometimes called "Rıza the Philosopher." Syed Tanvir Wasti, "Feylesof Rıza," *Middle Eastern Studies* 38, no. 2 (April 2002): 83–100.

110. It was claimed that Rıza Tevfik "knows the Hebrew language and the Judeo-Spanish dialect to perfection." "From Abroad," *Jewish Chronicle*, July 9, 1909, 11.

111. "The Turkish Parliamentary Delegation," *Jewish Chronicle*, July 23, 1909, 13–14. In 1911, Rıza Tevfik was again interviewed by the Anglo-Jewish paper. "Zionism and the Turkish Jews," *Jewish Chronicle*, August 4, 1911, 14. Talat Bey, another Muslim deputy from Edirne, was constantly accused of having pro-Zionist inclinations (accurately or not). Mim Kemal Öke, "Young Turks, Freemasons, Jews and the Question of Zionism in the Ottoman Empire (1908–1913)," *Studies in Zionism* 7, no. 2 (1986): 199–218.

112. "Le Cinquantenaire de l'A.I.U.: Entre Associations," *L'Aurore*, May 20, 1910, 3; "Sionisme et Dignité: Lettre d'Andrinople," *L'Aurore*, June 10, 1910, 2.

113. AAIU, Turquie, IV E, Algranti, June 3, 1910.

114. "Kyen lo Kulpa," *El Meseret*, July 7, 1910.

115. "Protestation," *L'Aurore*, July 15, 1910, 2.

116. "Sionisme et Dignité: Lettre d'Andrinople," *L'Aurore*, June 10, 1910, 2. The quote is not from Sciuto's speech but rather the commentary of "M.S."

117. Benbassa and Rodrigue, *Sephardi Jewry*, 118–21.

118. "Notas i Impresyones de Vyaje en Bulgarya," *La Boz de la Verdad*, September 12, 1912, 2.

119. Haim Kaufman, "Jewish Sports in the Diaspora, Yishuv, and Israel: Between Nationalism and Politics," in *Israel Studies* 10, no. 2 (Summer, 2005): 147–67. The Istanbul club was founded by Jews of German and Austrian extraction and was initially called *Israelitischer Turnverein Konstantinopel*. The Plovdiv club was initially called *HaGibor*.

120. AAIU, Turquie, XI. E., Mitrani, July 12, 1909.

121. "Impresyones de Viaje: Andrinople," *HaShofar*, July 17, 1909, 329–30; *Annuaire oriental* 29 (1909): 1713.

122. AAIU, Turquie, XI E., Mitrani, July 12, 1909.

123. Benjamin Arditti, *Vidni evrei v Bŭlgariiá* 3 (Tel Aviv, 1969), 7–18; Moshe David Gaon, *ha-'Itonut b'Ladino: Bibliyografyah: shelosh me'ot 'itonim* (Jerusalem, 1965), 120; "Komite Sentral de los Tsiyonistos de Bulgarya," *HaShofar*, May 14, 1909, 260–61.

124. "Impresyones de Viaje," *HaShofar*, July 17, 1909, 330.

125. "Impresyones de Vyaje," *HaShofar*, July 17, 1909, 330.

126. AAIU, Turquie, I. H. 1b, Cercle Israélite to JCA Paris, May 31, 1908.

127. AAIU, Turquie, XI. E., Mitrani, July 12, 1909.

128. "Impresyones de Vyaje," *HaShofar*, July 31, 1909, 339.

129. Makabi's mission statement spoke of "the spread of gymnastics and the perpetuation of national Jewish sentiment (*hissiyat-ı milliye-i musevi*)." See Murat Yıldız, *The Ottoman World of Sport: Refashioning Bodies, Men, and Communities in Late Imperial Istanbul* (Austin, forthcoming), 61.

130. The president of the Edirne branch was "Dr. Adjoubel." "Lettre d'Andrinople," *L'Aurore*, November 11, 1910, 2.

131. "Entre Maccabis," *L'Aurore*, November 15, 1910, 1–2.

132. "Andrinople: A la Maccabi," *L'Aurore*, January 6, 1911, 3.

133. "La 'Macabi' de Philippopoli," *L'Aurore*, July 23, 1909, 2.

134. "Echos," *L'Aurore*, April 25, 1911, 2.

135. "En Syudad," *La Boz de la Verdad*, August 31, 1911, 1. The Ladino title of the play is *Neshev Purim, Komedia en un akto*. For a transliterated edition, see Elena Romero, *El Teatro de los sefardíes orientales* 3 (Madrid, 1979), 975–82. Catalan also directed the Talmud Torah in Çorlu from 1911 to 1912. "Çorlu," *La Boz de la Verdad*, November 16, 1911, 1; and "El Profesor Djudyo i el Evreyo," *La Boz de la Verdad*, December 4, 1911, 1.

136. AAIU, Turquie, XII. E., Mitrani, February 7, 1912.

137. TNA, FO 195/2364, No. 28, Samson to Lowther, May 1, 1911.

138. "Avizo de la Makabi," *La Boz de la Verdad*, November 6, 1911, 2.

139. TNA, FO 195/2364, No. 28, Samson to Lowther, May 1, 1911.

140. AAIU, Turquie, IV. E., Algranti, June 3, 1910. Traditionally, Edirne is called "Andrinople" in French and "Adrianople" in English. For the Edirne community's reputation for being loyal Alliancists, see AAIU, Turquie, XII. E., Mitrani, March 25, 1912.

141. "Echos," *L'Aurore*, February 21, 1911, 2; *Bulletin de la Grande Loge de district XI et de la Loge de Constantinople N. 678, I.O.B.B.* (February 1911–February 1913): 9–12, 59–83; Rıfat Bali, "Bir Yahudi Dayanışma ver Yardımlaşma Kurumu: B'nai B'rith XI Bölge Büyük Locası Tarihçesi ve Yayın Organı Hamenora Dergisi," *Müteferrika*, no. 8–9 (Spring-Summer 1996): 46; *Almanach Israelite 5688* (Thessaloniki), 103, from JMG Collection, inv .no.1981.091.1 By 1913, the district had twenty lodges. Ottoman Jews often styled B'nai B'rith as Béné-Bérith.

142. Rodrigue, *French Jews, Turkish Jews*, 134–35.

143. "L'Ordre des Béné-Bérith: Fondation d'une loge à Constantinople," *L'Aurore*, March 3, 1911, 1.

144. *Bulletin de la Grande Loge* (February 1911–February 1913): 23–24, 81–83. For the clinic in the 1930s, see CAHJP, TR/Ed/52. At some point, the former home of one Moise Taranto became the Bikur Holim pharmacy. "Necrologia," *La Boz de Türkiye*, June 15, 1942, 383.

145. *Bulletin de la Grande Loge* (February 1911–February 1913): 23–24, 81–83.

146. The opposition party, Hürriyet ve İtilaf Farkısı, had scant support from Jewish leaders. Ali Birinci, *Hürriyet ve İtilaf Fırkası: 2. Meşrutiyet Devrinde İttihat ve Terakki'ye Karşı Çıkanlar* (Istanbul, 1990), 51, 224. Also see Kayalı, "Elections and the Electoral Process," 265–86; TNA, FO 195/2270, No. 75, Samson to O'conor, September 30, 1908, and No. 95, Samson to O'conor, December 31, 1908.

147. Niego, *Cinquante Années de Travail*, 30–31.

148. The Bulgarian lodges created their own subdistrict in 1914, but the larger Eastern District continued to function. *Bulletin de la Grande Loge* (February 1913–December 1921).

149. In 1908, "many" Bulgarian Jews visited the Edirne boys' school, one of whom donated 300 kilograms of meat to the free lunch program. AAIU, Turquie, XI. E., Mitrani, March 4, 1908.

150. Rodrigue, "Jewish Enlightenment and Nationalism," 81; "The First Journal Devoted to the Sephardi Past Appears in Edirne (1888)," in Julia Phillips Cohen and Sarah Abrevaya Stein, eds., *Sephardi Lives: A Documentary History, 1700–1950* (Stanford, 2014), 392–93. Mitrani later published the Ladino newspaper *Karmi Sheli* (1890–1891).

151. Julia Phillips Cohen, "*La Boz de la Verdad*," *Encyclopedia of Jews in the Islamic World*, ed. Norman A. Stillman (Brill, 2010); Niego, *Cinquante Années de Travail*, 345–52. For an overview of the modern Ladino press, see Olga Borovaya, *Modern Ladino Culture: Press, Belles Lettres, and Theater in the Late Ottoman Empire* (Bloomington, 2012), 23–74.

152. AAIU, Grèce, I. E. 14, Barishac, May 18, 1890; AAIU, Bulgarie XXV. E. 240, Barishac, April 14, 1904.

153. AAIU, Turquie, IV. E. 67.1, Barishac, March 14, 1905, June 12, 1905, June 13, 1905.

154. They were still there in 1908. AAIU, Turquie, XIV. E., Ungar, June 20, 1908.

155. The article appeared in 1908. AAIU, Turquie, XI. E., Mitrani, December 28, 1909.

156. "La Direksyon del Jurnal" and "Avizo," *La Boz de la Verdad*, November 24, 1911, 2. Also see the masthead. Sometime in 1911, Razon became the sole printer. A. Roditti was the newspaper's "administrator." "Protestation," *L'Aurore*, July 15, 1910, 2.

157. Elias Canetti, *The Tongue Set Free* (London, 2011), 88. According to the masthead of *La Boz de la Verdad*, an annual subscription cost 40 kuruş in the city of Edirne, 50 kuruş in the rest of Edirne Province, and 15 francs beyond the province.

158. AAIU, Turquie, VII. E., Guéron, October 3, 1912.

159. For others who used this phrase, see AAIU, Turquie, XII. E., Haim Aron Levy et al., March 25, 1912.

160. "En Nuestra Komunidad," *La Boz de la Verdad*, August 10, 1911, 1; "Letra de la Syudad," *La Boz de la Verdad*, September 14, 1911, 1; "Letra de la Syudad," *La Boz de la Verdad*, December 4, 1911, 2.

161. "Algunos Detayos Sobre la Komunidad de Saloniko," *La Boz de la Verdad*, December 7 [*not* 4], 1911, 1. Barishac presumably wrote all articles that lacked bylines, as this was common practice for editors of Ladino newspapers. Borovaya, *Modern Ladino Culture*, 23–74.

162. AAIU, Turquie, XI. E., Mitrani, February 8, 1910.

163. Solomon Abrahamn Rosanes, *Korot ha-Yehudim b'Turkiya u-b'Artzot ha-Kedem* 5 (Jerusalem, 1930–1945), 389–91.

164. "Kirk Kilise," *La Boz de la Verdad*, August 28, 1911, 1; "Notas Sobre Saloniko i Refleksyones Sobre Nuestra Komunidad," *La Boz de la Verdad* September 19, 1911, 1.

165. "Provinces," *L'Aurore*, May 15, 1910, 3; "S.M.I. le Sultan à Andrinople," *L'Aurore*, November 4, 1910, 1.

166. "En la Komunidad: La Rekonsilyasyon," *La Boz de la Verdad*, December 21, 1911, 1.

167. AAIU, Turquie, VII. E., Guéron, October 3, 1912, and May 16, 1913.

168. Regarding "the people" of a given Jewish community, see the following articles in *La Boz de la Verdad*: "Korespondensya Djudyo," December 4, 1911, 2; "El Sirkulo Yisraelita," December 14, 1911, 1; "En el Sirkulo Yisraelita: La Rekonsilyasyon," December 18, 1911, 2; "En la Komunidad: La Rekonsilyasyon," December 21, 1911, 1; and "Notas de Mustafa-Pasha," December 28, 1911, 2.

169. For use of the term *"puevlo Otomano,"* see "En Bulgarya: Notas de Viaje," *La Boz de la Verdad*, September 5, 1912.

170. "En Bulgarya: Notas de Viaje," *La Boz de la Verdad*, September 5, 1912, 2; "Las Eleksyones i los Djudyos: Impresyones de Viaje en Bulgarya," *La Boz de la Verdad*, September 10, 1912, 1.

171. "En Bulgarya: Notas de Viaje," *La Boz de La Verdad*, September 5, 1912, 1.

172. However, Barishac would later call Edhem Ruhi a "famous antisemite." "A la Atensyon del Konsistoryo: Edhem Ruhi i los Djudyos," *La Boz de la Verdad*, May 7, 1914, 2.

173. "En Bulgarya: Notas de Viaje," *La Boz de La Verdad*, September 5, 1912, 1.

174. "El Kolera En Edirne," *La Boz de la Verdad*, August 21, 1911, 1; "A la Atensyon del Kuerpo Rabiniko," *La Boz de la Verdad*, September 28, 1911, 2.

175. "En Syudad: Adizyones a la Alyansa," *La Boz de la Verdad*, December 7 [*not* 4], 1911, 2.

176. "Los Djudyos," *La Boz de la Verdad*, December 4, 1911, 1.

177. Charles Kurzman, *Democracy Denied, 1905–1915: Intellectuals and the Fate of Democracy* (Cambridge, 2008), 24–33, 40–43, 51–52. Kurzman mentions Ahmet Rıza and Cahid Yalçın as examples of CUP intellectuals who were part of this intellectual class.

178. For networks of Sephardi publicists (who corresponded in French) see Borovaya, *Modern Ladino Culture,* 23–136.

179. "Provinces," *L'Aurore*, January 2, 1910, 3.

180. "Las eleksyones i los Djudios: Impresyones de Viazhe en Bulgaria," *La Boz de la Verdad*, September 10, 1912. Barishac's claim to be "Ottoman and Jewish at the same time" resonates with what Sarah Abvrevaya Stein sees in the late-Ottoman Ladino press: "a

modern sense of Ottoman Jewishness that was at once multiple and essentialist." "Creating a Taste for News: Historicizing Judeo-Spanish Periodicals of the Ottoman Empire," *Jewish History* 14, no. 1 (2000): 11.

181. In at least one case, Barishac did not criticize the *content* of Nahum's politics so much as the chief rabbi's call for Jews to vote as a bloc (for the CUP). This practice showed a lack of civic responsibility and earned Jews "many enemies among the [empire's] Turks, Arabs, and Greeks." "Las eleksyones i los Djudios: Impresyones de Viazhe en Bulgaria," *La Boz de la Verdad*, September 10, 1912.

182. "En la Kapitala: El Medjlis Djismani," *La Boz de la Verdad*, September 11, 1911, 1.

183. "Notas de Viaje: Ksanti," *La Boz de la Verdad*, September 7, 1911, 1.

184. "El Antisemitismo," *La Boz de la Verdad*, December 18, 1911, 1. In the Third Chamber of Deputies, all members of parliament from Edirne Province were Muslim except for two Armenians from the Tekirdağ district and one Armenian from the Gelibolu district.

185. "El Antisemitismo," *La Boz de la Verdad*, December 18, 1911, 1. On these parliamentary debates, see Louis Fishman, "Understanding the 1911 Ottoman Parliament Debate on Zionism in Light of the Emergence of a 'Jewish Question,'" in *Late Ottoman Palestine: The Period of Young Turk Rule*, ed. Yuval Ben-Bassat and Eyal Ginio (London, 2011), 103–20.

186. "En la Kamara: Los Djudyos, Un Chiko Insidente," *La Boz de la Verdad*, January 11, 1912, 2.

187. AAIU, Bulgarie, XXXV. E., Barishac in Gumuldjina, April 14, 1904.

188. Karkason, "An Ambivalent Coexistence."

189. "Bulgarya: Kalumniya de la Sangre en Stanimaka," *La Boz de la Verdad*, March 26, 1912.

190. In Edirne, local authorities ordered the dismissal of all teachers holding Italian citizenship, including an employee of the Alliance girls' school. AAIU, Turquie, XII. E., Mitrani, January 12, 1912, and May 3, 1912.

191. "Chikas Informasyones Lokales," *La Boz de la Verdad*, October 19, 1911, 1.

192. "Los Djudyos," *La Boz de la Verdad*, December 4, 1911, 1.

193. "Los Djudyos," *La Boz de la Verdad*, December 4, 1911, 1.

194. "El Yeni Edirne," *La Boz de la Verdad*, December 25, 1911, 2. The Zionist press in Istanbul also condemned *Yeni Edirne*. "Snobisme Antisémetique," *L'Aurore*, December 8, 1911, 1.

195. "En el Yeni Edirne," *La Boz de la Verdad*, December 28, 1911, 1. But a few months later, *Yeni Edirne* made a scandal of an incident at the Alliance girls' school involving a Muslim student and her Italian-Jewish teacher. AAIU, Turquie, XII. E., Mitrani, May 14, 1912.

196. Mustafa Şevket (Dağdiveren) would go on to become mayor of Edirne and a founder of the *Trakya-Paşaeli Müdâfaa-i Hukuk Cemiyeti*. See Chapter 4.

197. Ender Bilar, *Edirne'nin Basın-Yayın Tarihi, 1361–2006* 1 (Edirne, 2006), 105, 111; "Avizo", *La Boz de la Verdad*, November 24, 1911, 2. Also see the mastheads of both newspapers.

198. Circa 1910, Mustafa Şevket supported the Osmanlı Demokrat Firkası. TNA, FO 195/2335, Samson March 31, 1910, No. 17.

199. For more on Mehmet Şeref (Aykut), see Chapter 4 and especially Chapter 5. I could not determine if he is the lawyer "Şeref Bey" mentioned elsewhere in Chapter 2.

200. For another example, see "Konversyon Eskandaloza," *La Boz de la Verdad*, October 19, 1911, 1.

201. "Notas de Viaje: En Sufuli," *La Boz de la Verdad*, September 4, 1911, 2; "Sobre la Linya de Saloniko," *La Boz de la Verdad*, September 11, 1911, 1; "Dimoteka: A la Atensyon del Gran Rabno de Turkiya," *La Boz de la Verdad*, September 14, 1911, 1; "Las Konversyones," *La Boz de la Verdad*, October 26, 1911, 1; "El Evreyo," *La Boz de la Verdad*, November 9, 1911, 1; "En la Komunidad," *La Boz de la Verdad*, November 24, 1911, 1; "Dedeağaç," *La Boz de la Verdad*, November 30, 1911, 1; "En la Fraternite," *La Boz de la Verdad*, December 11, 1911, 1.

202. "Nuestro Djurnal Baptizado por Sinyor David Fresko," *La Boz de la Verdad*, March 26, 1912.

203. Benbassa and Rodrigue, *Sephardi Jewry*, 125–26.

204. "El Kongreso Tsiyonisto," *La Boz de la Verdad* August 21, 1911, 2.

205. Like Barishac, Rıza Tevfik Bey had cooled on the CUP by 1911. Wasti, "Feylesof Rıza."

206. "Notas i Impresyones de Viaje en Bulgarya," *La Boz de la Verdad*, September 12, 1912, 2. Also, I found no instances of Barishac describing his Jewish opponents as "assimilationists"—an epithet that was popular among Zionists in Salonica (and elsewhere). Cohen, *Becoming Ottomans*, 109.

207. "El Profesor Djudyo i el Evreyo," *La Boz de la Verdad*, December 4, 1911, 1. Mitrani was a common surname in the Edirne region. Solomon and Moise were not closely related.

208. "Los Profesores de Ebreo," *La Boz de la Verdad*, November 16, 1911, 1. The Ladino article included a quote in ancient Greek. See Chapter 4 for Mitrani's. activities during the Greek occupation of Edirne.

209. Dimitar Voinikov, *The Bulgarians in the Easternmost Part of the Balkan Peninsula: Eastern Thrace* (Sofia, 2014), 79.

210. For Edhem Ruhi's biography, see https://www.biyografya.com/biyografi/7165.

211. One precedent was described by Istanbul's *Jurnal Israelit* in 1861: That year, local Purim celebrations got out of hand to the point that Jews attacked Ottoman police. Julia Phillips Cohen, "A Model *Millet*? Ottoman Jewish Citizenship at the End of Empire," in Abigail Green and Simon Levis Sullam, eds., *Jews, Liberalism, Antisemitism: A Global History* (Cham, 2020), 217.

212. The words "brasserie" and "cabaret" are from Moise Mitrani's French-language report. AAIU, Turquie, XI. E., Mitrani, June 24, 1910.

213. BOA, DH/EUM/THR 00037_00060_001.

214. TNA, FO 195/2335, No. 32, Samson to Lowther, June 21, 1910; No. 34, Samson to Lowther, June 30, 1910; AAIU, Turquie, IV. E., Algranti, June 22–23, 1910; AAIU, Turquie, XI. E., Mitrani, June 24, 1910.

215. TNA, FO 195/2335, No. 32, Samson to Lowther, June 21, 1910; No. 34, Samson to Lowther, June 30, 1910; AAIU, Turquie IV. E., Algranti, June 22–23, 1910; AAIU, Turquie XI. E., Mitrani, June 24, 1910. In the Ottoman document written by the police chief, his name appears as Ahmet Naci. Probably his full name was Cemal Ahmet Naci. The president of the Jewish communal council was Jacob Pappo.

216. AAIU, Turquie XI. E., Mitrani, June 24, 1910.

217. AAIU, Turquie, IV. E., Algranti to JCA, March 20, 1911. *La Boz de la Verdad* said it was "a few" beers, according to a reprint of the article that appeared in French: "L'incident d'Andrinople," *L'Aurore*, July 15, 1910, 1. For the proximity of police headquarters to the park, see Rıfat Osman, *Edirne Rehnüması* (Edirne, 2013), 75.

218. TNA, FO 195/2335, No. 32, Samson to Lowther, June 21, 1910.

219. AAIU, Turquie, XI. E., Mitrani, June 24, 1910. The *vali* gave a highly improbable account of the story to *Le Jeune Turc*, a Jewish newspaper in Istanbul. It was reprinted in "L'incident d'Andrinople," *L'Aurore*, July 15, 1910, 1.

220. It seems unlikely that people would be so rash as to shoot from their own homes. The police chief's claim resembles anti-Jewish tropes found in the Russian Empire around this time. See Oleg Budnitskii, "Shots in the Back: On the Origin of the Anti-Jewish Pogroms of 1918–1921," in *Polin: Studies in Polish Jewry Vol 14: Focusing on Jews in the Polish Borderlands*, ed. Antony Polonsky (London, 2001), 187–201.

221. BOA, DH/EUM/THR 00037_00060_001.

222. AAIU, Turquie, XI. E., Mitrani, June 24, 1910.

223. TNA, FO 195/2335, No. 32, Samson to Lowther, June 21, 1910; AAIU, Turquie, XI. E., Mitrani, June 24, 1910.

224. AAIU, Turquie, IV. E., Algranti, June 22–23, 1910; AAIU, Turquie XI. E., Mitrani, June 24, 1910.

225. The story was translated and printed in full in "L'incident d'Andrinople," *L'Aurore*, July 1, 1910, 1–2.

226. TNA, FO 195/2335, No. 32, Samson to Lowther, June 21, 1910; AAIU, Turquie, IV. E., Algranti, June 22–23, 1910; AAIU, Turquie, XI. E., Mitrani, June 24, 1910.

227. AAIU, Turquie, IV. E., Algranti, July 17, 1910.

228. AAIU, Turquie, XI. E., Mitrani, June 24, 1910.

229. TNA, FO 195/2335, No. 41, Samson to Lowther, July 27, 1910.

230. "L'incident d'Andrinople," *L'Aurore*, July 1, 1910, 1–2.

231. AAIU, Turquie, XI. E., Mitrani, July 8, 1910; "A la Atensyon del Konsistoryo: Edhem Ruhi i los Djudyos," *La Boz de la Verdad*, May 7, 1914, 2. The Plovdiv paper was Edhem Ruhi's *Balkan*. Soon, the Turkish press in Edirne assumed a more pacifying tone. "L'incident d'Andrinople," *L'Aurore*, July 15, 1910, 1.

232. AAIU, Turquie, IV. E., Algranti, June 26, 1910. *La Boz de la Verdad* claimed that the bill was written in Turkish and posted to an Armenian church. "L'incident d'Andrinople," *L'Aurore*, July 1, 1910, 1.

233. "L'incident d'Andrinople," *L'Aurore*, July 1, 1910, 1–2.

234. BOA, DH/EUM/THR 00037_00060_001.

235. AAIU, Turquie, IV. E., Algranti, June 26, 1910.

236. "Après l'incident," *L'Aurore*, July 29, 1910, 1.

237. AAIU, France XVI. F. 27, Mitrani, annual report for the 1909–1910 school year. As for Barishac, he criticized the community's meek response and the lack of action from the Jewish deputies in parliament. "El Antisemitismo," *La Boz de la Verdad*, December 18, 1911, 1.

238. Cohen, *Becoming Ottomans*, 1–18; Cohen, "A Model *Millet*?," 222.

239. TNA, FO 195/2335, No. 34, Samson to Lowther, June 30, 1910.

240. "Provinces," *L'Aurore*, September 23, 1910, 3. The story was picked up from *La Boz de la Verdad*.

241. "Por la Difunta Kaza Derokada," *La Boz de la Verdad*, November 16, 1911, 2.

242. AAIU, Turquie, IV. E., Algranti, March 28, 1911. The term "Edirne Incident" may have been an allusion to the 1703 revolt against Sultan Mustafa II, which is known in Turkish as the "Edirne Vakası."

243. TNA, FO 195/2335, No. 41, Samson to Lowther, July 27, 1910.

244. "L'incident d'Andrinople," *L'Aurore*, July 1, 1910, 1–2.

Chapter 3

1. Quote is from AAIU, France, XVI. F. 27, Mitrani, August 6, 1913. See also AAIU, Turquie, VII. E., Guéron, January 4, 1912, and May 22, 1913; *Bulletin de la Grande Loge de district XI et de la Loge de Constantinople N. 678, I.O.B.B.* (February 1911–February 1913): 81–83; and *Bulletin de l'Alliance Israélite Universelle*, 3rd ser., no. 38 (1913): 128–58. The new Alliance schools included a girls' school in Dimetoka (1910), a girls' school in Kırklareli (1910), a mixed school in Gümülcine (1910), and a boys' school in Çorlu (1912). There were also plans to build a Jewish school in Karaağaç.

2. AAIU, Turquie, XI. E., Mitrani, January 8, 1914; Avigdor Levy, "The Siege of Edirne (1912–1913) as Seen by a Jewish Eyewitness: Social, Political, and Cultural Perspectives," in *Jews, Turks, Ottomans: A Shared History, Fifteenth through the Twentieth Century*, ed. Avigdor Levy (Syracuse, 2002), 192; Devi Mays, *Forging Ties, Forging Passports: Migration and the Modern Sephardi Diaspora* (Stanford, 2020), 67–68.

3. Justin McCarthy, "The Population of Ottoman Europe Before and After the Fall of the Empire," in *IIIrd Congress on the Social and Economic History of Turkey: Princeton University, 24–26 August, 1983*, ed. Lowry and Hattox (Istanbul, 1990), 286; A. A. Pallis, "Racial Migrations in the Balkans during the Years 1912–1924," *Geographical Journal* 66, no. 4 (October 1925): 330.

4. H. Yıldırım Ağanoğlu, *Osmanlı'dan Cumhuriyet'e Balkanlar'ın Makus Talihi: Göç* (Istanbul, 2001), 338.

5. This is not to deny that many refugees maintained emotional ties with their native lands. In Bulgaria, descendants of refugees from Eastern Thrace have complex and diverse understandings of the Turkish-Bulgarian border. See Valentina Ganeva-Raycheva, "Migration, Territories, Heritage: Discourses and Practices in Constructing the Bulgarian-Turkish Border," in *Migration, Memory, Heritage: Socio-cultural Approaches to the Bulgarian-Turkish Border*, ed. Valentina Ganeva-Raycheva and Meglena Zlatkova (Sofia, 2012), 29–64.

6. To the extent that the government displaced certain borderland populations, these policies could affect people of all religions. In 1860, for example, Ottoman foreign minister Ali Paşa proposed removing Belgrade's *Muslim* population from the violent borderland so that the city's Muslim quarter could be "expropriated or destroyed" as part of a fortification plan. Burcu Özgüven, "*Palanka* Forts and Construction Activity in the Late Ottoman Balkans," in *The Frontiers of the Ottoman World*, ed. A. C. S. Peacock (Oxford, 2009), 178.

7. Pieter M. Judson, *Guardians of the Nation: Activists on the Language Frontiers of Imperial Austria* (Cambridge, 2006), 18.

8. While I focus on Jews who remained in Edirne Province, Devi Mays makes a similar argument about Jews throughout the Ladino-speaking Sephardi diaspora, in *Forging Ties, Forging Passports*, 55–56.

9. İpek Yosmaoğlu, *Blood Ties: Religion, Violence, and the Politics of Nationhood in Ottoman Macedonia, 1878–1908* (Ithaca, 2014), 17.

10. Eyal Ginio claims that the Balkan Wars represent "the first total war of the Ottoman state." "Mobilizing the Ottoman Nation during the Balkan Wars (1912–1913): Awakening from the Ottoman Dream," *War in History* 12, no. 2 (2005): 156. The term "total war" entered the mainstream with the appearance of Erich Ludendorff's 1935 book *Der totale Krieg*. Describing the Balkan Wars, Mark Biondich uses the older term *Volkskrieg*. "The Balkan Wars: Violence and Nation-Building in the Balkans, 1912–13," *Journal of Genocide Research* 18, no. 4 (2016): 389–404.

11. For more on civic Ottomanism, see Michelle U. Campos, *Ottoman Brothers: Muslims, Christians, and Jews in Early Twentieth-century Palestine* (Stanford, 2011), 1–7.

12. Taner Akçam, "The Young Turks and the Plans for the Ethnic Homogenization of Anatolia," in *Shatterzone of Empires: Coexistence and Violence in the German, Habsburg, Russian, and Ottoman Borderlands*, ed. Omer Bartov and Eric D. Weitz (Bloomington, 2013), 260.

13. Ivo Andrić, *The Bridge on the Drina*, translated from the Serbo-Croat by Lovett F. Edwards (Chicago, 1977), 229.

14. Erik J. Zürcher, *Turkey: A Modern History* (London, 2017) 103–7; M. Şükrü Hanioğlu, *A Brief History of the Late Ottoman Empire* (Princeton, 2008), 170–73. Before the Balkan Wars, the Ottoman Empire in Europe had also bordered Greece, Serbia, Montenegro, and Habsburg Bosnia.

15. Richard C. Hall claims that before the war, a Bulgarian staff officer used his post in the Edirne consulate to investigate the city's fortifications. *The Balkan Wars, 1912–1913: Prelude to the First World War* (London, 2000), 20, 39. In her journal, Angèle Guéron claimed that "intelligence" from local Christians allowed the Bulgarian army to quickly encircle Edirne. Levy, "The Siege of Edirne," 164–65.

16. For a Greek Orthodox soldier in the Ottoman army who was recognized for displaying bravery the Battle of Lüleburgaz, see Ginio, "Mobilizing the Ottoman Nation," 164.

17. Dimitar Voinikov, *The Bulgarians in the Easternmost Part of the Balkan Peninsula— Eastern Thrace* (Sofia, 2014), 279–82.

18. Erik J. Zürcher says that Christian soldiers deserted the Ottoman army "in droves," and that Christian civilians were widely seen as potential spies and saboteurs. *Turkey*, 106–7. Also see AAIU, Turquie, I. C. 3 (Siège d'Andrinople), Guéron, March 26, 1913.

19. Fikret Adanır, "Non-Muslims in the Ottoman Army and the Ottoman Defeat in the Balkan War of 1912–1913," in *A Question of Genocide: Armenians and Turks at the End of the Ottoman Empire*, ed. Ronald Grigor Suny, Fatma Müge Göçek, and Norman M. Naimark (Oxford, 2011), 113–25.

20. Eyal Ginio, "'Ottoman Jews! Rush to Save Our Homeland!' Ottoman Jews in the Balkan Wars (1912–1913)" [in Hebrew], *Pe'amim* 105/106 (2005/2006), 18–20; Kazım Karebekir, *Edirne Hatıraları* (Istanbul, 2009), 54.

21. For example, see AAIU, Turquie, I. C. 3 (Siège d'Andrinople), Guéron, November 10, 1912. In a broader context, Julia Phillips Cohen discusses the notion of Ottoman Jews as a "model community." *Becoming Ottomans: Sephardi Jews and Imperial Citizenship in the Modern Era* (Oxford, 2014), xi–xii, 16.

22. Ahmet Efiloğlu, "The Exodus of Thracian Greeks to Greece in the Post–Balkan War Era," in *War and Collapse: World War I and the Ottoman State*, ed. M. Hakan Yavuz and Feroz Ahmad (Salt Lake City, 2016), 330; Avraam Moshe Tadjer, *Notas istorikas sovre los djudyos de Bulgaria i la komunita de Sofya* (Sofia, 1932), 181.

23. According to Moise Mitrani, more than 500 Jewish families—perhaps 2,750 individuals—fled the city of Edirne for Istanbul. *Bulletin de l'Alliance* (1913): 79.

24. Carnegie Endowment for International Peace, *Report of the International Commission to Inquire into the Causes and Conduct of the Balkan Wars* (Washington, DC, 1914), 126. See also Levy, "The Siege of Edirne," 161–64.

25. Eighty Jewish families fled Çorlu for Istanbul and sixty Jewish families fled Tekirdağ for Istanbul. *American Jewish Yearbook 5674*, ed. Herbert Friedenwald and H.G. Friedman (Philadelphia, 1913), 194.

26. For a discussion of the document and its author (Elya Elgazi), see Eyal Ginio, "Ottoman Jews in the Balkan Wars," 13–16. For the document itself, see Eliezer Papo, *Ve-hitalta le-vinkha ba-yom ha-hu: parodyot Sefaradiyot-Yehudiyot 'al ha-Hagadah shel Pesaḥ* 2 (Jerusalem, 2012), 21–43.

27. For more on the *muhajir* phenomenon in the Ottoman Empire, see Vladimir Hamed-Troyansky, *Empire of Refugees: North Caucasian Muslims and the Late Ottoman State* (Stanford, 2024).

28. Eyal Ginio, "Jewish Philanthropy and Mutual Assistance During the Balkan Wars: Between Ottomanism and Communal Identities" (Unpublished, 2017).

29. "Ottoman Jews and the War: Patriotic Demonstrations," *The Jewish Chronicle*, October 11, 1912, 16; Karebekir, *Edirne Hatıraları*, 208.

30. "Kirk-kilise," *La Boz de la Verdad*, August 28, 1911, 1.

31. "Por los Soldados Djudyos," *La Baz de la Verdad*, March 26, 1912, 2; "En Syudad," *La Boz de la Verdad*, March 29, 1912, 2.

32. For a ballad about a mother who lost her son in the Battle of Lüleburgaz, see "O Madre Mia," performed by Voice of the Turtle on the album *From the Shores of the Golden Horn: Music of the Spanish Jews of Turkey* (Somerville, MA: Titanic, 1989), track 5. For Ottoman-Jewish soldiers who died or became prisoners of war, see Ginio, "Ottoman Jews in the Balkan Wars," 18–22. Of Bulgaria's 45,000 Jews, 4,200 fought in the Balkan Wars, and 400 died. *American Jewish Yearbook 5674*, 190, 206.

33. "Verso la Amerika," *La Boz de la Verdad*, September 2, 1912, 1; Erok Haker, *Once Upon a Time Jews Lived in Kırklareli: The Story of the Adato Family, 1800–1934* (Istanbul, 2003).

34. Levy's article builds on an earlier series by Rıfat Bali, the first installment of which is "Edirne Muhasarası Sırasında Tutulmuş Bir Günlük—I," *Tarih ve Toplum: Aylık Ansiklopedik Dergi* 32, no. 190 (September 1999): 35–43.

35. Levy, "The Siege of Edirne," 162–70.

36. *American Jewish Yearbook 5674*, 193.

37. Levy, "The Siege of Edirne," 166–70, 183–85. "Three thousand Jews were obliged to seek refuge in the schools," including the Alliance boys' school. *American Jewish Yearbook 5674*, 193.

38. Eyal Ginio, "Constructing a Symbol of Defeat and National Rejuvenation: Edirne (Adrianople) in Ottoman Propaganda and Writing during the Balkan Wars," in *Cities into Battlefields: Metropolitan Scenarios, Experiences and Commemorations of Total War*, ed. Stefan Goebel and Derek Keene (Burlington, 2011), 83–99.

39. AAIU, Turquie, I. C. 3 (Siège d'Andrinople), Guéron, March 26, 1913.

40. Cengiz Şişman, "Galante, Abraham (Avram)," *Encyclopedia of Jews in the Islamic World*.

41. Abraham Galanté, *Turcs et Juifs: Etude Historique, Politique* (Istanbul, 1932), 43–45. Professionally, Sévère was an engineer.

42. 1906–1907 Ottoman Census, from Kemal H. Karpat, *Ottoman Population 1830–1914: Demographic and Social Characteristics* (Madison, 1985), 162–69; *Bulletin de l'Alliance Israélite Universelle*, 3rd ser., no. 37 (1912): 99–128.

43. AAIU, Turquie, XI. E., Mitrani, August 25, 1910.

44. AAIU, Turquie, II. C., Saul Cohen, November 11, 1912, and November 23, 1912.

45. AAIU, Turquie, II. C., Saul Cohen, November 23, 1912, and December 1, 1912.

46. AAIU, Turquie, II. C., David Levy, May 9, 1913. The occupation grew especially intense after January 1913, when the brief armistice came to an end.

47. AAIU, Turquie, II. C., David Levy, July 22, 1913.

48. When an international Jewish delegation visited Tekirdağ in the winter of 1913, it counted only 110 Jewish families—slightly less than half of the prewar figure. Tadjer, *Notas istorikas*, 181.

49. AAIU, Turquie, II. C., David Levy, February 20, 1913, May 2, 1913, and July 22, 1913.

50. AAIU, Turquie, II. C., David Levy, May 9, 1913. In February 1913, Levy lodged a complaint with the city prefect and sought compensation for the damage and theft committed by the Bulgarian soldiers.

51. AAIU, Turquie, II. C., David Levy, July 22, 1913.

52. See the AIU online database of personnel: http://www.archives-aiu.org/aiu/index.htm.

53. AAIU, Turquie II., C, David Levy, August 6, 1913. For similar accounts, see Mays, *Forging Ties, Forging Passports*, 57–58.

54. AAIU, Turquie II., C, David Levy, August 6, 1913. What is more, Levy was the son-in-law of the Orientalist Joseph Halévy. See the AIU online database: http://www.archives-aiu.org/aiu/index.htm. Hans-Lukas Kiesler argues that, beginning in 1913, Talat Paşa was de facto leader of the empire. *Talaat Pasha: Father of Modern Turkey, Architect of Genocide* (Princeton, 2018), 32–33, 47, 108, 193, 321.

55. AAIU, Turquie II. C., David Levy, August 6, 1913.

56. Adanır, "Non-Muslims in the Ottoman Army," 124.

57. For more on İskeçe/Xanthi, see TNA, FO 195/2456, No. 22, O'Reilly to Grey, January 12, 1914, Enclosure, Heard's "Report on the Situation in Western Thrace," December 23, 1913.

58. FO 195/2454, Samson, December 31, 1913; A.A. Pallis, "Racial Migrations in the Balkans during the Years 1912–1924," 326–27. To this day, the Western Thrace region of Greece maintains a large Muslim minority. For a study of this population, see Olga Demetriou, *Capricious Borders: Minority, Population, and Counter-Conduct Between Greece and Turkey* (New York, 2013).

59. For example, see Carnegie Endowment, *Report of the International Commission*, 78–108, 135–47, 158–207.

60. TNA, FO 195/2454, No. 15, Badetti, received August 19, 1913.

61. Tevfik Bıyıklıoğlu, *Trakya'da Milli Mücadele* I (Ankara, 1992), 81; Zürcher, *Turkey*, 107.

62. Levy, "The Siege of Edirne," 186–91; TNA, FO 195/2454, No. 33, Samson, August 12, 1913.

63. E. Ashmead-Bartlett, "Atrocities of the Bulgarian Army: Crimes in Thrace," *Daily Telegraph*, August 21, 1913, 9.

64. Justin McCarthy acknowledges that "murder of civilians was far less in Edirne than in other conquered cities." *Death and Exile*, 143.

65. Carnegie Endowment, *Report of the International Commission*, 117. The mayor of occupied Edirne was a local Bulgarian Christian. Darin Stephanov, "The Beautiful and the Brutal: Bulgarian Images of Odrin (Edirne) and the Contours of the Ethnonational Mindset," in *The Heritage of Edirne in Ottoman and Turkish Times: Continuities, Disruptions and Reconnections*, ed. Brigit Krawietz and Florian Riedler (Berlin, 2020), 375n100.

66. Pierre Loti, *Turquie Agonisante* (Paris, 1913), 182–93; Carnegie Endowment, *Report of the International Commission*, 115–16. However, the Carnegie Report adds that the library at Selimiye Mosque was broken into and robbed.

67. AAIU, Turquie, I. C. 3 (Siège d'Andrinople), Guéron, March 27, 1913.

68. By one count, Sofia's population was 82,621 and Edirne's was 80,000. *American Jewish Yearbook 5674*, 200.

69. Tadjer, *Notas istorikas*, 181–82.

70. Ginio, "Jewish Philanthropy," 10n3. Of the Jews who stayed in Istanbul, some applied for *protegé* status at the Spanish consulate, claiming that they did not want to become Bulgarian citizens. Dozens were successful, and some even obtained Spanish citizenship a few years later. Pablo Martín Asuero, "The Spanish Consulate in Istanbul and the Protection of the Sephardim (1804–1913)," in *Quaderns de la Mediterrània* 8 (2007): 175–77.

71. Destinations included Edirne (Odrin), Kırklareli (Lozengrad), and Mustafapaşa (Svilengrad). The first boatload of 320 refugees left Istanbul on May 24, 1913. See "El Repatriamyento de los Refujiados Djudyos en Konstantinopla," *El Tiempo*, May 14, 1913, 4, and "El Repatriamyento de los Refujiados Israelitas," *El Tiempo*, May 26, 1913, 7, and "The Repatriation of Jewish War Refugees," *Jewish Chronicle*, May 30, 1913, 14.

72. One such family arrived in Kırklareli to find that Bulgarian officers had been billeted to their home. Haker, *Once Upon a Time Jews Lived in Kırklareli*, 122.

73. *Bulletin de l'*Alliance (1912): 57–62.

74. *American Jewish Yearbook 5674*, 195. The yearbook reports an allocation of $65,000 for the refugees in Istanbul and "more" than $25,000 for the Jews of Edirne.

75. *American Jewish Yearbook 5674*, 196.

76. Gabriel Arié in Sofia, May 15, 1913, and May 22, 1913, from *A Sephardi Life in Southeastern Europe: The Autobiography and Journals of Gabriel Arié, 1863–1939*, ed. Esther Benbassa and Aron Rodrigue (Seattle, 1998), 230, 235. Arié estimated that between 30,000 and 35,000 Jews had been added to Bulgaria's existing Jewish population of about 40,000.

77. AAIU, France, XVI. F. 27, Mitrani, August 6, 1913.

78. Ginio, "Ottoman Jews in the Balkan Wars," 5. The dictionary was published by Albert Pipano.

79. AAIU, Turquie VII. E., Guéron, May 14, 1913.

80. "Ben Israel" [sic], "Journal du siège d'Adrianople," *Almanach national au profit de l' hôpital de Hirsch* 6 (1914): 192–94.

81. "Ben Israel" [sic], "Journal du siège d'Adrianople," 199–200.

82. Eyal Ginio, *The Ottoman Culture of Defeat: The Balkan Wars and their Aftermath* (Oxford, 2016), 1–23.

83. For more on Moise Cohen, see Jacob M. Landau, *Tekinalp, Turkish Patriot, 1883–1961* (Leiden, 1984). Also see Chapter 2 of this book.

84. AAIU, Turquie VII. E., Guéron, May 16, 1913, and March 3, 1915; AAIU, Turquie XII. E., Mitrani, February 7, 1915, and January 9, 1915.

85. AAIU, Turquie VII. E. 146, Guéron, February 12, 1919, and February 22, 1919.

86. İzel Rozental, "'Zavallı Ancel' Halam," *Şalom*, June 16, 2021.

87. Bıyıklıoğlu, *Trakya'da Milli Mücadele*, 71; and "Adrianople: Deputation in London," *Daily Telegraph*, August 19, 1913, 9. Sometimes breaking into two groups, the delegates visited Vienna, Rome, Paris, London, Saint Petersburg, and Berlin. Bıyıklıoğlu says that the delegation included a Jew named "Hayim Bahares," but that is almost certainly a misspelling of "Hayim Behmoiras," a lawyer discussed in Chapter 2.

88. Some fled directly across the border, others via Istanbul. Carnegie Endowment, *Report of the International Commission*, 127, 130–33. Contemporary Bulgarian accounts claimed that 30 percent of Eastern Thrace's Bulgarian population was killed. Theodora Dragostinova, "Competing Priorities, Ambiguous Loyalties: Challenges of Socioeconomic Adaptation and National Inclusion of the Interwar Bulgarian Refugees," *Nationalities Papers* 34, no. 5 (Cambridge, 2019), 553. Also see Fuat Dündar, *Modern Türkiye'nin Şifresi: İttihat ve Terakki'nin etnisite mühendisliği, 1913–1918* (Istanbul, 2008), 187–88; and Ryan Gingeras, "A Last Toehold in Europe: The Making of Turkish Thrace, 1912–1923," in *War and Collapse: World War I and the Ottoman State*, ed. Yavuz and Ahmad (Salt Lake City, 2016), 384.

89. "Treaty of Peace Between Bulgaria and Turkey," in *American Journal of International Law* 8, no. 1, Supplement: Official Documents (January 1914): 37.

90. TNA, FO 195/2454, No., 40, Samson to Mallet, December 31, 1913; Dündar, *Modern Türkiye'nin Şifresi*, 188–91; Gingeras, "A Last Toehold in Europe," 384. Voinikov recounts how his family was forced to leave Eastern Thrace for Bulgaria in September 1913. *The Bulgarians*, 307–8.

91. FO 195/2454, No. 40, Samson to Mallet, December 31, 1913. For the convention itself, see Alexandre Antoniadès, *Le Developpement économique de la Thrace* (Athens, 1922), 167–69.

92. Stephen P. Ladas, *The Exchange of Minorities: Bulgaria, Greece, and Turkey* (New York, 1932), 18; C. A. Macartney, *National States and National Minorities* (London, 1934), 432; Antoniadès, 171–74. The commissioners met seven times in the spring of 1914 before their work was cut short by the outbreak of World War I.

93. Pallis, "Racial Migrations," 328. At the end of 1913, Edirne's British consul claimed that no Bulgarian villages remained in the province, save for three Bulgarian-Catholic settlements near Tekirdağ. TNA, FO 195/2454, No. 40, Samson to Mallet, December 31, 1913. But apparently even these settlements soon petered out. Gingeras, "A Last Toehold in Europe," 384, 400n50.

94. Carnegie Endowment, *Report of the International Commission*, 128. Also, many Orthodox Greeks fled Bulgarian Western Thrace for Ottoman Eastern Thrace. TNA, FO 2454, No. 40, Samson to Mallet, December 31, 1913.

95. TNA, FO 2454, No. 40, Samson to Mallet, December 31, 1913; TNA, FO 195/2456, No. 17, Samson to Mallet, March 31, 1914; Ahmet Efiloğlu, "The Exodus of Thracian Greeks," 332–33.

96. Taner Akçam, *The Young Turks' Crime Against Humanity: The Armenian Genocide and Ethnic Cleansing in the Ottoman Empire* (Princeton, 2012), 69.

97. TNA, FO 195/2456, No. 17, Samson to Mallet, March 31, 1914. Also partially quoted in Gingeras, "A Last Toehold in Europe," 385.

98. In April 1914, the Interior Ministry sent a cable to the provincial government of Edirne, demanding a halt to the "attacks the immigrants are alleged to have committed." Akçam, *The Young Turks' Crime*, 72.

99. Yannis G. Mourelos, "The 1914 Persecutions and the First Attempt at an Exchange of Minorities between Greece and Turkey," *Balkan Studies* 26, no. 2 (1985): 393.

100. Akçam, *The Young Turks' Crime*, 71.

101. TNA, FO 195/2456, No. 36, Samson to Mallet, June 30, 1914; TNA, FO 195/2458, No. 356, Dussi, April 4, 1914.

102. Dündar, *İttihat ve Terakki'nin Müslümanları iskân politikası, 1913–1918* (Istanbul, 2001), 69.

103. Akçam calls this the "dual-track mechanism." *The Young Turks' Crime*, 63. The situation in Edirne became so heated that would-be assassins fired on the *vali* while he was holding his seven-year-old son, killing the latter. Halil Menteşe, *Osmanlı Mebusan Meclisi Reisi Halil Menteşe'nin Anıları* (Istanbul, 1986), 166.

104. Akçam, *The Young Turks' Crime*, 71–89. By the time the Ottoman Empire entered World War I, only about 138,000 Orthodox Greeks remained in Edirne Province. Ladas, *The Exchange of Minorities*, 15–16.

105. Akçam, *The Young Turks' Crime*, 88–89, 99–113.

106. NARA, RG 84, Adrianople 1915–1916, No. 166, Allen to Ravndal, March 5, 1916.

107. Pallis estimates that the Greek population of Edirne Province was 253,000 in 1912, 138,000 in 1915, and 53,000 in 1917. "Racial Migrations," 327–30.

108. Carnegie Endowment, *Report of the International Commission*, 128–30.

109. Suny, *They Can Live in the Desert*, xi–xxi, 281–327, 350–65; Norman Naimark, "Preface," in *A Question of Genocide*, xiii–xix; Taner Akçam, *A Shameful Act: The Armenian Genocide and the Question of Turkish Responsibility* (New York, 2006), 1–13, 149–204.

110. Fuat Dündar claims that, with the exception of certain elites, the Armenian population of Edirne Province was not deported. *Crime of Numbers: The Role of Statistics in the Armenian Question, 1878–1918* (New Brunswick, 2010), 150–51; and "Pouring a People into the Desert," in *A Question of Genocide,* 283–84. Citing Dündar, Ronald Grigor Suny repeats this claim in *They Can Live in the Desert but Nowhere Else* (Princeton, 2015), 320–21, 354. It is unclear where Dündar got this notion, which is refuted by other sources (see below).

111. NARA, RG 84, Adrianople 1915–1916, No. 36, Charles E. Allen to G. Bie Ravndal, October 16, 1915.

112. NARA, RG 84, Adrianople 1915–1916, No. 54, Allen to Ravndal, October 29, 1915.

113. NARA, RG 84, Adrianople 1915–1916, No. 64, Allen to Ravndal, November 5, 1915. The detail about the bazaar is from Raymond Kévorkian, *The Armenian Genocide: A Complete History* (London, 2011), 545–50.

114. Kévorkian, *The Armenian Genocide*, 545–50; Roy Arakelian, *Edirne (Adrianupolis) ve Ermeni toplumu = Andrinople (Edirne) et sa communauté Arménienne* (Istanbul, 2016), 65–69; NARA, RG 84, Adrianople 1915–1916, No. 64, Allen to Ravndal, November 5, 1915.

115. Raymond Kévorkian, *Le Génocide des Arméniens* (Paris, 2006), 917; Karpat, *Ottoman Population*, 162–69. Most of the six thousand Armenians who returned after World War I would leave again in 1922, at the close of the Greco-Turkish War. See Chapter 4.

116. Nurten Çetin, "Osmanlı Devleti'nin Birinci Dünya Savaşı'nda İtilaf Devletleri Vatandaşlarına Yönelik Uygulamalarından Biri: Sürgün (Edirne Örneği)," *Trakya Üniversitesi Edebiyat Fakültesi Dergisi* 3, no. 5 (January, 2013): 75–94. In Great Britain, at least, the detained Ottoman citizens included Jews from Edirne. NARA, RG 84, Adrianople 1915–1916, No. 93, Allen to Ravndal, December 5, 1915. For more on the wartime treatment of Ottoman Jews in Entente states, see Sarah Abrevaya Stein, *Extraterritorial Dreams: European Citizenship, Sephardi Jews, and the Ottoman Twentieth Century* (Chicago, 2016), 73–96.

117. NARA, RG 84, Adrianople 1915–1916, Brie to Allen, November 1, 1915; NARA, RG 84, Adrianople 1915–1916, Allen to Deutsche OrientBank, January 4, 1916; NARA, RG 84, Adrianople 1915–1916, No. 51, Allen to Hoffman Philip, February 16, 1916. Most of these "Russians and Italians" were from Edirne and Tekirdağ. Among the Italian citizens were Sephardim, and among the Russian citizens were Ashkenazim.

118. Dündar, *İttihat ve Terakki'nin Müslümanları iskân politikası*, 250. Mehmet Akif Bey's exact words were, *"Biz tehciri komşularımızdan öğrendik."*

119. Dündar, *Modern Türkiye'nin şifresi*, 184.

120. AAIU, France, XVI. F. 27, Mitrani, January 1, 1920. In Kırklareli, many Jewish young men left for the Americas, seeking jobs in places such as Cuba and New York. "Korespondensya de Kirklisse," *La Boz de la Verdad*, June 4, 1914, 2; "Komunidad Renyegada de sus Ijoz," *La Boz de la Verdad*, July 9, 1914, 1.

121. In September 1913, the Ottomans ceded to Bulgaria the towns of Gümülcine, Dedeağaç, İskeçe, and Mustafapaşa (among others). In October 1915, the Ottomans also ceded Karaağaç and Dimetoka (among other towns).

122. For instance, when Malko Tarnovo (Tırnovacık) found itself on the Bulgarian side of the border in 1913, the largely Bulgarian-Christian population realized that "all means of living"—pastures for livestock grazing, forests that supplied timber and charcoal, the market towns of Edirne and Tekirdağ—remained in the Ottoman Empire. Voinikov, *The Bulgarians*, 109.

123. Beginning in January 1913, the de facto rulers of the Ottoman Empire were the "Three Pashas": Interior Minister Mehmed Talat Paşa, War Minister Ismail Enver Paşa, and Navy Minister Ahmed Cemal Paşa.

124. H. Girard, "L'église Bulgare Catholique de Thrace et de Bulgaria," *Échos d'Orient* 16, no. 98 (1913): 68–69; Charles Fabrègues, "Le Vicariat Apostolique Bulgare de Thrace," in

Échos d'Orient 7, no. 44 (1904): 38. The city that is now Zagreb, Croatia, was then part of Austria-Hungary and called Agram (in German). A convent in that city was linked to the Sisters of Agram school in Edirne.

125. AAIU, Turquie, I. C. 3.1 a, Guéron, January 19, 1914, and January 25, 1914; AAIU, Turquie, VII. E., Guéron, February 5 1914, February 24, 1914, and March 11, 1914. For a controversy about these Jewish students participating in the Catholic school's 1910 Corpus Christi parade, see Chapter 2.

126. "El Konflicto Turko-Grego," *La Boz de la Verdad*, May 18, 1914, 2; "Los Deputados Gregos," *La Boz de la Verdad*, May 21, 1914, 2; "Los Gregos de Trasa," *La Boz de la Verdad*, May 25, 1914, 2.

127. "Albert Alfassa a la Frontyera," *La Boz de la Verdad*, May 14, 1914, 2. It is unclear when, where, or how Alfassa became a Greek citizen.

128. "La Kestyon Alfasa," *La Boz de la Verdad*, May 21, 1914, 2.

129. "El Gran Rabno Bejarano onde Enver Pasha," *La Boz de la Verdad*, June 29, 1914, 1. For more on Bejarano and Enver Paşa's relationship, see "Echos," *L'Aurore*, August 16, 1918, 2.

130. "Albert Alfassa," *La Boz de la Verdad*, July 9, 1914, 1.

131. "Albert Alfassa," *La Boz de la Verdad*, July 27, 1914, 1.

132. "1,200,000 Djudyos Ekspulsados," *La Boz de la Verdad*, August 4, 1915, 2. For more on this event, see Eric Lohr, "The Russian Army and the Jews: Mass Deportation, Hostages, and Violence during World War I," *Russian Review* 60, no. 3 (July, 2001): 404–19.

133. Quoted in Kévorkian, *The Armenian Genocide*, 547–48.

134. While my focus is on Thrace, it is worth noting that Jews were among the refugees and migrants who left Macedonia for the Ottoman Empire after their hometowns became Greek, Serbian, or Bulgarian. "Turkos i Djudyos de Makedonya Emigran en Turkya," *La Boz de la Verdad*, March 12, 1914, 4.

135. Eyal Ginio, "Challenging Communal Boundaries in Late Ottoman Thrace: Jews and Muslims in Dimetoka (Didymoteicho)," *Jewish Social Studies* 27, no. 3 (Fall 2022): 92.

136. AAIU, Turquie, XII. E., Mitrani, January 8, 1914, and January 30, 1914.

137. "Los Djudyos de Mustafa Pasha," *La Boz de la Verdad*, March 30, 1914, 1; "En Syudad," *La Boz de la Verdad*, April 30, 1914, 2.

138. "Las Familyas de Mustafa Pasha," *La Boz de la Verdad*, April 6, 1914, 1; "En Syudad: Rengrasyamyentos Publikos," *La Boz de la Verdad*, April 20, 1914, 2.

139. "Novidades Lokales," *La Boz de la Verdad*, June 25, 1914, 2. Similar arrangements were being made for displaced Muslims and Bulgarian Christians. Ladas, *The Exchange of Minorities*, 18–20.

140. "Ultima Ora," *La Boz de la Verdad*, June 29, 1914, 3.

141. "En Uzunköprü: El Hakim Efendi Abre Una Inkuesta," *La Boz de la Verdad*, July 13, 1914, 2. Perhaps the quote also referenced recent persecutions faced by Jewish peddlers in villages around Dimetoka. The persecutions ceased after the chief rabbi of the Ottoman Empire spoke to Talat Paşa and Rabbi Bejarano spoke to Hacı Adil Bey. "El Gran Ravno

de Turkya i la Komunidad de Demotika," *La Boz de la Verdad*, March 16, 1914, 2; and "En Demotika," *La Boz de la Verdad*, March 30, 1914, 2.

142. Many Jews were sent from Gelibolu to Tekirdağ. AAIU, Turquie, XCIII. E., President of the Jewish Community of Tekirdağ, June 9, 1920; Also see Mays, *Forging Ties, Forging Passports*, 62.

143. Dündar, *Modern Türkiye'nin Şifresi*, 386–88, 394. Dündar counts these incidents as part of a larger "expulsion and deportation of Jews" that occurred in the Ottoman Empire between 1914 and 1917. But this is an exaggeration.

144. NARA, RG 84, Adrianople 1915–1916, No. 14, Allen to Ravndal, October 2, 1915; NARA, RG 84, Adrianople 1915–1916, Ravndal to Allen, November 1, 1915.

145. Taylan Esin, "19. Yüzyılın Sonunda Osmanlı İmparatorlu'nda Kurulan Musevi İskan Birliği (JCA) Çiftlikleri." *Toplumsal Tarih* no. 249 (September 2014): 22–33.

146. NARA, RG 84, Adrianople 1915–1916, Allen to Deutsche Orientbank, A.G., January 4, 1916. For more on Russian Jews in the late Ottoman Empire, see Sarah M. Zaides, *Tevye's Ottoman Daughter: Ashkenazi and Sephardi Jews at the End of* Empire (Istanbul, 2022).

147. NARA, RG 84, Adrianople 1915–1916, No. 1, Allen to Ravndal, September 30, 1915.

148. *Almanach Israelite, 5683*, 113–13.

149. Nos. 15 and 17, Allen to Ravndal, October 4, 1915.

150. NARA, RG 84, Adrianople 1915–1916, No. 16, Allen to Ravndal, October 4, 1915.

151. Also, some of these people were interned in Kırklareli. NARA, RG 84, Adrianople 1915–1916, No. 28, Allen to Ravndal, October 9, 1915; NARA, RG 84, Adrianople 1915–1916, No. 50, Allen to Ravndal, October 25, 1915; NARA, RG 84, Adrianople 1915–1916, No. 106, Allen to Ravndal, December 17, 1915.

152. NARA, RG 84, Adrianople 1915–1916, No. 79, Allen to Ravndal, November 20, 1915.

153. NARA, RG 84, Adrianople 1915–1916, No. 74, Allen to Ravndal, November 16, 1915.

154. NARA, RG 84, Adrianople 1915–1916, No. 53, Allen to Ravndal, October 27, 1915; NARA, RG 84, Adrianople 1915–1916, No. 79, Allen to Ravndal November 20, 1915; NARA, RG 84, Adrianople 1915–1916, No. 97, Allen to Ravndal, December 10. 1915. In Italian, Simone is a masculine name pronounced with three syllables. It comes from the Hebrew name Shimon.

155. No. 163, Allen to Ravndal, February 24. 1916.

156. See Chapter 2.

157. For more on "royal alliance," see Lois C. Dubin, "Yosef Hayim Yerushalmi, the Royal Alliance, and Jewish Political Theory," *Jewish History* 28, no. 1 (2014): 51–83.

158. Before the Balkan Wars, Jews worked with Ottoman officials *and* Christian leaders to prevent the Dimetoka livestock fair from occurring on the Jewish sabbath (see Chapter 1). But when a similar issue emerged in 1914, Jews only petitioned the central Ottoman authorities. "En Syudad: El Bazar de Demotika de Nuevo en Shabat," *La Boz de la Verdad*, July 9, 1914, 2; "En Syudad: El Bazar de Demotika," *La Boz de la Verdad*, July 13, 1914, 2.

159. Zürcher, *Turkey*, 116.

160. Ginio, "Constructing a Symbol of Defeat," 83–99.

161. Eyal Ginio, "Paving the Way for Ethnic Cleansing: Eastern Thrace during the Balkan Wars (1912–1913) and their Aftermath," in *Shatterzone of Empires*, 295.

162. "Seremoniya Funebre a la Okazyon de la Aniversaryo de la Kayida de Edirne en Poder de los Bulgaros," *La Boz de la Verdad*, March 30, 1914, 1. For the speech given by Ahmed Rıza Paşa, commander of the 2nd Army Corps, see TNA, FO 195/2456, No. 17, Enclosure No. 2, Samson to Mallet, March 31, 1914.

163. Julia Phillips Cohen, *Becoming Ottomans: Sephardi Jews and Imperial Citizenship in the Modern Era* (New York, 2014), 15–16.

164. For a theoretical discussion of cultural and political community, see Bernard Yack, "The Myth of the Civic Nation," *Critical Review: A Journal of Politics and Society* 10, no. 2 (Spring 1996): 193–211.

165. "En la Kapitala: El Medjlis Djismani," *La Boz de la Verdad*, September 11, 1911, 1.

166. Ernest Gellner, *Nations and Nationalism* (Ithaca, 1983), 1.

167. See Chapter 2.

168. "Avizo de la Makabi," *La Boz de la Verdad*, November 6, 1911, 2.

169. "La Makabi en Konstantinopla i la Lengua Ebreyiko," *La Boz de la Verdad*, March 16, 1914, 1; "La Fiesta de la Makabi," *La Boz de la Verdad*, June 11, 1914, 1–2.

170. *La Boz de la Verdad*, July 16, 1914.

171. One such article said, "We recommend this hotel to our fellow residents in [the city of] Edirne, our fellow residents of the province, and residents of Bulgaria who are visiting Palestine." See "En Yafa: Otel Balkan 'Or Hadash,'" *La Boz de la Verdad*, July 16, 1914, 4.

172. AAIU, Turquie, XII. E., Mitrani, July 17, December 20, 1921.

173. "En Syudad: Despozorios," *La Boz de la Verdad*, March 5, 1914, 2; "En Syudad: Kazamyentos," *La Boz de la Verdad*, May 21, 1914, 2; "Kazamyento," *La Boz de la Verdad*, June 11, 1914, 2; "Kazamyento," *La Boz de la Verdad*, June 29, 1914, 2.

174. "Shumla: Anunsio," *La Boz de la Verdad*, June 25, 1914, 2.

175. But, as noted in Chapter 1, this job could be dangerous. See "Una Ninya Djudya Edirneliya de 14 Anyos Violada por Dos Mansevos en Tatar-Bazardjik," *La Boz de la Verdad*, July 9, 1914, 1.

176. "Novedades Lokales," *La Boz de la Verdad*, June 21, 1915, 1. For more on this society, see Chapter 2.

177. AAIU, Turquie, XI. E., Mitrani, March 4, 1908.

178. See Chapter 2.

179. Among the speakers was Rabbi Abraham Danon, who spoke lovingly about his hometown of Edirne. *Bulletin de la Grande Loge de district XI et de la Loge de Constantinople N. 678, I.O.B.B.* (February 1913–December 1921): 62–73.

180. Tadjer, *Notas istorikas*, 140–41.

181. Donations made their way to needy Jews in Edirne, Gelibolu, Kırklareli, Lüleburgaz, Tekirdağ, Dimetoka, and elsewhere. Instrumental to these efforts were Henry

Morgenthau and Abram Elkus—American ambassadors in Istanbul who were also members of B'nai B'rith. See *Bulletin de la Grande Loge* (February 1913–December 1921): 134–47, 233–38.

182. AAIU, Turquie, XII. E., Mitrani, January 9, 1919; *Bulletin de la Grande Loge* (February 1913–December 1921): 239–44; "Southeastern Front," *Air Service Journal*, September 13, 1917, 316; Mays, *Forging Ties, Forging Passports*, 69.

183. AAIU, Turquie, XII. E., Mitrani, January 9, 1919; *Bulletin de la Grande Loge* (February 1913–December 1921): 239–44.

184. Zürcher, "The Ottoman Conscription System, 1844–1914," *International Review of Social History* 43, no. 3 (December 1998): 437–49.

185. By August 1915, 300 Jews from the Kırklareli region and 120 from the Çorlu region had been placed in work gangs. Mehmet Beşikçi, *The Ottoman Mobilization of Manpower in the First World War: Between Voluntarism and Resistance* (Leiden, 2012), 133. According to a satirical Ladino Haggadah published in Istanbul after the war, Jews were made to do demolition work on "the old streets of Edirne and Silivri." Nisim Sh'T Eli, *Haggadah de la Gerra* (Istanbul, 1919).

186. AAIU, France, XVI. F. 27, Mitrani, January 1, 1920; Aron Rodrigue, *French Jews, Turkish Jews: The Alliance Israélite Universelle and the Politics of Jewish Schooling in Turkey, 1860–1925* (Bloomington, 1990), 155. In Kırklareli, the Alliance girls' school was requisitioned for a few months. AAIU, Turquie, XCIV. E., Rosa Avigdor, October 27, 1914, and January 24, 1915.

187. NARA, RG 84, Adrianople 1915–1916, No. 166, Charles E. Allen to Ravndal, March 5, 1916; AAIU, Turquie, XII. E., Mitrani, January 9, 1919.

188. Bıyıkoğlu, *Trakya'da Milli Mücadele*, 99–106. At this point, Ottoman soldiers stationed in Edirne could not even use the local train station, which was in (Bulgarian) Karaağaç: İ. Hakkı Sunata, *Gelibolu'dan Kafkaslara: Birinci Dünya Savaşı Anılarım* (Istanbul, 2003), 231–32.

189. Also, merchants of all religions benefited from Bulgaria's decision to drop its 30 percent ad valorem tax on goods destined for Istanbul. "Novedades del Interior," *El Tiempo*, November 3, 1915, 166.

190. "Novedades Lokales," *La Boz de la Verdad*, June 21, 1915, 1; *Bulletin de la Grande Loge* (February 1913–December 1921): 139. Rachel and Diamandi Bejarano worked for the Red Crescent in Edirne. Bella, Rosa, and Estréa Semah, along with Zimboul and Inès Mitrani, worked for the Red Cross in Karaağaç.

191. Tadjer, *Notas istorikas*, 196–97; *Osmanlı'dan Cumhuriyet'e Hilal-i Ahmer İcraat Raporları*, ed. Murat Uluğtekin and M. Gül Uluğtekin (Ankara, 2013), 62–63.

192. Kemal Karpat, "Jewish Population Movements in the Ottoman Empire, 1862–1914," in *The Jews of the Ottoman Empire*, ed. Avigdor Levy (Princeton, 1994), 403–4. The German-language writer Elias Canetti was born in Ruse in 1905. He claims that during his childhood, "most of the Sephardim" in Bulgaria "were still Turkish subjects." *The Tongue Set Free* (London, 2011), 5. He also claims that in 1915, his mother presented their Ottoman

passports to a Romanian customs official as they crossed from Romania to Austria-Hungary. *The Tongue Set Free*, 104.

193. Tadjer, *Notas istorikas*, 196–97. Pipano also authored the above-mentioned Ladino-Bulgarian dictionary.

194. AAIU, France, XVI. F. 27, Mitrani, January 1, 1920.

195. See Chapter 2.

196. NARA, RG 84, Adrianople 1915–1916, No. 1, Allen to Ravndal, September 30, 1915; NARA, RG 84, Adrianople 1915–1916, No. 37, Allen to Ravndal, October 16, 1915.

197. BOA. HR. SYS., 2267/87, April 12, 1918; BOA. HR. SYS., 2267/90, June 5, 1918.

198. BOA. HR. SFR.(04), 925/22, November 28, 1918.

199. BOA. HR. SFR.(04), 644/36, Fethi Bey to Halil Menteşe. Reportedly, gold was also smuggled into Karaağaç by *kavasses* who worked in Edirne's Austro-Hungarian consulate. It is unlikely that any of these *kavasses* were Jewish.

200. Barishac was born in 1867. See Chapter 2.

201. Manlio Graziano, *What Is a Border?* (Stanford, 2018), 33.

Chapter 4

1. Following Devin Naar, I use "Hellenism" to indicate a form of Greek patriotism that emerged after World War I and that, at least according to some Greek Jews, was open to citizens of all religions. See Devin E. Naar, *Jewish Salonica: Between the Ottoman Empire and Modern Greece* (Stanford, 2016), 1–35.

2. Among the orphans was Davit Nae, who would go on to be a prominent member of the Communist Party of Turkey. Rıfat Bali, "Unutulmuş bir TKP'li Davit Nae," *Toplumsal Tarih* no. 202 (October 2010): 70–76. See also *Bulletin de la Grande Loge de district XI et de la Loge de Constantinople N. 678, I.O.B.B.* (February 1913–December 1921): 134–47, 270–74; and JDC Archives, 1921 report on "Adrianople," NY 1921–1932, File 446, number 83.09.

3. *Bulletin de la Grande Loge* (February 1913–December 1921): 134–47.

4. The hotel was in the Sirkeci neighborhood. "Matzah al Uzo de Andrinopla," *El Tiempo*, April 8, 1919, 481.

5. "Los Maftirin," *El Tiempo*, February 7, 1919, 352. When the Knesset Israel (or "Apollon") synagogue in Galata opened in 1923, it became the new venue for the *maftirim* and the synagogue of choice for many Jews from Edirne. "Le Frère Secrétaire du District XI à Andrinople," *Hamenora* 3, no. 2 (February 1925): 42. A diminished version of the *maftirim* choir continued to occasionally perform in Edirne. Albert Cohen, "Notas y Impresiones de Viaje: En la Comunidad Israelita de Edirne," *La Boz de Türkiye*, October 15, 1940, 112–13.

6. For a recent exception, see Nurten Çetin and V. Türkan Doğruöz, *Milli Mücadele'nin Yerel Tarihi 1918–1923, Cilt 10: Edirne, Kırklareli, Tekirdağ* (Ankara, 2023).

7. Called Sofulu in Turkish, Soufli was home to the massive Ceriano silk factory, which was purchased in 1920 by members of the (Jewish) Djivre family.

8. Shemtov Perahia made this speech on August 13, 1920. A typed, unpublished copy in French can be found in the Yad Ben-Zvi Archive, Juda Haim Perahia Collection, 0049.003/8. A Ladino version can be found in "Kavala i la Sinyatura de la Pas," *El Pueblo*, August 18, 1920, 1. Perahia was president of the Jewish National Fund in Kavala. "Kavala i la Sinyatura de la Pas," *El Pueblo*, August 18, 1920, 1.

9. For one mention of a "Jewish flag," see Erol Haker, *Once Upon a Time Jews Lived in Kırklareli: The Story of the Adato Family, 1800–1934* (Istanbul, 2003), 300–301. A version of today's Israeli flag was flown in 1897, at the first Zionist Congress in Basel, and a year later it became the official Zionist flag.

10. Esther Benbassa and Aron Rodrigue, *Sephardi Jewry: A History of the Judeo-Spanish Community, 14th–20th centuries* (Berkeley, 2000), 127–30; Rena Molho, "The Zionist Movement up to the First Panhellenic Zionist Conference," in *Salonica and Istanbul: Social, Political and Cultural Aspects of Jewish Life*, ed. Rena Molho (Istanbul, 2005), 165–86.

11. Compare what Tatjana Lichtenstein says about interwar Czechoslovakia, where Zionists "promoted Zionism as a form of national neutrality, an expression of ethnic Jewish pride and Czechoslovak patriotism." *Zionists in Interwar Czechoslovakia: Minority Nationalism and the Politics of Belonging* (Bloomington, 2016), 10.

12. For example, see: N. Fahri Taş, "Birinci Dünya Savaşı Sonrasında Fransızların Trakya'yı İşgali," *Atatürk Araştırma Merkezi Dergisi* 20, no. 60 (November, 2004): 660–74.

13. Taş, "Birinci Dünya Savaşı Sonrasında," 663–65.

14. First used by Greek leaders in 1844, the term "Megali Idea" referred to the goal of reviving the borders of the Byzantine Empire by extending Greece's territory into Epirus, Macedonia, Thrace, Western Asia Minor, and Crete.

15. Tevfik Bıyıklıoğlu, *Trakya'da Millî Mücadele* I (Ankara, 1955), 145, 200–203.

16. TNA, FO 608/118, No. 1066, Richard Webb, April 1, 1919. From 1918 to 1920, the Greek government worked with Allied authorities in Istanbul to repatriate 133,000 Orthodox Greeks to Eastern Thrace from Anatolia and Greece. A. A. Pallis, "Racial Migrations in the Balkans during the Years 1912–1924," *Geographical Journal* 66, no. 4 (October 1925): 329.

17. TNA, FO 608/118, No. 667, A. Calthorpe, May 5, 1919.

18. FO 608/118, September 3, 1919. This source claims that the Jewish community president was also a rabbi.

19. The *vali* of Edirne demanded the release of the four men. BOA. DH.EUM.AYŞ, 4/62/2–3 (June 8–9, 1919). For yet another account of the incident, see V. Türkan Doğruöz, *Millî Mücadelede Kırklareli* (Kırklareli, 2007), 11–13.

20. AAIU, Turquie XCIV. E., 1110.04, Conorté Canetti, May 31, 1920.

21. AAIU, Turquie XCIV. E. 1110.04, Conorté Canetti, June 18, 1920.

22. AAIU, Turquie XCIV. E. 1110.04, Conorté Canetti, June 18, 1920

23. After Canetti visited Kırklareli's Christian quarter to buy a fermented beverage called *boza*, rumors swirled that he had visited "the Greek Patriarch" to declare support for Greek annexation. AAIU, Turquie XCIV. E. 1110.04, Conorté Canetti, June 18, 1920.

The Ottoman chief rabbi had told the Jewish communities of Tekirdağ and Edirne that he would provide no voting guidance in the 1919 Ottoman elections, which constituted "an individual matter, not a communal one." "En la Komunidad de Andrinopla" and "En la Komunidad de Rodosto," *El Tiempo*, October 24, 1919, 45.

24. AAIU, Turquie XCIV. E. 1110.04, Conorté Canetti, June 18, 1920.

25. Benbassa and Rodrigue, *Sephardi Jewry*, 127–30; Rena Molho, "The Zionist Movement," 183.

26. However, the ceremony was cancelled by the "more reserved" community in the city of Edirne and/or the Ottoman Chief Rabbi in Istanbul, who insisted that Jews "do nothing to hurt the feelings of the Turks." TNA, FO 608/118, No. 922, Calthorpe, June 3, 1919.

27. John J. McTague, Jr., "Zionist-British Negotiations over the Draft Mandate for Palestine, 1920," *Jewish Social Studies* 42, no. 3/4 (Summer–Autumn, 1980): 283.

28. AAIU, Turquie XCIV. E. 1110.04, Conorté Canetti, June 18, 1920. Perhaps the girl was quoting a famous speech that Abraham Danon gave in 1892 at a Greek Orthodox club in Edirne. Tamir Karkason, "An Ambivalent Coexistence: Jews and Christians in Late Ottoman Edirne," *Jewish History* 38, nos. 1–2 (2024): 1–25.

29. Bernard Pierron, *Juifs et Chrétiens de la Grèce Moderne: Histoire des relations intercommunautaires de 1821 à 1945* (Paris, 1996), 176–78.

30. Circa 1922, Çorlu, Lüleburgaz, Babaeski, and Gelibolu had Shivat Tzion societies. *Almanach Israelite 5688* (Thessaloniki): 97–120, from the Jewish Museum of Greece Collection, inv.no.1981.091.1. Even before Elnekave's visit, there was a Hovevei Tzion (Lovers of Zion) society in Tekirdağ. "En la Komunidad Israelita de Rodosto," *El Tiempo*, February 28, 1919, 397.

31. "En Luleburgaz," *El Tiempo*, October 28, 1919, 53–54.

32. The ousted chief rabbi was Haim Nahum. See Esther Benbassa, *Haim Nahum: A Sephardic Chief Rabbi in Politics, 1892–1923* (Tuscaloosa, 1995).

33. Yitzhak Trani, "En la Provensya," *El Djudyo*, June 1, 1920, 3–4.

34. See the minutes of the First Conference of London: *Documents on British Foreign Policy, 1919–1939*, First Series, Vol. VII, 1920, ed. E. L. Woodward and Rohan Butler (London, 1958), 63–65. See also "La Okupasyon de la Tras: 30,000 Kilometros i 800,000 Abitantes Akordados a la Gresya," *El Tiempo*, May 4, 1920, 469.

35. AAIU, Turquie XCIV. E., 1110.04, Canetti, July 22, 1919.

36. For more on the pogroms, see Jeffrey Veidlinger, *In the Midst of Civilized Europe: The Pogroms of 1918–1921 and the Onset of the Holocaust* (New York, 2021).

37. See Chapter 2.

38. TNA, FO 371/4157, Samson, June 5, 1919. The founders of the association were Mustafa Şevket (Dağdeviren), Mehmet Şeref (Aykut), Mehmet Faik (Kaltakkıran), and Kasım Yolageldili. B. Cem Altınel, *Kuruluşunun 100. Yılında Trakya Paşaeli Müdafaa-i Hukuk Cemiyeti YöneticilerininYaşam Öyküleri* (Edirne, 2018), 15–16.

39. From September 1919 until January 1920—apparently the end of its run—the newspaper listed Yuda Razon as publisher. See the last page of each issue: http://www.osmanlicagazeteler.org.

40. TNA, FO 371/4157, No. 59, Samson, March 25, 1919.

41. Bıyıklıoğlu, *Trakya'da Millî Mücadele*, 71–72.

42. Bıyıklıoğlu, *Trakya'da Millî Mücadele*, 123–37.

43. "Soldados Djudyos en la Armada Kemalista," *El Tiempo*, September 14, 1923, 6. The article's source is *La Boz de la Verdad*, whose post-1922 issues are no longer extant, to my knowledge.

44. AAIU, Turquie XCIV. E., 1110.04, Conorté Canetti, May 24, 1920.

45. For local bandits joining the Turkish resistance movement, see Mihri Belli, *Mihri Belli'nin Anıları: "İnsanlar Tanıdım"* (Istanbul, 1989), 33–37.

46. The Jews of Çorlu were told to pay sixteen thousand Ottoman lira, and the Jews of Edirne were told to pay four thousand Ottoman lira. AAIU, Turquie XII. E., Mitrani, June 25, 1920. See also "Greece," *The Near East* 18, no. 478, July 1, 1920, 5.

47. AAIU, Turquie XCIV. E., 1110.04, Conorté Canetti, May 24, 1920, May 31, 1920, and June 3, 1920; AAIU, Turquie XCVI. E., 1125.02, Benjamin Bidjérano, May 31, 1920; AAIU, Turquie XII. E., Mitrani, June 25, 1920.

48. AAIU, Turquie XII. E., Mitrani, August 2, 1920. A separate detachment had already landed at the port of Tekirdağ. Edirne was now Adrianoúpolis, and Tekirdağ was now Raidestos.

49. AAIU, Turquie XII. E., Mitrani, August 2, 1920. In today's values, Alexander gave $10,500 to the Muslim community and $5,250 each to the Jewish and Armenian communities.

50. For more on Solomon Mitrani, see Chapter 2.

51. AAIU, Turquie, XII. E., Mitrani, August 2, 1920.

52. The Greek General Government of Thrace was divided into six prefectures: Adrianopolis (Edirne), Raidestos (Tekirdağ), Kallipolis (Gelibolu), Karànta Ekklisiès (Kırklareli), Evros, and Rhodope. See the 1920 Greek census: *Recensement de la Population de la Grèce au 19 Décembre 1920/1 Janvier 1921: Résultats Statistiques Généraux* (Athens, 1928).

53. Article 27 defined "the frontiers of Turkey" with Greece; article 95 mentioned "a national home for the Jewish people in Palestine." The treaty was rejected by Mustafa Kemal's nationalist movement.

54. Stefanos Katsikas, "*Millets* in Nation-States: The Case of Greek and Bulgarian Muslims, 1912–1923," *Nationalities Papers* 37, no. 2 (March 2009): 181–82; The quote is from Article 16 of the "Treaty Concerning the Protection of Minorities in Greece": http://www.forost.ungarisches-institut.de/pdf/19200810-2.pdf.

55. Naar, *Jewish Salonica*, 27; Rena Molho, "The Zionist Movement," 185; K. E. Fleming, *Greece: A Jewish History* (Princeton, 2008), 92. Around this time, Greek Law 2345 called for the appointment of a chief mufti of Greece to lead the country's Muslim community, but it

was never applied in practice. See Stefanos Katsikas, "*Millet* Legacies in a National Environment: Political Elites and Muslim Communities in Greece (1830s–1923)," in *State-Nationalisms in the Ottoman Empire, Greece, and Turkey: Orthodox and Muslims, 1830–1945*, ed. Benjamin C. Fortna et al. (New York, 2013), 55.

56. "G. Roussos, Minister of Foreign Affairs, to all Greek Embassies," September 4, 1924, in *Documents on the History of the Greek Jews: Records from the Historical Archives of the Ministry of Foreign Affairs*, ed. Photini Constantopoulou and Thanos Veremis (Athens, 1999), 111–12.

57. "Greece," *The Near East* 18, no. 491 (September 30, 1920): 461.

58. "En Andrinopla," *El Djudyo*, October 19, 1920, 3.

59. "Los Israelitas en Gresya," *El Tiempo*, September 21, 1920, 805.

60. "En Andrinopla," *El Djudyo*, March 1, 1921, 2.

61. "Thrace Jews and the Greek Administration," *Jewish Chronicle*, October 1, 1920, 11.

62. "Thrace Jews and the Greek Administration," *Jewish Chronicle*, October 1, 1920, 11.

63. Venizelos knew that he had strong support among the Orthodox Greeks of Thrace, and this was a factor in his decision to annex the region before the elections. Michael Llewellyn Smith, *Ionian Vision: Greece in Asia Minor, 1919–1922* (New York, 1973), 140–41.

64. AAIU, Turquie, XCIV. E., 1110.04, Canetti, October 24, 1922; George Th. Mavrogordatos, *The Stillborn Republic: Social Coalitions and Party Strategies in Greece, 1922–1936* (Los Angeles, 1983), 238; Smith, *Ionian Vision*, 150–51. "Old Greece" referred to the pre-1912 borders of the country.

65. Richard Clogg, *A Concise History of Greece* (Cambridge, 2021), 95.

66. Mark Mazower, *Salonica, City of Ghosts: Christians, Muslims, and Jews, 1430–1950* (New York, 2005), 319.

67. "Las Insinuasyones del Zheneral Zimbrakakyes," *El Pueblo*, November 24, 1920, 1.

68. These Jewish members of parliament had just been elected on the anti-Venizelist ticket. "The Jewish Deputies in the Greek Parliament," *Jewish Chronicle*, December 10, 1920, 10; "Anti-Semitism in Greece: Commander-in-Chief's Outburst," *Jewish Chronicle*, December 17, 1920, 10.

69. "Ultimas Novidades," *El Pueblo*, November 24, 1920, 2; "The Anti-Semitic Outburst in Thrace: Official Condemnation," *Jewish Chronicle*, January 7, 1921, 8.

70. Smith, *Ionian Vision*, 176.

71. Worth about US$15,000 today.

72. *Documents on the History of the Greek Jews*, 111. Eventually, the payment was made. AAIU, Turquie, XII. E., Mitrani, March 31, 1922.

73. For the situation of the Jews in Thessaloniki, see Sam Hassid, "Further on the 1920 Elections," *Jewish Museum of Greece Newsletter*, no. 41 (Autumn–Winter 1996) 5–7.

74. Alexandre Antoniadès, *Le Développement économique de la Thrace* (Athens, 1922), 62. Antoniadès himself was a deputy from Edirne.

75. Mavrogordatos, *The Stillborn Republic*, 238; "Los Eleksyones," *El Tiempo*, November 23, 1920, 145–46. However, the Turkish-Muslim deputies would soon defect from the Liberal Party.

76. Greek Parliament, *Mitroo Plirexousion, Gerousiaston kai Voulefton, 1822–1935* (Athens, 1986), 186–299. The Edirne prefecture also sent to parliament four Muslims and six Orthodox Greeks. Republic of Greece, Census Office, *Recensement de la Population de la Grèce au 19 Décembre 1920/1 Janvier 1921.*

77. AAIU, Turquie, XCIV. E., 1110.04, Canetti, October 24, 1922.

78. From the private archive of Avner Perez: Menahem Mitrani, untitled *djonk* written in soletreo script (Edirne, 1921): see the dedication to the son, Shlomo/Solomon. Also see AAIU, Turquie, XCIV. E., Solomon Mitrani, July 3, 1907. The seminary in Edirne operated from 1891 to 1898. See Rodrigue, "The Alliance Israélite Universelle and the Attempt to Reform," 62–69.

79. AAIU, Turquie, XCIV. E., Solomon Mitrani, July 20, 1906; AAIU, Turquie, XCIV. E., 1110.01 b, Rosa Mitrani [née Avigdor], April 22, 1912; AAIU, Turquie, XCIV. E., 1110.01 b, Rosa Mitrani [née Avigdor], April 24, 1912.

80. See Chapter 2.

81. *Bulletin de la Grande Loge* (February 1913–December 1921): 321. For diaspora nationalism in the Ottoman Empire, see Aron Rodrigue, "From *Millet* to Minority: Turkish Jewry," in *Paths of Emancipation: Jews, States, and Citizenship*, ed. Pierre Birnbaum and Ira Katznelson (Princeton, 2014), 255.

82. AAIU, Turquie, XII. E., Moise Mitrani, April 5, 1921. For a slightly different account, see "La Kolunya de la Sangre," *El Tiempo*, April 1, 1921, 524.

83. *El Tiempo* wrote that "the Jews of Edirne are celebrating their first Passover under the Greek regime, and in their prayers, they urge God to 'liberate' them from the slavery of the Pharaohs!" "La Kolunya de la Sangre," *El Tiempo*, April 1, 1921, 524.

84. "Greece," *The Near East*, April 7, 1921, 401.

85. AAIU, Turquie, XII. E., Moise Mitrani, April 5, 1921; "La Protestasyon de los Djudyos de Andrianopla," *El Tiempo*, April 15, 1921, 555.

86. AAIU, Turquie XII. E., Moise Mitrani, April 5, 1921. Ritual murder allegations would soon occur in Greek-occupied Izmir and even Thessaloniki. "La Kolunya de la Matansa Ritual en Salonika," *El Tiempo*, April 22, 1921, 572–73.

87. AAIU, Turquie XII. E., Moise Mitrani, April 5, 1921.

88. Just a few weeks prior, however, the chief rabbi of the Ottoman Empire had sought redress from a Greek commissioner in Istanbul after a Jewish notable in Kırklareli was jailed by the authorities. "El Gran Rabno Bejerano Onde el Alto Komisaryo Eleniko," *El Tiempo*, February 11, 1921, 411.

89. AAIU, Turquie, XCIV. E., Canetti, October 24, 1922. For more on efforts to replace the lira with the drachma, see AAIU, Turquie, XII. E., Moise Mitrani, November 5, 1920.

90. TNA, FO 371/6573, No. 13981, Reşid Paşa, December 21, 1921; AAIU, Turquie, XCIV. E., Canetti, October 24, 1922.

91. "Miting de Protestasyon: En Andrinopla," *El Djudyo*, May 31, 1921, 3; "Las Fiestas del Mandato en Saloniko i al Interior," *La Renasensia Djudya*, September 8, 1922, 1.

92. AAIU, France XVI. F. 27, Moise Mitrani, July 6, 1921.

93. This is consistent with Nicholas Stavroulakis's claim that "the Salonika Community was known for being a closed world, even to other Jews." Nicholas Stavroulakis, "The Jews of Greece: An Essay" (Athens, 1990), 52. Also, K. E. Fleming describes "a belated nationalization of Greece's Jews—a nationalization that became complete only with their departure from Greece." Fleming, *Greece*, 12.

94. AAIU, France, XVI. F. 27, Moise Mitrani, July 6, 1921; "El Sy. Shlomo Goldman: Profesor de Evreo i Konferansyado," *El Djudyo*, February 11, 1921, 4.

95. AAIU, France, XVI. F. 27, Moise Mitrani, July 6, 1921.

96. "Yom Achekel a Kirklissé," *L'Écho d'Andrinople,* May 20, 1921, 2.

97. AAIU, France, XVI. F. 27, Moise Mitrani, July 6, 1921; "Notas i Impresyones de Viaje," *El Djudyo*, July 29, 1921, 3; "Notas i Impresyones de Viaje," *El Djudyo*, August 2, 1921, 2; "Notas i Impresyones de Viaje," *El Djudyo*, August 9, 1921, 3. A week after writing about his trip to Eastern Thrace, Elnekave reported that a Shivat Tzion society had been founded in Kırklareli. "En Kirklesya," *El Djudyo*, August 19, 1921, 2.

98. AAIU, Turquie, XII. E., December 21, 1921. Mitrani claimed that B'not Tzion had already shut down, but other sources show that it soon resumed activity. "La Fiesta del Mandato Palestiyano en Andrinople," *La Fuersa*, September 8, 1922, 2.

99. AAIU, France, XVI. F. 27, Moise Mitrani, July 6, 1921.

100. See the mastheads of both newspapers.

101. AAIU, Turquie XII. E., Moise Mitrani, April 4, 1921.

102. AAIU, Maroc, XLVIII. E. 734, Nissim Behar, December 7, 1917, December 21, 1917, and January 3, 1918. The secretary's response is from December 21, 1917.

103. AAIU, Turquie, XII. E., Moise Mitrani, April 4, 1921. Behar was Mitrani's former student. AAIU, Turquie, XII. E., Moise Mitrani, April 5, 1921.

104. *L'Écho d'Andrinople* appears in the old card catalogue of the National Library of Greece, but the item itself seems to be lost. One issue exists in Stanford University Libraries, under the title *L'écho d'Andrinople: organe indépandant: journal politique, économique, littéraire & social*. Another issue exists here: AAIU, Turquie, XII. E. Mitrani, May 25, 1921. For Behar's "expulsion from Thrace," see AAIU, Turquie, XII. E. Mitrani, March 31, 1922.

105. "Les Arabes ont soif...!" *L'Écho d'Andrinople*, May 20, 1921, 1. The Jaffa riots claimed the lives of forty-seven Jews and forty-eight Arabs.

106. "Meeting de protestation," *L'Écho d'Andrinople*, May 20, 1921, 1–2. The protests had been ordered by the Zionist Federation of Greece, via telegram. "Miting de Protestasyon: En Andrinopla," *El Djudyo*, May 31, 1921, 3.

107. Also, the Istanbul-based Zionist Federation of the East had recently made Danon "commissar" of the Jewish National Fund in Thrace. *Almanach Israelite 5688*, 104.

108. "Meeting de protestation," *L'Écho d'Andrinople*, May 20, 1921, 1–2.

109. AAIU, Turquie, XII. E., Moise Mitrani, April 4, 1921.

110. Nessim Behar, "La Collaboration Vozikis-Tsoukalas," *L'Écho d'Andrinople*, October 21, 1921, 1.

111. AAIU, Turquie, XII. E., Mitrani, April 4, 1921.

112. "En Andrinopla," *El Djudyo*, March 1, 1921, 2.

113. AAIU, Turquie, XII. E., Moise Mitrani, December 20, 1921.

114. "El Djudayizmo a Ovra," *La Boz de la Verdad*, June 14, 1922, 2; "Novidades Diversas Lokales," *La Boz de la Verdad*, July 28, 1922, 1.

115. In the available issues of *La Boz de la Verdad* from the period 1921–1922, I found no mention of Arabs. In earlier runs of the newspaper, Barishac's treatment of Arabs in Syria/Palestine was rather sympathetic (see Chapter 2). Measured praise for the work of Greek administrators can be found in "Sr. Maksimos i la Trasa," *La Boz de la Verdad*, July 28, 1922, 1; "Kirklisse," *La Boz de la Verdad*, July 28, 1922, 2.

116. "En Provensya: Gumuldjine," *La Boz de la Verdad*, July 28, 1922, 2. Komotini was also in the Greek General Government of Thrace.

117. "No Piedramos Tiempo," *La Boz de la Verdad*, June 14, 1922, 1; "Fantezia: La Edukasyon Fizika," *La Boz de la Verdad*, June 14, 1922, 2.

118. Rodrigue, *French Jews, Turkish Jews*, 134–35.

119. AAIU, Turquie, XII. E., Moise Mitrani, May 5, 1915; April 24, 1919; November 18, 1919; December 19, 1919; April 20, 1920; July 13, 1920.

120. AAIU Turquie, XII. E., Mitrani, April 4, 1921. The pseudonym was "B. Jacob."

121. AAIU, Turquie, V. E. 83 b, Julie Beja, May 16, 1921.

122. According to Moise Mitrani, the Bejas attacked the Alliance for teaching too much French and not enough Hebrew. AAIU, France, XVI. F. 27, Mitrani, July 6, 1921.

123. AAIU, Turquie, XII. E., Moise Mitrani, December 20, 1921.

124. Rodrigue, *French Jews, Turkish Jews*, 161–66.

125. AAIU, Turquie, VII. E., Guéron, May 16, 1913, and March 3, 1915; AAIU, Turquie, XII. E., Mitrani, February 7, 1915, and Jan, 9, 1915.

126. The president was Moise Maim. AAIU, Turquie, XII. E., Mitrani, December 24, 1919.

127. AAIU, Turquie XII. E., Mitrani, January 9, 1919.

128. There were more girls than boys in the Jewish schools of Uzunköprü, Çorlu, Babaeski, and Xanthi. There were slightly more boys than girls in the Jewish schools of Edirne and Lüleburgaz. Data is unavailable for the other towns. The boys' and girls' schools of Gelibolu also had to merge. *Almanach Israelite 5688*, 97–122, 173–74.

129. AAIU, France, XVI. F. 27, Algranti, September 29, 1910; AAIU, France, XVI. F. 27, Moise Mitrani, July 6, 1921.

130. Smith, *Ionian Vision*, 244–49.

131. *Documents on British Foreign Policy, 1919–1939*, First Series, Vol. 15, International Conferences and Conversations, 1921, 125–452; Smith, *Ionian Vision*, 223; "La Sosyedad del Derecho de los Pueblos Desidyo el Returno a la Turkiya de Ismirna i de la Tras," *El Tiempo*, September 23, 1921, 934.

132. "Grande Ajitasyon en la Tras," *El Tiempo*, October 21, 1921, 39.

133. Nicéphore Moschopoulos, *La question de Thrace, ou le mensonge bulgare* (Athens, 1922), 452–53; Kostas Geregas, *Anamniseis ek Thrakis* (Athens, 1925), 107–8.

134. On the concept of making natural and human landscapes "legible" for the state, see James C. Scott, *Seeing Like a State: How Certain Schemes to Improve the Human Condition Have Failed* (New Haven, 1998).

135. CAHJP, GR/Xa 4, December 28, 1921 [27 Kislev 5682]. In June 1922, the Edirne community again reminded the president of the Xanthi community about taxes owed to the chief rabbinate. CAHJP, GR/Xa 4, June 5, 1922 [9 Sivan 5682].

136. CAHJP, GR/Xa 4, April 17, 1922 [19 Nisan 5686]. Indeed, Greek authorities soon gave thirty thousand drachmas to the Alliance school in Edirne. AAIU, Turquie, XII. E., Mitrani, May 16, 1922.

137. CAHJP, GR/Xa 4, Shapat Algoder in Edirne to the president of the Jewish community of Xanthi, March 7, 1922.

138. CAHJP, GR/Xa 4, Boton to president of the Xanthi Jewish community, the 20th of "I", 1922. The newspaper was called *La Fuersa*. By 1924, Boton had stopped publishing that newspaper and started another called *El Progreso*. See Yitzchak Kerem, "Xanthi," *Encyclopaedia Judaica* 21.

139. "Gregos i Djudyos: El Turno de la Kestyon Palestiniyana," *El Fuerso*, August 25, 1922, 1. The mayor's surname was Brokoumis, and his original Greek letter was published beside a Ladino translation.

140. Another example of a reinstated Ottoman institution was Edirne's religiously mixed municipal council, mandated by Article 15 of the Sèvres Treaty.

141. Dem. C. Svolopoulos, *Thrace Under the Hellenic Administration* (Athens, 1922), 51–56. Jews were also treated at the Greek hospital in Komotini. See Antoniadès, *Le Développement économique de la Thrace*, 100. In some cases, military doctors made house calls. AAIU, Turquie XCIV. E., Canetti, October 24, 1922.

142. AAIU, Turquie XII. E., Mitrani, January 9, 1919.

143. M. S. Eulambio, *The National Bank of Greece: A History of the Financial and Economic Evolution of Greece* (Athens, 1924), 168.

144. "El Arivo del Sr. Maksimos en Muestra Sivdad," *La Fuersa*, July 7, 1922, 2. The new branch was in the town of Keşan.

145. AAIU, Turquie, XI. E., Mitrani, May 11, 1909; AAIU, Turquie, XII. E., Mitrani, May 16, 1922; AAIU, France, Mitrani, July 12, 1922. In the spring of 1922, the government paid half of the school's sixty-thousand-drachma deficit and promised to make a second payment of thirty thousand. It is unclear whether this second payment was ever made.

146. Though it granted group rights to the Jewish communities of Greece, Greek Law 2456 was forceful on the topic of teaching Greek in Jewish schools. Naar, *Jewish Salonica*, 157.

147. AAIU, Turquie, XII. E., Mitrani, April 4, 1921, and March 31, 1922.

148. AAIU, Turquie, XII. E., Mitrani, March 31, 1922, and July 12, 1922; AAIU, France, XVI. F. 27., Mitrani, July 12, 1922.

149. AAIU, France, XVI. F. 27, Mitrani, July 6, 1921; AAIU, Turquie, XII. E., Mitrani, July 17, 1921.

150. AAIU, France, XVI. F. 27, Mitrani, January 1, 1920.

151. "Las Fiestas del Mandato en Saloniko i al Interior," *La Renasensia Djudia*, September 9, 1922, 1. The Zionist Federation of Greece had told the Zionist clubs of Edirne to arrange these celebrations. Following the ceremony in Edirne's Great Synagogue, attendees poured into the streets and joined members of Makabi in a parade through the Jewish quarter. "La Fiesta del Mandato Palestiyano en Andrinople," *La Fuersa*, September 8, 1922, 2.

152. Benbassa and Rodrigue, *Sephardi Jewry*, 129–30. The quote is in reference to the Istanbul community, but it also applies to Edirne. Also applicable is their claim about the community in Thessaloniki: "After the Greek occupation, Zionism operated as a Diaspora nationalism, more concerned with local problems than with emigration." Benbassa and Rodrigue, *Sephardi Jewry*, 142.

153. Geregas, *Anamniseis ek Thrakis*, 119–20. The relevant legislation was Law 2782.

154. AAIU, France, XVI. F. 27, Mitrani, July 12, 1922.

155. AAIU, Turquie, XCIV. E., 1110.04, Canetti, October 24, 1922.

156. Bıyıklıoğlu, *Trakya'da Millî Mücadele,* 403–4.

157. AAIU, Turquie, XCIV. E., 1110.04, Canetti, October 24, 1922. Canetti was one of these Jews, but he was saved at the last minute by the intervention of Deputy Solomon Mitrani.

158. AAIU,Turquie, XII. E., Mitrani, September 21, 1922; AAIU, Turquie, XCVI. E., Benjamin Bidjérano, October 24, 1922.

159. The armistice was signed by the Grand National Assembly of Turkey, on the one hand, and Italy, France, and Britain, on the other. Greece acceded to the armistice on October 14, 1922.

160. Some wound up in Komotini and Xanthi, where Jewish schools and homes were among the buildings requisitioned to house the refugees. "Novedades Lokales," *La Fuersa*, October 20, 1922, 2. For more on the Christian departures from Eastern Thrace, see AAIU, Turquie XCIV. E. 1110.04, Canetti, October 24, 1922; AAIU, Turquie XII. E. Mitrani, October 19, 1922; AAIU, Turquie XCVI. E., Benjamin Bidjérano, October 24, 1922; "Belçika Konsolosuna İthaf," *Paşaeli*, July 30, 1923.

AAIU, Turquie XCIV. E. 1110.04, Canetti, October 24, 1922.

161. Smith, *Ionian Vision*, 319.

162. AAIU, Turquie, XCIV. E. 1110.04, Canetti, October 24, 1922.

163. For Ernest Hemingway's firsthand account, see "A Silent, Ghastly, Procession," *Toronto Daily Star*, October 22, 1922, in Ernest Hemingway, *Dateline Toronto: The Complete Toronto Star Dispatches, 1920–1924,* ed. William White (New York, 1985), 232.

164. Bıyıklıoğlu, *Trakya'da Millî Mücadele,* 458–59; AAIU, Turquie, XII. E., Mitrani, October 19, 1922; AAIU, Turquie, XCIV. E. 1110.04, Canetti, October 24, 1922.

165. AAIU, Turquie, XII. E., Mitrani, October 19, 1922.

166. AAIU, Turquie, XCIV. E., 1110.04, Canetti, October 24, 1922.

167. AAIU, Turquie, XCVI. E., Benjamin Bidjérano, October 24, 1922. For more on "Circassian Greeks," see Anton Popov, "From Pindos to Pontos: The Ethnicity and Diversity of Greek Communities in Southern Russia," *Bulletin: Anthropology, Minorities, Multiculturalism* 5 (January 2004): 88. For the role of nonlocals in violence occurring in Izmir at this time, see Reşat Kasaba, "İzmir 1922: A Port City Unravels," in *Modernity and Culture: From the Mediterranean to the Indian Ocean*, ed. Leila Fawaz and C. A. Bayly (New York, 2002), 204–24.

168. AAIU, Turquie, XCIV. E., 1110.04, Canetti, October 24, 1922.

169. At the end of the Greco-Turkish War, departing Greek soldiers murdered Muslims and Jews alike in Western Anatolia. "Alleged Greek Atrocities," *Jewish Chronicle*, September 22, 1922, 18. Edirne Jews raised funds for their beleaguered coreligionists in Izmir. "Jews in Smyrna," *Jewish Chronicle*, September 29, 1922, 12.

170. Veidlinger, *In the Midst of Civilized Europe*, 2. Veidlinger goes on to say that these pogroms marked "the real beginning of the Holocaust" that occurred during World War II.

171. As Kathryn Ciancia puts it, "In many ways, Jews *were* the towns." *On Civilization's Edge: A Polish Borderland in the Interwar World* (New York, 2021), 107. In the early twentieth century, Ukraine's three million Jews represented 12 percent of the overall population. Veidlinger, *In the Midst of Civilized Europe*, 11.

172. Oleg Budnitskii, "Shots in the Back: On the Origin of the Anti-Jewish Pogroms of 1918–1921," in *Polin: Studies in Polish Jewry Vol 14: Focusing on Jews in the Polish Borderlands*, ed. Antony Polonsky (London, 2001), 187–201.

173. "A 'Zone of Violence': The Anti-Jewish Pogroms in East Galicia in 1914–1915 and 1941," Alexander V. Prusin, *The Shatterzone of Empires: Coexistence and Violence in the German, Habsburg, Russian, and Ottoman Borderlands*, ed. Bartov and Weitz (Bloomington, 2013), 367–70.

174. Budnitskii, "Shots in the Back," 187–88, 198–200.

175. Bıyıklıoğlu, *Trakya'da Millî Mücadele*, 462.

Chapter 5

1. Avigdor Levy, "The Siege of Edirne (1912–1913) as Seen by a Jewish Eyewitness: Social, Political, and Cultural Perspectives," in *Jews, Turks, and Ottomans: A Shared History, Fifteenth through the Twentieth Century*, ed. Avigdor Levy (Syracuse, 2002), 156; Republic of Turkey, Directorate of Statistics, *General Census of the Population, October 28, 1927*, Booklet II (Ankara, 1929), 110–13; Kemal H. Karpat, *Ottoman Population 1830–1914: Demographic and Social Characteristics* (Madison, 1985), 162–69.

2. *General Census of the Population, October 28, 1927*, Booklet II, 110–13. Eastern Thrace's large Greek Orthodox population mostly left at the end of the 1919-1922 Greco-Turkish War, while another eighteen thousand left following the 1923 Convention on the Exchange

of Populations. Onur Yıldırım, *Diplomacy and Displacement: Reconsidering the Turco-Greek Exchange of Populations, 1922–1934* (New York, 2006), 129.

3. Zeynep Kezer, *Building Modern Turkey: State, Space, and Ideology in the Early Republic* (Pittsburghs, 2015), 114–15.

4. In addition to drawing Turkey's northwestern border, the Treaty of Lausanne confirmed the country's southern and northeastern borders, which had been taking shape in diplomatic agreements since 1921. Alexander E. Balistreri, "Revisiting Millî: Borders and the Making of the Turkish Nation State," in *Regimes of Mobility: Borders and State Formation in the Middle East, 1918–1946*, ed. Jordi Tejel and Ramazan Hakkı Öztan (Edinburgh, 2022), 29–58.

5. Aron Rodrigue, "From *Millet* to Minority: Turkish Jewry" in *Paths of Emancipation: Jews, States, and Citizenship*, ed. Pierre Birnbaum (Princeton, 2014), 238–61.

6. Laws excluding non-citizens from certain occupations were often implemented to exclude Christian and Jewish citizens. Speros Vryonis Jr., *The Mechanism of Catastrophe: The Turkish Pogrom of September 6–7, 1955, and the Destruction of the Greek Community of Istanbul* (New York, 2005), 32–33; Rıfat Bali, *Xenophobia and Protectionism: A Study of the 1932 Law Reserving Majority of Occupations in Turkey to Turkish Nationals* (Istanbul, 2013). For an argument that Jews were "on the periphery of Turkishness"—as opposed to beyond it—see Soner Çağaptay, *Islam, Secularism, and Nationalism in Modern Turkey: Who Is a Turk?* (London, 2006), 158–60.

7. Two examples are Hatice Bayraktar, "The Anti-Jewish Pogrom in Eastern Thrace in 1934: New Evidence for the Responsibility of the Turkish Government," *Patterns of Prejudice* 40, no. 2 (2006); and Ayhan Aktar, "Trakya Yahudi Olaylarını 'Doğru' Yorumlamak," *Tarih ve Toplum*, no. 155 (1996). For a more comprehensive review of the literature, see Berna Pekesen, "The Anti-Jewish Pogrom in 1934: Problems of Historiography, Terms and Methodology," in *The Heritage of Edirne in Ottoman and Turkish Times: Continuities, Disruptions and Reconnections*, ed. Birgit Krawietz and Florian Riedler (Berlin, 2020).

8. In the 1927 census, combined Jewish population for the provinces of Edirne, Kırklareli, and Tekirdağ stood at 8,557, and the Jewish population of Çanakkale Province was 1,845. *General Census of the Population, October 28, 1927*, Booklet II, 110–13. In the 1935 Census, these numbers had fallen to 5,972 and 1,583, respectively. Republic of Turkey, Directorate of Statistics, *General Census of the Population, October 20, 1935* (Ankara, 1937), 193–97. Berna Pekesen says that "the number of Jews living in Thrace and the Dardanelles region declined by almost 50 percent" immediately after the 1934 attacks, but this can only be true if the 1927 census undercounted Thrace's Jewish population or if the 1935 census inflated the number of Jews still in the region. "The Anti-Jewish Pogrom in 1934," 412–13.

9. Hatice Bayraktar, "The Anti-Jewish Pogrom," 97; Pekesen, "The Anti-Jewish Pogrom in 1934," 413.

10. Bayraktar, "The Anti-Jewish Pogrom," 102; Ayhan Aktar, "Conversion of a 'Country' into a 'Fatherland,'" in *Nationalism in the Troubled Triangle: Cyprus, Turkey, and Greece* (New York, 2010), 23–24.

11. Ayşegül Aydın and Cem Emrence, *Zones of Rebellion: Kurdish Insurgents and the Turkish State* (Ithaca, 2015), 77.

12. I say "roughly" because Çanakkale Province includes territory in northwestern Asia Minor, while the vilayet of Edirne had always been limited to Europe.

13. Cemil Koçak, *Umumi Müfettişlikler, 1927–1952* (Istanbul, 2003), 127–29.

14. Bayraktar, "The Anti-Jewish Pogrom," 95–111.

15. Koçak, *Umumi Müfettişlikler,* 127–29.

16. Bayraktar, "The Anti-Jewish Pogrom," 101–4.

17. Bayraktar, "The Anti-Jewish Pogrom," 110–11. For more on this map, see Sertaç Şen, "Marshaling Development: Turkish Thrace in the Interwar Years," *Diyâr* 4, no. 2 (2023): 232–61.

18. Ramazan Hakkı Öztan, "Settlement Law of 1934: Turkish Nationalism in the Age of Revisionism," *Journal of Migration History* 6 (2020): 97.

19. Law No. 2510, T.C. Resmi Gazete, no. 2733, June 21, 1934, 4003–9.

20. For theories on the intended zoning of the country, see Erol Ülker, "Assimilation, Security and Geographical Nationalization in Interwar Turkey: The Settlement Law of 1934," *European Journal of Turkish Studies* 7 (2008): 24–33; and Uğur Ümit Üngor, *The Making of Modern Turkey: Nation and State in Eastern Anatolia, 1913–1950* (Oxford, 2011), 152–53.

21. Rıfat N. Bali, *1934 Trakya Olayları* (Istanbul, 2014), 150–55. By July 1, 1934, Jews from Çanakkale were in Istanbul. "Las Persekusyones, Pogromes, i Ekspulsyones en Turkya komo las Kozas se Pasaron," *La Vara*, August 10, 1934, 3. Thank you, Joana Bürger, for showing me these articles in *La Vara*.

22. NARA, SD 867.4016 Jews/9, Skinner, June 29, 1934.

23. Atila, "İktisadi Savaş," *6 Ok* 1, no. 15 (June 30, 1934): 3. From Bali, *Trakya Olayları*, 149.

24. TNA, FO, 424/279, FC 28, no. 2: Loraine, July 7, 1934, and Kapsalis, July 5, 1934. From *Documents in the History of the Greek Jews: Records from the Historical Archives of the Ministry of Foreign Affairs*, ed. Constantopoulou and Veremis (Athens, 1999), 241–42.

25. "La Persekusyones, Pogromes, i Ekspulsyones en Turkya komo las Kozas se Pasaron," *La Vara*, August 10, 1934, 3.

26. Sources insisting on the occurrence of rape include Avner Levi, "*Ha-fraot b'Yehudei Trakya*, 1934," *Pe'amim* 20 (1984): 111–31; "La Persekusyones, Pogromes, i Ekspulsyones en Turkya komo las Kozas se Pasaron," *La Vara*, August 10, 1934, 3; NARA, RG59 Records of the Department of State Relating to the Internal Affairs of Turkey 1930–1944, 867.4016/Jews/8: July 27, 1934. Erol Haker denies the occurrence of rape. *Once Upon a Time Jews Lived in Kırklareli: The Story of the Adato Family, 1800–1934* (Istanbul, 2003), 227–45.

27. However, one newspaper article claimed that three Jewish children died of illness on the journey out of Eastern Thrace: "Jewish Deportees from Turkey in Fearful Flight," *Jewish Telegraphic Agency*, July 6, 1934, 5.

28. "La Persekusyones, Pogromes, i Ekspulsyones en Turkya komo las Kozas se Pasaron," *La Vara*, August 10, 1934, 3; Bali, *Trakya Olayları*, 182–86.

29. "Bulgarian Exiles Flee from Turkey," *New York Times*, July 8, 1934, 15.

30. Bali, *Trakya Olayları*, 186–89. According to *La Vara* (published in New York City), the Athens government told Greek consuls in Turkey to stop giving visas to Turkish Jews, but "hundreds" of Jewish refugees still wound up in Thessaloniki. "La Grega Defiende de Dar Vizas a Djudyos de Turkia," *La Vara*, September 14, 1934, 1. Orestiada had been the Greek name for Karaağaç, a historically non-Muslim suburb of Edirne. When Turkey annexed this suburb from Greece in 1923, residents moved en masse to a new settlement across the river and called it Nea Orestiada (New Orestiada).

31. "Jews Fear New Attacks: Turks Continue Expulsions," *Jewish Daily Bulletin*, July 8, 1934, 1; Bali, *Trakya Olayları*, 186–89.

32. Bayraktar, "The Anti-Jewish Pogrom," 97.

33. Bali, *1934 Trakya Olayları*, 451.

34. Anna M. Mirkova, *Muslim Land, Christian Labor: Transforming Ottoman Imperial Subjects into Bulgarian National Citizens, 1878–1939* (Budapest, 2017), 211.

35. Bali, *Trakya Olayları*, 450–51. When Law 2510 described the immigrants who urgently needed to be settled, it used the word *muhacir*, which has Islamic resonances. In contrast, the law used the word *mülteci* to describe "those seeking temporary refuge, with no intention of settling." In his speech, Kaya used the more neutral word for "immigrant": *göçmen*. But given the context, there is little doubt that he was referring to Muslim immigrants, specifically.

36. Bali, *Trakya Olayları*, 54–57; Şen, "Marshaling Development," 232–61.

37. Esther Benbassa and Aron Rodrigue, *Sephardi Jewry: A History of the Judeo-Spanish Community, 14th–20th Centuries* (Berkeley, 2000), 163.

38. *Hamenora* 8, no. 1 (January 1930): 49–52; *Hamenora* 8, no. 10–11 (October–November 1930): 333–42; *Bulletin de la Grande Loge de district XI et de la Loge de Constantinople N. 678, I.O.B.B.* (February 1913–December 1921): 66, 134–47. The orphanage was called Avi Yetomim (Father of the Orphans). Schools included the Alliance school and a more religious institution called Mahazike Torah (Holders of the Torah). The charities were called Ozer Dalim (Assistance for the Poor) and Matan B'seter (Secret Charity). The worker's syndicate was called Hevra Hapoalim.

39. According to Moise Mitrani, the city of Edirne's Jewish population was about 20,000 in 1912, 8,000–9,000 in 1919, 7,000 in 1925, 6,500 in 1927, and 6,000 in 1929. AAIU, France, XVI F 27, Mitrani, January 1, 1920, and September 19, 1929; AAIU, Turquie, XII. E., Mitrani, January 9, 1919, and January 9, 1925. The 1927 census counted about 6,098 Jews in Edirne Province, 978 in Kırklareli Province, and 1,481 in Tekirdağ Province. *General Census of the Population, October 28, 1927*, Booklet II, 110–13.

40. AAIU, Turquie, XII. E., Mitrani, January 9, 1919, and April 7, 1925. In 1934, Edirne member of parliament Mehmet Şeref (Aykut) recalled how the club had committed an unforgiveable act of betrayal by "kicking out all Turks" during the Armistice period. His anti-Jewish letter appears in Mehmet Pınar's *Tek Parti Döneminde Trakya'da Siyasi Hayat ve Yahudiler, 1930–1934* (Ankara, 2016), 247–71. Also see Rıfat N. Bali,

Edirne Mebusu Mehmet Şeref Aykut'un Munis Tekinalp'e Mektubu, 20 Nisan 1934 (Istanbul, 2023).

41. Yomtov Alkabes, "El Sionizmo en Turkia," *La Verdad*, August 24, 1951, 2.

42. *Bulletin de la Grande Loge* (February 1913–December 1921): 134–47. Members wrote the name of their club in the French style: *Acharon*.

43. *Bulletin de la Grande Loge* (February 1913–December 1921): 134–37, 270–74; *Hamenora* 2, nos. 2–3 (February–March 1924): 44; Bali, "Bir Yahudi Mali ve Sosyal Yardımlaşma Kurumu: Dersaadet Küçük İstikrazat Sandığı," *Tarih ve Toplum*, no. 160 (April, 1997): 45–54. As lodge president, Israel Danon oversaw the establishment of the fund in the early 1920s. The American Jewish Joint Distribution Committee (JDC) was the leading source of capital.

44. "Fondation de la Loge Bénoth Bérith Havatzeleth Hacharon No. 677 Andrinople," *Hamenora* 3, no. 3 (March 1925): 72–73; "District d'Orient N. XI: Composition des Bureaux por l'Exercise 1925," *Hamenora* 3, no. 5 (May 1925): 160; "Loge Hacharon: Rapport sur la section des Bénoth-Bérith 'Havatzeleth,'" *Hamenora* 8, no. 1 (January 1930): 49; AAIU, Turquie, XII. E., Mitrani, February 29, 1925.

45. The lodge is referenced in a document from 1939: CAHJP, TR/Ed/220.

46. CAHJP, TR/Ed/138. The name of Eastern District's organ was *HaMenora*. To a lesser extent, the Alliance also helped Jews preserve these interstate networks. For example, the Jewish community in Didymoteicho, Greece, sometimes asked the Alliance school director in Edirne to petition Paris on its behalf. AAIU, Turquie, XII. E., Mitrani, October 23, 1924.

47. I. S. Penakoff, "The Persecution of Jews in Eastern Thrace," *Slovo*, July 30, 1934. A French translation can be found in T. C. Cumhurbaşkanlığı Devlet Arşivleri Başkanlığ, Hariciye Vekaleti, 30/10/242/634/23, 2–3.

48. AAIU, Turquie, XII. E., Mitrani, April 30, 1924; "Palestine Emigration from Turkey," *JTA News Bulletin*, June 6, 1924, 6.

49. *Annuaire commercial turc* 1 (1924–1925): 59–60.

50. *Şark Ticaret Yıllığı/Annuaire oriental* (1934): 452.

51. In Izmir Province—where Jews also constituted 3–4 percent of the population—about 80 percent of commercial firms were owned by Muslims, 13 percent by Jews, and 7 percent by Christians. *Annuaire commercial turc* 1 (1924–1925): 119–30.

52. This document is known as the "index notebook" (*fihrist defteri*). Thank you to İsmail Eser for making it available.

53. This document is known as the "main notebook" (*esas defteri*). Thank you to İsmail Eser for making it available.

54. "The Greek Consulate in Adrianople to the Greek Embassy in Ankara," July 3, 1934, in *Documents on the History of the Greek Jews*, 239–40; TNA, FO 424/279, FC 28, no. 11, Percy Loraine to John Simon, July 22, 1934.

55. *Annuaire oriental* (1929): 1018–20; *Annuaire oriental* (1934): 452.

56. Also, Murat Koraltürk notes that while Jews were more prevalent in industries involving imports, Muslim landowners in Edirne achieved vertical integration in industries

in which all inputs were local. *Erken Cumhuriyet Döneminde Ekonominin Türkleştirilmesi* (Istanbul, 2011), 191–202.

57. YIVO, record group 3335.2, box 19 of 25, folder 184 (American Jewish Relief Fund), "Comparative balance sheet for Adrianople, Turkey," August 31, 1924, Table III, 3–4. About 45 percent of loans were for amounts lower than fifty Turkish lira.

58. CAHJP, TR/Ed/341. The remaining 40 percent of people in my sample had various other jobs.

59. Çağlar Keyder and others speak of a "Moslem bourgeoisie" or "Moslem commercial class" that replaced the Christian bourgeoisie after 1923. *State and Class in Turkey: A Study in Capitalist Development* (London, 1987), 91–95. Also see Zafer Toprak, *Türkiye'de Ekonomi ve Toplum (1908–1950): Milli İktisat-Milli Burjuvazi* (Istanbul, 1995).

60. Albert Cohen, "Notas y Impresiones de Viaje," *La Boz de Türkiye*, October 1. 1940, 93–95.

61. Pekesen, "The Anti-Jewish Pogrom in 1934," 429.

62. This builds on previous scholarship such as Rıfat N. Bali, "The 1934 Thrace Events: Continuity and Change within Turkish State Policies Regarding Non-Muslim Minorities: An Interview with Rıfat N. Bali," *European Journal of Turkish Studies*, no. 7 (2008); Bali, *1934 Trakya Olayları*; and Jacob Daniels, "Prelude to a Turkish Anomaly: Eastern Thrace Before the 1934 Attacks on Jews," *Antisemitism Studies* 1, no. 2 (Fall 2017): 364–96.

63. "La Manifestasyon de los Djudyos de Chorlu al Nuevo Governador de Andrinopla," *El Tiempo*, November 3, 1922, 91–92. The *vali*'s remarks were published in *Tevhid'i Evkar* on November 2, 1922, and appear in Abraham Galante's *Turcs et Juifs: étude historique, politique* (Istanbul, 1932), 81–82.

64. "The Anti-Jewish Campaign in Turkey: Chief Rabbi's Protests," *Jewish Chronicle*, December 22, 1922, 22. The *vali* was Şakir Bey. The local chief rabbi was Meir Behmoiras—the same who had welcomed King Alexander of Greece two years prior, on that very *bimah*.

65. The *vali* was interviewed by *El Telegrafo*, but I quote a reprint: "Una Entrevista kon Shakir Bey, Governador Djeneral de la Tras," *El Tiempo*, December 12, 1922, 182. Around this time, the Jewish community of Edirne threw a celebration for the *vali* in the hall of Cercle Israélite. AAIU, Turquie, XII. E., Mitrani, January 10, 1923.

66. "Jews in Turkey: Fleeced by Kemalists," *Jewish Chronicle*, November 24, 1922, 18; AAIU, Turquie, XII. E., Mitrani, November 30, 1922. Mitrani claimed that "the new masters of Eastern Thrace" asked the Jewish community to pay thirty thousand Turkish liras to the national cause.

67. B. Cem Altınel, *Kuruluşunun 100. Yılında Trakya Paşaeli Müdafaa-i Hukuk Derneği Yoneticilerinin Yaşam Öyküleri* (Edirne, 2018), 15–53.

68. A year later, Jewish notables were pressured to pay a disproportionate share of the expenses related to celebrations marking the anniversary of Turkish forces retaking Edirne. AAIU, Turquie, XII. E., Mitrani, December 16, 1923.

69. Altınel, *Kuruluşunun 100. Yılında*, 43–46.

70. "El Antisemismo de Algunos Djurnales Turkos," *El Telegrafo*, May 26, 1924, 2. This was a reprint from *La Boz de la Verdad*.

71. Cengiz Bulut, *Trakya-Paşaeli Müdafaa-i Hukuk Cemiyeti Kurucularından Kasım Yolageldili, 1874–1936* (Edirne, 2019), 88–103.

72. Bulut, *Kasım Yolageldili*, 146–50; *Annuaire commercial turc* 1 (1924–1925): 59–60; *Annuaire Oriental* (1927): 79–80; *Annuaire oriental* (1929): 1019–20. In the 1924–1925 edition of the commercial yearbook, Kasım Yolageldili was listed as a grain producer who also engaged in animal husbandry and agriculture. His son Cevat was listed as a cereal merchant and army provisioner, while his son Mustafa was listed as an army provisioner and road contractor. The 1927 and 1929 yearbooks simply listed a firm called "Kasım Yolageldilizade and Co.," under the headings of "Cereal Merchants" and "Flour Merchants."

73. Hasan Adnan Önelçin, *Trakya Basını* (Tekirdağ, 1972), 26. Kasım also had a son named Muhittin Yolageldili who wrote for *Paşaeli* (and later *Edirne Postası*). Bulut, *Kasım Yolageldili*, 161.

74. Avner Levi, *Toldot ha-Yehudim ba-Republikah ha-Turkit: ma'amadam ha-politi ve-ha-mishpati* (Jerusalem, 1992).

75. The Istanbul paper was *İleri*. See "Un Atako Grosyero del Periodiko Turk 'Ileri' kontra los Djudyos," *El Tiempo*, December 5, 1922, 163–65. Later, anti-Jewish articles appeared in the Istanbul paper *Tevhid-i Evkar*: "La Prensa Turka i Los Djudyos de Turkiya," *El Tiempo*, October 5, 1923, 47–49.

76. When *Paşaeli* claimed that Kırklareli Jews had supported the Greek occupation, *İkdam* reprinted the article—but with a refutation written by a Jew from Eastern Thrace who was studying medicine in Istanbul. "La Prensa Turka i Los Djudyos de Turkiya," *El Tiempo*, October 5, 1923, 47–49. For an anti-Jewish story reprinted by *Vakit*, see "El Kazo del Merkador Djudyo Barokas i de Murad Efendi de Rodosto," *El Tiempo*, August 7, 1923, 825.

77. For a synopsis of *Paşaeli*'s articles, see "La Prensa Turka i Los Djudyos de Turkiya," *El Tiempo*, October 5, 1923, 47–49.

78. "El Kazo del Merkador Djudyo Barokas i de Murad Efendi de Rodosto," *El Tiempo*, August 7, 1923, 825.

79. Bitter at losing the deal, the Muslim merchant convinced the municipal council to ban the Jew from the bourse, but other Muslim merchants intervened and had their Jewish colleague reinstated. "El Kazo del Merkador Djudyo Barokas i de Murad Efendi de Rodosto," *El Tiempo*, August 7, 1923, 825.

80. "En la Tras Oriental: La Kampanya Anti-Djudya del Pasha Ili," *El Tiempo*, September 7, 1923, 935. The president of Turkish Hearths in Edirne even called *Paşaeli*'s articles "contemptible." "En la Tras Oriental: La Kampanya Anti-Djudya del Pasha Ili," *El Tiempo*, September 7, 1923, 935.

81. Barishac made these claims on the witness stand in *Paşaeli*'s criminal trial. "En Andrinopla: El Proseso Kontra el Djurnal Turko 'Pasha Ili'," *El Tiempo* October 16, 1923, 83.

82. Eventually, the *vali* intervened and allowed the Jews to attend the fair. "Jews Persecuted in Turkey: An Anti-Semitic Campaign," *Jewish Chronicle*, July 18, 1923, 41.

83. "En Andrinopla: El Proseso kontra el Djurnal Turko 'Pasha Ili'," *El Tiempo* October 16, 1923, 83.

84. "En Andrinopla: El Proseso kontra el Djurnal Turko 'Pasha Ili'," *El Tiempo* October 16, 1923, 83. As mentioned in Chapter 4, a small number of Jews in Kırklareli were killed by self-described Turkish Nationalist fighters in 1920. But it is unclear if these fighters—or perhaps bandits—were local.

85. AAIU, Turquie, XI. E., Mitrani, December 16, 1923.

86. The delegation consisted of Barishac, the local chief rabbi, the president of the communal council, and the president of the Jewish general assembly. The governor was Naci Bey. "Una Delegasyon Komunal Onde el Vali de Andrinopla," *El Tiempo*, September 7, 1923, 935.

87. "En Andrinopla: El Proseso Kontra el Djurnal Turko 'Pasha Ili,'" *El Tiempo* October 16, 1923, 83; "Prosesos de Prensa: El Proseso Kontra el Pasha Ili," *El Tiempo*, October 23, 1923, 107; "El Pasha Ili Aze Amyenda Onorable ma el Parkito Entent auna Aksyon Kontra su Aksyon," *El Tiempo*, September 7, 1923, 935.

88. Bulut, *Kasım Yolageldili*, 132; AAIU, Turquie, XII. E., Mitrani, December 16, 1923.

89. "El Antisemismo de Algunos Djurnales Turkos," *El Telegrafo*, May 26, 1924, 2. This was a reprint from *La Boz de la Verdad*.

90. *Annuaire commercial turc* 1 (1924–1925): 59–60; *Annuaire oriental* (1927): 78–80; *Annuaire oriental* (1929): 1018–20.

91. AAIU, Turquie, XII. E., Moise Mitrani, June 28, 1923. Moise Mitrani claimed that the Muslim teacher was bullying two female students, and when Rosa Mitrani intervened she was accused of "insulting the Turkish nation."

92. *La Boz de la Verdad* appears in the 1927 edition of *Annuaire oriental* but not the 1928 edition.

93. "En Palestina Estamos?" *El Telegrafo*, July 21, 1924, 2. This was a reprint from *La Boz de la Verdad*.

94. Sezen Sevgil, "Edirne Milletvekili Mehmet Şeref Aykut ve Birinci TBMM'deki Faaliyetleri," master's thesis, Trakya University, 2016, 34–35.

95. Pınar, *Tek Parti Döneminde*, 247–50.

96. See Chapter 4.

97. Pınar, *Tek Parti Döneminde*, 247–71. For more on Cohen and Galante, see Chapter 2 and Chapter 3.

98. Galanté, *Turcs et Juifs*, 84–85.

99. Founded in 1927, *Edirne Milli Gazete* at this time was run by İbrahim Akıncıoğlu, CHF party chief for Edirne Province. İlkay Öz, *Mülksüzleştirme ve Türkleştirme: Edirne Örneği* (Istanbul, 2020), 79.

100. "Bu da benden," *Edirne Postası*, August 17, 1933, 1. The article carried the following subtitle: "In the year 1933, there is not, and cannot be, a Jewish question in Turkey—certainly not in Edirne."

101. "Edirne Musevi Gençliği," *Edirne Postası*, September 14, 1933, 1.

102. Pınar, *Tek Parti Döneminde*, 247–71; Rıfat N. Bali, *Edirne Mebusu Mehmet Şeref Aykut'un Munis Tekinalp'e Mektubu*.

103. Pınar, *Tek Parti Döneminde*, 263.

104. When a married couple holding Moroccan citizenship protested their dismissal from the Alliance school in Kırklareli, officials in Ankara almost shut down the entire Alliance network in Thrace. AAIU, Turquie, XII. E., Mitrani, May 25, 1923, and June 28, 1923. Also see Rodrigue, *French Jews, Turkish Jews: The Alliance Israélite Universelle and the Politics of Jewish Schooling in Turkey, 1860–1925* (Bloomington, 1990), 161–66.

105. AAIU, Turquie, XII. E., Mitrani, June 28, 1923.

106. Senem Aslan, "'Citizen, Speak Turkish!': A Nation in the Making," *Nationalism and Ethnic Politics* 13, no. 2 (2007): 245–72.

107. Rıfat N. Bali, *Cumhuriyet Yıllarında Türkiye Yahudileri: Bir Türkleştirme Serüveni, 1923–1945* (Istanbul, 2000), 143–45.

108. "La Campagne contre les Juifs en Turquie: Les Incidents d'Andrinople," *Israël*, May 4, 1928, 3; "Les misères des Juifs de Turquie," *L'Aurore*, May 3, 1928, 1.

109. Aslan, "'Citizen, Speak Turkish!,'" 261–64. In Eastern Thrace, 93 percent of the Jewish population had marked Ladino as their mother tongue in the 1927 census. *General Census of the Population, October 28, 1927*, Booklet II, 116–21.

110. In 1933, Edirne Jews formed the Commission for Speaking Turkish and the Turkish Cultural Association. Rıfat N. Bali, "Edirne Yahudileri," in *Edirne: Serhattaki Payitaht*, ed. Emin Nedret İşli and M. Sabri Koz (Istanbul, 1998), 220. Also see "Musevi Vantandaşlarımızın Yeni Bir Teşekkülü," *Edirne Milli Gazete*, December 4, 1933. Meanwhile, the rabbi of Kırklareli urged his congregation to "speak the beloved language of the noble Turkish race." Soner Çağaptay, "Race, Assimilation, and Kemalism: Turkish Nationalism and the Minorities in the 1930s," *Middle Eastern Studies* 40, no. 3 (May, 2004): 95.

111. Aslan, "'Citizen, Speak Turkish!,'" 257, 260. Aslan calls the campaign "an attempt to create a new social and economic hierarchy."

112. The local stakeholders included students, the inspector of primary education, and the editor-in-chief of *Edirne Postası*. Aslan, "'Citizen, Speak Turkish!,'" 261–64.

113. Bali, *Trakya Olayları*, 150.

114. It is worth adding that the municipalities of Edirne, Tekirdağ, and Lüleburgaz banned the public use of languages other than Turkish in 1936. Çağaptay, "Race, Assimilation, and Kemalism," 86–101.

115. In Eastern Thrace, the SCF won the municipal councils of Lüleburgaz, Vize, and a few other towns. "Turquie: La situation politique des Juifs," *Israël* (November 7, 1930): 5. Also see Pınar, *Tek Parti Döneminde*, 150, 222–23; and Bali, "1930 Yılı Seçimleri ve Serbest Fırka'nın Azınlık Adayları," *Tarih ve Toplum*, no. 167 (November 1997): 27–34.

116. Pınar, *Tek Parti Döneminde*, 142–43; and Bulut, *Trakya-Paşaeli Müdafaa-i Hukuk Cemiyeti*, 104.

117. Statism (*devletçilik*) was one of Kemalism's "six arrows." The other five were republicanism (*cumhuriyetçilik*), populism (*halkçılık*), nationalism (*milliyetçilik*), laicism (*laiklik*), and reformism (*inkılapçılık*). For more on Kemalism, see Nathalie Clayer et al., *Kemalism: Transnational Politics in the Post-Ottoman World* (London, 2019).

118. According to the 1927 census, in the Edirne region 15,647 people worked in the agricultural sector, 2,177 worked in the "industrial" sector, and 2,149 worked in the commercial sector. *General Census of the Population, October 28, 1927*, Booklet II, 102.

119. Avner Levi, "1934 Trakya Yahudileri Olayı Alınamayan Ders," *Tarih ve Toplum*, no. 151 (1996): 10–17. Germany was Turkey's main trading partner in the 1930s.

120. Ayhan Aktar, "Trakya Yahudi Olaylarını 'Doğru' Yorumlamak," *Tarih ve Toplum*, no. 155 (1996): 49; Corry Guttstadt, *Turkey, the Jews, and the Holocaust* (Cambridge, 2013), 56–61.

121. The paper was called *Milli İnkılap*. Erdem Güven and Mehmet Yılmazata, "Milli İnkılap and the Thrace Incidents of 1934," *Journal of Modern Jewish Studies* 13, no. 2 (July 2014): 190–211.

122. Aktar, "Trakya Yahudi," 49.

123. In Turkey, Jewish, Armenian, and Greek Orthodox leaders "renounced" the minority rights of their respective communities in 1926, but they were probably pressured to do so by the state. Bali, *Cumhuriyet Yıllarında Türkiye Yahudileri*, 95–112.

124. Ramazan Hakkı Öztan describes this process as the "collapse of the Versailles order." "Settlement Law of 1934," 91. Similarly, Mirkova traces a "gradual dissolution of the post-World War I order" that was manifest by the mid-1930s in Turkey, Bulgaria, and beyond. *Muslim Land, Christian Labor*, 208.

125. In Bulgaria, various governments demanded changes to the border with Yugoslavia, and paramilitary organizations sought the annexation of Greek Thrace. Yonca Köksal, "Transnational Networks and Kin States: The Turkish Minority in Bulgaria, 1878–1940," *Nationalities Papers* 38, no. 2 (2010): 196–97; Mirkova, *Muslim Land, Christian Labor*, 195, 203–4, 208–9; Öztan, 93–95. In 1939, Turkey annexed Hatay from the French mandate of Syria.

126. For more on "demographic engineering," see Uğur Ümit Üngör, *The Making of Modern Turkey: Nation and State in Eastern Anatolia, 1913–1950* (Oxford, 2011).

127. For a general overview, see Renée Hirschon, "The Consequences of the Lausanne Convention: An Overview," in *Crossing the Aegean: An Appraisal of the 1923 Compulsory Population Exchange between Greece and Turkey*, ed. Renée Hirschon (New York, 2003), 13–20.

128. Stephen P. Ladas, *The Exchange of Minorities: Bulgaria, Greece and Turkey* (New York, 1932), 705, 712; Onur Yıldırm, *Diplomacy and Displacement: Reconsidering the Turco-Greek Exchange of Populations, 1922–1934* (New York, 2006), 141, 146; and İbrahim Erdal, *Mübadele: Uluslaşma Sürecinde Türkiye ve Yunanistan 1923-1925* (Istanbul, 2006), 352. A total of about 356,000 Muslims were expelled from Greece to Turkey following the 1923 Convention. Hirschon, "The Consequences of the Lausanne Convention," 14.

129. "Los Israelitas de Chataldja," *El Tiempo*, December 7, 1923, 329; and "Expulsions of Jews from Thrace," *Jewish Chronicle*, December 7, 1923. Also see Mark Mazower, *Salonica, City of Ghosts: Christians, Muslims, and Jews, 1430–1950* (New York, 2005), 324.

130. Both displacements were facilitated by a "voluntary" population exchange agreement that Greek and Bulgarian leaders had signed in 1919. Theodora Dragostinova, *Between Two Motherlands: Nationality and Emigration among the Greeks of Bulgaria, 1900–1949* (Ithaca, 2011), 117–156. Also see Mirkova, *Muslim Land Christian Labor*, 193, 211.

131. Nikola Minov, "Cursed in Heaven: The Colonization of the Aromanians in Southern Dobruja," in *Borders, Boundaries and Belonging in Post-Ottoman Space in the Interwar Period*, ed. Ebru Boyar and Kate Fleet (Boston, 2023), 53–83.

132. Vezi Metin Omer, "Why did They Leave? Perceptions on the Turkish Emigration from Dobrogea to Turkey (1918–1940)," *International Journal of Political Science & Urban Studies* 7, no. 1 (March 2019): 42–54; and Kemal Karpat, "The Hijra from Russia and the Balkans: The Process of Self-Definition in the Late Ottoman State," in *Muslim Travellers: Pilgrimage, Migration, and the Religious Imagination*, ed. Dale Eickelman and James Piscatori (Berkeley, 1990), 148–50.

133. Mirkova, *Muslim Land, Christian Labor*, 189–93, 208, 211; Öztan, "Settlement Law of 1934," 96. For full text of the 1925 Treaty of Friendship between Bulgaria and Turkey, see http://www.forost.ungarisches-institut.de/pdf/19251018-1.pdf.

134. League of Nations, *League of Nations Treaty Series* 153, no. 7 (London, 1934–1936), 153.

135. The article was published on December 3, 1933. See Leyla Amzi-Erdoğdular, "Muslim Migration and Nation-Building in Interwar Yugoslavia and Turkey," in *Borders, Boundaries and Belonging in Post-Ottoman Space in the Interwar Period*, ed. Ebru Boyar and Kate Fleet (Boston, 2023), 263.

136. Damla Demirözü, "The Greek-Turkish Rapprochement of 1930 and the Repercussions of the Ankara Convention in Turkey," *Journal of Islamic Studies* 19, no. 3 (September 2008): 309–24. The treaty also settled all outstanding property claims related to the Population Exchange.

137. Thrasyvoulos Papastratis, "The Image of the Jews through the Local Newspapers in the Prefecture of Evros, 1924–1940," paper presented at the International Symposium on the Jews in Demotica before and after the Shoah, Didymoteicho, Greece, May 6, 2023.

138. Papastratis, "The Image of the Jews through the Local Newspapers in the Prefecture of Evros"; Zeynep Kaşlı, "Negotiating History and Diversity in a Border Province: The Non-Muslim Urban Past in Today's Edirne," in *Contested Spaces in Contemporary Turkey: Environmental, Secular and Urban Politics*, ed. Fatma Müge Göçek (London, 2018), 113.

139. Around six thousand Jews lived in Plovdiv, but that city was over one hundred miles from the border. Simon Marcus and Emil Kalo, "Plovdiv," *Encyclopaedia Judaica* 16, ed. Michael Berenbaum and Fred Skolnik (Macmillan Reference USA, 2007), 241–42.

140. I. S. Penakoff, "The Persecution of Jews in Eastern Thrace," *Slovo*, July 30, 1934. A French translation can be found in T. C. Cumhurbaşkanlığı Devlet Arşivleri Başkanlığ, Hariciye Vekaleti, 30/10/242/634/23, 2–3.

141. B., "Inhospitable Thrace," *Mir*, July 30, 1934. A French translation can be found in T. C. Cumhurbaşkanlığı Devlet Arşivleri Başkanlığ, Hariciye Vekaleti, 30/10/242/634/23, 2–3.

142. Mirkova, *Muslim Land Christian Labor*, 193, 208–11, 220–23. Among Bulgaria's Turkish-speaking population, Sofia supported leaders who opposed Mustafa Kemal and the secular Turkish Republic. Ebru Boyar and Kate Fleet, "A Dangerous Axis: The 'Bulgarian Müftü', the Turkish Opposition and the Ankara Government, 1928–36," *Middle Eastern Studies* 44, no. 5 (2008): 775–89.

143. Mazower, *Salonica, City of Ghosts*, 384–86; Minna Rozen, *The Last Ottoman Century and Beyond: the Jews in Turkey and the Balkans 1808–1945* 1 (Tel Aviv, 2005), 242.

144. Marco Dogo, "Loyalty Sorely Tried: The Jews and the Bulgarian State (1878–1935)," in *The Jews and the Nation-States of Southeastern Europe from the 19th Century to the Great Depression: Combining Viewpoints on a Controversial Story*, ed. Tullia Catalan and Marco Dogo (Newcastle, 2016), 95–96. Writing in Sofia on December 31, 1934, a prominent Bulgarian Jew claimed that "uncertainty about the future leads many Jewish families to contemplate liquidating their businesses in Bulgaria and moving to Palestine." Esther Benbassa and Aron Rodrigue, *A Sephardi Life in Southeastern Europe: The Autobiography and Journal of Gabriel Arié, 1863–1939* (Seattle, 1998), 276–77.

145. Aron Rodrigue, "L'Etat impérial ottoman et les politiques de déportation," in *Le temps de l'état: mélanges offerts à Pierre Birnbaum*, ed. Bertrand Badie and Yves Deloye (Paris, 2007), 185–202. See also Reşat Kasaba, *A Moveable Empire: Ottoman Nomads, Migrants, and Refugees* (Seattle, 2009).

146. H. Yıldırım Ağanoğlu, *Osmanlı'dan Cumhuriyet'e Balkanlar'ın Mâkus Talihi: Göç* (Istanbul, 2001), 338; Abdullah Saydam, *Kırım ve Kafkas Göçleri, 1856–1876* (Ankara, 1997), 131.

147. See Chapter 1.

148. Rodrigue, "L'Etat impérial ottoman," 185–202.

149. Stefan Winter, "The Kızılbaş of Syria and Ottoman Shiism," in *The Ottoman World*, ed. Christine Woodhead (New York, 2012), 171–72.

150. Şeyhmus Diken, *İsyan Sürgünleri* (Istanbul, 2005), 89–94, 210–13; and Malmisanij, *Diyarbekirli Cemilpaşazadeler ve Kürt Milliyetçiliği* (Istanbul, 2004), 210–13.

151. "Un Atako Grosyero del Periodiko Turk 'Ileri' Kontra los Djudyos," *El Tiempo*, December 5, 1922, 163–65; and "La Prensa Turka i Los Djudyos de Turkiya," *El Tiempo*, October 5, 1923, 47–49.

152. Pınar, *Tek Parti Döneminde*, 263–64.

153. Helmut Walser Smith, *The Butcher's Tale: Murder and Anti-Semitism in a German Town* (New York, 2002), 132.

154. For more on CUP policies in Anatolia after the Balkan Wars, see Taner Akçam, "The Young Turks and the Plans for the Ethnic Homogenization of Anatolia," in *Shatterzone of*

Empires: Coexistence and Violence in the German, Habsburg, Russian, and Ottoman Borderlands, ed. Omer Bartov and Eric D. Weitz (Bloomington, 2013), 258–79.

155. For more on this affair, see Faik Ökte, *The Tragedy of the Turkish Capital Tax* (London, 1987).

156. For more on this pogrom, see Vryonis, *The Mechanism of Catastrophe*.

Conclusion

1. AAIU, Turquie, XLIV. E. 511, Conorté Canetti, February 20, 1923. Canetti was in the town of Kırklareli.

2. Albert Cohen, "Notas y Impresiones de Viaje," *La Boz de Türkiye*, October 1. 1940, 93–95.

3. Moise Mizrahi, "En la Comunidad İsraelita de Edirne," *La Boz de Türkiye*, January 1, 1944, 171.

4. Juda Romano, *La Boz de Türkiye*, April 1, 1949.

5. Rıfat N. Bali, "Edirne Yahudileri," in *Edirne: Serhattaki Payitaht*, ed. Emin Nedret İsli and M. Sabri Koz (Istanbul, 1998), 208–9.

6. The meaning of this "nationalism" in quotes is a central topic of this book. For one treatment, see Aron Rodrigue, "From *Millet* to Minority: Turkish Jewry," in *Paths of Emancipation: Jews, States, and Citizenship*, ed. Pierre Birnbaum and Ira Katznelson (Princeton, 2014), 238–61.

7. Put differently, local Jews resisted the notion that these new nation-states were "identity spaces." For territory as "identity space" versus territory as "decision space," see Charles S. Maier, *Once Within Borders: Territories of Power, Wealth, and Belonging since 1500* (Cambridge, 2016), 1–13.

8. Jeremy Adelman and Stephen Aron, "From Borderlands to Borders: Empires, Nation-States, and the Peoples in between in North American History," *American Historical Review* 104, no. 3 (June 1999): 814–41.

9. Arguably, these conflicts date to the Middle Ages. Certainly, they were evident by the nineteenth century. In addition to Chapter 1 of this book, see R. J. Crampton, *A Concise History of Bulgaria* (Cambridge, 2005), 9–28.

10. For more on the Turkish-Bulgarian border during the Cold War, see Kapka Kassabova, *Border: A Journey to the Edge of Europe* (Minneapolis, 2017). For more on Turkey's geopolitical place during the Cold War, see Zaur Gasimov, "'The Turkish Wall': Turkey as an Anti-Communist and Anti-Russian Bulwark in the Twentieth Century," in *Rampart Nations: Bulwark Myths of East European Multiconfessional Societies in the Age of Nationalism*, ed. Liliya Berezhnaya and Heidi Hein-Kircher (New York, 2019), 186–206.

11. At least this applies to the successor states of the Habsburg, Ottoman, and Romanov empires. I am not so sure it applies to San Diego and Buffalo, for example. As discussed in the Introduction, the borderlands of North America are, to an extent, typologically different from the borderlands of Eurasia.

12. For more on the notion of "difference" in the Ottoman Empire, see Aron Rodrigue, "Difference and Tolerance in the Ottoman Empire: Interview by Nancy Reynolds," *Stanford Humanities Review* 5, no. 1 (1996): 81–92.

13. For a study that complicates this generalization, see Devin E. Naar, *Jewish Salonica: Between the Ottoman Empire and Modern Greece* (Stanford, 2016).

14. Orit Bashkin, *Impossible Exodus: Iraqi Jews in Israel* (Stanford, 2017), 6–7; Joel Beinin, "Jews as Native Iraqis: An Introduction," Foreword to Nissim Rejwan, *The Last Jews in Baghdad: Remembering a Lost Homeland* (Austin, 2004), xviii–xix; Joel Beinin, *The Dispersion of Egyptian Jewry: Culture, Politics, and the Formation of a Modern Diaspora* (Berkeley, 1998), 63–83.

15. For the emergence of the "minority" category in Turkey, see Rodrigue, "Reflections on Millets and Minorities: Ottoman Legacies," in *Turkey between Nationalism and Globalization*, ed. Riva Kastoryano (New York, 2013), 36–46.

16. The term "Muslim bourgeoisie" is discussed in Chapter 5.

17. In his 2008 historiography of Ottoman Jewry, Yaron Ben-Naeh recommends eight areas for future research, one of which is "physical mobility within the Ottoman Empire and outside its borders." I think his call remains to be heeded. "The Historiography of Ottoman Jewry," *Journal of Jewish Studies* 69, No. 1 (Spring 2008): 130.

18. With that said, two scholars have gestured in this direction. See Sarah Abrevaya Stein, *Family Papers: A Sephardic Journey through the Twentieth Century* (New York, 2019); and Devi Mays, *Forging Ties, Forging Passports: Migration and the Modern Sephardi Diaspora* (Stanford, 2020).

Epilogue

1. CAHJP, TR/Ed/207, President of the Jewish Community in Edirne to President of the Jewish Community in Istanbul, September 8, 1939.

2. CAHJP, TR/Ed/207, Edirne Jewish Community to President of the Istanbul Jewish Community, January 15, 1940.

3. AAIU, Turquie, XII. E., Mitrani to Paris, June 25, 1920; Corry Guttstadt, *Turkey, the Jews, and the Holocaust* (Cambridge, 2013), 22–25.

4. Frederick B. Chary, *The Bulgarian Jews and the Final Solution, 1940–1944* (Pittsburgh, 1972), 35. Guttstadt says that the original order for deporting Bulgaria's four thousand foreign Jews was given in February 1939 and "reissued' in September 1939. *Turkey, the Jews, and the Holocaust*, 152n37.

5. CAHJP, TR/Ed/207, President of the Jewish Community in Edirne to President of the Jewish Community in Istanbul, September 8, 1939.

6. CAHJP, TR/Ed/207, President of the Jewish Community in Edirne to President of the Jewish Community in Istanbul, September 8, 1939.

7. CAHJP, TR/Ed/207, Jewish Community of Plovdiv to President of the Jewish Community in Edirne, January 12, 1940.

NOTES TO THE EPILOGUE

8. CAHJP, TR/Ed/207, President of the Jewish Community in Edirne to President of the Jewish Community in Istanbul, September 8, 1939.

9. CAHJP, TR/Ed/207, Secretary of the Jewish Community in Edirne to the Central Jewish Consistory of Bulgaria in Sofia, January 17, 1940.

10. CAHJP, TR/Ed/207, Edirne Chief Rabbinate to the President of the Jewish Community in Istanbul, January 15. 1940. It is possible that this letter was also written by Yuda Romano.

11. CAHJP, TR/Ed/207, Unsigned letter to the Foreign Ministry in Ankara, undated. References to the cold weather suggest that it was written in the winter of 1939–1940. Also see CAHJP, TR/Ed/207, İzak Mizrahi in Edirne to the Interior Ministry in Ankara, undated.

12. Guttstadt, *Turkey, the Jews, and the Holocaust*, 55.

13. Guttstadt, *Turkey, the Jews, and the Holocaust*, 48–55.

14. Guttstadt, *Turkey, the Jews, and the Holocaust*, 152.

15. CAHJP, TR/Ed/207, President of the Jewish Community in Edirne to President of the Jewish Community in Istanbul, February 21, 1940.

16. CAHJP, TR/Ed/207, Edirne Chief Rabbinate to President of the Jewish Community in Istanbul, January 15. 1940.

17. CAHJP, TR/Ed/207, President of the Jewish Community in Edirne to President of the Jewish Community in Istanbul, September 8, 1939.

18. CAHJP, TR/Ed/207, Edirne Chief Rabbinate to the President of the Jewish Community in Istanbul, January 15. 1940.

19. CAHJP, TR/Ed/207, President of the Jewish Community in Edirne to President of the Jewish Community in Istanbul, September 8, 1939; CAHJP, TR/Ed/207, Secretary of the Jewish Community in Edirne to the Central Jewish Consistory of Bulgaria in Sofia, January 17, 1940.

20. CAHJP, TR/Ed/207, President of the Jewish Community in Edirne to President of the Jewish Community in Istanbul, February 21, 1940.

21. CAHJP, TR/Ed/207, President of the Jewish Community in Edirne to President of the Jewish Community in Istanbul, February 21, 1940.

22. CAHJP/TR/Ed/207, President of the Jewish Community in Edirne to President of the Jewish Community in Istanbul, February 14, 1940.

23. CAHJP/TR/Ed/207, President of the Jewish Community in Edirne to President of the Jewish Community in Istanbul, February 14, 1940. Sami Ginsburg had also been the dentist of Sultan Abdülhamid II. For more on Ginsburg (Günzberg), see Rıfat N. Bali, *Sarayın ve Cumhuriyetin Dişçibaşısı: Sami Günzberg* (Istanbul, 2007).

24. CAHJP/TR/Ed/207, President of the Jewish Community in Edirne to President of the Jewish Community in Istanbul, February 23, 1940.

25. Hannah Arendt, *The Origins of Totalitarianism* (New York, 1966), 283.

26. The quoted phrase is from CAHJP/TR/Ed/207, Edirne Chief Rabbinate to unknown recipient, March 11, 1940.

27. CAHJP/TR/Ed/207, President of the Central Consistory of Bulgarian Jewry to the Chief Rabbinate in Edirne, March 22, 1940. In the 1940s, Yuda Romano was affiliated with the Jewish Agency and helped Jews from Bulgaria and Greece switch trains in Edirne as part of their voyages to Palestine/Israel. Rıfat N. Bali, "Edirne Yahudileri," in *Edirne: Serhattaki Payitaht*, ed. Emin Nedret İsli and M. Sabri Koz (Istanbul, 1998), 224–25.

28. Marco Nahon, *Birkenau, The Camp of Death* (Tuscaloosa, 1989), 17–18.

29. Aron Rodrigue, "Sephardim and the Holocaust" (Washington, DC, 2005), 9–10.

30. Nahon, *Birkenau, The Camp of Death*, 27–39. Nahon was one of the few survivors from Didymoteicho.

31. Guttstadt, *Turkey, the Jews, and the Holocaust*, 290–91.

32. Also, in December 1940, Edirne Jews helplessly read about the *Salvator*, a small ship carrying over 300 Sephardim that sank near Silivri on its way from Varna to Palestine. Chary, *The Bulgarian Jews*, 36. For a list of the 211 passengers who drowned, see CAHJP/TR/Ed/207, President of the Jewish Community in Edirne to President of the Jewish Community in Istanbul, February 21, 1940.

33. For a general discussion of the tax, see Faik Ökte, *The Tragedy of the Turkish Capital Tax* (London, 1987). For the implications of the tax in Edirne, see İlkay Öz, *Mülksüzleştirme ve Türkleştirme: Edirne Örneği* (Istanbul, 2020).

Bibliography

Archives

Archives of the Alliance Israélite Universelle (AAIU), Paris
Archives of the American Joint Distribution Committee (JDC), New York
Başbakanlık Osmanlı Arşivi (BOA) & T. C. Cumhurbaşkanlığı Devlet Arşivleri, Istanbul
Central Archives for the History of the Jewish People (CAHJP), Jerusalem
Jewish Museum of Greece (JMG) Collection, Athens
The National Archives, UK (TNA), London
National Archives and Records Administration, USA (NARA), Washington, DC
Private Collection of Avner Perez, Ma'ale Adumim, West Bank
Yad Ben-Zvi Archives (YBZ), Jerusalem
YIVO Institute for Jewish Research (YIVO), New York

Published Primary Sources: Serials

Âfitab
Air Service Journal
Almanach Israelite
Almanach national au profit de l'hôpital de Hirsch
American Jewish Yearbook
American Journal of International Law
Annuaire commercial turc
Annuaire oriental du commerce de l'industrie de l'administration et de la magistrature
Annual report of the Council of the Corporation of Foreign Bondholders

L'Aurore
La Boz de la Verdad
La Boz de Türkiye
Bulletin de la Grande Loge de district XI et de la Loge de Constantinople N. 678, I.O.B.B.
Bulletin de l'Alliance Israélite Universelle
Ha-Carmel
Daily Telegraph
El Djudyo
L'Écho d'Andrinople
Échos d'Orient
The Economist
The Economist Monthly Trade Supplement
Edirne Milli Gazete
Edirne Postası
La Epoka
La Fuersa
The Fortnightly Review
Istanbul Kalendaryo
Israël
Jewish Chronicle
JTA News Bulletin
Ha-Magid
Hamenora
El Meseret
The Near East
The New York Times
Paşaeli
El Pueblo
La Renasensia Djudya
Ha-Shofar
El Telegrafo
El Tiempo
Trakya Paşaeli
La Vara
La Verdad
Yeni Edirne
Yeni Edirne Gazetesi
Yosef Da'at/El Progreso

Published Primary Sources: Reports, Legal Documents, and Censuses

Antoniadès, Alexandre. *Le Developpement économique de la Thrace*. Athens: Typos, 1922.

Carnegie Endowment for International Peace. *Report of the International Commission to Inquire into the Causes and Conduct of the Balkan Wars.* Washington, DC: The Endowment, 1914.

Geographical Section of the [British] Naval Intelligence Division, Naval Staff/Admiralty, *A Handbook of Bulgaria.* London: His Majesty's Stationery Office, 1920.

Greek Parliament, *Mitroo Plirexousion, Gerousiaston kai Voulefton, 1822–1935.* Athens: Greek Parliament, 1986.

League of Nations, *League of Nations Treaty Series* CLIII, no. 7. London: Harrison & Sons, 1934–1936.

Moschopoulos, Nicéphore. *La question de Thrace, ou le mensonge bulgare.* Athens: Typos, 1922.

Republic of Greece, Census Office. *Recensement de la Population de la Grèce au 19 Décembre 1920/1 Janvier 1921: Résultats Statistiques Généraux.* Athens: Imprimerie Nationale, 1928.

Republic of Turkey, Directorate of Statistics. *General Census of the Population, October 28, 1927.* Booklet II. Ankara: Hüsnütabiat Matbaası, 1929.

Republic of Turkey, Directorate of Statistics. *General Census of the Population, October 20, 1935.* Ankara: Mehmet Ihsan Basımevi, 1937.

Svolopoulos, Dem. C. *Thrace Under the Hellenic Administration.* Athens: Typos, 1922.

Young, George. *Corps de droit Ottoman: Recueil des codes, lois, règlements, ordonnances et actes les plus importants du droit intérieur, et d'études sur le droit coutumier de l'Empire Ottoman* 3. Oxford: Clarendon, 1906.

Published Primary Sources: Memoirs, Literature, Compilations, and Critical Editions

Andrić, Ivo. *The Bridge on the Drina*, translated from the Serbo-Croat by Lovett F. Edwards. Chicago: University of Chicago Press, 1977.

Ayala, Amor. *Los sefardíes de Bulgaria: Estudio y edición crítica de la obra "Notas Istorikas" de Avraam Moshe Tadjer.* Berlin: De Gruyter, 2017.

Belli, Mihri. *Mihri Belli'nin Anıları: "İnsanlar Tanıdım".* Istanbul: Milliyet Yayın, 1989.

Benbassa, Esther, and Aron Rodrigue eds. *A Sephardi Life in Southeastern Europe: The Autobiography and Journals of Gabriel Arié, 1863–1939.* Seattle: University of Washington Press, 1998.

Canetti, Elias. *The Tongue Set Free.* London: Granta, 2011.

Cohen, Julia Phillips, and Sarah Abrevaya Stein, eds. *Sephardi Lives: A Documentary History, 1700–1950.* Stanford, CA: Stanford University Press, 2014.

Constantopoulou, Photini, and Thanos Veremis, eds. *Documents on the History of the Greek Jews: Records from the Historical Archives of the Ministry of Foreign Affairs.* Athens: Kastaniotis Editions, 1999.

Denman, Fatma Kılıç, ed. *Yeni Harflerle Kadın: II. Meşrutiyet Döneminde bir Jön Türk Dergisi (1908–1909).* Istanbul: Kadın Eserleri Kütüphanesi ve Bilgi Merkezi Vakfı, 2010.

Eli, Nisim Sh'T. *Haggadah de la Gerra*. Istanbul: Sosyeta Anonima de Papeteria i de Imprimiria, 1919.

Geregas, Kostas. *Anamniseis ek Thrakis, 1920–1922*. Athens: Mati, 1925.

Güran, Tevfik, ed. *Osmanlı Dönemi Tarım İstatistikleri, 1909, 1913 ve 1914: Tarihi İstatistikler Dizisi 3*. Ankara: T.C. Başbakanlık Devlet İstatistik Enstitüsü, 1997.

Hemingway, Ernest. *Dateline Toronto: The Complete Toronto Star Dispatches, 1920–1924*, ed. William White. New York: Scribner's, 1985.

Karebekir, Kazım. *Edirne Hatıraları*. Istanbul: YKY, 2009.

Kazancıgil, Ratip, Nilüfer Gokçe, and Musa Öncel, eds. *Edirne il Yıllığı: Edirne Vilâyet Sâlnâmesi H.1319-M.1901*. Edirne, Turkey: Edirne Valiliği Kültür Yayınları, 2014.

Loti, Pierre, *Turquie Agonisante*. Paris: Calmann-Lévy, 1913.

Menteşe, Halil. *Osmanlı Mebusan Meclisi Reisi Halil Menteşe'nin Anıları*. Istanbul: Hürriyet Vakfı Yayınları, 1986.

Mevsim, Hüseyin, ed. *Bulgar Gözüyle Edirne*. Istanbul: Kitap Yayınevi, 2012.

Nahon, Marco. *Birkenau, The Camp of Death*. Tuscaloosa: University of Alabama Press, 1989.

Niego, Joseph. *Cinquante Années de Travail dans les œuvres Juives: Allocutions et Conférences*. Istanbul: L. Babok & Fils, 1933.

Papo, Eliezer, ed. *Ve-hitalta le-vinkha ba-yom ha-hu: Parodyot Sefaradiyot-Yehudiyot al ha-Hagadah shel Pesah 2*. Jerusalem: Mekhon-Ben Tsevi, 2012.

Rodrigue, Aron, ed. *Jews and Muslims: Images of Sephardi and Eastern Jewries in Modern Times*. Seattle: University of Washington Press, 2003.

Romero, Elena, ed. *El Teatro de los Sefardíes Orientales 3*. Madrid: CSIC, 1979.

Sunata, İ. Hakkı. *Gelibolu'dan Kafkaslara: Birinci Dünya Savaşı Anılarım*. Istanbul: Türkiye İş Bankası, 2003.

Uluğtekin, Murat, and M. Gül Uluğtekin, eds. *Osmanlı'dan Cumhuriyet'e Hilal-i Ahmer İcraat Raporları*. Ankara: Türk Kızılayı Derneği, 2013.

Upward, Allen. *The East End of Europe: A Report of an Unofficial Mission to the European Provinces of Turkey on the Eve of the Revolution*. New York: E. P. Dutton, 1909.

Woodward, E. L., and Rohan Butler, eds. *Documents on British Foreign Policy, 1919–1939*, First Series, Vol. VII, 1920. London: Her Majesty's Stationery Office, 1958.

Secondary Literature

Aarbakke, Vemund. "Urban Space and Bulgarian-Greek Antagonism in Thrace, 1870–1912." In *Balkan Heritages: Negotiating History and Culture*, edited by Maria Couroucli and Tchavdar Marinov, 29–44. Burlington, VT: Ashgate, 2015.

Adanır, Fikret. "Non-Muslims in the Ottoman Army and the Ottoman Defeat in the Balkan War of 1912–1913." In *A Question of Genocide: Armenians and Turks at the End of the Ottoman Empire*, edited by Ronald Grigor Suny, Fatma Müge Goçek, and Norman M. Naimark, 113–25. Oxford: Oxford University Press, 2011.

Adelman, Jeremy, and Stephen Aron. "From Borderlands to Borders: Empires, Nation-States, and the Peoples in between in North American History." *American Historical Review* 104, no. 3 (June, 1999): 814–41.

Ağanoğlu, H. Yıldırım. *Osmanlı'dan Cumhuriyet'e Balkanlar'ın Makus Talihi: Göç.* Istanbul: Kum Saati, 2001.

Ahmad, Feroz. "The Special Relationship: The Committee of Union and Progress and the Ottoman-Jewish Political Elite, 1908–1918." *Jews, Turks, Ottomans: A Shared History,* edited by Avigdor Levy. Syracuse, NY: Syracuse University Press, 2002.

Ahmad, Feroz. *The Young Turks and the Ottoman Nationalities: Armenians, Greeks, Albanians, Jews, and Arabs, 1908–1918.* Salt Lake City: University of Utah Press, 2014.

Akçam, Taner. *A Shameful Act: The Armenian Genocide and the Question of Turkish Responsibility.* New York: Metropolitan Books, 2006.

Akçam, Taner. *The Young Turks' Crime Against Humanity: The Armenian Genocide and Ethnic Cleansing in the Ottoman Empire.* Princeton, NJ: Princeton University Press, 2012.

Aktar, Ayhan. "Trakya Yahudi Olaylarını 'Doğru' Yorumlamak." *Tarih ve Toplum,* no. 155 (November 1996): 45–56.

Aktar, Ayhan. "Conversion of a 'Country' into a 'Fatherland.'" In *Nationalism in the Troubled Triangle: Cyprus, Turkey, and Greece.* New York: Palgrave, 2010.

Alroey, Gur. *An Unpromising Land: Jewish Migration to Palestine in the Early Twentieth Century.* Stanford, CA: Stanford University Press, 2014.

Altaras, Nesi. "The Jews of Van-Urmia: Remembering Borderland Migrations (1914–18)." *Jewish Social Studies: History, Culture, Society* 28, no. 1 (Winter 2023): 79–115.

Altınel, B. Cem. *Kuruluşunun 100. Yılında Trakya Paşaeli Müdafaa-i Hukuk Cemiyeti Yöneticilerinin Yaşam Öyküleri.* Edirne, Turkey: Edirne Belediyesi, 2018.

Amzi-Erdoğdular, Leyla. "Muslim Migration and Nation-Building in Interwar Yugoslavia and Turkey." In *Borders, Boundaries and Belonging in Post-Ottoman Space in the Interwar Period,* edited by Ebru Boyar and Kate Fleet. Boston: Brill, 2023.

Anzaldúa, Gloria. *Borderlands/La Frontera: The New Mestiza.* San Francisco: Aunt Lute Books, 1987.

Arakelian, Roy. *Edirne (Adrianupolis) ve Ermeni toplumu = Andrinople (Edirne) et sa communauté Arménienne.* Istanbul: Paros Yayıncılık, 2016.

Arditti, Benjamin. *Vidni evrei v Bŭlgariĭa* 3. Tel Aviv: 1969.

Arendt, Hannah. *The Origins of Totalitarianism.* New York: Harcourt, 1966.

Aslan, Senem. "'Citizen, Speak Turkish!': A Nation in the Making." *Nationalism and Ethnic Politics* 13, no. 2 (2007): 245–72.

Arslanboğa, Kadir. "Osmanlı Devleti'nde Uluslararası Bir Fuar: Uzuncaabad-Hasköy Panayırı'nın 1769 ile 1818 Yıllarına ait Gümrük Gelirleri." *Uluslararası Sosyal Araştırmalar Dergisi* 8, no. 36 (February 2015): 774–86.

Astourian, Stephan H., and Raymond H. Kévorkian, eds. *Collective and State Violence in Turkey: The Construction of a National Identity from Empire to Nation-State.* New York: Berghahn, 2021.

Asuero, Pablo Martín. "The Spanish Consulate in Istanbul and the Protection of the Sephardim (1804–1913)." *Quaderns de la Mediterrània* 8 (2007): 169–78.

Ateş, Sabri. *Ottoman-Iranian Borderlands: Making a Boundary, 1843–1914.* Cambridge: Cambridge University Press, 2013.

Aydın, Ayşegül, and Cem Emrence. *Zones of Rebellion: Kurdish Insurgents and the Turkish State.* Ithaca, NY: Cornell University Press, 2015.

Balcı, Sezai, and Ahmet Yadi. *Osmanlı Bürokrasisinde Yahudiler.* Istanbul: Libra Kitapçılık ve Yayıncılık, 2013.

Bali, Rıfat N. "Bir Yahudi Dayanışma ver Yardımlaşma Kurumu: B'nai B'rith XI Bölge Büyük Locası Tarihçesi ve Yayın Organı Hamenora Dergisi." *Müteferrika*, no. 8–9 (Spring-Summer 1996): 41–60.

Bali, Rıfat N. "Bir Yahudi Mali ve Sosyal Yardımlaşma Kurumu: Dersaadet Küçük İstikrazat Sandığı." *Tarih ve Toplum*, no. 160 (April 1997): 45–54.

Bali, Rıfat N. "1930 Yılı Seçimleri ve Serbest Fırka'nın Azınlık Adayları." *Tarih ve Toplum*, no. 167 (November 1997): 27–34.

Bali, Rıfat N. "Edirne Yahudileri." In *Edirne: Serhattaki Payitaht*, edited by Emin Nedret İsli and M. Sabri Koz, 205–27. Istanbul: Yapi Kredi Yayinlari, 1998.

Bali, Rıfat N. *Cumhuriyet Yıllarında Türkiye Yahudileri: Bir Türkleştirme Serüveni, 1923–1945.* Istanbul: İletişim, 1999.

Bali, Rıfat N. "Edirne Muhasarası Sırasında Tutulmuş Bir Günlük—I." *Tarih ve Toplum* 32, no. 190 (October 1999): 35–43.

Bali, Rıfat N. "Edirne Muhasarası Sırasında Tutulmuş Bir Günlük—II." *Tarih ve Toplum* 32, no. 191 (November 1999): 15–24.

Bali, Rıfat N. "Edirne Muhasarası Sırasında Tutulmuş Bir Günlük—III." *Tarih ve Toplum* 32, no. 192 (December 1999): 26–30.

Bali, Rıfat N. "Edirne Muhasarası Sırasında Tutulmuş Bir Günlük—IV." *Tarih ve Toplum* 32, no. 193 (January 2000): 34–38.

Bali, Rıfat N. *Sarayın ve Cumhuriyetin Dişçibaşısı: Sami Günzberg.* Istanbul: Kitabevi, 2007.

Bali, Rıfat N. "The 1934 Thrace Events: Continuity and Change within Turkish State Policies Regarding Non-Muslim Minorities: An Interview with Rıfat N. Bali." By Alexandre Toumarkine and Nikos Sigalas. *European Journal of Turkish Studies*, no. 7 (2008).

Bali, Rıfat N. "Unutulmuş bir TKP'li Davit Nae." *Toplumsal Tarih* no. 202 (October 2010): 70–76.

Bali, Rıfat N. *1934 Trakya Olayları.* Istanbul: Libra Kitapçılık ve Yayıncılık, 2012.

Bali, Rıfat N. *Xenophobia and Protectionism: A Study of the 1932 Law Reserving Majority of Occupations in Turkey to Turkish Nationals.* Istanbul: Libra, 2013.

Bali, Rıfat N. *Edirne Mebusu Mehmet Şeref Aykut'un Munis Tekinalp'e mektubu (20 Nisan 1934)*. Istanbul: Libra Kitapçılık ve Yayıncılık, 2023.

Balistreri, Alexander E. "Revisiting Millî: Borders and the Making of the Turkish Nation State." In *Regimes of Mobility: Borders and State Formation in the Middle East, 1918–1946*, edited by Jordi Tejel and Ramazan Hakkı Öztan, 29–58. Edinburgh: Edinburgh University Press, 2022.

Baramova, Maria, Grigor Boykov, and Ivan Parvev, eds., *Bordering Early Modern Europe*. Wiesbaden, Germany: Harrassowitz Verlag, 2015.

Bartov, Omer, and Eric D. Weitz. "Introduction: Coexistence and Violence in the German, Habsburg, Russian, and Ottoman Borderlands." In *Shatterzone of Empires: Coexistence and Violence in the German, Habsburg, Russian, and Ottoman Borderlands,* ed. Omer Bartov and Eric D. Weitz, 1–20. Bloomington: Indiana University Press, 2013.

Bashkin, Orit. *Impossible Exodus: Iraqi Jews in Israel*. Stanford, CA: Stanford University Press, 2017.

Baud, Michiel, and Willem Van Schendel. "Toward a Comparative History of Borderlands." *Journal of World History* 8, no. 2 (Fall, 1997): 211–42.

Baykal, Bekir Sıtkı. *Edirne'nin Uğramış Olduğu İstilâlar*. Ankara: Türk Tarih Kurumu, 1965.

Bayraktar, Hatice. "The Anti-Jewish Pogrom in Eastern Thrace in 1934: New Evidence for the Responsibility of the Turkish Government." *Patterns of Prejudice* 40, no. 2 (2006): 95–111.

Beinin, Joel. *The Dispersion of Egyptian Jewry: Culture, Politics, and the Formation of a Modern Diaspora*. Berkeley: University of California Press, 1998.

Beinin, Joel. "Jews as Native Iraqis: An Introduction." Foreword to Nissim Rejwan, *The Last Jews in Baghdad: Remembering a Lost Homeland*. Austin: University of Texas Press, 2004.

Bemporad, Elissa. *Becoming Soviet Jews: The Bolshevik Experiment in Minsk*. Bloomington: Indiana University Press, 2013.

Benbassa, Esther. "Associational Strategies in Ottoman Jewish Society in the Nineteenth and Twentieth Centuries." In *The Jews of the Ottoman Empire*, edited by Avigdor Levy, 457–84. Princeton, NJ: Darwin, 1994.

Benbassa, Esther. *Haim Nahum: A Sephardic Chief Rabbi in Politics, 1892–1923*. Translated by Miriam Kochan.Tuscaloosa: University of Alabama Press, 1995.

Benbassa, Esther, and Aron Rodrigue. *Sephardi Jewry: A History of the Judeo-Spanish Community, 14th–20th Centuries*. Berkeley: University of California Press, 2000.

Benlisoy, Stefo. *İstanbul'un Irgatları: II. Meşrutiyet'te Sosyalist Bir İşçi Örgütü*. Istanbul: İstos, 2018.

Ben-Naeh, Yaron. "The Historiography of Ottoman Jewry." *Journal of Jewish Studies* 69, no. 1 (Spring 2008): 109–33.

Berberian, Houri. *Roving Revolutionaries: Armenians and the Connected Revolutions in the Russian, Iranian, and Ottoman Worlds*. Oakland: University of California Press. 2019.

Beşikçi, Mehmet. *The Ottoman Mobilization of Manpower in the First World War: Between Voluntarism and Resistance*. Leiden: Brill, 2012.
Bilar, Ender. *Edirne'nin Basın-Yayın Tarihi, 1361–2006*, 1. Edirne: Edirne Valiliği, 2006.
Biondich, Mark. "The Balkan Wars: Violence and Nation-Building in the Balkans, 1912–13." *Journal of Genocide Research* 18, no. 4 (2016): 389–404.
Birinci, Ali. *Hürriyet ve İtilaf Fırkası: 2. Meşrutiyet Devrinde İttihat ve Terakki'ye Karşı Çıkanlar*. Istanbul: Dergâh Yayınları, 1990.
Bıyıklıoğlu, Tevfik. *Trakya'da Milli Mücadele*. Ankara: Türk Tarih Kurumu, 1992.
Borovaya, Olga. *Modern Ladino Culture: Press, Belles Lettres, and Theater in the Late Ottoman Empire*. Bloomington: Indiana University Press, 2012.
Boyar, Ebru. *Ottomans, Turks, and the Balkans: Empire Lost, Relations Altered*. London: I. B. Tauris, 2007.
Boyar, Ebru, and Kate Fleet. "A Dangerous Axis: The 'Bulgarian Müftü', the Turkish Opposition and the Ankara Government, 1928–36." *Middle Eastern Studies* 44, no. 5 (2008): 775–89.
Boyar, Ebru, and Kate Fleet. "Introduction." In *Borders, Boundaries and Belonging in Post-Ottoman Space in the Interwar Period*, edited by Ebru Boyar and Kate Fleet, 1–12. Leiden: Brill, 2023.
Budnitskii, Oleg. "Shots in the Back: On the Origin of the Anti-Jewish Pogroms of 1918–1921." In *Polin: Studies in Polish Jewry Vol 14: Focusing on Jews in the Polish Borderlands*, edited by Antony Polonsky, 187–207. London: Littman Library of Jewish Civilization, 2001.
Bulut, Cengiz. *Trakya-Paşaeli Müdafaa-i Hukuk Cemiyeti Kurucularından Kasım Yolageldili, 1874–1936*. Edirne, Turkey: T.C. Edirne Valiliği, 2019.
Campos, Michelle U. *Ottoman Brothers: Muslims, Christians, and Jews in Early Twentieth-Century Palestine*. Stanford, CA: Stanford University Press, 2011.
Can, Cemil Cahit, and Ender Bilar. *Edirne Bilbliyografyası*. Edirne, Turkey: Trakya Üniversitesi Rektörlüğü Yayınları, 2009.
Caron, Vicki. *Between France and Germany: The Jews of Alsace-Lorraine, 1871–1918*. Stanford, CA: Stanford University Press, 1988.
Chary, Frederick B. *The Bulgarian Jews and the Final Solution, 1940–1944*. Pittsburgh: University of Pittsburgh Press, 1972.
Chotzidis, Angelos A. "The Impact of the Ottoman Public Debt Administration on the Economies of Epirus, Macedonia and Thrace: A Preliminary Approach." (unpublished conference paper).
Ciancia, Kathryn. *On Civilization's Edge: A Polish Borderland in the Interwar World*. New York: Oxford University Press, 2021.
Clayer, Nathalie, Fabio Giorni, and Emmanuel Szurek. *Kemalism: Transnational Politics in the Post-Ottoman World*. London: I. B. Tauris, 2019.
Clogg, Richard. *A Concise History of Greece*. Cambridge: Cambridge University Press, 2021.
Cohen, Julia Phillips. *Becoming Ottomans: Sephardi Jews and Imperial Citizenship in the Modern Era*. Oxford: Oxford University Press, 2014.

Cohen, Julia Phillips. "A Model Millet? Ottoman Jewish Citizenship at the End of Empire." In *Jews, Liberalism, Antisemitism: A Global History*, edited by Abigail Green and Simon Levis Sullam, 209–29. Cham, Switzerland: Palgrave Macmillan, 2020.

Crampton, R. J. *A Concise History of Bulgaria*. Cambridge: Cambridge University Press, 2005.

Çağaptay, Soner. "Race, Assimilation, and Kemalism: Turkish Nationalism and the Minorities in the 1930s." *Middle Eastern Studies* 40, no. 3 (May, 2004): 86–101.

Çağaptay, Soner. *Islam, Secularism, and Nationalism in Modern Turkey: Who Is a Turk?* London: Routledge, 2006.

Çakır, Ali. "Kırklareli/Pavli Panayırından Kakava Şenliklerine Yaşamı Kutlarken," in *Rakı Gastronomisi: Türkiye'nin Cilingir Sofrası*. Istanbul: Overteam Yayınları, 2017.

Çetin, Nurten. "Osmanlı Devleti'nin Birinci Dünya Savaşı'nda İtilaf Devletleri Vatandaşlarına Yönelik Uygulamalarından Biri: Sürgün (Edirne Örneği)." *Trakya Üniversitesi Edebiyat Fakültesi Dergisi* 3, no. 5 (January 2013): 75–94.

Çetin, Nurten, and V. Türkan Doğruöz. *Milli Mücadele'nin Yerel Tarihi 1918–1923*, Vol. 10: Edirne, Kırklareli, Tekirdağ. Ankara: Türkiye Bilimler Akademesi, 2023.

Çetinkaya, Doğan. *The Young Turks and the Boycott Movement: Nationalism, Protest and the Working Classes in the Formation of Modern Turkey*. London: I. B. Taurus, 2013.

Dağlıoğlu, Emre Can. "Silk-Made Capitalism: Local Networks and Financial Control in the Late Ottoman Empire." PhD diss., Stanford University, forthcoming.

Daniels, Jacob. "Prelude to a Turkish Anomaly: Eastern Thrace Before the 1934 Attacks on Jews." *Antisemitism Studies* 1, no. 2 (Fall 2017): 364–96.

Danon, Dina. *The Jews of Ottoman Izmir: A Modern History*. Stanford, CA: Stanford University Press, 2020.

Darling, Linda. "The Mediterranean as a Borderland." *Review of Middle East Studies* 46, no. 1 (Summer 2012): 54–63.

Demetriou, Olga. *Capricious Borders: Minority, Population, and Counter-Conduct Between Greece and Turkey*. New York: Berghahn Books, 2013.

Demir, Mehtap. "Maftirim: Osmanlı Müzik Kültüründe Sefarad Paraliturjik Müziği." *Ç.Ü. Sosyal Bilimler Enstitüsü Dergisi* 26, no. 2 (2017): 313–32.

Demirözü, Damla. "The Greek-Turkish Rapprochement of 1930 and the Repercussions of the Ankara Convention in Turkey." *Journal of Islamic Studies* 19, no. 3 (September 2008).

Der Matossian, Bedross. "Formation of Public Sphere(s) in the Aftermath of the 1908 Revolution among Armenians, Arabs, and Jews," Faculty Publications, Department of History, University of Nebraska-Lincoln (2012): 189–219.

Detrez, Raymond. *Historical Dictionary of Bulgaria*. London: Scarecrow, 1997.

Diken, Şeyhmus. *İsyan Sürgünleri*. Istanbul: İletişim, 2005.

Dinçer, Sinan. "An Exclusionary Border Regime: The Ottoman Case, 1890–1914." In *Borders and Mobility Control in and between Empires and Nation-States*, edited by Jovan Pešalj, Annemarie Steidl, Leo Lucassen, and Josef Ehmer, 184–218. Leiden: Brill, 2023.

Dogo, Marco. "Loyalty Sorely Tried: The Jews and the Bulgarian State (1878–1935)," in *The Jews and the Nation-States of Southeastern Europe from the 19th Century to the Great Depression: Combining Viewpoints on a Controversial Story*, edited by Tullia Catalan and Marco Dogo. Newcastle, UK: Cambridge Scholars, 2016.

Doğruöz, V. Türkan. *Milli Mücadelede Kırklareli*. Kırklareli, Turkey: Kırklareli Belediyesi Kültür Yayınları, 2007.

Dolbee, Samuel. *Locusts of Power: Borders, Empire, and Environment in the Modern Middle East*. Cambridge: Cambridge University Press, 2023.

Dragostinova, Theodora. *Between Two Motherlands: Nationality and Emigration among the Greeks of Bulgaria, 1900–1949*. Ithaca, NY: Cornell University Press, 2011.

Dragostinova, Theodora. "Competing Priorities, Ambiguous Loyalties: Challenges of Socioeconomic Adaptation and National Inclusion of the Interwar Bulgarian Refugees." *Nationalities Papers*, 34, no. 5 (2019): 549–74.

Dubin, Lois C. "Yosef Hayim Yerushalmi, the Royal Alliance, and Jewish Political Theory." *Jewish History* 28, no. 1 (2014): 51–83.

Dudala, Halina. "Jews in Upper-Silesian Grammar Schools in the Second Half of the Nineteenth and Early Twentieth Century." In *Jews in Silesia*, edited by Marcin Wodinski and Janusz Spyra, 79–97. Krakow: Ksiegarnia Akademicka, 2001.

Dündar, Fuat. *İttihat ve Terakki'nin Müslümanları iskân politikası, 1913–1918*. Istanbul: İletişim, 2001.

Dündar, Fuat. *Modern Türkiye'nin Şifresi: İttihat ve Terakki'nin Etnisite Mühendisliği, 1913–1918*. Istanbul: İletişim, 2008.

Dündar, Fuat. *Crime of Numbers: The Role of Statistics in the Armenian Question, 1878–1918*. New Brunswick, NJ: Transaction, 2010.

Dündar, Fuat. "Pouring a People into the Desert." *A Question of Genocide: Armenians and Turks at the End of the Ottoman Empire*, edited by Ronald Grigor Suny, Fatma Müge Göçek, and Norman M. Naimark, 276–84. Oxford: Oxford University Press, 2011.

Efiloğlu, Ahmet. "The Exodus of Thracian Greeks to Greece in the Post–Balkan War Era." In *War and Collapse: World War I and the Ottoman State*, edited by M. Hakan Yavuz and Feroz Ahmad, 330–56. Salt Lake City: University of Utah Press, 2016.

Efron, John M. *German Jewry and the Allure of the Sephardic*. Princeton, NJ: Princeton University Press, 2016.

Ellis, Matthew H. "Over the Borderline? Rethinking Territoriality at the Margins of Empire and Nation in the Modern Middle East (Parts I and II)." *History Compass* 13, no. 8 (2015): 411–34.

Emekci, Cennet. "Kozahane ve İpek Fabrikaları Üzerine Bir Araştırma: Edirne Kozahane Restorasyonu." Master's thesis, Trakya University, 2011.

Erdal, İbrahim. *Mübadele: Uluslaşma Sürecinde Türkiye ve Yunanistan 1923–1925*. Istanbul: IQ Kültür Sanat, 2006.

Erickson, Edward J. *Defeat in Detail, The Ottoman Army in the Balkans, 1912–1913*. Westport, CT: Praeger, 2003.

Eser, Ümit. *Nationalist Schism in the Empire: Tanzimat Reforms and the Establishment of the Bulgarian Exarchate*. Istanbul: Libra Kitapçılık ve Yayıncılık, 2019.

Esin, Taylan. "19. Yüzyılın Sonunda Osmanlı İmparatorlu'nda Kurulan Musevi İskan Birliği (JCA) Çiftlikleri." *Toplumsal Tarih* no. 249 (September 2014): 22–33.

Eulambio, M. S. *The National Bank of Greece: A History of the Financial and Economic Evolution of Greece*. Athens: S. C. Vlastos, 1924.

Findley, Carter Vaughn. *Turkey, Islam, Nationalism, and Modernity: A History, 1789–2007*. New Haven, CT: Yale University Press, 2010.

Fishman, Louis. "Understanding the 1911 Ottoman Parliament Debate on Zionism in Light of the Emergence of a 'Jewish Question.'" In *Late Ottoman Palestine: The Period of Young Turk Rule*, edited by Yuval Ben-Bassat and Eyal Ginio, 103–20. London: I. B. Tauris, 2011.

Fleming, K. E. *Greece: A Jewish History*. Princeton, NJ: Princeton University Press, 2008.

Galanté, Abraham. *Turcs et Juifs: étude historique, politique*. Istanbul: Haim, Rozio & Co., 1932.

Galanté, Abraham. *Türkler ve Yahudilar: Tarihi, Siyasi araştırma*. Istanbul: Gözlem 1995.

Ganeva-Raycheva, Valentina. "Migration, Territories, Heritage: Discourses and Practices in Constructing the Bulgarian-Turkish Border." In *Migration, Memory, Heritage: Socio-cultural Approaches to the Bulgarian-Turkish Border*, edited by Valentina Ganeva-Raycheva and Meglena Zlatkova, 29–64. Sofia: IEFSEM-BAS, 2012.

Gaon Moshe David, *Ha-Itonut b'Ladino: Bibliyografyah: shelosh me'ot itonim*. Jerusalem: Mekhon Ben Zvi b'Universitah HaIvrit, 1965.

Gasimov, Zaur. "'The Turkish Wall': Turkey as an Anti-Communist and Anti-Russian Bulwark in the Twentieth Century." In *Rampart Nations: Bulwark Myths of East European Multiconfessional Societies in the Age of Nationalism*, edited by Liliya Berezhnaya and Heidi Hein-Kircher, 186–206. New York: Berghahn Books, 2019.

Gellner, Ernest. *Nations and Nationalism*. Ithaca, NY: Cornell University Press, 1983.

Genç, Mehmet. *Osmanlı İmparatorluğu'nda Devlet ve Ekonomi*. Istanbul: Ötüken, 2013.

Gerber, Haim. *Crossing Borders: Jews and Muslims in Ottoman Law, Economy and Society*. Istanbul: Isis, 2008.

Gingeras, Ryan. "A Last Toehold in Europe: The Making of Turkish Thrace, 1912–1923." In *War and Collapse: World War I and the Ottoman State*, edited by M. Hakan Yavuz and Feroz Ahmad, 371–404. Salt Lake City: University of Utah Press, 2016.

Ginio, Eyal. "Mobilizing the Ottoman Nation during the Balkan Wars (1912–1913): Awakening from the Ottoman Dream." *War in History* 12, no. 2 (2005): 156–77.

Ginio, Eyal. "'Ottoman Jews! Rush to Save our Homeland!' Ottoman Jews in the Balkan Wars (1912–1913)." [In Hebrew.] *Pe'amim* 105/106 (2005/2006): 5–28.

Ginio, Eyal. "Constructing a Symbol of Defeat and National Rejuvenation: Edirne (Adrianople) in Ottoman Propaganda and Writing during the Balkan Wars." In *Cities into Battlefields: Metropolitan Scenarios, Experiences and Commemorations of Total War*, edited by Stefan Goebel and Derek Keene, 83–99. Burlington, VT: Ashgate, 2011.

Ginio, Eyal. "Paving the Way for Ethnic Cleansing: Eastern Thrace during the Balkan Wars (1912–1913) and Their Aftermath." In *Shatterzone of Empires: Coexistence and Violence in the German, Habsburg, Russian, and Ottoman Borderlands*, edited by Omer Bartov and Eric D. Weitz, 283–97. Bloomington: Indiana University Press, 2013.

Ginio, Eyal. *The Ottoman Culture of Defeat: The Balkan Wars and their Aftermath*. London: Hurst, 2016.

Ginio, Eyal. "Jewish Philanthropy and Mutual Assistance During the Balkan Wars: Between Ottomanism and Communal Identities." Unpublished, 2017.

Ginio, Eyal. "Challenging Communal Boundaries in Late Ottoman Thrace: Jews and Muslims in Dimetoka (Didymoteicho)." *Jewish Social Studies* 27, no. 3 (Fall 2022): 88–122.

Gökatalay, Semih. "Economic Nationalism of the Committee of Union and Progress Revisited: The Case of the Society for the Ottoman Navy." *Nationalities Papers* 48, no. 5 (September 2020): 942–56.

Gratien, Chris. *The Unsettled Plain: An Environmental History of the Late Ottoman Frontier*. Stanford, CA: Stanford University Press, 2022.

Graziano, Manlio. *What Is a Border?* Stanford, CA: Stanford University Press, 2018.

Grunwald, Kurt. *Türkenhirsch: A Study of Baron Maurice de Hirsch, Entrepreneur and Philanthropist*. Jerusalem: Israel Program for Scientific Translations, 1966.

Guidotti-Hernandez, Nicole M. "Borderlands Scholarship for the Twenty-First Century." *American Quarterly* 68, no. 2 (June, 2016): 487–98.

Gutman, Aryeh. "Outline of the Society and Organization of the Adrianople Community: 16th and 17th Centuries." Master's thesis, Tel Aviv University, 2016.

Gutman, David. "Travel Documents, Mobility Control, and the Ottoman State in an Age of Global Migration, 1880–1915." *Journal of the Ottoman and Turkish Studies Association* 3, no. 2 (November 2016): 347–68.

Guttstadt, Corry. *Turkey, the Jews, and the Holocaust*. Cambridge: Cambridge University Press, 2013.

Habermas, Jürgen. *The Structural Transformation of the Public Sphere: An Inquiry into a Category of Bourgeois Society*. Cambridge, MA: MIT Press, 1991.

Haker, Erol. *Once Upon a Time Jews Lived in Kırklareli: The Story of the Adato Family, 1800–1934*. Istanbul: Isis, 2003.

Haker, Erol. *Edirne, Its Jewish Community, and Alliance Schools, 1867–1937*. Istanbul: Isis, 2006.

Hall, Richard C. *The Balkan Wars, 1912–1913: Prelude to the First World War*. London: Routledge, 2000.

Hamed-Troyansky, Vladimir. *Empire of Refugees: North Caucasian Muslims and the Late Ottoman State*. Stanford, CA: Stanford University Press, 2024.

Hanioğlu, M. Şükrü. *A Brief History of the Late Ottoman Empire*. Princeton, NJ: Princeton University Press, 2008.

Hanioğlu, M. Şükrü. "The Second Constitutional Period, 1908–1918." In *Cambridge History of Turkey*, 4 (Turkey in the Modern World), edited by Reşat Kasaba, 62–111. Cambridge: Cambridge University Press, 2008.

Hassid, Sam. "Further on the 1920 Elections." *Jewish Museum of Greece Newsletter*, no. 41 (Autumn–Winter 1996): 5–7.

Herzog, Christopher. "Migration and the State: On Ottoman Regulations Concerning Migration since the Age of Mahmud II." In *The City in the Ottoman Empire: Migration and the Making of Urban Modernity*, edited by Ulrike Freitag, Malte Fuhrmann, Nora Lafi, and Florian Riedler, 117–34. London: Routledge, 2011.

Hirsch, Marianne, and Leo Spitzer. *Ghosts of Home: The Afterlife of Czernowitz in Jewish Memory*. Berkeley: University of California Press, 2010.

Hirschon, Renée. "'Unmixing Peoples' in the Aegean Region." In *Crossing the Aegean: An Appraisal of the 1923 Compulsory Population Exchange between Greece and Turkey*, edited by Renée Hirschon, 3–12. New York: Berghahn Books, 2003.

Issawi, Charles. *The Economic History of Turkey, 1800–1914*. Chicago: University of Chicago Press, 1980.

Jensen, Peter Kincaid. "The Greco-Turkish War, 1920–1922." *International Journal of Middle East Studies* 10, no. 4 (November 1979): 553–65.

Judson, Pieter M. *Guardians of the Nation: Activists on the Language Frontiers of Imperial Austria*. Cambridge, MA: Harvard University Press, 2006.

Kamayor, Roysi Ojalvo. *Turkey's Jewish Heritage Revisited: Architectural Conservation and the Politics of Memory*. Istanbul: Libra Kitapçılık ve Yayıncılık, 2018.

Karabatak, Haluk. "Türkiye Azınlık Tarihine Bir Katkı: 1934 Trakya Olayları ve Yahudiler." *Tarih ve Toplum*, no. 146 (February 1996): 68–80.

Karagedikli, Gürer. "In Search of a Jewish Community in the Early Modern Ottoman Empire: The Case of Edirne Jews (c. 1686–1750)." Masters thesis, Bilkent University, 2011.

Karakışla, Yavuz Selim. "The 1908 Strike Wave in the Ottoman Empire." *Turkish Studies Association Bulletin* 16, no. 2 (September 1992): 153–77.

Karkason, Tamir. "An Ambivalent Coexistence: Jews and Christians in Late Ottoman Edirne." *Jewish History* 38, nos. 1–2 (2024): 1–25.

Karkason, Tamir. "Printing and Modernity: The Activities of the Dorshei Ha-Haskalah Association ('Seekers of the Enlightenment,' 1879–1889) to Revive Hebrew-Alphabet Printing in Edirne." *Ladinar: Studies in the Literature, Music & the History of the Sephardic Jews* 11 (2020): 131–54.

Karkason, Tamir. "Maskilic Families in the Ottoman Empire." *Journal of Jewish Studies* 74, no. 2 (2023): 429–54.

Karkason, Tamir. "An Ambivalent Coexistence: Jews and Christians in Late Ottoman Edirne," *Jewish History* 38, nos. 1–2 (2024).

Karpat, Kemal H. *Ottoman Population 1830–1914: Demographic and Social Characteristics*. Madison: University of Wisconsin Press, 1985.

Karpat, Kemal H. "The Hijra from Russia and the Balkans: The Process of Self-Definition in the Late Ottoman State." In *Muslim Travellers: Pilgrimage, Migration, and the Religious Imagination*, edited by Dale Eickelman and James Piscatori. Berkeley: University of California Press, 1990.

Karpat, Kemal H. "Jewish Population Movements in the Ottoman Empire, 1862–1914." In *Studies on Ottoman Social and Political History: Selected Articles and Essays*, edited by Kemal H. Karpat. Leiden: Brill, 2002.

Karpat, Kemal H. "Comments on Contributions and the Borderlands." In *Ottoman Borderlands: Issues, Personalities and Political Changes*, edited by Kemal H. Karpat and Robert W. Zens, 1–14. Madison: Center of Turkish Studies at University of Wisconsin, 2003.

Kasaba, Reşat. *A Moveable Empire: Ottoman Nomads, Migrants, and Refugees*. Seattle: University of Washington Press, 2009.

Kasaba, Reşat. "İzmir 1922: A Port City Unravels." In *Modernity and Culture: From the Mediterranean to the Indian Ocean*, edited by Leila Fawaz and C. A. Bayly, 204–29. New York: Columbia University Press, 2002.

Kassabova, Kapka. *Border: A Journey to the Edge of Europe*. Minneapolis: Graywolf, 2017.

Kaşlı, Zeynep. "Negotiating History and Diversity in a Border Province: The Non-Muslim Urban Past in Today's Edirne." In *Contested Spaces in Contemporary Turkey: Environmental, Secular and Urban Politics*, edited by Fatma Müge Göçek. London: I. B. Tauris, 2018.

Katsikas, Stefanos, "Millet Legacies in a National Environment: Political Elites and Muslim Communities in Greece (1830s–1923)." In *State-Nationalisms in the Ottoman Empire, Greece, and Turkey: Orthodox and Muslims, 1830–1945*, edited by Benjamin C. Fortna, Stefanos Katsikas, Dimitris Kamouzis, and Paraskevas Konortas, 47–70. New York: Routledge, 2013.

Kaufman, Haim. "Jewish Sports in the Diaspora, Yishuv, and Israel: Between Nationalism and Politics." *Israel Studies* 10, no. 2 (Summer 2005): 147–67.

Kayalı, Hasan. "Elections and the Electoral Process in the Ottoman Empire, 1876–1919." *International Journal of Middle East Studies* 27, no. 3 (August 1995): 265–86.

Kayalı, Hasan. *Arabs and Young Turks: Ottomanism, Arabism, and Islamism in the Ottoman Empire, 1908–1918*. Berkeley: University of California Press, 1997.

Kayıcı, Haluk. *Salnamelere Göre Idari, Sosyal ve Ekonomik Yapısıyla Edirne Sancağı*. Edirne, Turkey: T. C. Edirne Valiliği, 2013.

Keegan, John. *A History of Warfare*. New York: Alfred A. Knopf, 1993.

Kévorkian, Raymond H. *Le Génocide des Arméniens*. Paris: Odile Jacob, 2006.

Kévorkian, Raymond H. *The Armenian Genocide: A Complete History*. London: I. B. Tauris, 2011.

Keyder, Çağlar. *State and Class in Turkey: A Study in Capitalist Development*. London: Verso, 1987.

Kezer, Zeynep. "Spatializing Difference: The Making of an Internal Border in Early Republican Elazığ, Turkey." *Journal of the Society of Architectural Historians* 73, no. 4 (December 2014): 507–27.

Kezer, Zeynep. *Building Modern Turkey: State, Space, and Ideology in the Early Republic*. Pittsburgh: University of Pittsburgh Press, 2015.

Kiesler, Hans-Lukas. *Talaat Pasha: Father of Modern Turkey, Architect of Genocide*. Princeton, NJ: Princeton University Press, 2018.

Klein, Janet. *The Margins of Empire: Kurdish Militias in the Ottoman Tribal Zone*. Stanford, CA: Stanford University Press, 2011.

Koçak, Cemil. *Umumi Müfettişlikler, 1927–1952*. Istanbul: İletişim, 2003.

Konortas, Paraskevas. "Nationalism vs Millets: Building Collective Identities in Ottoman Thrace." In *Spatial Conceptions of the Nation: Modernizing Geographies in Greece and Turkey*, edited by P. Nikiforos Diamandouros, Thalia Dragonas and Çağlar Keyder, 161–80. London: Tauris Academic Studies, 2010.

Konortas, Paraskevas. "Nationalist Infiltrations in Ottoman Thrace (ca. 1870–1912): The Case of the *Kaza* of Gumuljina." In *State-Nationalisms in the Ottoman Empire, Greece, and Turkey: Orthodox and Muslims, 1830–1945*, edited by Benjamin C. Fortna, Stefanos Katsikas, Dimitris Kamouzis, and Paraskevas Konortas, 73–100. New York: Routledge, 2013.

Koraltürk, Murat. *Erken Cumhuriyet Döneminde Ekonominin Türkleştirilmesi*. Istanbul: İletişim, 2011.

Kozelsky, Mara. "The Crimean War and the Tatar Exodus." In *Russian-Ottoman Borderlands: The Eastern Question Reconsidered*, edited by Lucien J. Frary and Mara Kozelsky, 165–83. Madison: University of Wisconsin Press, 2014.

Köksal, Yonca. "Local Demands and State Policies: General Councils (Meclis-i Umumi) in the Edirne and Ankara Provinces, 1867–1872." *Middle Eastern Studies* 53, no. 3 (2017): 470–85.

Köksal, Yonca. *The Ottoman Empire in the Tanzimat Era: Provincial Perspectives from Ankara to Edirne*. London: Routledge, 2019.

Krawietz, Birgit, and Florian Riedler. "Approaching Edirne: Dis-/Connections and Attractions." In *The Heritage of Edirne in Ottoman and Turkish Times: Continuities, Disruptions and Reconnections*, edited by Birgit Krawietz and Florian Riedler, 469–83. Berlin: De Gruyter, 2020.

Kurzman, Charles. *Democracy Denied, 1905–1915: Intellectuals and the Fate of Democracy*. Cambridge, MA: Harvard University Press, 2008.

Ladas, Stephen P. *The Exchange of Minorities: Bulgaria, Greece, and Turkey*. New York: Macmillan, 1932.

Lampe, John R., and Marvin R. Jackson. *Balkan Economic History, 1550–1950*. Bloomington: Indiana University Press, 1982.

Landau, Jacob M. *Tekinalp, Turkish Patriot, 1883–1961*. Leiden: Nederlands Historisch-Archaeologisch Instituut te İstanbul, 1984.

Lehmann, Matthias. *The Baron: Maurice de Hirsch and the Jewish Nineteenth Century*. Stanford, CA: Stanford University Press, 2022.

Levi, Avner. "Ha-Fraot b'Yehudei Trakya, 1934." *Pe'amim* 20 (1984): 111–31.

Levi, Avner. *Toldot ha-Yehudim b'Republikah ha-Turkit: ma'amadam ha-politi veha-mishpati*. Jerusalem: Lafir, ha-'amutah le-ḳidum, 1992.

Levi, Avner. "1934 Trakya Yahudileri Olayı: Alınamayan Ders." *Tarih ve Toplum*, no. 151 (July 1996): 10–17.

Levy, Avigdor. "The Siege of Edirne (1912–1913) as Seen by a Jewish Eyewitness: Social, Political, and Cultural Perspectives." In *Jews, Turks, Ottomans: A Shared History, Fifteenth through the Twentieth Century*, edited by Avigdor Levy, 153–93. Syracuse, NY: Syracuse University Press, 2002.

Lichtenstein, Tatjana. *Zionists in Interwar Czechoslovakia: Minority Nationalism and the Politics of Belonging*. Bloomington: Indiana University Press, 2016.

Livanios, Dimitris. "Beyond 'Ethnic Cleansing: Aspects of the Functioning of Violence in the Ottoman and Post-Ottoman Balkans." *Southeast European and Black Sea Studies* 8, no. 3 (2008): 189–203.

Locke, John. "Second Treatise of Government" (1689). In *John Locke, Two Treatises of Government*, edited by Peter Laslett. Cambridge: Cambridge University Press, 1988.

Lohr, Eric. "The Russian Army and the Jews: Mass Deportation, Hostages, and Violence during World War I." *Russian Review* 60, no. 3 (July 2001): 404–19.

Macartney, C. A. *National States and National Minorities*. London: Oxford University Press, 1934.

MacDermott, Mercia. *A History of Bulgaria, 1395–1885*. New York: Frederick A. Praeger, 1962.

Maier, Charles S. *Once Within Borders: Territories of Power, Wealth, and Belonging since 1500*. Cambridge, MA: Harvard University Press, 2016.

Makdisi, Ussama. *Age of Coexistence: The Ecumenical Frame and the Making of the Modern Arab World*. Oakland: University of California Press, 2019.

Malmisanij. *Diyarbekirli Cemilpaşazadeler ve Kürt Milliyetçiliği*. Istanbul: Avesta, 2004.

Marshall, Gül Aldıkaçtı, *Shaping Gender Policy in Turkey*. Albany: State University of New York Press, 2013.

Martinez, Oscar J. "The Dynamics of Border Interaction: New Approaches to Border Analysis." In *Global Boundaries*, Vol. 1, edited by Clive H. Schofield. New York: Routledge, 1994.

Martinez, Oscar J. *Border People: Life and Society in the U.S.-Mexico Borderlands*. Tucson: University of Arizona Press, 1994.

Mau, Steffen. *Sorting Machines: The Reinvention of the Border in the 21st Century*. Translated by Nicola Barfoot. Cambridge: Polity Press, 2023.

Mavrogordatos, George Th. *The Stillborn Republic: Social Coalitions and Party Strategies in Greece, 1922–1936*. Los Angeles: University of California Press, 1983.

Mays, Devi. "Recounting the Past, Shaping the Future: Ladino Literary Representations of World War I." In *World War I and the Jews: Conflict and Transformation in Europe, the*

Middle East, and America, edited by Marsha L. Rozenblit and Jonathan Karp, 201–21. New York: Berghahn Books, 2017.

Mays, Devi. *Forging Ties, Forging Passports: Migration and the Modern Sephardi Diaspora*. Stanford, CA: Stanford University Press, 2020.

Mazower, Mark. *Salonica, City of Ghosts: Christians, Muslims, and Jews, 1430–1950*. New York: Alfred A. Knopf, 2005.

McCarthy, Justin. "The Population of Ottoman Europe Before and After the Fall of the Empire." In *IIIrd Congress on the Social and Economic History of Turkey: Princeton University, 24–26 August, 1983*, edited by Heath Lowry and Ralph Hattox. Istanbul: Isis, 1990.

McCarthy, Justin. *Death and Exile: The Ethnic Cleansing of Ottoman Muslims, 1821–1922*. Princeton, NJ: Darwin, 1995.

McCourt, John. *The Years of Bloom: James Joyce in Trieste, 1904–1920*. Madison: University of Wisconsin Press, 2000.

McTague, John J., Jr., "Zionist-British Negotiations over the Draft Mandate for Palestine, 1920." *Jewish Social Studies* 42, no. 3/4 (Summer–Autumn, 1980): 281–92.

Meininger, Thomas A. *Ignatiev and the Establishment of the Bulgarian Exarchate: 1864–1872*. Madison, WI: Logmark Editions, 1970.

Methodieva, Milena B. "The Debate on Parliamentarism in the Muslim Press of Bulgaria, 1895–1908." In *The First Ottoman Experiment in Democracy*, edited by Christoph Herzog and Malek Sharif. Würzburg, Germany: Ergon Verlag, 2010.

Migdal, Joel S. "Mental Maps and Virtual Checkpoints: Struggles to Construct and Maintain State and Social Boundaries." In *Boundaries and Belonging: States and Societies in the Struggle to Shape Identities and Local Practices*, edited by Joel S. Migdal, 3–23. Cambridge: Cambridge University Press, 2004.

Mirkova, Anna M. *Muslim Land, Christian Labor: Transforming Ottoman Imperial Subjects into Bulgarian National Citizens, 1878–1939*. Budapest: Central European University Press, 2017.

Molho, Rena. "The Zionist Movement up to the First Panhellenic Zionist Conference." In *Salonica and Istanbul: Social, Political and Cultural Aspects of Jewish Life*, edited by Rena Molho, 165–86. Istanbul: Isis, 2005.

Moss, Kenneth B. *An Unchosen People: Jewish Political Reckoning in Interwar Poland*. Cambridge, MA: Harvard University Press, 2021.

Mourelos, Yannis G. "The 1914 Persecutions and the First Attempt at an Exchange of Minorities between Greece and Turkey." *Balkan Studies* 26, no. 2 (1985): 389–413.

Naar, Devin E. *Jewish Salonica: Between the Ottoman Empire and Modern Greece*. Stanford, CA: Stanford University Press, 2016.

Naar, Devin E. "The 'Mother of Israel' or the 'Sephardi Metropolis'? Sephardim, Ashkenazim, and Romaniotes in Salonica." *Jewish Social Studies* 22, no. 1 (Fall 2016): 81–129.

Nadel, Ira B., *Joyce and the Jews: Culture and Texts*. Iowa City: University of Iowa Press, 1989.

Namyslo, Aleksandra. "The Religious Life of Katowice Jews in the Inter-War Period." In *Jews in Silesia*, edited by Marcin Wodinski and Janusz Spyra, 125–38. Krakow: Ksiegarnia Akademicka, 2001.

Nassi, Gad. *Jewish Journalism and Printing Houses in the Ottoman Empire and Modern Turkey*. Istanbul: Isis, 2001.

Nathan, Naphtali. "Notes on the Jews of Turkey." *Jewish Journal of Sociology* 6 (1964): 172–89.

Necipoğlu, Gülru. *The Age of Sinan: Architectural Culture in the Ottoman Empire*. London: Reaktion, 2005.

Nugent, Paul. "Border Towns and Cities in Comparative Perspective." In *A Companion to Border Studies*, edited by Thomas M. Wilson and Hastings Donnan, 557–72. Malden, MA: Wiley-Blackwell, 2012.

Odabaşı, Pınar. "Ottoman Edirne in the Early 20th Century: War, Diplomacy and Violence in the Western Borderlands of the Empire on the Eve of the Nation-State." PhD diss., University of Akron, forthcoming.

Omer, Vezi Metin. "Why Did They Leave? Perceptions on the Turkish Emigration from Dobrogea to Turkey, 1918–1940." *International Journal of Political Science & Urban Studies* 7, no. 1 (2019): 43–54.

Osman, Rifat. *Edirne Rehnüması*. Edirne: Edirne Valiliği, 2013.

Öke, Mim Kemal. "Young Turks, Freemasons, Jews and the Question of Zionism in the Ottoman Empire (1908–1913)." *Studies in Zionism* 7, no. 2 (1986): 199–218.

Ökte, Faik. *The Tragedy of the Turkish Capital Tax*. Translated by Geoffrey Cox. London: Croom Helm, 1987.

Önelçin, Hasan Adnan. *Trakya Basını*. Tekirdağ, Turkey: Tekirdağ Halkevi Yayınları, 1972.

Öz, İlkay. *Mülksüzlestirme ve Türklestirme: Edirne Örnegi*. Istanbul: İletişim Yayınları, 2020.

Özbek, Nadir. "Modernite, Tarih ve İdeoloji: II. Abdülhamid Dönemi Tarihçiliği Üzerine Bir Değerlendirme." *Türkiye Araştırmaları Literatür Dergisi* 2, no. 1 (2004): 71–90.

Özer, Mustafa. *The Ottoman Imperial Palace in Edirne (Saray-ı Cedîd-i Âmire): A Brief Introduction*. Translated by Catherine Bobbitt. Istanbul: Bahçeşehir University Press, 2014.

Özgüven, Burcu. "Palanka Forts and Construction Activity in the Late Ottoman Balkans." In *The Frontiers of the Ottoman World*, edited by A.C.S. Peacock, 171–87. Oxford: Oxford University Press, 2009.

Öztan, Ramazan Hakkı. "Settlement Law of 1934: Turkish Nationalism in the Age of Revisionism." *Journal of Migration History* 6 (2020): 82–103.

Palairet, Michael. *The Balkan Economies c. 1800–1914*. Cambridge: Cambridge University Press, 1997.

Pallis, A.A. "Racial Migrations in the Balkans during the Years 1912–1924." *Geographical Journal* 66, no. 4 (October 1925): 315–31.

Papademitriou, Tom. *Render unto the Sultan: Power, Authority, and the Greek Orthodox Church in the Early Ottoman Centuries.* Oxford: Oxford University Press, 2015.

Papastratis, Thrasyvoulos. "The Image of the Jews through the Local Newspapers in the Prefecture of Evros, 1924–1940." Paper presented at the International Symposium on the Jews in Demotica before and after the Shoah, Didymoteicho, Greece, May 6, 2023.

Peacock, A. C. S. "Introduction: The Ottoman Empire and Its Frontiers." In *The Frontiers of the Ottoman World*, edited by A. C. S. Peacock, 1–27. Oxford: Oxford University Press, 2009.

Peçe, Uğur. *Island and Empire: How Civil War in Crete Mobilized the Ottoman World.* Stanford, CA: Stanford University Press, 2024.

Pekesen, Berna. *Nationalismus, Türkisierung und das Ende der Jüdischen Gemeinden in Thrakien.* Munich: R. Oldenbourg Verlag, 2012.

Pekesen, Berna. "The Anti-Jewish Pogrom in 1934: Problems of Historiography, Terms and Methodology." In *The Heritage of Edirne in Ottoman and Turkish Times: Continuities, Disruptions and Reconnections*, edited by Birgit Krawietz and Florian Riedler, 412–31. Berlin: De Gruyter, 2020.

Penslar, Derek J. "Introduction: The Press and the Jewish Public Sphere." *Jewish History* 14, no. 1 (2000): 3–8.

Penslar, Derek J. *Shylock's Children: Economics and Jewish Identity in Modern Europe.* Berkeley: University of California Press, 2001.

Peremeci, Osman Nuri. *Edirne Tarihi.* Edirne, Turkey: Bellek Yayınları, 2011.

Pérouse, Jean-François. "Region versus Metropolis: Thrace and Sprawling Istanbul." In *The Heritage of Edirne in Ottoman and Turkish Times: Continuities, Disruptions and Reconnections*, edited by Birgit Krawietz and Florian Riedler, 469–83. Berlin: De Gruyter, 2020.

Pešalj, Jovan, Annemarie Steidl, Leo Lucassen, and Josef Ehmer. "Introduction." In *Borders and Mobility Control in and between Empires and Nation-States*, edited by Jovan Pešalj, Annemarie Steidl, Leo Lucassen, and Josef Ehmer, 1–11. Leiden: Brill, 2023.

Pierron, Bernard. *Juifs et Chrétiens de la Grèce Moderne: Histoire des relations intercommunautaires de 1821 à 1945.* Paris: Harmattan, 1996.

Piketty, Thomas. *Capital in the Twenty First Century.* Cambridge, MA: Belknap Press, 2014.

Pınar, Mehmet. *Tek Parti Döneminde Trakya'da Siyasi Hayat ve Yahudilar, 1930–1934.* Ankara: Grafiker, 2016.

Popescu, Bogdan G. *Imperial Borderlands: Institutions and Legacies of the Habsburg Military Frontier.* Cambridge, UK: Cambridge University Press, 2024.

Popov, Anton. "From Pindos to Pontos: The Ethnicity and Diversity of Greek Communities in Southern Russia." *Bulletin: Anthropology, Minorities, Multiculturalism* 5 (January 2004): 84–90.

Pursley, Sara. "'Lines Drawn on an Empty Map': Iraq's Borders and the Legend of the Artificial State" (Parts 1 and 2). *Jadaliyya*, June 2, 2015. https://www.jadaliyya.com/Details/32140.

Protić, Stojan M. *The Aspirations of Bulgaria*. London: Simpkin, Marshall, Hamilton, Kent, 1915.

Prusin, Alexander V. "A 'Zone of Violence': The Anti-Jewish Pogroms in Eastern Galicia in 1914–1915 and 1941." In *Shatterzone of Empires: Coexistence and Violence in the German, Habsburg, Russian, and Ottoman Borderlands*, edited by Omer Bartov and Eric D. Weitz, 362–77. Bloomington: Indiana University Press, 2013.

Quataert, Donald. *Social Disintegration and Popular Resistance in the Ottoman Empire, 1881–1908: Relations to European Economic Penetration*. New York: New York University Press, 1983.

Quataert, Donald. *Ottoman Manufacturing in the Age of the Industrial Revolution*. Cambridge: Cambridge University Press, 1993.

Rahme, Joseph G. "Namık Kemal's Constitutional Ottomanism and Non-Muslims." *Islam and Christian-Muslim Relations* 10, no. 1 (1999): 23–39.

Riedler, Florian. "Building Modern Infrastructures on Ancient Routes: Road and Rail Development in 19th-Century Edirne." In *The Heritage of Edirne in Ottoman and Turkish Times: Continuities, Disruptions and Reconnections*, edited by Birgit Krawietz and Riedler, 435–68. Berlin: De Gruyter, 2020.

Rivlin, Bracha. *Pinkas ha-kehilot. Yavan: entsiklopedyah shel ha-yishuvim ha-Yehudim le-min hivasdam ve-'ad le-ahar Sho'at Milhemet ha-'Olam ha-Sheniyah*. Jerusalem: Yad Vashem, 1998.

Rodrigue, Aron. "Jewish Society and Schooling in a Thracian Town: The Alliance Israélite Universelle in Demotica, 1897–1924." *Jewish Social Studies* 45, no. 3/4 (Summer–Autumn 1983): 263–86.

Rodrigue, Aron. "The Alliance Israélite Universelle and the Attempt to Reform Jewish Religious and Rabbinical Instruction in Turkey." In *L'"Alliance" dans les communautés du bassin mediterranéen à la fin du 19ème siècle et son influence sur la situation sociale et curturelle*, edited by Simon Schwarzfuchs, LVI–LXI. Jerusalem: Misgav Yerushalayim, 1987.

Rodrigue, Aron. *French Jews, Turkish Jews: The Alliance Israélite Universelle and the Politics of Jewish Schooling in Turkey, 1860–1925*. Bloomington: Indiana University Press, 1990.

Rodrigue, Aron. "Difference and Tolerance in the Ottoman Empire: Interview by Nancy Reynolds." *Stanford Humanities Review* 5, no. 1 (1996): 81–92.

Rodrigue, Aron. "The Ottoman Diaspora: The Rise and Fall of Ladino Literary Culture." In *Cultures of the Jews: A New History*, edited by David Biale, 863–85. New York: Shocken Books, 2002.

Rodrigue, Aron. "Jewish Enlightenment and Nationalism in the Ottoman Balkans: Barukh Mitrani in Edirne in the Second Half of the Nineteenth Century." In *Minorities in the Ottoman Empire*, edited by Molly Greene, 129–41. Princeton, NJ: Markus Wiener, 2005.

Rodrigue, Aron. *Sephardim and the Holocaust*. Washington, DC: United States Holocaust Memorial Museum, 2005.

Rodrigue, Aron. "L'Etat impérial ottoman et les politiques de deportation." In *Le temps de l'état: Mélanges offerts à Pierre Birnbaum*, edited by Bertrand Badie and Yves Deloye. Paris: Fayard, 2007.

Rodrigue, Aron. "Reflections on Millets and Minorities: Ottoman Legacies." In *Turkey Between Nationalism and Globalization*, edited by Riva Kastoryano, 36–46. London: Routledge, 2013.

Rodrigue, Aron. "From Millet to Minority: Turkish Jewry." In *Paths of Emancipation: Jews, States, and Citizenship*, edited by Pierre Birnbaum and Ira Katznelson, 238–61. Princeton, NJ: Princeton University Press, 2014.

Rosanes, Salomon Abraham. *Divrei Yemei Yisrael b'Torgama* 1–3. Sofia: Husiatin, 1907–1914.

Rosanes, Salomon Abraham. *Korot ha-Yehudim b'Turkiya u-b'Artzot ha-Kedem* 1–6. Jerusalem: Mosad ha-Rav Kuk, 1930–1945.

Rozen, Minna. *The Last Ottoman Century and Beyond: the Jews in Turkey and the Balkans, 1808–1945*, vol. 1. Tel Aviv: Tel Aviv University Press, 2005.

Rushworth, Dennis. "Mapping in Support of Frontier Arbitration: Delimitation and Demarcation." *IBRU Boundary and Security Bulletin* (Spring 1997): 61–64.

Sahara, Tetsuya. "The Ottoman City Council and the Beginning of the Modernization of Urban Space in the Balkans." In *The City in the Ottoman Empire: Migration and the Making of Urban Modernity*, edited by Ulrike Freitag, Malte Fuhrmann, Nora Lafi, and Florian Riedler, 26–50. London: Routledge, 2011.

Sahlins, Peter. *Boundaries: The Making of France and Spain in the Pyrenees*. Berkeley: University of California Press, 1989.

Saydam, Abdullah. *Kırım ve Kafkas Göçleri, 1856–1876*. Ankara: Türk Tarih Kurumu, 1997.

Scott, James C. *Seeing Like a State: How Certain Schemes to Improve the Human Condition Have Failed*. New Haven, CT: Yale University Press, 1998.

Sevgil, Sezen. "Edirne Milletvekili Mehmet Şeref Aykut ve Birinci TBMM'deki Faaliyetleri." Master's thesis, Trakya University, 2016.

Sezgin, Paméla J. Dorn. "Hakhamim, Dervishes, and Court Singers: The Relationship of Ottoman Jewish Music to Classical Turkish Music." In *The Jews of the Ottoman Empire*, edited by Avigdor Levy, 585–632. Princeton, NJ: Darwin, 1994.

Singer, Amy. "Enter, Riding on an Elephant: How to Approach Early Ottoman Edirne." *Journal of the Ottoman and Turkish Studies Association* 3, no. 1 (May 2016): 89–109.

Smith, Michael Llewellyn. *Ionian Vision: Greece in Asia Minor, 1919–1922*. New York: St. Martin's, 1973.

Spector, Shmuel, and Bracha Freundlich. *Lost Jewish Worlds: The Communities of Grodno, Lida, Olkieniki, Vishay*. Jerusalem: Yad Vashem, 1996.

Stavroulakis, Nicholas. "The Jews of Greece: An Essay." Athens: Talos Press, 1990.

Stein, Sarah Abrevaya. "Creating a Taste for News: Historicizing Judeo-Spanish Periodicals of the Ottoman Empire." *Jewish History* 14, no. 1 (2000): 9–28.

Stein, Sarah Abrevaya. "The Permeable Boundaries of Ottoman Jewry." In *Boundaries and Belonging: States and Societies in the Struggle to Shape Identities and Local Practices*, edited by Joel S. Migdal, 49–70. Cambridge: Cambridge University Press, 2004.

Stein, Sarah Abrevaya. *Extraterritorial Dreams: European Citizenship, Sephardi Jews, and the Ottoman Twentieth Century*. Chicago: University of Chicago Press, 2016.

Stein, Sarah Abrevaya. *Family Papers: A Sephardic Journey Through the Twentieth Century*. New York: Farrar, Straus and Giroux, 2019.

Stern, Eliyahu. *Jewish Materialism: The Intellectual Revolution of the 1870s*. New Haven, CT: Yale University Press, 2018.

Stoianovich, Traian. "The Conquering Balkan Orthodox Merchant." *Journal of Economic History* 20, no. 2 (June 1960): 234–313.

Stravoulakis, Nicholas. *The Jews of Greece: An Essay*. Athens: Talos, 1990.

Sugar, Peter F. "Railroad Construction and the Development of the Balkan Village in the Last Quarter of the 19th Century." In *Nationality and Society in Habsburg and Ottoman Europe*, 485–98. Brookfield, VT: Variorum, 1997.

Suny, Ronald Grigor. *They Can Live in the Desert but Nowhere Else*. Princeton, NJ: Princeton University Press, 2015.

Şen, Sertaç K. "Marshaling Development: Turkish Thrace in the Interwar Years." *Diyâr* 4, no. 2 (2023): 232–61.

Şenoğuz, H. Pınar. *Community, Change and Border Towns*. London: Routledge, 2019.

Taş, N. Fahri. "Birinci Dünya Savaşı Sonrasında Fransızların Trakya'yı İşgali." *Atatürk Araştırma Merkezi Dergisi* 20, no. 60 (November 2004): 660–74.

Tejel, Jordi, and Ramazan Hakkı Öztan. "Introduction: Regimes of Mobility in Middle Eastern Borderlands, 1918–46." In *Regimes of Mobility: Borders and State Formation in the Middle East, 1918–1946*, edited by Jordi Tejel and Ramazan Hakkı Öztan, 1–25. Edinburgh: Edinburgh University Press, 2022.

Teller, Adam. "Revisiting Baron's 'Lachrymose Conception': The Meanings of Violence in Jewish History." *AJS Review* 38, no. 2 (November 2014): 431–39.

Tercatin, Baruch, and Lucian-Zeev Herşcovivi. *Prezențe rabinice în perimetrul românesc: secolele XVI–XXI*. Bucharest: Hasefer, 2008.

Ther, Philipp. "Caught in Between: Border Regions in Modern Europe." In *Shatterzone of Empires: Coexistence and Violence in the German, Habsburg, Russian, and Ottoman Borderlands*, edited by Omer Bartov and Eric D. Weitz, 485–502. Bloomington: Indiana University Press, 2013.

Todorova, Maria. *Imagining the Balkans*. Oxford: Oxford University Press, 2009.

Tokel, Meliha. *Tarihte ve günümüzde Edirne Yahudi cemaati*. Master's thesis, Marmara Üniversitesi, 2010.

Topal, Alp Eren. "Ottomanism in History and Historiography: Fortunes of a Concept." In *Narrated Empires: Perceptions of Late Habsburg and Ottoman Multinationalism*, edited by Johanna Chovanec and Olof Heilo, 77–98. Cham, Switzerland: Palgrave Macmillan, 2021.

Toprak, Zafer. *Türkiye'de Ekonomi ve Toplum (1908–1950): Milli İktisat-Milli Burjuvazi*. Istanbul: Tarih Vakfı Yurt Yayınları, 1995.

Toprak, Zafer. "1934 Trakya Olaylarında Hükümetin ve CHF'nin Sorumluluğu." *Toplumsal Tarih*, no. 34 (October 1996): 19–25.

Ury, Scott. *Barricades and Banners: The Revolution of 1905 and the Transformation of Warsaw Jewry*. Stanford, CA: Stanford University Press, 2012.

Ülker, Erol. "Assimilation, Security and Geographical Nationalization in Interwar Turkey: The Settlement Law of 1934." *European Journal of Turkish Studies* 7 (2008).

Ünal, Hasan. "Ottoman Policy during the Bulgarian Independence Crisis, 1908–9: Ottoman Empire and Bulgaria at the Outset of the Young Turk Revolution." *Middle Eastern Studies* 34, no. 4 (October 1998): 135–76.

Üngor, Uğur Ümit. *The Making of Modern Turkey: Nation and State in Eastern Anatolia, 1913–1950*. Oxford: Oxford University Press, 2011.

Varol-Bornes, Marie-Cristine. "Un erudito entre dos lenguas: el 'castellano' de Hayim Bejarano en el prólogo a su refranero glosado." In *Los sefardíes ante los retos del mundo contemporáneo: identidad y mentalidades*, edited by Paloma Díaz-Mas and María Sánchez Pérez, 113–27. Madrid: CSIC, 2010.

Veidlinger, Jeffrey. *In the Midst of Civilized Europe: The Pogroms of 1918–1921 and the Onset of the Holocaust*. New York: Metropolitan Books, 2021.

Voinikov, Dimitar. *The Bulgarians in the Easternmost Part of the Balkan Peninsula—Eastern Thrace*. Sofia, Bulgaria: Orbell, 2014.

Vryonis, Speros, Jr. *The Mechanism of Catastrophe: The Turkish Pogrom of September 6–7, 1955, and the Destruction of the Greek Community of Istanbul*. New York: Greekworks.com, 2005.

Wasti, Syed Tanvir. "Feylesof Rıza." *Middle Eastern Studies* 38, no. 2 (April 2002): 83–100.

Winter, Stefan, "The Kızılbaş of Syria and Ottoman Shiism." In *The Ottoman World*, edited by Christine Woodhead, 171–83. New York: Routledge, 2012.

Wippel, Steffen. "Edirne as a Secondary City: Global Reconfiguration of the Urban." In *The Heritage of Edirne in Ottoman and Turkish Times: Continuities, Disruptions and Reconnections*, edited by Birgit Krawietz and Florian Riedler, 484–533. Berlin: De Gruyter, 2020.

Yack, Bernard. *The Problems of a Political Animal: Community, Justice, and Conflict in Aristotelian Political Thought*. Berkeley: University of California Press, 1993.

Yack, Bernard. "The Myth of the Civic Nation." *Critical Review: A Journal of Politics and Society* 10, no. 2 (Spring, 1996): 193–211.

Yıldız, Murat. *The Ottoman World of Sport: Refashioning Bodies, Men, and Communities in Late Imperial Istanbul*. Austin: University of Texas Press, forthcoming.

Yalımov, İbrahim. "The Bulgarian Community and the Development of the Socialist Movement in the Ottoman Empire During the Period 1876–1923." In *Socialism and Nationalism in the Ottoman Empire, 1876–1923*, edited by Mete Tunçay and Erik J. Zürcher. London: British Academic, 1994.

Yıldırım, Onur. *Diplomacy and Displacement: Reconsidering the Turco-Greek Exchange of Populations, 1922–1934*. New York: Routledge, 2006.

Yılmaz, İlkay. *Ottoman Passports: Security and Geographic Mobility, 1876–1908*. Syracuse, NY: Syracuse University Press, 2023.

Yosmaoğlu, İpek. "Chasing the Printed Word: Press Censorship in the Ottoman Empire, 1876–1913." *Turkish Studies Association Journal* 27, no. 1 (2003): 15–49.

Yosmaoğlu, İpek. *Blood Ties: Religion, Violence, and the Politics of Nationhood in Ottoman Macedonia, 1878–1908*. Ithaca, NY: Cornell University Press, 2014.

Zaides, Sarah M. *Tevye's Ottoman Daughter: Ashkenazi and Sephardi Jews at the End of Empire*. Istanbul: Libra Kitapçılık ve Yayıncılık Ticaret A.Ş., 2022.

Zürcher, Erik J. "The Ottoman Conscription System, 1844–1914." *International Review of Social History* 43, no. 3 (December 1998): 437–49.

Zürcher, Erik J. "The Young Turks: Children of the Borderlands?" In *Ottoman Borderlands: Issues, Personalities and Political Changes*, edited by Kemal Karpat and Robert W. Zens, 275–86. Madison: Center of Turkish Studies at University of Wisconsin, 2003.

Zürcher, Erik J. "The Late Ottoman Empire as Laboratory of Demographic Engineering." In *Le Regioni Multilingui come Faglia e Motore della Storia Europea nel XIX–XX Secolo*, Naples, September 16–18, 2008.

Zürcher, Erik J. *Turkey: A Modern History*. London: I.B. Tauris, 2017.

Zürcher, Erik J. "Greek and Turkish Refugees and Deportees, 1912–1924." In *Leiden Project Working Papers Archive*. Online, 3.

Index

Abdülhamid II, 29, 53–54, 56, 61, 65, 71, 75, 77, 115
Abramowitz, Maurice, 72, 75
acculturation, 65
Adil Bey (Arda), Hacı, 104, 110
agency, 7, 19–20, 154–55, 178
agricultural settlements, Jewish, 45–47, 74, 112; Fethiköy Çiftliği, 47. *See also* productivization
Ağrı Rebellion, 174. *See also* Kurds
Alexander of Greece, 129–30, 132
Alexandroupoli, 34, 37, 48–49, 66, 99, 109, 119, 131, 142, 171, 186
Alfassa, Albert, 6–7, 110
Alfassa, Anna, 113
Alfassa, Sarah, 113
Alliance Israélite Universelle: apprenticeship program, 45, 47–48; as a communal welfare institution, 43, 111; critics of, 76, 136–41; establishment of and support for its schools, 37, 41, 53, 79, 90; its school buildings during wartime, 95, 98, 118; Muslim students and alumni, 82, 88, 98–99, 165; nationalism and, 134, 140–41, 143–44, 155, 164, 166–67; related clubs and associations, 37, 39, 65–68, 155; rivalry with Zionists, 69, 71–74, 101–2, 139–41, 144; role of school directors, 44, 62–64, 95, 97, 125; values of, 61, 78, 87. *See also* women and girls, education of
Alpullu, 154, 159
American Jewish Joint Distribution Committee (JDC), 159
Americas, Sephardi migration to, 18, 43, 109, 157. *See also* refugees and migrants, Jewish
Anglo-Jewish Association, 101
Ankara, 8, 148–49, 151, 154, 160–61, 164, 167, 169, 172–74, 180, 184–85; Treaty of, 171
annexation of Edirne to Greece. *See* occupation of Edirne by Greece
Annuaire oriental, 158–59

289

antisemitism, 14–15, 19, 50, 57, 70, 76, 79–82, 110, 127, 134, 147–48, 150, 152–55, 162–66, 169, 175
Arendt, Hannah, 185
Armenian Christians: 29, 31, 33, 42–43, 45, 50, 54, 58, 67, 71, 81, 87, 93, 97, 99–100, 104, 129–31, 133, 141, 145–46, 158, 167, 171, 175; genocide of, 18, 107–9, 111, 151
Asenovgrad, 81
Ashkenazi Jews, 13–15, 17, 30, 32n72, 46–47, 48n179, 66–67, 69, 71–72, 83, 111–12, 148, 185
askeri. See military, presence in the Edirne region
assimilation, 7, 14, 47, 56, 83n206, 102, 152, 166, 168, 179. *See also* integrationism
associational life, Jewish, 16–17, 37, 39, 53, 65–75, 77–78, 117, 127, 136, 139–40, 144, 148, 155–56
Atatürk, Mustafa Kemal, 19, 126, 151, 154, 157, 162, 164, 168, 185
Athens. *See* Greece
Atsız, Nihal, 169
Auschwitz-Birkenau, 186. *See also* Holocaust
Austria, 186
Austria-Hungary. *See* Habsburg Empire
Aykut, Mehmet Şeref. *See* Şeref (Aykut), Mehmet
Azaria, Behor, 71–72, 78, 84
Azaria family, 36, 44

Babaeski, 32, 107, 135, 153, 163
Baghdad, 80. *See also* Iraq
Balkan, 56, 84, 87n231
Balkan Pact of 1934, 170
Balkan Wars, 3, 18, 28, 31, 42, 47, 51–52, 60, 64, 78, 90–106, 109–11, 114–16, 129, 142, 166, 173–75; Siege of Edirne, 92–95, 129. *See also* occupation of Edirne by Bulgaria

Balfour Declaration, 15, 18, 127–28, 130
banks and bankers, 39–42, 46, 64, 116, 119, 140, 143, 159, 166
Barishac, Josef, 76–84, 87, 95, 104–5, 110, 115–16, 119–21, 136–40, 144, 162–63, 165. See also *La Boz de la Verdad*
Barokas family, 32
Behar, Bohor, 39
Behar, Moise (Moshe), 85, 88
Behar, Nissim, 136–40, 144. See also *L'Écho d'Andrinople*
Behmoiras, Haim Efendi, 61, 66, 87, 104
Behmoiras, Jacques, 74
Behmoiras, Rabbi Meir, 127, 130–31, 137, 141–42
Beirut, 75, 86, 88
Beja, Julie, 137–41
Bejarano, Rabbi Haim Moshe, 50, 61–64, 72–73, 77–78, 86–87, 95, 109–10, 113–14, 127. *See also* chief rabbinate of Edirne
Bejarano, Sévère, 96
belediye meclisi, 60, 100
Belgrade. *See* Serbia
Benbassat, Michel, 70
Benbassat, Nissim, 74
Bikur Holim, 53, 70–71, 74, 155. *See also* healthcare
blood libel. *See* ritual murder allegation
borderlands: academic literature on, 9–13, 23; empires and, 4–5; Jews and, 7–8, 11, 13–15, 20, 55, 96, 102, 109–11, 114, 121, 123, 147–48, 177–81; journalism in, 56, 79, 84; nation-states and, 19, 148, 150–51, 154, 169–78, 180; political nature of, 16–17; violence in, 91–92, 108
borders: changing functions of, 178–79; demarcation of, 59; emergence of, 26–30, 92–93, 118; identity and, 5–6, 18, 52, 55, 91, 121, 178–79; mobility across, 22–23, 27, 58, 78–79, 119–20, 127, 134, 181, 183,

186; national security and, 14, 19, 107, 152–53; territorial revisionism and, 169–73. *See also* refugees and migrants
Bosnia and Herzegovina, 48, 84
Boton, Izak (Izakino) de, 82, 143
boycotts, 48–50, 87, 105, 153, 163–65, 167. *See also* economic warfare
Britain, 24–26, 99, 101, 137, 107–8, 124–26, 126, 137, 144, 146, 149, 165; ambassador of, 158; consul/consulate of, 25, 29, 40, 48, 56, 58, 73, 85–88, 96, 106
Bucharest. See *Romania*
Bulgaria: autonomy of, 27, 57, 179; boycotts against, 48–49; independence of, 18, 29, 48, 54, 58–59; Jews of, 12, 35, 70–71, 75, 78–79, 83–84, 98, 100–102, 111, 113, 117, 119, 143, 183, 186; Sofia, 24, 29–30, 48, 58, 97, 100, 119–20, 170, 172, 184. *See also* occupation of Edirne by Bulgaria
Bulgarian Catholics, 70, 110
Bulgarian Exarchate, 26–27, 48
Bulgarian Orthodox Christians, 29, 31, 37, 40, 48, 50, 52, 54, 56–59, 81, 93, 100, 103–5, 131, 146, 157, 170, 172, 178
Burgas, 75, 100, 117
Byzantine Empire, 24, 30
B'nai B'rit, 39, 41, 73–75, 101, 111, 117, 122, 133, 139, 155–56
B'nai Tzion, 136–37, 143. *See also* Zionism
B'not Tzion, 136. *See also* Zionism

Campbell Riots, 173
Canetti, Conorté, 125–28
Canetti, Elias, 76, 119n192
capitalism, free-market, 168
Catalan, Nissim, 73, 83
Cemal Bey, 85–87
Cercle de la Bienfaisance, 66–67, 72
Cercle Israélite, 39, 66–67, 72, 74, 77, 86, 155
chambers of commerce, 154, 157–59, 162

cheese production, 39, 42n143, 160
chickpeas, 40
chief rabbinate of Edirne, 15, 35, 37, 53, 61–62, 77–78, 86–87, 94, 110, 114, 142, 155, 183
chief rabbinate of the Ottoman Empire, 49–50, 62, 77, 80, 110, 112, 127
Chiprut, Yitzhak, 116
cholera, 29n48, 43n148, 103, 111
citizenship, 6, 29, 31, 41, 49, 54, 56–57, 59, 61, 71, 79, 82, 101–2, 108, 112–14, 119, 130, 174, 183–84
class. *See* socioeconomic class
Cohen, Moise (Tekinalp), 82, 103, 165–66
Cold War, 178–79
Committee of Union and Progress (CUP), 6, 10, 18, 51, 54, 56–60, 62, 65–67, 69, 75, 77–78, 80, 82, 84, 89, 104, 106–9, 114
communal council, Jewish, 16, 39, 60–61, 78, 85, 87–88, 137, 155–56
communism, 152, 171
Constantine I of Greece, 132
Constantinople. *See* Istanbul
Constanţa, 100
constitutionalism, 54, 56, 60–61, 71, 73–74, 78–81, 84, 88–89
Counterrevolution of 1909, 68
court trials, 86, 163
Crete, 49, 84
Crimea, 173
Cumhuriyet, 170
Cumhuriyet Halk Partisi (CHP). *See* Republican People's Party
Çanakkale, 34, 151–54, 167
Çatalca, 46–47, 170
Çorlu, 32–33, 37, 39–41, 94, 96–98, 108, 124, 127, 129, 136, 146, 153–54, 161, 170

Danon, Abraham, 45, 65, 74–76, 133
Danon, Aron, 137, 144
Dedeağaç. *See* Alexandroupoli

demarcation of borders. *See* borders, demarcation of
diaspora nationalism, 15, 133. *See also* nationalism, Jewish
Didymoteicho, 31–34, 36–37, 39, 45, 47, 49–52, 76, 118, 144
Dimetoka. *See* Didymoteicho
Diyarbakır, 151–52
Djivre family, 32, 123n7
Dorshei Haskalah, 45, 65–66, 72
Drama, 28

Eastern Europe, Jews of. *See* Ashkenazi Jews
Eastern Rumelia, 27–29, 32, 54, 56, 59
ebraizantes. *See* Hebrew, instruction of
economic warfare, 23, 47–52, 153, 167. *See also* boycotts
economy, Jews in the. *See* occupational profiles
Ecumenical Patriarch of Constantinople, 26, 48, 50, 127
Edhem Ruhi, 56, 79, 84
Edirne: Armistice period and, 124–28; Balkan Wars and, 90–103; Bulgarian occupation of, 3–6, 16, 92–103, 110; economic history of, 23–30; former capital of the Ottoman Empire, 24; Greek annexation of, 128–48; modern political history of, 55–60; settlement patterns in the city of, 30–32; settlement patterns in the province of, 32–38; Turkish Republic and, 149–69, 175–76, 182–86; World War I and, 107–8, 112–21; World War II and, 182–86; Young Turk Revolution and, 53–55
Edirne Delegation (Edirne Heyeti), 103–5, 107, 119
Edirne Incident (1910), 84–88
Edirne Milli Gazete, 165, 167

Edirne Postası, 166–67
education, Jewish. *See* Alliance Israélite Universelle. *See also* Talmud Torah
Egypt, 42, 75, 156, 179
El Djudyo, 83, 127
El Progreso, 143n138
El Pueblo, 132
El Tiempo, 76, 83
elections: Ottoman, 57, 59–60, 74–75, 126; Greek, 131–33; Turkish, 168. *See also* parliament
Elnekavé, David, 127, 135–36
Emine Semiye, 66
Enez, 25
England. *See* Britain
entertainment. *See* Fevaid Theater; Reşadiye Bahçesi
Enver Paşa, 62, 110
Eski Zağra. *See* Stara Zagora
ethnic cleansing, 3, 5–6, 9–10, 12, 18, 91, 97–99, 104–9, 114, 146–49, 155, 168–69, 175, 177, 179–80. *See also* refugees and migrants
European Union, 2, 179
Evros, 171

fairs, 25, 36–37, 47, 49–52, 163, 171–72
Fethi Bey, 163
Ferdinand I of Bulgaria, 101
Fevaid Theater, 73
Filibe. *See* Plovdiv
fire of 1905, 27, 30, 53, 61, 76
France, 24–25, 30, 37–38, 45–46, 56, 64, 66, 68, 71–72, 74, 78, 87, 101, 108–9, 118, 124, 126, 130, 134, 137, 139, 143–44, 146, 149, 155–57, 166
Fraternité Scolaire, 66–67, 69, 72
Free Republican Party, 168
Freedom and Accord Party. *See* Liberal Entente

Galante, Abraham, 96, 165–66
garbanzo beans. *See* chickpeas
Gelibolu, 34, 36–38, 42, 96, 104, 112
Gallipoli. *See* Gelibolu
Gallipoli campaign. *See* World War I
gender, 15, 18, 54, 139, 164; patriarchy of the Jewish community, 95. *See also* women and girls
general assembly, Jewish, 39, 78, 138–39
General Inspectorate, First, 151
General Inspectorate, Second, 150–52, 171
General Inspectorate of Thrace. *See* General Inspectorate, Second
Germany, 14, 25, 30, 117, 175; Nazi, 169, 179, 182–83, 186
Ginsburg, Sami, 185
Goldmann, Shlomo, 135–36
Gounaris, Dimitrios, 132
governors. *See vali* of Edirne Province
Great Britain. *See* Britain
Greco-Turkish War, 124, 128–29, 141, 145–46, 161, 184
Greece: boycotts against, 49, 51; government of, 6, 106, 124, 129–34, 141, 145, 149, 170–71; in the Balkan Wars, 92–93, 105–7; in World War II, 186; its war of independence, 179; Jews of, 11, 82, 122–23, 130, 132, 156; northeast border of, 1–2, 21, 145–46, 153, 178, 182. *See also* occupation of Edirne by Greece
Greek, teaching and speaking, 8, 131, 143–44
Greek Orthodox Christians: 6, 18–19, 23, 26, 31, 34–37, 45, 48–51, 54, 57, 66, 93, 97–100, 103–8, 110, 112, 118, 124–27, 129–34, 141, 145–47, 167–70, 175; Jewish commercial rivalry with, 35, 39, 45, 49–52, 57
Greek Thrace. *See* Thrace, Western
Guéron, Angèle, 3–5, 12, 62, 64–66, 69, 73, 76, 86–87, 89, 94–95, 99–103, 140

Guéron, Isaiah, 64
Gümülcine. *See* Komotini

Habsburg Empire, 1, 9, 13–14, 21, 29, 48–49, 66, 70, 84, 91, 107, 111, 117, 148
Haifa, 62. *See also* Palestine
Hakkı Bey, İsmail, 81
Halévy, Joseph, 98n54
Halfon, Jacob, 39, 41
halitzah, 35n96, 64
Halutzei Tzavah, 67, 117. *See also* military conscription
HaShofar, 71, 78, 84
Haskalah, 16, 37, 44–45, 66, 74–76, 89
Haskovo, 119, 172
Hayrabolu, 108, 113
Hebrew: teaching and speaking, 7, 17, 61, 66–67, 69–70, 79, 83, 130, 133, 135–36, 138–39, 144; press, poetry, and literature, 13, 16, 53, 65–66, 75–76
healthcare, 53, 70–71, 74, 143, 155. *See also* Bikur Holim
Herzl, Theodor, 116, 135. *See also* Zionism
Hilfsverein der Deutschen Juden, 100–101
Hitlerism, 166, 169, 185
Hizmet-i Nisvan, 66
Holocaust, 182–86
Hovevei Tzion, 127n30. *See also*, Zionism

imams, 167
industrial factories and filatures, 36, 38, 44, 159, 160, 162, 166
integrationism, 18, 54, 56, 61–62, 64–65, 71, 84, 102, 178
intellectuals, 77, 80
İnönü, İsmet, 185
İskeçe. *See* Xanthi
Ioannina, 122
Iraq, 151, 179. *See also* Baghdad
Israel, State of, 180, 182

Istanbul, 1, 6, 8, 10, 12, 15–18, 23–24, 26–27, 29–30, 32–34, 37–38, 41, 43, 45, 47, 49–50, 61–62, 68–76, 80, 83, 87–89, 93–95, 97–104, 108–11, 117–20, 122, 124–29, 133–36, 138, 145, 149–51, 153–54, 156–58, 160–62, 167–70, 174–77, 180, 182–83, 185
Italo-Ottoman War, 59–60, 82
Italy, 30, 36, 59, 82, 108, 113–14, 149, 151, 156, 166
Ivaylovgrad, 36
Izmir, 12, 16, 33, 38, 41, 43, 46, 69, 75, 80, 107, 124, 131, 145–46, 150, 158, 180

Jaffa, 45, 74, 116. *See also* Palestine
Jewish Colonization Association, 46–47, 74. *See also* agricultural settlements, Jewish
Jewish National Fund
Jewish question, 15, 69, 152, 166n100

Kahn, Yehuda, 70
Kaleiçi neighborhood, 30–31, 85
Karaağaç, 1, 30–31, 33, 36, 38, 71, 75–76, 90, 93, 107, 113, 118–20, 184–86
Karaso, Samuel, 99
Karmi, 75
Kastanies, 1, 171–72
Kavala, 123
kayades, 80, 87
Kazanlak, 73
Kemal, Mustafa. *See* Atatürk, Mustafa Kemal
Kemal, Namık, 26, 56
Kemalism, 152, 172. *See also* Atatürk, Mustafa Kemal
Keşan, 36, 153
Kırklareli, 3, 32–33, 36–38, 40, 42–44, 60, 94–95, 108, 112, 125–27, 129–30, 133–35, 139, 145–46, 151, 153–54, 156, 168, 175
Komotini, 34, 36–37, 40–42, 48–49, 57, 76, 81, 99, 123, 139, 142, 186

Kurds, 151–52, 174
Kurdzhali, 172

La Boz de la Verdad: advocating Jewish interests, 49–51, 80–82, 87, 110–12, 162, 164; closing of, 164; critiquing community members and institutions, 77–80; founding and agenda of, 8, 76, 136, 138; on Bulgarian Jewry, 78–79; on Jewish emigration, 43; on Zionism, 83, 116–17, 138–40; open letters in, 165; using the discourse of Islamic Ottomanism, 115; various reporting of, 40, 86, 117. *See also* Ladino press
La Fourmi, 66
lachrymose conception of Jewish history, 8, 181
Ladino literature and songs, 73, 94, 118n185, 164
Ladino press: combatting antisemitism, 76–77, 80–82; comparing communities, 10–13, 25, 33, 78–79; in Istanbul, 15, 33, 76, 133, 138, 161; in Izmir, 69; in Plovdiv, 13, 71, 78, 84; in Thessaloniki, 15, 25, 132; in Xanthi, 82, 143; origins in Edirne, 53, 75–76, 65; using democratic discourse, 57, 72, 78–80; war reportage, 94. *See also La Boz de la Verdad*
language politics, 7–8, 19, 62, 67, 79, 83, 96, 102–3, 131, 136, 138, 143–44, 167
Lausanne, Treaty of, 149–50
Law 1041, Turkish, 184
Law 1312, Turkish, 184
Law 2510, Turkish, 152–53, 171
League of Nations, 130, 133, 143, 146, 169
Lebanon, 174. *See also* Beirut
Lesbos, 186
Levi, Yaakov, 76
Levy, David, 97–99
Levy, Simone, 113
Liberal Entente, 80–81

INDEX 295

Liberal Republican Party. *See* Free Republican Party
London. *See* Britain
Loupo, Samuel, 45–46
Lüleburgaz, 33, 124–25, 127, 136, 153–54, 167
L'Aurore, 69–70, 83, 87, 89
L'Écho d'Andrinople, 136–39

Macedonia, 36, 92, 106, 110, 132
Mades, Haim, 67
maftirim, 16, 61, 122, 133
Makabi, 70–73, 75, 116, 144. *See also* physical education and gymnastics
Malkara, 107
markets, covered, 31, 42, 166
matzah, 133, 142, 167
meclis-i umumi, Jewish. *See* general assembly, Jewish
meclis-i umumi, vilayet, 60
Mehmed V, 62, 64, 77, 85
merchants, 3, 15–16, 24–26, 35–42, 44, 48–52, 55, 61, 97–99, 110, 116, 118, 122–23, 129, 134, 142, 146, 149, 158–59, 161–67, 175, 181
migration. *See* refugees and migrants
military: conscription, 7, 43, 67, 73, 93–94, 98, 118; presence in the Edirne region, 23–24, 31, 39–41, 45, 154
millet, model, 88
millet system, 11, 15, 26–27, 56–57, 72, 130, 142, 150
minorities and minority rights, 4–5, 8–9, 19, 108, 130, 133, 143–44, 148–50, 167, 169–73, 175, 178, 180
Mitrani, Barukh, 75–76, 81
Mitrani family, 32
Mitrani, Moise, 7–8, 37, 62, 67, 71–73, 77, 85–88, 90, 95, 111, 136, 138–41, 144–46
Mitrani, Rosa (née Avigdor), 3–4, 7–8, 95, 137–40, 156, 164
Mitrani, Salomon (Shlomo), 83, 130, 133–34, 142

Mizrahi, Robert, 6, 29
Montreux Convention, 154
Mudanya Armistice, 145–46
Mudros Armistice, 123, 125
muftis, 87, 115
muhacir, 94, 185. *See also* refugees and migrants, Muslim
municipal council. See *belediye meclisi*
murder of local Jews, 129, 146, 163
Muslim bourgeoisie, 52, 158, 160–61, 164, 166–69, 180
Muslims, Turkish, 2–3, 6, 11–12, 18–19, 21–23, 25–32, 34, 36–37, 39–40, 43, 45–49, 51–52, 56–59, 62, 68–69, 74, 81–82, 84, 87, 90–91, 93–100, 103–6, 109–21, 124–34, 138–39, 141, 145, 148–51, 154, 158–74, 179–80, 186
Mustafapaşa. *See* Svilengrad
mübadiller. *See* population exchange between Greece and Turkey; refugees and migrants, Muslim

Nahum, Rabbi Haim, 62, 77, 80, 110, 112
nationalism: 4, 15, 21–23, 52, 56, 66–67, 84, 92, 116, 148, 179–80; Armenian, 67; Bulgarian, 5, 26–27, 57, 66, 70, 148; Greek, 5, 127, 148; Jewish, 15, 18, 55, 61, 65, 70–71, 75–76, 80, 83, 116, 120, 126–27, 130, 133, 138–39, 144–45, 148, 178; Ottoman, 5, 10, 49, 54–56, 114–16; Turkish, 7–8, 10–11, 19–20, 52, 61, 82, 103, 148, 150, 165, 167–68. *See also* Zionism
nationalization of industry, 29, 173
Nea Orestiada, 153, 171
Niego, Joseph, 46, 74, 111–12, 117
Nordau, Max, 131

occupation of Edirne by Bulgaria, 3–6, 16, 92–103, 110. *See also* Balkan Wars
occupation of Edirne by Greece, 7–8, 10, 18, 122–48

296   INDEX

occupational profiles, Jewish, 39, 42–43, 157–60
oil wrestling, 153
Okyar, Fethi, 168
Or Zion, 72. *See also* Zionism
Orhun, 169
orphanages, Jewish, 44, 64, 122, 144, 155–56
Ottoman Empire: dissolution of, 2, 92–93, 122–24, 130, 155; European lands of, 21, 24, 92–93, 179; first capitals of, 1, 24, 95; Jews in the administration of, 6, 29, 60, 119–20; lack of deep-seated antisemitism in, 147–48, 169, 175; northwestern border of, 5, 24, 54; patriotism for, 3, 92–96; population management in, 30, 150, 173–75. *See also* Committee of Union and Progress (CUP)
Ottomanism, 66, 80, 92, 114–15, 178
Ottoman-Turkish press. *See* Turkish-language press

Palestine, 15, 69–70, 73, 83, 126–27, 135–39, 143–44, 156–57, 164–65, 185
Palestinian Arabs, 83, 137–38
Pappo family, 36
Pappo, Joseph Jacob, 39, 60
Paris. *See* France
Paris Peace Conference, 128
parliament, Jews in, 7, 57, 60, 80–81. *See also* elections
passports, 28–29, 119, 184
Paşaeli, 8, 162–65
Pazardzhik, 117
peasants, Jews and, 33, 36, 39, 41, 148, 162, 166, 171
Philippopolis. *See* Plovdiv
physical education and gymnastics, 67, 139
Pipano, Albert, 102n78, 119
Pınarhisar, 93
Plovdiv, 12, 25, 27, 38, 56, 70–71, 73, 75, 78–79, 83–84, 87, 100, 113, 117, 143, 183. *See also* Bulgaria, Jews of

pogroms, 14, 128, 137, 146, 148, 171, 173, 175. *See also* Thrace Events of 1934
Poland, 5, 13–14, 25, 147, 183
population numbers, 2, 23, 27n40, 31–34, 104–5, 107–8, 149, 151, 155n39, 177
population exchange: between Bulgaria and the Ottoman Empire, 104–5, 111–13; between Greece and the Ottoman Empire, 106–7; between Greece and Turkey, 6, 169–70; between Greece and Bulgaria, 170n130
productivization, 44–48. *See also* agricultural settlements, Jewish
Próodos, 171–72
protests, 49, 84–85, 87–88, 135, 137, 141, 167
public spheres, 54, 60, 65–67, 76, 88–89

railroads and railway companies, 17, 23, 27–31, 34–35, 37–38, 41–43, 59, 71, 93, 99–101, 107–8, 118, 124, 135–36, 140, 154, 183–86
rape. *See* sexual violence
Razon, Yuda, 8, 76, 128, 136, 162, 165
Red Crescent Society, 3, 66, 95, 118–19
Red Cross Society, 118–19
refugees and migrants: 91; Christian, 99, 104–8, 110, 114, 124, 145–46, 157, 169–70, 172; Jewish, 32, 43, 93–94, 97–98, 100–101, 108–14, 153–55, 157, 171–72; Muslim, 47, 59, 90, 93–94, 97, 99, 104–6, 110, 151–52, 154, 169–70, 172–74, 183–85
Republican People's Party, 152, 154, 165, 168
Resettlement Law of 1934. *See* Law 2510, Turkish
Reşadiye Bahçesi, 68, 85, 87, 164
ritual murder allegation, 81, 133–34, 162, 175
rivers and riverine commerce, 24–26, 30–33, 118–20, 129, 186
Romania: 25, 46, 61–62, 71, 83, 100, 149, 170, 179
Romaniot Jews, 30

Romano, Presidio, 83
Romano, Yuda, 183, 185
royal alliance, 114
Rumeli. *See* Ottoman Empire in Europe
Rusçuk. *See* Ruse
Ruse, 61, 75–76, 101
Russian Empire, 9, 13–14, 21, 25, 27, 46–47, 67, 71, 82–83, 107–8, 110–12, 146–48, 173–74
Russo-Ottoman Wars, 25, 27, 32, 61–62, 82

Sabuni neighborhood, 30–31, 39, 82
Salonica. *See* Thessaloniki
Samuel, Nissim B., 40
San Remo Resolution, 127
Saray, 112
Serbia, 24, 30, 74–75, 92, 174, 179
Siege of Edirne. *See* Balkan Wars
Sciuto, Lucien, 69–70, 72, 77, 89
Selimiye Mosque, 1–2, 31, 49, 64, 100–101
Semah, Rabbi Abraham, 49, 61, 72. *See also* chief rabbinate of Edirne
Sephardi Jews: arrival in Edirne, 30; historiography of, 4, 8, 75, 181; identity of, 11, 17, 91–92, 115, 121, 179; in the Holocaust, 182–86; networks of, 11, 17, 65, 91–92, 96, 116–21, 143, 156–57, 179–80; social change among, 123, 137, 139–40
Serres, 34
Settlement Law of 1934. *See* Law 2510, Turkish
sexual violence, 44, 100, 153, 184
Sèvres, Treaty of, 130, 141
Shivat Tzion, 127, 136. *See also* Zionism
Shoah. *See* Holocaust
Shumen, 98, 117
Siege of Edirne. *See* Balkan Wars
Silistra, 100
Silivri, 47, 50–51, 94, 112
silk industry, 16, 24–25, 27, 34, 36, 38–39, 44, 60, 142, 163, 166
Sisters of Agram School, 45, 110

Smolyan, 172
smuggling, 28, 120, 171
Smyrna. *See* Izmir
socialism, 43
socioeconomic class, 38–44, 52, 54, 158, 160–61, 164, 166–69, 180
Sofia. *See* Bulgaria
Sofulu. *See* Soufli
Soufli, 34, 36–38, 123, 142
Stara Zagora, 61, 117
statism, 160, 168. *See also* nationalization of industry
Stergiadis, Aristeidis, 131
sultans, 1, 26, 35, 53, 62, 77, 85, 115, 119
sürgün, 30, 174
Svilengrad, 33, 40, 46, 59, 73, 76, 81, 111–12, 133
synagogues, 27–28, 30, 45, 53, 61–62, 86, 122, 127, 130, 137, 144, 153, 161
Syria, 83, 108, 151, 156
Şakir (Kesebir), Mehmet, 161
Şarköy, 36–37
Şeref (Aykut), Mehmet, 82, 128, 165–66, 175
Şevket (Dağdeviren), Mustafa, 82, 128n38
Şevket Paşa, Mahmud, 62
Şükrü Kaya, 106, 151, 154

Talat Paşa, 10, 62, 88, 98, 103, 106–7, 110, 112, 114
Tali (Öngören), İbrahim, 151–52, 155, 157
Talmud Torah, 40, 53, 73, 76, 81, 133
Tamim-i Lisan-ı Osmani Cemiyeti, 68. *See also* Turkish, teaching and speaking
Tatars, 173
Tekinalp, Munis. *See* Moise Cohen
Tekirdağ, 6, 33, 37–38, 42–43, 46–47, 94, 97–99, 104, 106–8, 110, 112–13, 127, 136, 151, 153, 162, 186
territoriality, 29–30
Tevfik Bey, Rıza, 69, 83

Thessaloniki, 10, 15, 17, 25, 28, 33–34, 36, 38, 41, 42–43, 48, 52, 69, 71, 73, 75–77, 80, 82, 89, 102, 122, 124, 126, 128, 130–32, 134–35, 139, 143, 146, 153, 173, 180, 186
Thrace, Eastern, 3, 18–19, 46, 93–94, 96, 104, 106–7, 109, 118, 122–33, 135–36, 141–43, 145–61, 163, 166, 168–69, 171–75, 177–80, 183, 186
Thrace Events of 1934, 3–4, 8, 19, 34, 150–54, 157, 160, 165–67, 169, 171–72, 175–76
Thrace, Western, 18, 34, 93, 99, 109, 118, 129, 142–43, 149, 170, 186
Thracians, ancient, 24
Toledo family, 36, 44
trade, international, 25–28, 36, 58–60, 169n119
Trakya Paşaeli, 128, 165
Treblinka, 186
Tunisia, 45–46
Turkey, Republic of, 1–5, 7–8, 11, 16, 19, 32, 37, 61, 91, 96, 148–58, 162, 165–66, 168–86
Turkification. *See* nationalism, Turkish
Turkish, teaching and speaking, 7–8, 19, 62–64, 67–68, 73, 96, 102–3, 119, 133, 143, 167–68. *See also* language politics
Turkish Hearths (Türk Ocakları), 163–64
Turkish Nationalist Movement, 124, 161; Association for the Defense of Rights in Thrace, 128–29, 145, 161
Turkish Thrace. *See* Thrace, Eastern
Turkish-language press, 8, 12, 15, 19, 35, 56–57, 82, 84, 87, 99, 165–68, 170, 174
Tzeirei Tzion, 136, 144. *See also* Zionism

Ungar, Sara, 58
Union des Associations Israélites, 101
United Kingdom. *See* Britain

United States of America: ambassador of, 117n181, 153; consul/consulate of, 107, 112–14. *See also* Americas, Sephardi migration to
Uzundzhovo, 25
Uzunköprü, 32–33, 36, 110, 112, 119, 124, 127, 135–36, 153, 162–63, 166, 174–75

vali of Edirne Province, 6, 29, 35, 56, 59, 62, 64, 66, 87, 95, 104, 109–10, 161, 163, 167
Varlık Vergisi, 175, 186
Venizelos, Eleftherios, 6, 124, 130–32, 171, 175
Vienna. *See* Austria; Habsburg Empire
vilayet idare meclisi, 49–50, 60–61
Vima tis Thraki, 171
Vize, 36, 112
Vouzikis, Charilaos, 133–34, 138

Warsaw. *See* Poland
Wealth Tax. *See Varlık Vergisi*
wealth transfer, 107–8, 118, 129, 151–54, 161, 167, 175, 183, 186
Wilson, Woodrow, 128
women and girls: education of, 3, 37, 44, 53, 62–63, 70, 74, 78, 102, 110, 137, 140; engaging with modern politics, 103; in clubs and associations, 66, 156; in political ceremonies, 63–64, 129–30; in the workplace, 10, 36, 44, 55, 58, 62, 66, 117, 137, 139–41, 164; rights of, 64–65; volunteering during war, 94–96, 118–19. *See also* gender
World War I, 10, 13–14, 18, 90, 74, 90, 92, 107–8, 112, 116–18, 120, 122–24, 128–29, 147–48, 152, 155, 166, 169, 174; Gallipoli campaign, 107–8, 112, 117–21
World War II, 13, 178–79, 182–86. *See also* Holocaust

Xanthi, 32, 34, 36, 82, 96, 99, 123, 142–43, 186

Yambol, 98, 117
Yeni Asır, 82
Yeni Edirne, 58, 82
Yolageldili, Cevat, 162
Yolageldili, Kasım, 161–66, 168
Yolageldili, Mustafa Kasım, 162–63
Yosef Da'at/El Progreso, 75
Young Ottomans, 26, 55
Young Turk Revolution, 2, 5, 6–7, 17–18, 20–21, 23, 28–29, 32, 43, 47–48, 54–55, 57–58, 60–62, 65–66, 73, 78, 82, 84, 89, 177

Young Turks. *See* Committee of Union and Progress
Yugoslavia, 149, 156, 170. *See also* Serbia

Zionism, 4–5, 7–8, 10, 15, 18–19, 55, 61, 65, 69–75, 81–83, 89, 102, 116–17, 123–24, 126–28, 131, 135–41, 143–45, 148, 155, 157, 178; World Zionist Organization, 15, 69, 126, 131
Zionist Federation in London, 137; Zionist Federation of the East, 126–28, 135; Zionist Federation of Greece, 126, 128, 135, 144; Zionist Organization of Bulgaria, 70–71, 83
Zymvrakakis, Emmanouil, 132

STANFORD STUDIES IN JEWISH HISTORY AND CULTURE

Jessica Marglin and Daniel Schwartz, Editors

This series features novel approaches to examining the Jewish past in the form of innovative work that brings the field into productive dialogue with the newest scholarly concepts and methods. Open to a range of disciplinary and interdisciplinary approaches, from history to cultural studies, this series publishes exceptional scholarship balanced by an accessible tone, illustrating histories of difference and addressing issues of current urgency. Books in this list push the boundaries of Jewish Studies and speak compellingly to a wide audience of scholars and students.

John M. Efron, *All Consuming: Germans, Jews, and the Meaning of Meat*
2025

Elizabeth Imber, *Uncertain Empire: Jews, Nationalism, and the Fate of British Imperialism*
2025

Paris Papamichos Chronakis, *The Business of Transition:
The Jewish and Greek Merchants of Salonica, 1882-1919*
2024

Naomi Seidman, *Translating the Jewish Freud: Psychoanalysis in Hebrew and Yiddish*
2024

Ariel Evan Mayse, *Laws of the Spirit: Ritual, Mysticism,
and the Commandments in Early Hasidism*
2024

Immanuel Etkes, *The Invention of a Tradition: The Messianic Zionism of the Gaon of Vilna*
2024

Viola Alianov-Rautenberg, *No Longer Ladies and Gentlemen:
Gender and the German-Jewish Migration to Mandatory Palestine*
2024

Susan Rubin Suleiman, *Daughter of History: Traces of an Immigrant Girlhood*
2023

Sandra Fox, *The Jews of Summer: Summer Camp and Jewish Culture in Postwar America*
2023

David Biale, *Jewish Culture Between Canon and Heresy*
2023

Alan Verskin, *Diary of a Black Jewish Messiah: The Sixteenth-Century Journey of David Reubeni through Africa, the Middle East, and Europe*
2023

Aomar Boum, Illustrated by Nadjib Berber, *Undesirables: A Holocaust Journey to North Africa*
2023

Dina Porat, *Nakam: The Holocaust Survivors Who Sought Full-Scale Revenge*
2023

Christian Bailey, *German Jews in Love: A History*
2023

Matthias B. Lehmann, *The Baron: Maurice de Hirsch and the Jewish Nineteenth Century*
2022

Liora R. Halperin, *The Oldest Guard: Forging the Zionist Settler Past*
2021

Samuel J. Spinner, *Jewish Primitivism*
2021

Sonia Gollance, *It Could Lead to Dancing: Mixed-Sex Dancing and Jewish Modernity*
2021

Golan Y. Moskowitz, *Wild Visionary: Maurice Sendak in Queer Jewish Context*
2020

Julia Elsky, *Writing Occupation: Jewish Émigré Voices in Wartime France*
2020

Alma Rachel Heckman, *The Sultan's Communists: Moroccan Jews and the Politics of Belonging*
2020

Clémance Boulouque, *Another Modernity: Elia Benamozgh's Jewish Universalism*
2020

Devi Mays, *Forging Ties, Forging Passports: Migration and the Modern Sephardi Diaspora*
2020

For a complete listing of titles in this series, visit the Stanford University Press website, www.sup.org.

The authorized representative in the EU for product safety and compliance is:
Mare Nostrum Group
B.V Doelen 72
4831 GR Breda
The Netherlands

www.ingramcontent.com/pod-product-compliance
Lightning Source LLC
Chambersburg PA
CBHW031757220426
43662CB00007B/438